Sign Wars

CRITICAL PERSPECTIVES
A Guilford Series

Edited by
DOUGLAS KELLNER
University of Texas, Austin

POSTMODERN THEORY: CRITICAL INTERROGATIONS
Steven Best and Douglas Kellner

A THEORY OF HUMAN NEED
Len Doyal and Ian Gough

PSYCHOLANALYTIC POLITICS, SECOND EDITION:
JACQUES LACAN AND FREUD'S FRENCH REVOLUTION
Sherry Turkle

POSTNATIONAL IDENTITY: CRITICAL THEORY AND
EXISTENTIAL PHILOSOPHY IN HABERMAS, KIERKEGAARD, AND HAVEL
Martin J. Matustik

THEORY AS RESISTANCE:
POLITICS AND CULTURE AFTER (POST)STRUCTURALISM
Mas'ud Zavarzadeh and Donald Morton

POSTMODERNISM AND SOCIAL INQUIRY
David R. Dickens and Andrea Fontana, Editors

MARXISM IN THE POSTMODERN AGE:
CONFRONTING THE NEW WORLD ORDER
Antonio Callari, Stephen Cullenberg, and Carole Biewener, Editors

AFTER MARXISM
Ronald Aronson

THE POLITICS OF HISTORICAL VISION: MARX, FOUCALT, HABERMAS
Steven Best

LEWIS MUMFORD AND THE ECOLOGICAL REGION:
THE POLITICS OF PLANNING
Mark Luccarelli

ROADS TO DOMINION: RIGHT-WING MOVEMENTS
AND POLITICAL POWER IN THE UNITED STATES
Sara Diamond

SIGN WARS: THE CLUTTERED LANDSCAPE OF ADVERTISING
Robert Goldman and Stephen Papson

Sign Wars

THE CLUTTERED LANDSCAPE
OF ADVERTISING

Robert Goldman
Stephen Papson

THE GUILFORD PRESS / New York   London

© 1996 The Guilford Press
A Division of Guilford Publications, Inc.
72 Spring Street, New York, NY 10012

Printed in the United States of America

This book is printed on acid-free paper.

Last digit is print number: 9   8   7   6   5   4   3   2   1

An earlier version of Chapter 2 appeared in *Theory, Culture, and
Society*, August 1994, 11(3), pp. 23–53. © 1994 by Sage Publications.
An earlier version of Chapter 6 appeared in *Humanity and Society*,
August 1992, 16(3), pp. 390–413. © 1992 by The Association for
Humanist Sociology.

Library of Congress Cataloging-in-Publication Data

Goldman, Robert, 1949–
    Sign wars : the cluttered landscape of advertising / Robert
Goldman and Stephen Papson.
       p.   cm. — (Critical perspectives)
    Includes bibliographical references and index.
    ISBN 1-57230-014-0 (hard). — ISBN 1-57230-034-5 (pbk.)
    1. Advertising.   2. Cynicism.   3. Advertising—Social aspects.
I. Papson, Stephen.   II. Title.   III. Series: Critical perspectives
(New York, N.Y.)
    HF5821.G583   1995
    659.1′042—dc20   95-9396
                                                CIP

Preface

"SIGN WARS" refers to an advertising culture composed of swirling contests between competing sets of images. "Sign wars" points toward the current state of advertising, along with the cultural contradictions set in motion by the commodity logic that drives these sign contests. This book's title thus derives from our theoretical perspective on advertising, one that views it as a site for producing commodity sign values. Or, as Nike's director of advertising makes the point from a practitioner's point of view, "The work we do has to create what I call a warm nuclear glow around the brand. We have to sell everything with a swoosh [Nike's logo] attached to it" (Lauren Haworth, May 17, 1993, p. 17).

As capitalist competitions have escalated into new forms and new regions, it is not at all surprising that a Hobbesian war of each against all has made its way into the semiotic zone of advertising images. We see sign competitions as essential ingredients in "maturing" consumer-goods markets. As advances in production and distribution techniques level out industries, brand parity results. Consumers often face making choices between products that differ little in price or function. Enter the commodity sign, an overall image or tag line attached to a brand-name product by advertisers to create an additional axis of difference in the consumer marketplace. In the world of parity goods, if the sign doesn't stand out, neither will the product. Battles in the cola wars, the phone wars, credit card wars, and so on, have become less about the products themselves than about their signifying imagery. The weapons of choice in the contemporary sign wars are aesthetic differentiation and aesthetic attack.

The continuous jockeying for position pressures advertisers to try and outdo each other in fashioning aesthetically distinctive and desirable signs. At every turn, the pressure is on to find fresher, more desirable, and more spectacular images to enhance the value of products. White-bread culture will simply no longer do. As sign value competitions intensify, advertisers invent new strategies and push into fresh cultural territory, looking for "uncut" and "untouched" signs. Under such circumstances no meaning system is sacred, because the realm of culture has been turned into a giant mine. Advertisers routinely raid cultural formations for the raw materials they need to construct new, more valuable signs. And then, just as quickly as they appear, signs are abandoned to make way for their replacements. To keep advertising's commodity-sign machine purring requires continuously scouring the landscape for new signifying materials. Indeed, advertising now chews up signs from other discourses so rapidly that it has begun to cannibalize its own system.

As with any war, there is not only something to be won here, but also much to be lost. When advertisers tap into, extract, and appropriate new cultural styles and images for the purpose of placing them in association with their commodities, they also risk a hemorrhaging of meaning. Paradoxically, the more intensely advertisers compete for the most valuable signs, the faster their signs cease to sizzle. The circulation of signs accelerates, driving a compulsive and reckless search for unoccupied cultural spaces and more spectacular signifying styles in order to be noticed. The turnover of ad campaigns quickens, the half-life of sign values shrinks, the clutter of images accumulates, and a new kind of cultural junk heap has taken shape. Add to this mix the rise of cynical, jaded viewers of both the baby boomer and Generation X persuasions—viewers angry at being repeatedly positioned by commercials over the years to accept false assumptions—and you get a crisis of advertising.

Our study covers the period from the mid-1980s through the early 1990s, when the stakes in these sign contests rocketed upward and advertisers began attacking each other's signs with mounting intensity. The Introduction and Chapter 1 cover the basic processes of constructing sign values, devoting particular attention to the logic of appropriation in ads; the numerous strategies for competitively differentiating (and one-upping) sign values; and the cultural contradictions that develop when meaning is treated as a raw resource and a disposable commodity. We have taken some familiar sign war contests from recent years to show how our theoretical perspective conceptualizes the sign wars terrain of contemporary advertising. As advertisers tackle the fundamental problems of sign differentiation amid the debris of sign clutter, they relentlessly search for new signifying strategies to differentiate themselves. Successful strategies are quickly copied by competitors, pushing the circuit of appropriation, stylization, and depreciation along.

Chapter 2 presents an overview of what we call the stage of hyperadvertising. In recent years advertisers have put semiotic techniques into the foreground, sometimes going so far as to turn the encoding strategy itself into a new sign value. This stage began when advertising "realism" emerged to counter criticisms that advertising constructed unreal worlds with little relevance for everyday life. Realist codes including the shaky camera, jump cuts, and decentered subjects became so exaggerated that a new style emerged. The cutting edge of advertising moved toward a self-reflexive hyperrealism that focused on its own encoding devices, and presupposed a self-aware and media-savvy attitude on the part of viewers.

Chapters 3, 4, and 5 examine three contemporary modes of addressing viewers: Chapter 3 concerns the alienated mode, Chapter 4 examines ads framed around issues of memory and nostalgia, and Chapter 5 probes authenticity as a mode of hailing viewers. Each of these modes represents a specially targeted response to the crisis of commodity culture aimed at different audiences. Because the relationship of signs to commodities is an arbitrary one that is continuously being reconstructed, it is fragile and its credibility is tenuous. Sure enough, after decades of this advertising, audiences have become jaded and cynical. No sign is worth an affective investment if the meaning the viewer derives from it evaporates too quickly. Chapter 3 examines how advertisers have altered their mode of address to appease viewer alienation by self-consciously drawing attention to advertising's subtexts. Paradoxically, the more that advertisers engage in flashy self-reflexive postures to deny their own participation in the conventional advertising project, the more they promote viewer cynicism toward advertising itself—until even cynicism is turned into a sign.

Chapter 4 explores the flip side of jadedness: how some advertising redirects fears of cultural and social crisis into more traditional forms of address. Signifiers of history, memory, and tradition provide important frames for advertising aimed at people who nostalgically yearn for a sense of sociocultural place and moral certitude. Saturn's 1994 consumer "Homecoming" ads speak to this desire to belong to a community—a community of Saturn buyers shown trekking to Spring Hill, Tennessee, to be joined under the sign, the logo, of Saturn. Ironically, an economy of individuated commodity signs has cut against the grain of community and tradition. This advertising genre turns history and memory into signifiers that mark the spots where history and memory have been emptied of meaning, leaving their shells to signify the categories of "history" and "memory," while diverting attention from the actual relations that link a present to a past.

Alienation and authenticity are so closely related in the cultural economy of sign value contests that at times we talk about the alienation of authenticity and the authenticity of alienation. Images of authenticity dot the advertising landscape because questions of authenticity and individuality remain a paramount theme in commodity culture. Chapter 5 explores the codes and ideologies of authenticity found in commercials. The advertisers' quest for signifiers of authenticity is a self-defeating one, because as soon as new decontextualized representations of authenticity register on the screen they begin to appear inauthentic and fabricated. So advertisers chew up and spit out signifiers of authenticity, then move on to formerly out-of-bounds cultural constructions. Every new bogus claim of authenticity erodes the credibility of such claims, but intensifies the desire for this elusive moment in commodity culture.

Historically, one institutional goal of advertising has been to facilitate a more predictable flow of commodity circulation. Over the long run, however, this system of continuous consumption based on possessing commodity signs has taken a toll on ecosystems. Chapter 6 looks at how advertising mediates mounting concerns about the environmental degradation that results from high-intensity consumption. "Green marketing" attaches signifiers of ecologically correct consumption to commodities as a response to the crisis of overconsumption. Such advertising invests goods with the sign of an ecologically concerned consumer, while also legitimating corporations as environmentally concerned.

Over the last several decades the relationship of advertising to corporate legitimacy has changed. For the most part, advertising has come to lodge the question of legitimacy in the corporate sign. Chapter 7 presses the question of how corporations engage advertising for purposes of legitimating their power. Unlike the approach taken in hailing the wary and disengaged in consumer-goods ads, corporate ads continue to present elaborate narratives of good citizenship, patriotism, environmental safety, positive "employee" relations, and technological innovation. Over the years, these narratives have become more and more tightly abbreviated and compressed in the form of signifiers. Today, the legitimacy of corporate power is invested in signs. From the perspective of critical theory, we cannot help but wonder whether all this stifles a sphere of public discourse. Yet, strangely enough, when corporations put all their eggs in the sign basket, the corporate sign may well become the site of new contestations.

While this book is not exclusively about network television advertisements, we do draw most of our examples from that medium. Unfortunately, we are not able to provide the reader with the actual text of every commercial to which we refer. At best we have provided frozen frames supported by captioning. We've had to make thousands of choices concerning which commercials to draw upon, which frames to use, what size to make them, where to place them, and how to caption them. Despite our efforts to construct a text that incorporates the actual textual object-images of analysis, we were faced with numerous limitations: single discontinuous frames are only a fragment of the commercial; the codes of color turn to black and white; voice tones and music can only be described; editing rhythms disappear; and so on. In short, critical codes that influence the process of constructing meaning in television ads cannot be fully reproduced here.

Finally, we must remind the reader to be cognizant of our own framing activity. Our analyses of ads draw heavily on a tradition that stresses the power involved in framing images that have been removed from context. Please note well that we have engaged in a critical framing project ourselves.

Sign wars rage on even as we write. Nearly every week there appears a new manifestation of the market struggle to establish the premiere sign of the moment. As we near the end of this project in the spring of 1995 we have been frustrated that we are unable to include a discussion of each new round of the escalating advertising contests that we call sign wars. In our final rewriting we added some last-minute examples. Ironically, as we write about the accelerated decrepitude of commodity signs, the velocity of this process ensures the accelerated decrepitude of this book. By the time it reaches the bookstores, it may be more about advertising history than contemporary advertising.

Acknowledgments

Thanks to Doug Kellner for his support of our work, not just in this project, but over the long haul. From the Lewis & Clark end, thanks to Julia Reid for her editorial counsel on the early chapters. To Arjan Schütte, Edward Ames, Ivan Drucker, Joy Turner, Ann Wehr, and Adam Weisberg for their trenchant insights and their playful, though cynical, critical spirits. To Arjan Schütte and Kristin Boden-Mackay for their guidance and support in assembling documents that integrated written text with television images via the computer. Finally, thanks to Sharon Smith for anchoring a way of life that permits projects like this; and to Clea, our little buddy, quietly monitoring each page, each day.

From the St. Lawrence end, thanks to Jean Deese for managing and decoding the sometimes difficult long distance electronic transfers of materials in our early days of internet experience. Thanks also to Mary Haught for her invaluable, and ever-present, clerical support.

Contents

Introduction: Advertising in the Age of Accelerated Meaning

WE'VE seen them thousands of times. They are commodity signs. The most familiar include the Coke insignia, the McDonald's arches, the Levi's 501 emblem, the Nike "swoosh." Commodity signs find their source in advertisements.

Today most television viewers have long since become acclimated to advertisements. We take them for granted. We decipher ads routinely, automatically, even absentmindedly, in what Walter Benjamin once called a "state of distraction." Ordinarily, little attention is paid to the codes that enable us to make sense of advertisements. Yet the transparency of these advertising codes is critical to our daily routine of reading and deciphering ads.

When we as viewers step back from this process of making and taking meaning from ads, it becomes apparent to us that the process depends on how we understand the advertisement itself as a framework for telling a particular kind of story. Once the commercial narrative framework is accepted as unproblematic, we are able to routinely decipher and evaluate the combinations of meanings that commercials advance as potential sign currency. We rarely pause to consider the assumptions imposed by the advertising framework since our attention is usually fixed on solving the particular riddle of each ad as it passes before us on the screen; just as importantly, our attention is usually fixed on the question of whether or not we like the ad. The vast majority of ads offer viewers few satisfactions from deciphering; but the few ads that do excite decoding pleasures place their products in line to realize profitable sign values.

Stripped of its glamour, advertising is a kind of cultural mechanics for constructing commodity signs. Advertisements are structured to boost the value of commodity brand names by attaching them to images that possess social and cultural value: brand-name commodity + meaning of image = a commodity sign. Constructing this currency of commodity images requires that advertisements take the form of semiotic equations into which disconnected signifiers and signifieds are entered and then recombined to create new equivalencies. Ads invite viewers to perceive an exchange between otherwise incommensurate meaning systems, and they must be structured to steer interpretation in that direction if they are to fulfill their purpose.

Advertisements are always commodity narratives. John Berger and Judith Williamson have each described the general curve of the commodity narrative expressed through the advertisement. According to Berger, "The spectator-buyer is meant . . . to imagine herself transformed by the product into an object of envy for others, an envy which will then justify her loving herself."[1] Consumer ads typically tell stories of success, desire, happiness, and social fulfillment in the lives of the people who consume the right brands. Interpreting the stories that ads tell is always conditional on how they address, or "hail," us—how we are positioned, how the commodity is positioned. When ads hail us, they *appellate* us, naming us and inviting us to take up a position in relation to the advertisements. Consumer ads greet us as

"Appellation" and "alreadyness." This Nike ad hails viewers in terms of an "alreadyness" of "facts" about themselves as individuals. This particular ad was extremely effective in this regard, as evidenced by the volume of mail Nike received from women who recognized themselves in these lines.

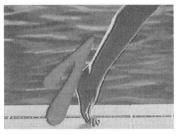

This Special K ad told of a relationship between eating cereal and gaining the look (body shape) you want. The narrative is a slightly modified version of the "envy and desire" script iterated in Berger's quote above. This concluding scene defined the Special K sign in terms of the arched foot and calf of the model. The product sign now stands for the object of desire that supposedly comes with purchase of the product. Notice how the sign is literally formed as a combination of meaning systems: half product lettering and half product outcome. The calf is transformed into a marker of desire realized through the sign of Special K. Because of the relationship between the viewer and the object of desire, the calf portion of the sign functions as a closing form of appellation.

Like the Special K image, these Citicorp images offer a study in the formation of a commodity sign. Here the sign is formed by joining an image of the Citicorp Tower with the reflection of portraits of people who are labeled as "Americans" (like ourselves) who "want to succeed."

individual viewers with what seem to be our own (*already*) ideological assumptions and personalities.[2]

Judith Williamson, in her pathbreaking book *Decoding Advertisements,* cracked open the operation of the advertising framework. She calls this the *metastructure,* "where meaning is not just 'decoded' within one structure, but transferred to create another."[3] This metastructure sets up tacit rules guiding these transfers; the metastructure is the framework within which sign currencies are assembled. Within this framework, advertisers attempt to engineer the transfers of meanings and values necessary to generate commodity signs. The *commodity sign* is formed at the intersection between a brand name and a meaning system summarized in an image.

We are socialized into recognition of sign values at an early age. A 1991 study of 6-year-old children confirmed the potential potency of sign values when it reported that children were as familiar with Joe Camel's link to cigarettes as they were with the Mickey Mouse logo and its connection to the Disney Channel.[4] In today's consumer-goods markets, products require signs that add value to them. Product standardization makes it imperative that products attach themselves to signs that carry an additional element of value. Nike captured a larger market share of the sneaker industry than Reebok did between 1986 and 1993 because Nike effectively harnessed the power of Michael Jordan's image while Reebok failed to counter with a superior or even an equal stream of imagery. In this kind of industry, everything depends on having a potent, differentiated image.

In the hotly competitive advertising industry, advertisers struggle to differentiate their images. For years, advertisers relied on a formula for joining the meaning of a brand-name product to the meaning of a socially charged image, vying for viewer attention by devising visually distinctive styles of joining meanings. The formula's success led to expanded usage until it began to provoke sustained consumer resistance. Late 1970s polling data registered rising consumer complaint about feeling "manipulated" and "insulted" by ads. In the late 1980s, advertisers responded with a wave

"Blah, blah, blah . . ." A clever sign wars ad puts down all the big name brand ads by exposing the reified formula used by one and all (in *Details* magazine).

of more "realist looks" in ads. But the problem of advertising clutter continued unabated and eventually pressured advertisers to adopt advertising narratives that were more abbreviated, oblique, and ambiguous. By the late 1980s, a new cultural cutting edge of advertising emerged as advertisers began to indulge in self-reflective banter to win back the favor of disenchanted viewers. An avant-garde of advertisers—most notably Wieden & Kennedy and Chiat/Day—bypassed the clutter by stylistically differentiating their methods of narrative representation. What advertisers once sought to conceal in their ads, they now boldly compete to utter aloud. Where advertisers once sought to maximize the transparency of the framework, they now try to jar viewers into interpretive quandaries as a way of keeping them engaged in the ads. Some ads now humorously caution viewers to remember that a sign is just a sign, and not the product itself. Replicas already abound. For example, a current, extra-hip Sprite commercial has jumped on the bandwagon to position its sign against other folks' advertising claims that soda pop can make you popular, give you athletic ability, or "make me more attractive to the opposite sex, though I wish it would." "If I need a badge I'll

Sprite's campaign lampoons the typical advertising hype that one can secure athletic accomplishments, sex appeal, popularity, or status badges by consuming commodity signs.

become a security guard," declares the youthful, black, inner-city narrator. "If I need a refreshing drink, I'll obey my thirst. Image is nothing!"

Advertising campaigns have even attempted to disrupt the taken-for-granted semiotic framework that supports the usual advertising assumptions concerning the correspondence between commodities and social outcomes.[5] Already, imitators have adopted the tactic of disregarding coding rules associated with video editing, so that sequences of images are not ordered according to conventional narrative expectations. But how far can advertisers go in creating narrative confusion without undermining the goals of advertising? What happens when viewers can no longer figure out what the point of an ad is? Ambiguous and oblique ads may temporarily solve problems of clutter, but how effective are such ads in establishing commodity signs? In today's consumer-goods markets, the competition in images has evolved into a stage that we call *sign wars*. Today, advertisers seem caught between the Scylla of fetishized formulas that annoy and alienate viewers, and the Charybdis of clever self-reflexivity that regains viewer attention at the risk of blowing apart the whole system of sign value.

Sign Wars: Constructing Sign Values

We titled this book *Sign Wars* to emphasize the theme that corporate competition in selling consumer commodities has become centered on the image, the look, the sign. The sign value of the commodity gives a brand name its zip, its meaning. Over the years the cycle of this sign competition has begun to race along, while its density and intensity has escalated. Our study of sign wars explores what happens when meaning is systematically commodified and becomes subject to an economic circuit of exchange and devaluation.

We look at consumer-goods ads as exercises in sign construction. We view advertising as a system of sign values. A sign value is generally equal to the desirability of an image. A sign value establishes the relative value of a brand where the functional difference between products is minimal. Contemporary ads operate on the premise that signifiers and signifieds that have been removed from context can be rejoined to other similarly abstracted signifiers and signifieds to build new signs of identity. This is the heart of the commodity sign machine. No cultural analysis of advertising today can ignore the mercurial process of recombining meaning systems in order to generate additional value and desirability for brand-name commodities.

The necessity of differentiating products motivates sign competition. The competition to build images that stand out in media markets is based on a process of routinely unhinging signifiers from signifieds so that new signifier–signified relationships can be fashioned. This process occurs with such rapidity and frequency that we

Timex competes with Swatch in a sign war based on stylistic contests waged by combining "colorful" meaning systems with their wristwatch. These scenes from a Timex commercial offer a textbook example of photographically unhinging and rehinging signifiers and signifieds. Each scene joins an arbitrarily chosen image—pink flamingos; surfing the sky; and a "Southwest" cactus scene—with the Timex product.

scarcely notice it anymore. But, slow down the videotape and the process becomes blatant as advertisers associate meaning systems that otherwise would not occupy the same space: for example, the sleek, phallic grace and power of a fighter jet in a steep climb is joined to an image of a female diver in a Diet Coke ad. The fighter jet is unhinged from its usual context and some of its connotations—sleekness, phallic grace, and power—can now be rehinged to the signified of the cola via the signifier of the gracefully arched female form. Stating the process in this linear march-step fashion makes it seem very mechanistic and formulaic, and to a certain extent it is.

Ads ask us to choose and construct our identities out of our consumption choices. What are the cultural consequences of continuously unhinging and recombining signifiers and signifieds to hail these identities? And what happens when the process of hinging and unhinging accelerates? By the mid-1980s, the average duration of television ad campaigns decreased to less than 13 weeks, as images were taken up and abandoned at an increasingly frenetic pace. That pace has not abated, and viewers are no longer surprised by the MTV-style of mutating images—a style based on an overfamiliarity with media formulas and clichés, and a frenzy of images thrown at us at ever-accelerating speeds until the speed itself is the primary signifier. As Moore remarks:

> Advertising is picking up speed. After more than 45 years of watching television commercials, after more than a decade of MTV and video games, viewers are used to a barrage of visual stimuli. In fact, younger viewers demand it. So television commercials move blindingly fast: Sometimes hundreds of images are crammed into 30 seconds. To follow the story in Nike's 1993 Super Bowl ad, in which

[Michael] Jordan and Bugs Bunny battle Marvin the Martian and his flock of giant green chickens, you probably needed super-slow motion on your VCR. . . . What's pushing this frenetic pace? . . . Zapping. Viewers armed with remote controls can, and will, zap an ad that doesn't hold their interest. They also flash among channels, following the action on several. "They look at little snippets. Then they lean on that thing [the remote control] and they do their own editing at home. They're able to glean the content of six shows instead of one." As a result, commercials have started to skip around, too. "In the past [ad producers] paid the minutest attention to continuity. Now you can shorthand a lot," Sann says. In fact, if you don't, "you're going to bore people and they're going to shut you off."[6]

The appetite of advertising—what we call the commodity sign industry—for new meanings and styles is voracious. The production and reproduction of competitive sign values require the continuous search for cultural matter that might have fresh value. The economy of images drives cultural turnover, eroding the premise that anything carries lasting value (except perhaps the famous iconic trinity of Elvis, Marilyn, and James Dean).

Ads vary widely in the stylistic strategies used to compete in the field of sign value. In the jeans industry, ads for Bongo jeans or Shawnee jeans or Steel jeans are structured by mechanical formulas for making sign values out of fetishized glamour looks. At the other end of the spectrum, Diesel jeans ads construct convoluted, angry, and self-conscious images about cynical and jaded consumption, yet continue to tease with the fetish character of glamour. Practices of sign production have grown more extreme with each passing season in parity industries like the fashion and footwear industries, where jeans and sneakers are distinguished mostly by their signs. With brand names like Get Used or Damaged or Request jeans the sign is the primary commodity—where the commodity, the social relation, and the sign are collapsed into a single signifying field.

In a mature sign economy, allusions to previous ad campaigns become rampant and imagery is fashioned out of bits and pieces of previous signs and media representations, including ads, TV shows, movies, and music videos. When this logic of sign articulation escalates too far, it results in absurd campaigns that race along on the pure logic of pastiche—drawing together and combining meanings that otherwise seem ludicrous in the same sentence. Case in point: Miller Lite's 1993 campaign combines meanings that do not go together—for example, sumo wrestlers with competition divers; rodeo bulldogging and divorce lawyers; recliner ski jumping; drag-strip racing and Wiener dogs—to create a unifying image that functions as an analogy for the combination of meanings that Miller Lite takes as its sign: "Tastes Great" and "Less Filling." While ads like this may seem brain-dead, they illustrate how the logic of constructing novel sign values edges us toward a postmodern world where recom-

Miller Lite: Wiener dog drag racing.

bining meanings to construct differentiated sign values results in a "wild and wacky" TV image world composed of a cut-and-paste culture.

The "look" has become an essential element of currency production because escalating market competition has made it renewable, ephemeral, and disposable. In 1990, Nike's advertising sign machine created a spin-off commodity—a commodity based solely on sign value; a commodity whose sign value eclipsed its use value. Nike put out a new line of T-shirts featuring images drawn from their successful TV ads starring Michael Jordan, Spike Lee, and Bo Jackson. The product targeted teen and preteen boys in a market defined by the circulation of images. Every six weeks, Nike released a new T-shirt with another "hot" image from their ad campaign.[7] This truly is planned obsolescence in the sign industry. This constant refreshing of signs illustrates the imperative of finding new spaces for signs and circulating them as quickly as possible. The same process reveals a fundamental social instability of sign value in a mature political economy of sign value.

The Logic of Appropriation

Advertising continuously appropriates meanings, which it chews up in the process of recontextualizing those meanings to fit commodities or corporations. Think of it as a giant harvesting machine—but instead of harvesting wheat, it harvests signifiers and signifieds of meaning. This harvest of uprooted meanings is delivered to a film editing studio, where it is reorganized according to the "scripts" (and agendas) of the advertiser. Advertising contributes in this way to a postmodern condition in which disconnected signs circulate at ever increasing rates, in which signifiers become detached from signifieds and reattached to still other signifieds.

Constructing a sign value retraces the path of meaning Roland Barthes describes as the transformation of language into myth.[8] It may be useful to walk through his formal grid for tracking the signifier, using an example from a Reebok campaign for the Blacktop shoe. The campaign drew on the referent system of "the blacktop"—a social and cultural space where inner-city youth play basketball. Appropriating signifiers for the purpose of constructing sign values tends to fetishize the signifier. What does this mean? Reebok's Blacktop campaign lifted the photo-

The DJ,

the chain-link fence,

and the fatboys

are turned into reified signifiers of Reebok's appropriation of the "hood," a.k.a. the "Blacktop."

graphic image of the chain-link fence and turned it into a signifier of inner city alienation. Similarly, Reebok has stolen and hollowed out rapper images in the form of the MC and the DJ and the "fatboys." When Reebok took the name of the socially structured space of the asphalt basketball court—the blacktop—and appropriated it as the name for their shoe, they not only sought to inflate the sign value of their shoe, they also turned the blacktop as a social and cultural space into what Barthes called a second-order signifier. Inside the semiotic space of the Reebok ads, the Blacktop (as defined by the chain-link image, the stylized MC image, etc.) has been turned into a reified signifier that marks the "place where legends are made" by Reebok.

Producing marketable commodity signs depends on how effectively advertisers are able to colonize and appropriate referent systems. Few referent systems are immune to this process, although the Bush White House aggressively combated consumer-goods advertising usage of the presidency because of its "sacred" status. Any referent system can be tapped, but remember that advertisers appropriate referent systems for the purpose of generating sign value, so they dwell on referent systems that they calculate might have value to their target audience. Celebrities are usually sought because they have high potential sign value. The referent systems that can pay off most handsomely when properly appropriated involve lifestyle and subcultures. In recent years advertising has appropriated nostalgia, hip-hop music, grunge, and feminist sensibilities. At our current stage of consumer culture, references to the images of these subcultures are drawn from the mass media more often than from daily life.

There exists no finite list of referent systems available for ads; there are as many as humans are capable of subjectively expressing. However, at any given moment, audiences will not be receptive to, and cannot recall, an infinite array of referent systems linked to brand names. At any rate, the issue is not whether all meaning systems will be used up, but rather how the sphere of cultural meaning has been turned over to the service of sustaining a system of commodities. The value-production process is insatiable as meaning systems are abstracted, appropriated, and carved up to fit the agendas of semiotic formulas necessary to fuel the engines of commodity sign production. Over the years, the velocity of this process of meaning circulation has accelerated, and the process of extracting sign value from any given meaning system has become subject to marginally diminishing returns. Ceaseless repetition of this circuit, the ceaseless replacement of images, has led to a rising cultural sensibility that meaning is insubstantial and ephemeral. Much of what has been written in marketing and reporting circles under the rubric of "Generation X" (members of the post-baby-boom generation) chronicles the culture of cynicism that has grown up in response to a cultural world characterized by the constant turnover of superficial meanings.

Sign values depend, then, on a system of cultural cannibalism. Though methods for producing sign values resist capsulation, we can distinguish some general approaches to appropriation. A common approach starts with the positive or "mimetic" appropriation of value. This frequently involves appropriating an image—a celebrity, a style, or the like—that is "hot" in terms of its potential market value. A second route relies on the negative signifier and the practice of counterpositioning, so that a sign value or a sign identity is established by sharply contrasting it with what it is not. A third maneuver adds the self-referential and media-referential domain. Here we enter into the logic of sign and code differentiation. A well-known combination of these strategies is the Energizer Bunny ad campaign, which is premised on using parody to harness the negative value of overused and irritating advertising genres. Like any system of currency, sign values only exist in relation to other values. Because sign values are constructed out of meaning, they must be articulated with reference to another system of value—a meaning system that is external to, and different from, the product. More and more frequently the referent system that is cannibalized to construct a new image comes from the land of television itself.

Effective sign values are rarely manufactured out of thin air. There are, of course, exceptions to this rule—for instance, Spuds MacKenzie for Bud Light. However, the risks associated

The Pepsi "Chillout" campaign gave us this failed sign. Pepsi's gesture unintentionally signified a mechanically overconformist consumer–product relationship.

with inventing an image are considerable, as Burger King (with Herb the Nerd) and Reebok (with its "UBU" campaign) found out. In each case the effort to invent a signifying image or gesture for their signs failed. Inventing a signifier without any basis in daily life (e.g., the Pepsi "summer chillout" gesture) is generally a recipe for sign failure in the contemporary era.

Value Added

Once upon a time, the Nike swoosh symbol possessed no intrinsic value as a sign, but value was added to the sign by drawing on the name and image value of celebrity superstars like Michael Jordan. Michael Jordan possesses value in his own right—the better his performances, the higher his value. The sign of Nike acquired additional value when it joined itself to the image of Jordan. Similarly, when Nike introduced a new shoe line named "Air Huarache" and wanted to distinguish its sign from those of other shoe lines, Nike adopted John Lennon's song "Instant Karma" as a starting point for the shoe's sign value. Nike justified drawing on Lennon's classic song by insisting that it was chosen because it dovetailed with Nike's own message of "self-improvement: making yourself better."[9]

No less common than drawing upon the value of a commodity classic like a famous song is the adoption of a subcultural style or image that has captured the popular imagination; the most pervasive current example of a signifying style appropriated for its sign value is rap or hip-hop music. This is almost invariably based on a cultural trickle-up process in which value is appropriated (it trickles up) while the critical ideological force of the style is dissipated (it trickles away). We emphasize that the mimetic approach to producing sign value works by sponging off other values.

Effective appropriation of a cultural moment or style is contingent on how the ad appellates (hails) its target audience members. An excellent example of appellation can be found in a series of McDonald's ads that hailed the viewer with a dude who speaks in the tongue and intonation of Southern California surfer-valley dudes immortalized and cleaned up in the movie *Bill & Ted's Excellent Adventure*. The "Excellent" campaign, by Leo Burnett USA of Chicago, offers viewers a permanently stoned, long-haired youth who wears the layered garb that signals membership in this subcultural totem group. In one ad he shares with viewers his analysis of navigation:

> *"In the past, when ancient old dudes cruised, they used the stars to lead their way. This was not a very excellent system because they were lost all day and ended up living in bogus caves. But luckily we dudes of today have a most excellent number of highways and very many busy streets, and even more excellent than that—they've all been built right next to a McDonald's."*

Another ad has him acting as a tourist guide, sitting astride a stone wall in front of a mansion as he discourses about the site. The content of his monologues is unimportant; it is the style with which they are delivered that defines the ads and their attitude.

> *"We have here a* major *casa. Home of seriously rich dudes. Now I know rich dudes have the most excellent manners. If we ask politely, well they're sure to invite us in. [He turns toward the mansion and yells out:] Yo, seriously rich dudes. May we come in and see your most excellent stuff? [When there is no reply, he turns back to us with a shrug:] Not home. Must've gone to McDonald's for apple pie or something."*

These ads begin and end with a wildly painted yellow "M" that extends beyond a red block. From its position in the lower right corner of the screen it is obvious that this replaces the ubiquitous golden arches logo of the fast-food giant. A change of this sort in a semiotic building block like the corporate logo should not be taken lightly. McDonald's here shows their moral flexibility to modify their corporate insignia to fit with the aesthetic preferences of a different target audience. Presenting this emblem at the start of the ad is as much a part of the hailing process as the youth who addresses us.

Generation X has recently become the hot topic in the advertising and marketing industries. It's risky hailing youth like this because if the representation does not ring true, then the advertiser has antagonized and estranged the viewer. Young and Rubicam Advertising's director of consumer research advises that when targeting youth, "You need to speak to them in their language and on their terms . . . Contrived 'hip' is the kiss of death with young people."[10] Constructing sign value by appropriating linguistic usage or gestures or music or clothing style also requires careful attention to the process of restyling, which deletes—"airbrushes"—negative moments. Ads that build on a borrowed speech usage or a gesture or a look are based on the tacit acknowledgment that subcultures are the source of authentic— read: desirable—signs. Authenticity must have a referent system to back it up. Whether it is rap or Generation X or punk or grunge, this process of producing sign value makes images palatable by stripping out—extracting—the essential political ideology that initially drove the expression of these discourses. What is left is mere surface.

Driven by the logic of hailing, the practice of cultural appropriation when situated within the framework of the advertisement seems to magically unfold into an equivalency between brand and cultural icon. In an attempt to appeal to the "twentysomething" audience, Chevrolet has recently laid claim to the history of rock 'n' roll as represented by the music of Jimi Hendrix. Chevrolet justified this act of appropriation as "a natural combination. Camaro and rock 'n' roll truly grew up together. For a quarter century, the car and music have been the life of the party." Chevrolet cements this new equivalency with the slogan "From the country that invented rock 'n' roll."[11]

Once a sign is appropriated it circulates between advertising discourse and everyday life in a stylized form—this kind of mediation invariably changes the sign's cultural meanings and associations. Whether or not these signifying efforts are successful in marketing terms, the signs thus produced tend to be reified images of social relations. Despite this, our critique of commodity signs cannot end with the simple assertion that these signs are nothing more than the alienated relations and desires denied people in their production relations. Historically, the cultural emphasis on consuming, owning, and wearing signs as an indicator of personal identity was well under way by the 1920s. Since then, the commodity self has offered an identity assembled out of the sign-objects that a person consumes. Individuals may seek to present an identity through the commodity signs they possess and wear.

Signwork has evolved as a key practice of what Erving Goffman termed "facework" in an impersonal urban society. The commodity self based on the packaging of self as a collection or ensemble of commodity signs is predicated on a certain degree of plasticity. At the very least, advertising has established the premise that the most gratifying social relations are those associated with the confident, and discriminating, sign user. While this contributes to rampant pseudoindividualism,[12] it is also true that commodity signs provide people with real social indicators of identity—after all, consumers do use signs to construct identities and to make invidious distinctions between themselves and others. This is one social consequence of positioning spectator-buyers to step into the advertising mirror.

Two generations ago, Sennett and Cobb examined how wearing badges to earn respect in our urban class-based society resulted in an array of social–psychological injuries.[13] Hebdige tracked how this, in turn, contributed to subcultural resistance to fashion codes, as youth bent the "approved" signs to suit their meanings (signs of disapproval). Hebdige adapted the concept of "bricolage" to describe the act of wearing meaning-laden objects (signs) in ways that seem to violate the cosmology (the moral hierarchies) of consumerism that binds the many signs into a cultural system.[14] As working-class political opposition has become closed off, opposition in the society of the spectacle is most readily expressed through the category of style. Though the code of commodity culture has always been able to reabsorb opposition and turn it into new commodity styles, the punk subculture's efforts at bricolage upped the ante, and advertisers eventually responded by appropriating and restyling the bricolaged look, and then turning it back into yet another commodity sign. Levi's advertising led the way, and others followed, into a period of "counterbricolage."[15]

This movement between bricolage and commodity counterbricolage has in its own right been a form of sign wars. Today, the appropriation process has grown so rapid that it can exploit and exhaust a subcultural movement before it has had time to develop—grunge is a case in point. Grunge has not only been thoroughly appropriated, its style stolen in a media blitz, the term itself has been adopted by the culture industry as a metaphor for what cultural analysts like ourselves call *bricolage*. Grunge has become a mass-media metaphor for the new style of mixing things that don't go together. In this brave new world of hyperappropriation, anything goes— retrolooks from any decade are thrown into the blender, as are the political sensibilities of any marginalized subculture—and everything becomes a mishmash.

Floating Signifiers and the Image Bank

The perpetual abstraction and recombination of images in pursuit of new currency has logically led to the creation of "image banks." Image banks are an institutionally rationalized approach to managing a marketplace of images for the construction of commodity signs in a stage of advanced sign competition. Banks deal in currency. The name *image bank* is indicative of the fact that images have become a free-floating and interchangeable currency. Image banks deal in stock photos—of mountain tops, sunsets, farm scenes, sea birds, and so on—that have been severed from meaningful context. Advertising agencies work with image banks because they provide a cost-cutting measure. Bankable images, catalogued and filed, are a reminder that signifiers and signifieds are no longer conceived of as necessarily or naturally conjoint. The same image or scenic representation may appear in multiple and diverse commodity narratives—for example, the same shot of

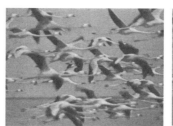 

Du Pont flamingos in flight   Kodak flamingos in flight

flamingo-like waterbirds in flight appears in a Du Pont ad to signify nature-not-yet-destroyed, while in a Kodak film commercial it signifies superior image quality. The image bank also signals a world where there is no necessary material ground—no necessary correspondence between image and referent system. The arbitrariness of the relationship between image signifiers and signifieds has reached a new plateau. A humorous instance of image bank abstraction gone haywire is illustrative. The advertising agency BBDO created a newspaper ad for Apple Computer that proved embarrassing when it discovered that the stock photo of an office building used in the ad was actually an image of the IBM Tower in Atlanta.[16]

Spirals of Referentiality, Speed, and Reflexivity

In the past, most ad campaigns (failures as well as successes) aimed at conveying a coherent and memorable symbolic value for their product by connecting it with an object of desire. But as these symbolic contests have escalated over the years, the turnover of images and symbols has accelerated and the reliance on media intertextuality has increased. This has contributed to an important cultural shift, the "substitution of referential density for narrative coherence."[17] Referential density means that frames become packed with multiple referents minus unifying threads that give the viewer clues about their relationships. Texts become defined not so much by the story they tell, but by the referential combinations they style. Style overwhelms story. Accelerated editing, a refusal to obey sequencing conventions, and a devotion to supermagnified close-ups—all place greater emphasis on the isolated signifier whose meaningfulness is now divorced from the contexts that initially gave meaning to it. Referential density is becoming a prominent characteristic of our cultural landscape, the result of a seemingly endless process of cannibalizing and lifting isolated images from previous media references and reassembling them in pastiche form. Indeed, advertising has shifted from an emphasis on narrative coherence such as that described by Roland Marchand as the "social tableaux"—stories about how to successfully live and act in modern society through the proper use of commodities to visual fascination. While narrative coherence has hardly vanished in the world of ads, its importance has diminished and the old stories have been abbreviated into tacit assumptions.

More and more today, ads either refer to other ads or are about the subject of advertising itself as a method of positioning the commodity brand name. This process is usually referred to as "media self-referentiality" and "intertextuality." Spirals of referentiality are a function of the continuous process of lifting meanings from one context and placing them into the advertising framework where they be-

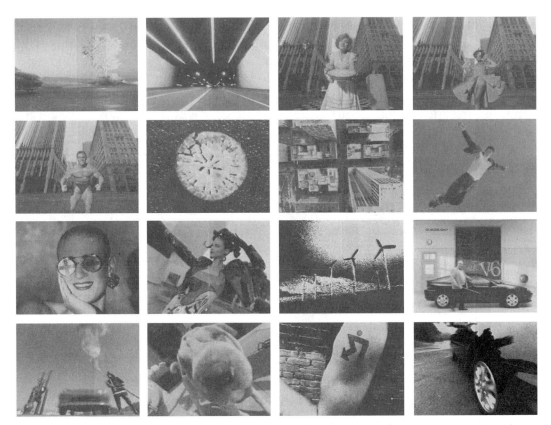

As commercials increase in referential density, images can be thrown together without any relationship to the image that comes before or after. These are but of a few of the arbitrary images that populate a 1992 Mazda ad. No order is implied by our layout.

come associated with another meaning system. Each time this occurs, meanings are modified and chains of signification are constructed. Let's take an apparently simple example of a bell. Initially, a bell may have meaning to you because it is located in the church near your home and you associate its ringing with the time of day when your mother called you home for dinner. In other words, its meaning was linked to its location and to your relationships with others. But as Walter Benjamin and John Berger have both shown, when a bell is photographed, the image is freed from its context and can be put to almost any service. Now the image can be used to signify a brand of tomatoes or it can be used to indicate "not-suburbia." Today, such an image has been used in a generic way to signify tourism or Europeanness. In fact, the placeless bell seen here is for us what we call a "Euro-signifier." We have just described what Barthes meant by second-order signifiers—that is, the bell now stands for Europeanness. Barthes understood that in the modern era this process of hinging and unhinging signifiers and signifieds could go on and on as the image of the bell gets lifted from its new context of generic tourism for use in yet another way. In this sense, advertising contributes to a world littered by second-order signifiers. The circuit of sign–value production is predicated on the diffusion of second-order signifiers. In advertising, harnessing the power of splitting the sign (much like an

The bell as Euro-signifier.

atom) releases significant potential energy as each signifying valence is steered toward recombination with another split sign to produce a new sign value. But this process also produces cultural by-products. In advertising, one result is an abnormally high level of second-order signifiers—what Barthes saw as the fundamental element of myth.

For decades, advertisers sought to avoid raising the subject of their ad's agenda or the power dynamic going on between text and viewer. Instead, the focus was on the glitter of the spectacular moment. But after decades of this, audiences have matured, become more media-literate, media-saturated, and media-cynical. The arbitrariness of the process eventually rises to the surface and can no longer be ignored. By the latter 1980s there emerged a genre of ads that played at being self-reflexive about the arbitrary process of meaning construction in ads. A new spiral emerged in which advertisers tried to top one another in how outrageous they can be in their self-reflexive acknowledgments.

Cultural Crisis and Contradiction

Where does this conversation about advertising culture fit in relation to changes in culture, the economy, and society? How are the spirals of speed, referential density, and media reflexivity related to the larger goings-on of our culture? We have previously argued that advertising has upheld culturally predominant ways of seeing things. Predominant ways of seeing are, however, almost always being contested or stretched by opposing social forces and relations. For example, in American society, patriarchy's long hegemony has recently been effectively contested by women who find patriarchal ways of seeing as too confining and repressive to meet their interests.

Saying that advertising tends to further the hegemony of commodity and market relations does not mean that advertisers are a wily ideological bunch intent on manipulating us politically. When we look at ads as an ideological site, we see ads as ideological in all the following senses: (1) as discourses that socially and culturally construct a world; (2) as discourses that disguise and suppress inequalities, injustices, irrationalities, and contradictions; (3) as discourses that promote a normative vision of our world and our relationships; and (4) as discourses that reflect the logic of capital. In this sense, ideology refers to the "meaning made necessary by the conditions of our society while helping to perpetuate those conditions."[18] Ads are ideological insofar as they construct socially necessary illusions and normalize distorted communication.[19] We are studying ads, then, because we think ads reveal some inner cultural contradictions of a commodity culture.

Advertisements offer rich social texts for investigating the socially constructed nature of hegemony because they are situated at the intersection of conflicting economic and cultural demands: on the one hand, advertisements must devote themselves to reproducing commodity relations (selling more products); on the other hand, they must engage the attention and interpretive participation of consumers by hailing them with images of their own "alreadyness." Ads thus can be made to reveal not only a dominant mode of representation, but also the self-contradictory representations of commodity culture.

This book focuses on two sides of the same coin: on sign wars, battles over the currency of images, and on the cultural contradictions of a political economy of sign value. As ideological discourses for understanding these cultural contradictions, ads can be made to speak a certain kind of truth about the commodity culture that produces them. To the extent that ads must give us back some sense of ourselves, they also unintentionally capture our cultural contradictions. Insofar as advertisers today feel the pressure to efficiently hail finely targeted audience segments, they must include signifiers of the self-contradictions manifested by this or that target group "persona" in their representations. In the last few years, in addition to the many ads that either try to suppress or disguise contradictions, we now have ads that literally swim in their self-reflexive awareness of issues of domination and power in commodity culture. Indeed, some ads now flaunt their own contradictoriness, or that of our culture, to gain attention for themselves. Today the practice of cultural criticism seems to be sponsored by commodity interests.

Herbert Marcuse's *One-Dimensional Man*, written in 1964, is the classic statement of the culture industry's capacity for containing opposition.[20] Marcuse argued that when culture was turned into commodity form it could contain contradictions and blunt critical alternative ways of seeing. He felt the process of commodifying language purged the vernacular of "class" from mass-mediated discourses, even though it remained an animating force in the landscape of everyday work life. Thirty years later, class has indeed been erased from public discourse, supplanted by the category of individual life-style; but the culture industry's capacity to contain crisis and contradiction has become disengaged from its capacity to redirect the language of resistance and opposition. While the evidence is compelling that advertising is able to appropriate and incorporate the language and visual representations of resistance, we are less convinced by the capacity of advertising to contain crisis tendencies.

Ironically, in a world where advertisers are forever struggling to stylistically differentiate themselves, more than ever before they depend on symbols of cultural opposition to drive the sign–value circuit. In fact, in the course of writing this book we have come to believe that while some advertising is aimed at containing contradictions (e.g., the environmental consequences of capitalist growth), advertising has itself become the site of new cultural crisis tendencies and emergent cultural contradictions, not the least of which is a profoundly privatized cynicism.

Advertising is in crisis, yet somehow it remains the voice of commodity hegemony. Its formulas have antagonized viewers. Its cultural products no longer merely incorporate opposition to produce images of harmony, although god knows there are plenty of advertisers who still try. While the advertising form has historically functioned as a site for ideologically masking social and cultural contradictions, the neat, clean, and tidy categories of the past have been sublated.

In this study, although we frequently stop to explore in-depth one particular ad or another, our argument emphasizes not the particular ad, but the system of ads— the sheer abundance of ads driven by the logic of capital and the reproduction of commodities. As a system, advertising produces sign wars, and sign wars will have real cultural consequences. Indeed, perhaps we should begin by asking what collective crises of meaning lie in store for a culture and society characterized by an increasing circulation velocity of images made necessary by sign wars.

Sign Wars

"*IMAGE* is everything!" shouts Andre Agassi, a celebrity tennis player endorsing Canon cameras. A major portion of the marketing world agrees. These days, objects of consumption that do not have an emblem, logo, or sign associated with them rarely have lasting market value. Today's corporate competition to sell commodities is centered on *the brand image, the look, the sign.*

> Image has become the predominant currency of television advertising these days. Increasingly campaigns are being reduced to strands of simple yet stylish scenes that speak volumes to viewers. Attitudes, values, characteristics, relative degrees of hipness and relevancy—all are communicated not so much by words anymore but by how you look, what you wear, what you do.[1]

This competitive stress on images—as signs—has made the sign war an increasingly familiar part of our electronic cultural landscapes of the 1980s and 1990s. A turning point in the nature and intensity of sign wars can be traced to the Coke vs. Pepsi cola wars of the early 1980s. Since then, sign wars have become routine and "cola wars" has become a generic term for sign/image competitions across product categories. Other such competitions include the beer wars (Miller vs. Bud vs. Coors), the sneaker wars (Nike vs. Reebok vs. LA Gear), the credit card wars (Visa vs. American Express vs. Mastercard), the phone wars (AT&T vs. MCI vs. Sprint), the car wars (Honda vs. Toyota vs. Saturn), and so on.

Though the most familiar sign wars may involve advertising campaigns that explicitly and pejoratively name their enemy—Pepsi named Coke; Apple named IBM; Stroh's named Bud; MCI named AT&T; Visa named American Express; Reebok named Nike—we see sign wars as a more generic phase in the maturation of a political economy of sign value. Usually, the firm that launches an explicit sign attack is trying to grab market share from the dominant firm in an industry. Challengers for market share are much more likely to take chances in sign wars; conversely, the leading firm in a market segment tends to publicly disregard its competitors in the industry.[2] If, however, a challenger's sign campaign successfully gains consumer attention, then the dominant firm will counterattack.

Exemplifying the attack and counterattack moves of the sign wars is the escalating negative advertising of long-distance phone carriers. AT&T monopolized the long-distance phone market until deregulation of the industry in 1984. Subsequently, MCI and Sprint slowly chipped away at AT&T's market share, such that by 1990 MCI had a 14.2% share and Sprint a 9.2% share, to AT&T's 65% share. With each point of market share worth $520 million in 1990, it is easy to see why these three firms spent nearly $1 billion on advertising in that year alone. AT&T and MCI went at it tooth and nail in ads that competed at signifying "real life" in order to establish themselves as *your* family's long-distance phone carrier.[3] After MCI introduced their home movie–style "Friends and Family" ad campaign, AT&T responded with aggressive counterads that sympathized with consumers whose names and numbers were given without their consent to harassing MCI telemarketers (in U.S. culture the telemarketer is a hated and despised figure who pesters, nags, and keeps you on the phone). AT&T's ads hammered away at the social blunder of giving the names of friends and family members to MCI phone sales, thus implicating MCI as a manipulator of personal relations. According to AT&T, with MCI you sell your soul and betray your loved ones. As MCI and Sprint have cut deeper into AT&T's market share in recent years, the sniping has grown increasingly nasty.[4] "It's very much like a political campaign. Except this campaign never ends," observed Thomas Messner, whose company made the MCI ads.[5] The similarity between the negative advertising of political campaigns, which have also become sign wars, and campaigns in maturing commodity markets has not been lost on industry executives who worry that mudslinging in campaigns for consumer goods will further damage the credibility of advertising in general. Castellanos has noted the congruence between political and advertising campaigns:

> MCI invites phone callers to hang up on AT&T. Coors asks beer drinkers to can Budweiser. Pizza Hut delivers a slice to Domino's. Ads for Tums give Rolaids heartburn. Why the negative, political-style edge? Survival. Blame not just the recession but maturing American markets. When growth stops, companies are left only one source of new customers—their rivals. The result? More political-style negative and comparative advertising. Market leaders have become threatened incumbents as consumers vote every day with their pocketbooks.[6]

This fierce advertising competition stems from the fact that long-distance phone services "are all so similar in quality and price that the main thing left to sell is some advertising wizard's image of what phone companies should be."[7]

Sign wars index the rationalization of advertising and marketing devoted to cultivating brand-name awareness. Sign wars heat up as it becomes more difficult to differentiate products by functionality, by price, or even by the accompanying imagery that constitutes sign value. Sign wars represent an escalation of sign competition pushed along by corporate concentration across national markets. As signs have taken off into new global markets, sign wars have flared across cultures, while intensifying in the United States, where image clutter has already saturated the marketplace. Image-centered competition in selling consumer goods has intensified in correspondence with the growing standardization of producing consumer goods. Image competition coupled with technological advance produces ever more spectacular images. As sign wars cruise along, *speed* becomes a critical variable in the competition—for example, AT&T reduced its advertising response time to a rival maneuver from a year in 1980 to weeks by 1990.[8]

Brand image has shifted from reputation based on product function to symbolic image value. Moving from product attributes to the powers of signification shifted the question of brands into the realm of psychology. Situating brand image "entirely inside consumers' minds"[9] bred an advertising style based on overstructured messages and intensive commodity fetishism. The formula is so familiar we take it for granted. In print ads, it follows this map: A caption is designed to make meaningful a relationship between product and image. The caption creates an axis of combination. We know that when placed within the framing boxes, images become partially unhinged from their previous meaning locations, and so we look to the instructions in the caption to discover how they might be recombined. Crudely, the combination of meanings accomplished in this chemical reaction is a commodity sign.

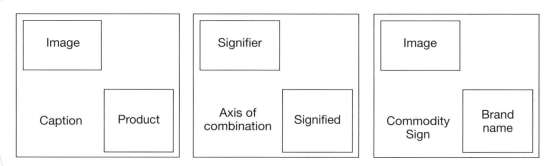

Mapping the logic of the commodity sign.

In the 1980s, brand-image management became a tool for cultivating product differentiation. Now well established, the strategic devotion to manipulating brand personalities divorced from the material attributes of products has contributed to creating wary and alienated viewers who "zap" ads and distrust promotions. Further, the escalating reliance on sign wars differentiation has also sped up the maturation process in numerous industries. For example, thanks both to sign wars and high-tech competition, the sneaker industry "reached a level of maturity in ten years for what's normally a fifty-year business cycle."[10] Besides engaging in aggressive contests to establish brand images, leading corporations now devote nearly as much effort to maintaining market share, a task that requires leading brands to continually

> invest in brand equity. Heavyweights put big money behind brand building. And it's less important whether such funds are categorized as advertising or sales promotion than whether they help underwrite creating and sustaining strong brand identity. Continuous investment is the rule of most heavyweights—which is why Coca-Cola is the world's most valuable trademark.[11]

"What's in a name?" asks one headline. The answer is "billions." Corporate mergers and takeovers in the 1980s prompted a recognition that it is crucial to measure the value of "intangibles": the value of the brand image. Marketers have refined their accounting methods to better calculate the value of brand images not just because a strong brand image means market share but also because brand images have become capital assets.[12]

> In many industries, a company's brand assets can easily exceed its tangible assets. In 1988, for example, Philip Morris Co. acquired Kraft Foods for $12.9 billion, including an estimated $11.6 billion for intangibles. Recent press reports estimate intangibles assets of $2.9 billion at Coca-Cola, $4.6 billion at Kodak, $5.3 billion at General Motors, and $8.5 billion at General Electric. One executive for Cadbury Schweppes stated that of the $220 million his firm paid to acquire the Hires and Crush soft-drink business from Procter & Gamble, only $20 million was for physical assets. The rest was "brand value."[13]

Though brand image has become a form of capital to be measured and managed, its extreme fluidity makes it subject to many forms of disruption. Sign value cannot be bottled and preserved. Brand equity dissipates quickly if left unattended; thus it requires dedicated maintenance. This is particularly difficult in competitive markets where a commodity sign is not only subject to sign wars, but also vulnerable to the dynamics of other competitive strategies. For example, price wars can effectively undo efforts at brand differentiation in markets characterized by minor product differentiation. If consumers can be certain that during any given month either Pepsi or Coke will undercut the other in terms of price, then consumers will have less interest in brand loyalty. As Bill Saporito notes, "For makers of consumer products, the danger of a price war is that brand equity—so expensive to build—erodes, and products become commodities, [again]."[14]

Sign Wars and Semiotics

Sign wars are economic activities! But they are economic activities in which the raw material worked into commodities is *Meaning* (our cultural fabric). As a form of cultural production, sign wars reduce meaning to a disposable economic resource.

Superimposed meaning systems form the Busch sign.

Day after day, ads combine and recombine signifiers and signifieds to define a sign currency that can be joined to commodities (products and services). It's a process geared to transferring meaning from one system (e.g., cowboys) to another (a brand-name commodity, such as Busch beer). Mechanically, an advertisement is a space where meaning is arranged so that transfers of meaning can take place. Advertisers try to steer these transfers to accomplish the transfer of value from one system (e.g., motherhood) to another (a brand-name commodity). They do not always succeed. And even when they do succeed, the cultural consequences of enacting these transfers of meaning do not end there, for they become another referential moment in what has become an unending chain of media-referential signification. Our study of sign wars tracks how the circuit of advertising breaks apart, reroutes, and recombines signifiers and signifieds. Exemplifying this fracturing and recombination of signifiers and signifieds, a recent Diet Coke campaign used new technology to insert old movie scenes featuring Gene Kelly, Humphrey Bogart, and Cary Grant into con-

Video magic lets Diet Coke mix and match celebrities, living and dead. Here, Paula Abdul appears as if she is dancing, singing, and socializing with Gene Kelly, Groucho Marx, and Cary Grant.

temporary scenes featuring celebrities such as Paula Abdul. While the original source of the clips remains significant (e.g., Gene Kelly dancing in *Anchors Aweigh*) it becomes secondary to the movie icon's simulated interaction with modern celebrities. The power of Diet Coke brings together signifying "entities" (not "persons" any longer because their placement in the ad has stripped them of that meaning and converted them into signifiers of media history) from different historical epochs and forces them into a "discourse" that celebrates the sign of Diet Coke.[15]

Advertisers often work in ways mindful of how the pioneer of semiotics, Saussure, approached his task, slicing everything into paired categories. Advertisers frequently define their positioning category by juxtaposing it against a negative signifier. One way to define sign value is in terms of what it is *not*. For example, auto repair chains like Midas typically define their value by ridiculing owners of independent garages as greasy, overweight, illiterate slobs. By contrast, Midas associates itself with imagery of clean-cut, slender, and well-mannered technicians. And, of course, countless items have been marketed to adolescent audiences using the juxtaposition, "What's *hot*. What's *not*."

Sign wars represent a mature stage of brand competition. With each successive round of sign competition, semiotics has become increasingly annexed as a tool and foregrounded as substance. Just as critics like ourselves have adopted semiotic strategies for decoding ads as texts, advertisers have begun to explicitly reveal the same strategies in their encoding process. The foregrounding of semiotic play set apart the 1989 Michelob Dry ad campaign that tried to establish a new commodity image via a series of semiotic equations ("What Dry Was . . . What Dry Is") aimed at redefining "dry" to mean Michelob's beer. Once Michelob Dry achieved recognition by representing itself via alternating paired oppositions of meanings, other beer advertisers played copycat in the quest to identify who they are by what they are not. It quickly became impossible to distinguish one beer ad from another, since they all used the same repetitive semiotic formula: for example, "This is [Miller time]. This is [not]." Already, the approach has become so formula-bound that its limited effectiveness depends on the stylized imagery used to fill the visual semiotic spaces. In the "not" space, the advertiser inserts speed-

Miller Lite's version of binary semiotic opposition. Silly archival footage signifies "not" Miller Lite, while a sextet of bikini-clad girls signifies Miller Lite.

ed up trash archival footage (in black and white) of silly stunts; in contrast, the space for marking the sign's identity carries a color image of the Busch "babe" or the Miller "babe" or the Coors "babe."

Of course, constructing mechanical semiotic oppositions as a method of reinforcing such singular messages has spread beyond the beer market. A current Sure deodorant commercial illustrates the basic semiotic formula. The technique consists of alternating sequences of paired oppositions between images of people labeled as: "Sure" (scenes of social confidence, a product user) versus "unsure" (someone unable to

Playtex uses the same technique of paired oppositions to juxtapose their bra's comfort with parodied fashion discomfort.

behave spontaneously without feeling uncertain and embarrassed, that is, not a product user). In a similar fashion, Yamaha valorizes itself by setting up obvious visual contrasts between "cool" (a Yamaha jet ski) and "uncool" (archival footage of tame 1950s water play).

A memorable instance of coming close to "pure" sign value was the Infiniti campaign that showed no product but only imagery that fed their brand awareness— their sign, their emblem, their logo. Because ad messages must stand out, the intro-

Metaphor as sign value: Infiniti's well-known "Zen" campaign relied heavily on visual metaphor.

ductory campaign for Infiniti showed no cars, but instead offered images of rocks, trees, and water accompanied by a voiceover consisting of a Zen-like philosophical discourse about our relationship with nature. The Infiniti campaign was predicated on differentiating itself from the contemporary fixation with flashy images—drawing attention to the alienated character of this fetish, quietly appearing to oppose it, and then pushing the fetish further still. The Infiniti campaign drew viewer attention because the product was absent; stated another way, the ad violated our expectation that images will be immediately joined to commodities. This campaign stood out because the viewer kept waiting for the payoff, the expected semiotic splicing of product and image.

It's a wild, wild semiotic world in advertising these days. The name of the game is to stand out, and the place where that is most likely to occur is in methods of signifying style. When there is no clear way of differentiating products or even positioning strategies, all that is left is style of signification constructed via technical adjustments in the image-production process—for example, a never-before-seen color tint, fonts that mutate, split screens, quick cuts, wild new colors, no depth of field. Style of signification is what has set Nike advertising apart—the company is recognized, as Bob Garfield has noted, for its "unique telling proposition."[16] We call this a "unique signifying style." Lost in the sign wars blur of "breakthrough" signifying styles is the truth that style has eclipsed substance.

Differentiation, Imitation, and the Circulation of Sign Values

Difference drives the sign machine. The dynamic between diffferentiation and imitation drives the circulation of sign values. When an advertiser successfully assembles a popular new sign value or a new signifying style, competitors try to imitate it. In this context, imitation triggers sign clones. Imitation can also exhaust the currency of the new sign value, setting in motion a renewed drive for a differentiated sign position. Imitation gives rise to sign and message clutter.

The dialectic of differentiation and imitation propels the advertising industry "in a world where innovations are easily copied and product differences slight. In the purgatory of parity goods, image is king. And in the quest for image, agency–client relationships are increasingly fragile."[17] Agency-hopping becomes the norm as clients desperately cast about for the image and style that will give them additional market share.

Clutter, clutter everywhere. There are "so many ads that individual commercials get lost in the electronic undergrowth."[18] When advertisements become a never-ending parade of images and no space is free from their appeal or their intrusion, then viewers respond by being less attentive. Viewers often watch no more than a few seconds of commercials before they switch channels.[19] Hence, advertisers "want to make their commercials zap-proof and memorable. TV viewers sit armed with remote control devices, ready to click their way through an infinite number of cable channels to avoid being subjected to boring commercials."[20] The dilemma faced by corporate advertisers today is how to cut through the clutter and get viewers to notice their message. Advertisers often respond with even more spectacular executions. One approach to the problem in magazine advertising has been to compound the clutter by creating continuous-page ad blocks.[21] There are many ways to beat clutter, but few approaches work very long "in the age of déjà . . . everything."[22] For instance, in 1989 advertisers discovered archival footage as a way of "busting through the clutter," but overuse quickly exhausted the new technique's ability to arrest our gaze.[23] Stylistic phenomena come and go, driven by the search for a differentiated look, and drained of interest by copycat advertisers. Levi's blued the landscape, and soon even K-Mart sported the look. Hand-held shaky cameras were the rage in the late 1980s, a favorite encoding device of the "realism" thing. Advertisers in the mid-1980s figured baby boomers would love 1960s Motown music with their cars, with their food, with everything.

The "quest for clutter-free space has taken Goodyear to the sky in a blimp and Oscar Mayer to the streets in a Wienermobile."[24] There are already plans underway to beam ads into the space of the nighttime sky, where they will be reflected off orbiting satellites, as advertisers search for new and as-yet-uncluttered spaces. Robert Hughes once spoke of the "shock of the new" as a way of framing modern art. In the obsessive quest to secure further consumption, advertising must continually seek new spaces to colonize and new ways to shock us into attentiveness. And what's more, the circuit seems to run faster—the new wears off more and more rapidly and we still can't get enough satisfaction. We have become addicted to the pleasures of abstracted meanings.

Sameness of product and advertising styles propels alternative advertising methods that obey the logic of sign differentiation. Here, sign value may be generated by transgressing conventional normative boundaries and/or coding boundaries—by going against the grain of other advertisements and signs. A diminishing range of unexplored referent systems drawn from daily life in conjunction with saturation of ad formulas prompted a movement toward self-reflexive advertising—ads that seek not to differentiate their product from one another, but their advertising method from that of their competitor. Typically, these new signifying styles have themselves usually been engulfed in a spiral of mimesis. From 1984 to 1986, the Levi's "501 Blues" campaign exemplified the success of a differentiated encoding style—a combination of camera and film-editing techniques that imparted a "truer" sense of a non-mediated reality. By violating the rigidly defined coding formulas that dominated advertising in the late 1970s and the early 1980s, the Levi's campaign identified itself *against* the fantasy consumption stories told by most ads. At first this new style was hip, but by the late 1980s even politicians were adopting it.

Ads of the late 1980s grew ever more elaborate in the unbridled effort to stand out amid the clutter. Like Reebok's "UBU" series these ads were cerebral, complex, and often garish, usually seeking to deny their own status as advertisements.[25] But their density soon created its own clutter, so by the early 1990s "simplicity" and "direct, even obvious advertising" returned. The reductive movement in advertising continued—with everything distilled out save the tacit encoding practices built into the advertising framework itself—while logos grew in size and prominence. Simpler ads were also cheaper to produce in a time of economic recession.[26] The direction of the corporate sign economy lurched back toward consolidating brand equity in the form of identifiable logos.[27]

Each year, print and TV advertising becomes more image-based. Meanwhile, text grows shorter—in part because it had become redundant and unnecessary, and in part because media-literate viewers had come to resent overly directive text. Of course, the amount of text in relation to images had been diminishing since the 1930s. In the late 1980s, captions and tag lines and voiceovers vanished and intentional ambiguity was introduced into the decoding process. In the reaction that followed, Wieden & Kennedy pioneered the use of scrolling type and jumbled combinations of fonts and font sizes in their 1992 Subaru campaign. Here was text to guide viewers' interpretation of the images that flowed next to it on screen. But this was no longer static text: these were mobile and playful words that now called attention to themselves as signs

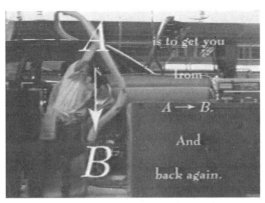

After years of eliminating text in favor of images, advertisers rediscovered fonts as images, thus turning written text into kinetic objects designed to arrest viewers' attention.

in their own right and not simply as functional carriers of meaning. Since then, customized fonts and moving type have saturated the advertising world. Elliott has observed that,

> In spot after spot sponsored by large marketers like A.T.&T., Citibank, Coca-Cola, Jaguar and Pepsi-Cola ... words seem to obey the unspoken commands of hyperactive lexicographers by rolling, floating, scrolling, dissolving, shrinking, expanding, leaping and hopping their way up, down and across the screen. Onscreen typography has become a potent strategy by which to capture the attention of restless viewers, who use their remote controls to graze among channels.[28]

In an age when floating signifiers predominate, the adoption of floating words began as a method of motivating viewers to become more involved in deciphering the ad message, but it was so rapidly imitated and with such indiscriminateness that it is no longer possible to differentiate the lettering styles or combinations of fonts of one brand from another. A technique like dancing fonts "becomes an end in itself, presented by ad creators more as a way to catch the attention of viewers rather than to define or set apart the product's message."[29] Jack Trout, a leading marketing consultant, worries that advertisers "are less concerned with the idea of what makes the product different and more concerned with what makes the advertising look different."[30]

Another familiar instance of this circuit of differentiation and mimesis in recent years involves the Eveready Energizer battery ads featuring the pink mechanical bunny who disrupts simulated commercials for stereotyped products.[31] The Energizer campaign established itself as the sign of irreverent parody by exposing the formulas and transgressing the coding boundaries of genre commercials on TV. No sooner had the Energizer ad campaign struck sign paydirt with its impious intruder than other advertisers began to parody the parody, thus tapping into the power of the Energizer sign value. The most notable rip-off of the Energizer bunny as a signifier was made by Coors Beer. Eveready responded by taking Coors to court for trademark infringement. Eveready was likewise approached by other firms who sought to share the Energizer mechanical bunny in joint promotions. In each case, Eveready sought to limit other uses of the bunny "to control the property, because we don't want to burn him out."[32] A burnt-out advertising sign loses potency, and its ability to add value to the brand name diminishes sharply.

Still, the most ubiquitous sign wars ads appear everyday for goods like beer, cars, and jeans. These ads are usually based on well-paved formulas for establishing sign values. While the goal of each campaign may be a differentiated sign value, the steering mechanism guiding these ads is a slavish devotion to what research departments say about the audience and the market. As a result, many campaigns aimed at cultivating an efficient sign value are actually quite undifferentiated. After all, in selling beer to young males few advertisers are willing to risk not showing an attractive and waiting female as the sign of their product. Circa 1990 it seemed that virtually every major beer brand offered their own stylized version of fantasy, having exhausted the realist approach to signifying beer brands. Some see parity advertising as the curse of parity products. Where products have no objective differences and consumers are unable to perceive differences that matter, advertisers feel "forced to be merely charming, to trade on image, to win friends."[33] Consumer goods, for the most part, require sign value. The few may differentiate themselves via this process, while the many are bandwagon jumpers who tilt the arrow back toward image parity. The irony of parity advertising is that it is pushed along by firms like AT&T and Coke as a means of maintaining brand equity and market share, but in the long run this makes it "curtains for brand equity."[34]

Attacking Signs: Strategies for Sign Wars

There are so many variations on the general methods of sign value construction that we cannot possibly specify every campaign strategy and technique for articulating sign values in the contest for market supremacy. Sign wars usually mean that advertisers try to position their sign (the summation of their image) as superior to the sign of their opposition. Hence, ads that contrast brand images try to position their sign as transcending that of their competitor. Barely a decade ago the cola wars introduced the primitive sign wars strategy of the blindfolded consumer product taste test. Though these ads seemed, at first glance, to be about whose product tasted better, they were really about showing that one sign, even when covered or concealed, shone through.

Today's sign war ads are more likely to show a sign transcending or surpassing the opposition sign, usually by relying on sly humorous twists. A short-lived, but notorious, sign war ad of this sort was the Reebok Pump ad that showed two bungee jumpers side by side. One wears Reebok Pumps and the other wears Nike shoes. They leap from a bridge into the void. While the Reebok wearer has a thrilling but safe leap because his Pumps fit snugly, the Nike wearer apparently falls out of his shoes to his death, since the final scene features the youth wearing the Reeboks suspended from a bungee cord, with a dangling pair of Nike shoes next to him. "The Pump from Reebok," a voiceover observes, "it fits a little better than the average athletic shoe." The ad was designed as a joke to reveal the semiotic superiority of the Reebok over the Nike sign. Though the ad was almost immediately yanked off the air because of outraged protests by parents, sources claimed that Reebok had to increase production 200% to meet demand created by the spot.[35]

Less ballyhooed, but no less an attack on its adversary's sign, was a Plymouth Laser RS Turbo ad that literally marked out the sign of

In this sign wars ad, Beneficial Finance constructed a semiotic juxtaposition between themselves and big banks that loan vast sums of money to dictators such as Noriega. In contrast to the Noriega image, Beneficial is represented by their devotion to the iconography of nuclear families like yours.

their competitor, Nissan Z. The Plymouth ad was shot entirely in extremely tight closeup of typewriter keys striking a fibrous bond paper surface. The key strikes and the letter *Z* appears on the page. This refers back to a Nissan Z ad that featured a similar closeup of rag bond paper as a voiceover narrated: "This is where we started, a clean sheet of paper. No boundaries, no rules, no preconceived ideas. . . . A car destined to leave its mark. . . ." As a chorus of voices mounts in intensity, a single typewriter key abruptly strikes the clean white page with a thunderous clap, leaving its mark: the letter *Z*. However, the Plymouth ad applies whiteout over the *Z* while a voiceover cautions that "if you think the Nissan ZX is faster from zero to sixty than any American car, [pause, the sound effects of screeching tires and five staccato banging sounds as the typewriter keys emphatically strike the page one letter at a time to spell out "LASER"], you stand corrected." Plymouth literally "corrects"—marks out and replaces—its rival's sign with its own.

Pepsi's construction of sign currency established a distinctive and recognizable style in their 1980s battles with Coke: the signifying style of Pepsi TV commercials became a brand benefit.[36] Pepsi ads were based on stories or jokes, usually made at Coke's expense. The popular "Shady Acres" ad shown during the 1990 Super Bowl worked as a joke because it was based on a narrative twist that openly acknowledges the nature of advertising for parity products. Pepsi starts us off by telling a joke about advertising and images. Pepsi points to their own parity industry, when the delivery guy shrugs and says "Coke, Pepsi, what's the difference?" Yet the remainder of the ad is devoted to showing a difference by yanking Coke's chain. After all, college frat boys who sip Coke are dozing off while lethargically going through the motions of playing bingo, while the residents of a nursing home guzzle Pepsi and boogie. The difference lies apparently in the sign of the object (Pepsi). The pleasure of the joke sells the sign. Pepsi's sign is energy and youthfulness, contrasted with the snail-paced tedium of the Coke universe where there is no viable sign—no hot signifiers, nothing but boredom! Pepsi stands out because of its *attitude*. Pepsi's primary commodity becomes the ads themselves—the ad was itself the pleasurable unit of consumption.

Frat boys who drink Coke play bingo; old folks who drink Pepsi boogie.

Pepsi told a similar joke in many of its ads. The Pepsi "Archaeology" ad jokes that in the future, the Coke bottle—once the world's most familiar commercial icon—will be an unidentifiable ancient relic when it is unearthed by archaeologists.

A future archaeology professor is stumped by the "find" of a dirt-encrusted Coca-Cola bottle.

By the 1980s, advertisers aimed as much at legitimating consumer choices as at creating them. In mature consumer-goods industries, a significant proportion of advertising aims at stealing market share from rivals and another portion aims at reinforcing consumer choices. Another Pepsi ad featured MC Hammer, the energetic rap music star, in concert, taking a sip from a Coke and then slipping into a syrupy, comatose Muzak sound to the dismay of his shocked audience. When an audience member rushes to his rescue by offering him a can of Pepsi, Hammer's voice and body returns to its former hip, rapping energy. Pepsi chips away at Coke's signifying claim ("Coke adds life") with a counterpoint (Coke annuls spirit) while also affirming Pepsi as the choice of those who possess energy and style.

Coke has taken aim at Pepsi less often, although their "Max Headroom" ads sought to silence the "P" word. In those ads, Coke invested considerable effort into repressing the signifying presence of Pepsi. Coke appropriated the Headroom character's popularity without maintaining his moral sensibility. Max Headroom had appeared as a critical and disruptive voice in a futuristic story about the culture of domination enforced by capitalist media corporations. An amalgam of the human spirit and computer-media technologies, Max Headroom as originally conceived was a stuttering, irreverent, truth-speaking cyber-spirit, the proverbial talking head. He defied authority and convention—playing the role of ideology critic in a closed society. But the Coke ad opens with Headroom on a theater screen as he turns his head toward the young crowd seating themselves and takes notice of them: "Hiya—wait—wait—waiting to see the show?" In a camera pan across the audience, we spy one Pepsi cup among a sea of Coke cups. Max has seen it too and as the camera backtracks he says: "Uh oh, I see the P word." Nervous laughter follows as everyone stretches to see who the offender is. The boy holding the cup sinks into his chair while his embarrassed date reacts by shooing him away to correct his grievous social faux pas. Max continues: "Listen to this. Next time

Can't Beat The Real Thing.

reach for a Coke, become a Cokeologist. What are you waiting for? Catch the wave!"
At Coke's direction, Max Headroom has moved from critic to shill, from dissident to
the voice of conformity, representative of Coke (the authoritarian state). Coke disguises social conformity under the sign of hipness (Headroom). As the ad ends, Max
vanishes, to be replaced by the more prosaic tones of a professional announcer. A
Coke and Pepsi can appear side by side and the Pepsi can slowly dissolves and disappears as the corporate voice flatly repeats Max's message: "Don't say the P word, and
catch the wave. Coke. The taste that wins the test."

Appropriating Rival Signifiers

Parity products invite sign wars based on signifier appropriation. A multistaged
episode in the automobile industry began with a series of Lexus ads featuring champagne glasses and ball bearings as visual measures of the superior engineering quality
of the Lexus vehicle. Shortly thereafter, Nissan Altima called attention to the Lexus
ball-bearing test in their ads—and then borrowed these signifiers to "demonstrate"
how the same test revealed that their car was as equally well engineered as the Lexus.
Since their product was priced substantially lower than the Lexus, their claim was
that the Nissan was a superior value.

Next, a BMW ad called attention to the
wine-glass test *and* the ball-bearing test
and denounced each as concocted and
irrelevant measures of driving performance. Instead, the BMW ad calls for
its own hairpin-turn test. These showy
visual measures, initially undertaken to
indicate the functional superiority (the
use value) of the product, quickly become mere signifiers of that superiority.
As each competitor tried to one-up
each other, they attempted to turn a
sign against their competitor and in

The wine-glass test.

their favor. Nissan appropriated the Lexus signifier, while BMW attacked the ball
bearings and champagne glasses as inappropriate signifiers; BMW then borrowed
them as indexical signs that point the "wrong way."[37]

A 1993 Honda Civic campaign took shape as a subtle sign wars campaign aimed
at Saturn, Toyota, and Subaru. One ad was predicated on a Toyota ad featuring someone grazing across the channels with their remote control device—the joke in the
Toyota ad is that the viewer cannot resist returning to the Toyota ad. Honda in turn

has someone grazing with a remote control device but no matter what channel the individual turns to he or she cannot escape the superiority of the Honda Civic. Honda appropriates the zapping reference and constructs its own version of intertextuality. What begins as an exercise in sign one-upsmanship continues by turning every zap into a sly reference to a competitor's ad. By mismatching images and voiceovers, Honda makes every other car maker's primary advertising signifier point to, and affirm, the superiority of Honda. The ad begins with a Toyota reference before a second channel depicts white-coated technicians from Mercedes, BMW, or Lexus confirming that Honda outperforms other cars. Zap. The next channel reveals the familiar scrolling copy of Subaru again "speaking" for Honda. And so it goes as we move through a compendium of cliché, shots from auto ads—the balloon sell-a-thon, the fast-talking local car barkers, and the de rigueur scene of women speaking knowledgeably of cars. The final scene is yet another jab at Toyota as the image breaks up, seen through the lines of the television screen.

A second ad starts with a typically mellow Honda voiceover as the camera surveys a showroom car. A small alien spacecraft hovers overhead, its anthropomorphized camera's eye recording the details and beauty of Honda's design. This alien spacecraft bears an amazing resemblance to a miniature planet Saturn, or perhaps it's

Honda Civic quietly roasts its rival by positioning an appreciative admirer of Honda's car technology.

just the sign of another car company. The voiceover quietly concludes that the "Honda Civic EX sedan is often admired by other car makers. Some we know. Some we don't." Grin and wink—Saturn thinks so much of our design they are willing to copy it and call it their own. This exemplifies rerouting a rival's signifier so that it carries a new signified—Honda took the Saturn image and resituated it to signify a spy and a copycat, albeit a copycat that appreciates superior automotive aesthetics.

Parody

Another sign wars strategy works off parody and spoof. Spoof and parody in ads rest on viewer familiarity with and recognition of other advertisements and signs. Advertising parodies are usually media-referential, referencing a specific ad campaign or a genre of ads. Again, the goal is to stand out, to differentiate one's ads from the clutter of other texts that lie all around—shows and ads and news and infomercials. Parody, when well executed, produces a catapult effect by taking advantage of the advertising expenditures of another advertiser. A devious parody of another ad can become a springboard to making a statement about oneself—for example, Snapple parodies a Gap ad featuring a pretentious but very hip poetry reading, showing instead a teenage girl reading her poem for an appreciative group of street people. By targeting viewers who think of themselves as highly media-literate, Snapple aims to develop their sign value as *irreverent* media-literate observers à la David Letterman. When Snapple ads rip the Gap ad and its pretension, they aim at hailing and positioning a totem group that sees itself as outside the accepted signs—as savvy enough to recognize the bullshit of other people's signs. The Letterman phenomena defines a cynical and ostensibly disruptive exposure of the spectacle (a concept discussed further in Chapter 5); he refuses to accept any sign—he positions himself as the sign of irreverence, the sign of refusal to be duped. He'll be stupid, by god, but he won't be duped. This kind of sardonic media-literate debunking is less an exercise in subverting the dominant ideology than another method of hailing.

While it is common to see a direct rival ridicule and mock the sign or icon of a competitor, it is less common to see them parody a rival's ads. For example, KFC ran ads lampooning a Ronald McDonald–type clown testifying before Congress, unable to answer questions concerning the actual value (nutritive and exchange value) of McD's food, and thereby testifying to the superiority of KFC. Parody and spoof often appear where there is no direct parity competition. Parody without parity, hah! Coors Light has parodied the Energizer parody and raided an upscale Chanel fantasy ad; Roy Rogers poked fun at Nissan's ball-bearing ad, itself an adaptation of a Lexus ad; Dollar Rent-a-Car retells a familiar Nike joke; and Pizza Hut poses as Reebok until they spring their joke. Leslie Nielsen, whose acting career was bolstered by parody films, has now become the star of parody ads for Coors Light and Dollar Rent-a-Car. The Dollar Rent-a-Car ad shows Nielsen stopping in his "old neighborhood" to play a game of pickup basketball. Aided by special effects, he soars into the air and jams the basketball over the heads of the befuddled players. One bewildered brother searching for an explanation for this magic mutters "It must be the shoes." The prior reference to the movie "White Men Can't Jump" gives way to this reference to the memorable Nike ads featuring Michael Jordan and "Mars Blackman" (Spike Lee). The ad concludes by cutting back to Nielsen, the b-ball hustler, grinning and saying "Nah, it's the car!"

The silliest recent spoof was a Roy Rogers takeoff on the automobile ads that roll a steel ball around the hood to demonstrate high engineering standards. The Roy Rogers ad rolls the steel ball around the edges of their roast beef sandwich, and a white-coated engineer solemnly pops a paper bag to indicate that the sandwich comes with an air bag. "We were really tired of the Nissan spot—as is the whole American population—which had been running entirely too much," said the copywriter who wrote the Roy Rogers ad. "The fact that there's absolutely no connection between a ball bearing and a sandwich is the essence of the joke," he said. "Car advertising takes itself terribly seriously, and fast-food advertising can't afford to."[38]

The king of advertising parody is the Energizer campaign of brazen takeoffs on the most banal advertising formulas. Their approach lures the viewer in with a cleverly executed facsimile, before springing the bunny and the joke. The Energizer bunny ads with their broad swipes at advertising genres for soap, cold remedies, bad music, and the like, spurred further advertising parodies. The ads positioned viewers to derive pleasure both from recognizing the references and from the joke itself of the bunny interrupting and disrupting ads associated with foot odor, hemorrhoids ("Sitigin"), or

The Energizer bunny marches across the ocean floor to disrupt a Jacques Cousteau-style ad genre: "Tonight on the Adventure Channel join explorer Marceau Su-la-may as he unlocks the mystery of the Great Barrier Reef."

Wall Street brokerage bluster. Not only do such parody ads position the advertiser on the viewer's side, they also provide a means of holding—arresting—the viewer's attention long enough to see where the narrative is going. The Energizer campaign has prompted others to get into the parody game because "advertisers realize they're talking to an increasingly media-literate audience."[39] Another example of this strategy is a 1993 Pizza Hut ad that lampoons a Reebok campaign. The Pizza Hut ad so carefully mimicked the photographic tone and feel of Reebok's somber and sincere "You Got the Love?" campaign that the first-time viewer was likely suckered in before Pizza Hut sprang the gag. The Pizza Hut voiceover even repeats the Reebok tag line, "You gotta have the love," before pausing and then saying, "but most important, you gotta have a ball."

These ads use parody to get instant recognition by drawing on the prior ad's appeal or lack of it. Those who have been parodied seldom appreciate it. In effect, their labor and their money fuels the parody. Some grin and bear it, others sue. The parodied companies usually claim that they have been economically damaged; the reason most often given is that parodies confuse consumers about what the "proper" associations are. Anheuser-Busch recently went so far as to sue a self-published mom-and-pop humor magazine for a parody entitled "Michelob Oily" because they claimed the magazine's readers "confused the parody with genuine Anheuser-Busch advertisements and trademarks."[40]

Jockeying for Position in the Fast Shoe Industry

The advertising contests between Nike, Reebok, L.A. Gear, British Knights, Converse, Avia, and Asics have been dubbed the "sneaker wars" in the popular press. We call it a sign war because it is a battle joined in terms of the meanings associated with images. No industry affords a better example of sign wars than the athletic shoe industry. Two factors have focused the competition in this industry: the technology of shoe design and advertising style.

For over a decade, sneaker advertising has been based on trying to extract sign value from sports and entertainment celebrities. In the celebrity sweepstakes, the rule of thumb has generally been that the bigger the celebrity, the more handsome the sign value. But with the emergence of Michael Jordan and Bo Jackson as advertising superstars, being a celebrity endorser was no longer enough; now the celebrity had to exude an attitude and a personality. Though everyone else jumped on the celebrity bandwagon, "the flood of sports celebrities . . . tended to cause confusion and made it hard for consumers to remember which sports stars wore what shoes."[41] Since 1989 Nike has been the leader in market share, with the former leader, Reebok International, in second place.[42] Nike has produced a series of winning campaigns since the late 1980s. Their imagery has dominated this market since the days when Michael Jordan teamed with "Mars Blackman" and the "Bo Knows" series was in its prime. These campaigns established Nike as a distinctive voice with a distinctive narrative style. Industry analysts credit Nike's success with their ability to position themselves as the sports performance shoe as opposed to a street fashion shoe. Further, Nike cornered the sign of authenticity in the fast shoe industry. Reebok, on the other hand, had less success with celebrity endorsers and was inconsistent in the image they projected—bouncing wildly from surreal individualists to body-shaping narcissists to wild and crazy daredevils. Reebok's string of inept

The sign of Nike's Air Jordan was established in a series of ads costarring Michael Jordan and Spike Lee (a.k.a. Mars Blackman).

commodity-sign ad campaigns has been the subject of countless stories since the "UBU" campaign debacle.[43] Our earlier discussion of brand equity helps to explain why Nike has taken the lead in a parity industry in which relatively little separates the shoes technologically or in design. Technological gimmicks and new fashion claims are regularly put forward, but as industry expansion slows, advertising has become more aggressive and the size of advertising budgets has become pivotal. The top three firms, Nike, Reebok, and L. A. Gear, controlled nearly 61% of market share in the athletic shoe industry in 1990. Their ad budgets dwarfed those of their smaller competitors, totaling an estimated $81 million in 1989, and they increased ad expenditures to over $115 million in 1990.[44]

With a history marked by meteoric shifts up and down the market-share ladder, L.A. Gear surged into third place with nearly 13% of market share in 1989. More than any company in the industry, L.A. Gear has pinned their brand imagery to celebrity endorsers and fashion glamour. At L.A. Gear, commodity fetishism reigns supreme. Their early success hinged on catering to teenybopper fashions with advertising dominated by svelte blondes in spandex. But by 1992, L.A. Gear's market share had slipped to less than 8% and their footwear sales plummeted, while Converse regained third place with 9% and rivals such as Keds, Asics, Adidas, Fila, Avia (owned by Reebok), and British Knights chipped away at L.A. Gear's share.[45] Still, the share of the market controlled by Nike and Reebok has continued to expand to 34% and 28%, respectively.[46]

Firms like Asics and British Knights have tried to grab market share from Nike and Reebok by "practicing the fine art of guerrilla warfare as its applies to marketing—trying to make a big splash on a limited budget. Asics produced a series of television advertisements that poke fun at its

Asics poked fun at Reebok's pump technology by showing a player resorting first to a bicycle pump and then, as his frustration mounts, to a hydraulic air compressor.

larger rivals."[47] A 1990 Asics Gel Spotlytes ad opens with a taller black ballplayer talking "trash" to a smaller player who is lacing up his Asics shoes. The smaller player wearing the Asics gel-cushioned shoes repeatedly dribbles past and jumps over a player who has been pumping up his shoes. Each time the Asics wearer dunks on the trash-talker, the latter turns to a bigger pump to pump up his shoes—moving from a bicycle pump, to an air compressor to pump up his jump. This ad offered an amusing instance of parody and sign one-upsmanship as Asics put down the Reebok Pump by appropriating the narrative of the Reebok sign and then turning the narrative to negate the sign value of Reebok's "Pump It Up" campaign. The subtext of this ad, equivalent to its "attitude" (its metacommunication), is "Forget the gimmicks, man, let's just play ball."

In the fast shoe industry, firms behind Nike and Reebok have sought to find alternative sign niches. For example, Donny Deutsch, who engineered a new ad campaign for British Knights, positioned its sign value in 1991 as follows: "We want to be seen as the sneakers for rebellious young people. . . . Reebok and Nike have become so mainstream they're the sneaker of choice for little old ladies." Because Nike had captured the signifying position of "authentic sports," British Knights opted for the alternative position of "authentic rebellion." The $15 million British Knights campaign played off the timeworn adolescent playground insult "Your mother wears army boots" for their campaign slogan, "Your mother wears Nike."[48] The campaign featured blue-haired little old ladies gossiping as they lounge around a tennis court in their Nikes. As Savan notes, "The poor ladies are crucified in order to define British Knights by what it isn't."[49]

Meanwhile ads for the Reebok Pump sneaker also aimed at Nike, with Reebok professional basketball endorsers like Dominique Wilkins referring to Nike's "Air" Jordan as he brags about the superiority of the Pump: "So Michael, my man, if you want to fly first class . . . pump up and *air* out." He then tosses away a Nike Air shoe. L.A. Gear's contribution to Nike-bashing had Karl Malone endorsing the Catapult model by declaring "Everything else is just hot *air*."[50]

In part, Nike and Reebok became the dominant shoe marketers because their media budgets dwarf what other competitors can spend. Not surprisingly, Asics and New Balance—each with less than 3% of market share—have both vied for a similar positioning niche. Asics's (1993) slogan, "You won't find our athletes on T-shirts or cereal boxes," positions them as more authentic (more serious) in their athletic pursuits than brands that operate a marketing colossus—Asics' athletes work out, and are too disciplined and dedicated to bother with the conspicuous consumption of signs. Similarly, New Balance ads circa 1991 featured "No celebrity endorsers." Firms with significantly smaller market shares than Nike and Reebok, without the coffers to pay millions for superstars or mega-advertising buys, play up our cultural distaste for excess, waste, and deception.

When it comes to selling basketball shoes, authenticity remains the key and Nike remains the king of authenticity. In 1991, Converse pursued this territory with a campaign entitled "It's What's Inside that Counts." Savan describes the campaign's ideology:

After eight months of research, Converse came up with "six key adjectives" to describe its "brand personality: 'confident, genuine, hardworking, tough, unselfish, and passionate.' " And so the measure of one's authenticity is not brash bravado, but the kind of realness gnawing through Converse's new print ad: "You can always spot a guy who wears Cons. Not by what's on his feet"—that would be too easy—"but rather, by what's in his soul. *He eats pain.*"[51]

The campaign deployed every coding device that might signify authenticity, but it made little impact in an industry saturated by such imagery. So in 1993 Converse returned to its roots and forged a counterpositioning move aimed at contesting the category of authenticity. The Converse All-Star shoe with canvas top predates the simulated leather and polyurethane revolution in athletic shoes and has a loyal following among some urban youth.[52] The current campaign has the tag line "So ugly, they're cool." Their spokesman is a coarse male who declares:

> *"There are a lot more whatchucall ugly people in this world than beautiful people, and there's a growing sense of strength in our collective ugliness. And it's frightening to some people. But we refuse to accept the standard television definition of what beauty is. We don't want to live in a beer commercial. We don't have permanent dramatic shadows that make our plain faces pretty. We don't have perfect airbrushed bodies, and we don't want 'em. The point is not to be beautiful. The point is to be yourself."*

Converse and the sign of "whatchucall ugly people." Can you say pseudo-individualism?

With this antifashion statement, Converse identifies itself as the ultimate badge for those who prefer to identify themselves as standing against the currents of the culture industry. True authenticity—being yourself—flies in the face of staged appearances. Converse actually raises the issue of fetishized commodity aesthetics in order to oppose the hegemony of beauty as defined by the television media. The real measure of identity and aesthetics lies, says Converse, in character—and Converse positions itself as having lots of character. According to Garfield, "In the mass marketing of individuality, nothing sells like character. It is the magic ingredient that enables a consumer to march to a different drummer, with several million identically clad consumers marching in lockstep behind him."[53] The four-four beat of pseudoindividualism marches on, this time wrapped in the differentiation of a torn-and-tattered visual aesthetic and framing device.

The ad's encoding strives to signify an antiaesthetic with images that look like this frame from the Converse ad shown above. The advertiser used the device of creating frames that reveal the irregularly torn openings for showing images of "ugly" persons. Each portrait is marked—literally—by the ripped frame and uneven, garish tints. Coarse and churlishly defiant, our narrator is even shown in one image in the photographic negative. Differentiation is sought by turning that which has previously had no cultural, social, economic, or political value into a value preference. And so, the rip and the tear, the garish tint, and the negatives are all turned into signifiers of what we want: to be ourselves. The final scene after "Mr. Ugly" has finished speaking is a product shot of feet in a pair of All-Stars that have been worn to a frazzle—they are ratty and defined by their holes. Over this image, the Converse logo appears from inside a crudely torn circular mortise, as if by executing the mortise so crudely it might seem less blatant. Converse has used ugliness to disguise their reliance on the most practiced formula for communicating commodity fetishism in the mass media: joining together an attitude and a brand image in a relationship of equivalence.

Reebok, Nike, Asics, and British Knight have all—during the current 1993 season—sought to appropriate the look and feel of the ghetto/the inner city/"the hood." Each has attached a different aesthetic to images signifying the black inner-city experience of basketball. Reebok embraced the hyperbole of "gangsta rap," and added some of their own. Nike has done multiple takes on the subject, from the thought-provoking reverie of a documentary short to jokes about middle-class coaching ideologies and how hopelessly unhip and out of touch they are. Asics has tried to appropriate the linguistic jive of the black men who play the "city game"—they be talkin' the worst junk in the city. And British Knight equips Derrick Coleman and Lloyd Daniels—two talented young NBA players who grew up on the city streets—with video camcorders so they can narrate video tours of their roots for us and declare these spaces as British Knight territory. Coleman's exaggeratedly amateurish effort at the authenticity of home movies ends with him woofing: "How'd you like that, Spike?" No matter which way the signifying trail bends, it still seems to refer back to Nike and Spike's turf.

Currently there are two prevailing signifying contests going on in the athletic shoe industry: one has to do with signifying *the hood* and the other has to do with signifying *authenticity*. These signifying contests speak volumes about colonizing the culture of the hood to fuel bourgeois conceits and pretensions about authenticity which are then made available in the form of a commodity sign. They speak, in spite of themselves, about definitions of self represented as style.[54] Though marketers endlessly gush over their unique technological-jargon advantage, the social meanings they signify are far more salient in determining their success. Subcultural responses to the experiences of class, race, and poverty provide the wellspring of sign value and market share. What happens when subcultural expressions of resistance to domination are drained of signifying value—at the very least, given an institutional tilt (shove) in the direction of *arrested development*? We have, after all, no idea of what punk or grunge or hip-hop as social and cultural movements might look like if they were not mined for their gold, do we?

Licensing and Ambush Advertising

Wherever there are organized systems of sign value, there is an invitation to counterfeiting. Disney is legendary for its obsessive enforcement of trademark privileges for its cultural properties, demanding, for example, that images of Mickey Mouse that parents painted on a New Zealand playground be removed. More recently, Universal Studios moved to enforce *Jurassic Park*'s hegemony of images by vigorously pursuing licensing agreements with Sega computer games, McDonald's, Kenner toys, and so on, while also establishing a 1-800 hotline to report counterfeit *Jurassic Park* images:

> Seen any rip-off dino merchandise lounging around? Then Universal Studios wants you to call 1-800-DINO-COP. The studio is eager to protect every last dime reaped from toys, T-shirts and other items linked to the mega-hit *Jurassic Park* . . . "You have to understand the uniqueness of this property," declares a Universal spokeswoman. Translation: Nobody but us should make a killing in dino merchandise. Alas, there's no reward for turning in bootleg dino wares. 'Tis just a "public service," a DINO-COP operator said.[55]

When firms pay to be the "official sponsor" of the Olympics, they are paying for the potential sign value of the Olympic games with which they can associate themselves. These sign deals, where a corporate sponsor pays for the monetary rights to the Olympics as a sign value, are based on the premise of exclusivity. Coke and Visa and Kodak paid for the official rights to exploit the sign systems associated with the Olympiad. They bid to be designated the "official" sign-product of the Olympics for their market niche—to call themselves the "official camera" or the "official candy bar" of the Olympics. So Coca-Cola outbid Pepsi for the right to tap into the value of Olympic symbolism, paying $33 million for the worldwide right to sport the Olympic symbol. When the stakes are so high, a particular hostile version of sign wars called "ambush" advertising flares. Fielding and Black note that "as the competition between rival firms has grown, so have accusations of ambush marketing—brand rivals 'piggybacking' on the exclusive sponsorship deals of the official sponsors."[56] Coke was predictably pissed-off by a Pepsi ad highlighting their celebrity endorser, Magic Johnson, and his participation on the U.S. Olympic basketball team. In the athletic footwear market, Reebok was the official sponsor. Like Pepsi, Converse ads made reference to its top endorsers—Larry Bird and Magic Johnson—and their teammates in their victorious march to Olympic gold. The U.S. Olympic Committee issued a "cease and desist letter" against Converse for infringing on Reebok's rights.[57] Another sign conflict to emerge from the 1992 Olympics was the flap over whether to force Michael Jordan, Charles Barkley, and four other members of "the Dream Team"—Nike endorsers all—to wear a Reebok-insignia jacket for the medal ceremony.

The most charged struggle to control the field of signification matched Visa International against American Express during the 1992 Winter and Summer Olympics. Under the cover of their official sponsorship of the Olympiad, for which they paid $20 million, Visa ran ads that explicitly pointed to the absence of American Express from the Olympic venue sites. In turn, American Express ran a campaign which though it did not explicitly name Visa or the Olympics was unmistakable in its references. The American Express television ads coyly mentioned Bar-celona and "fun and games" as travelers were reminded to bring their passports and American Express card, before concluding, "And remember, to visit Spain, you don't need a visa." Visa was predictably outraged that American Express had intruded on its official turf. Caught in the bind, the International Olympic Committee charged American Express with "parasite marketing" and attempting to "get a free ride off Visa, which is helping put on the event and helping to support American athletes."[58] American Express responded that they were merely running counterads made necessary by disinformation spread by Visa's ads, which repeatedly boasted that the Olympics "doesn't take American Express."

An American Express ambush ad, aired during the 1992 Winter Olympics: "You're here in the French Alps for all the winter fun and games. Having a good time. Everything's going smoothly. You're happy—because you've got friends over here. And you had the impression that lots of places didn't take The Card. Yeah. Right. The Card. The American Express Card. Don't leave home without it."

Litigating Sign Values

As competitors have grown more dependent on sign wars, there has been a corresponding tendency for these struggles to spill over into the legal arena where the ownership rights to images, logos, and signs are contested and enforced. Sign piracy and counterfeiting of designer fragrances and labels, Rolex watches, etc. can be expected to follow wherever there is a hot (valuable) piece of sign currency. Legal battles over the ownership and control of signs can be expected wherever sign currencies reign because the law is built around the logic of the commodity form.[59] Increasing semiotic litigation confirms the heightened importance of the sign relative to the commodity. The battles for control over the property rights to images and symbolic logos correspond to the centrality and primacy of sign values (images connected to commodities) in the marketplace.

In the realm of athletics, sign wars spill out past the ads into the sports arena itself. Recently, Nike sued Apex One, the NFL's official shoe brand, for participating in a "practice known as spatting, in which NFL players tape up their shoes and affix another logo to them." A federal judge ruled against Apex, which had also tried to disguise Russell jerseys to look like Apex jerseys.[60] A better-known case involved Eveready Battery Co. filing a lawsuit in federal court to prevent Coors Brewing Co. from airing a television commercial it claimed infringes on its rights as creator of the $55 million Energizer bunny campaign. The Coors ad, created by Foote, Cone, and Belding, has Leslie Nielsen imitating the mechanical bunny interrupting a Coors Light commercial by beating a bass drum that reads "Coors Light." A voiceover at the ad's conclusion states: "Coors Light . . . It Keeps Growing and Growing." Television watchers immediately recognized the allusion to the Energizer bunny, symbol for the Energizer brand battery, whose claim to fame is that it interrupts irritating genres of TV ads as it beats a bass drum. The pink, mechanical (battery-operated) bunny wears sunglasses and thongs and marches to the slogan: "Nothing outlasts the Energizer. It keeps going and going and going."

Ralston Purina Co., the corporate owner of the Energizer bunny, screamed sign rip-off. Eveready's CEO called the Coors ad "theft of our creative property." Coors replied that free speech protects the right to parody. "We have maintained all along that our commercial in no way will damage the Eveready Battery Co.," Coors said. "No company has a monopoly on the right to do a parody commercial. This is a light-hearted, fun commercial."[61] The arguments invoked by Ralston Purina and Coors present a microcosm of the logic of a political economy of sign value. Ralston Purina appealed to the logic of commodity relations to describe the bunny and the advertising format developed around the bunny's persona. "We've got a tremendous amount of equity in the bunny," said a Ralston Purina spokesman. "So we hope they would not use the commercial."[62] Energizer's attorney argued that "Coors is trying to take a free ride on the success of the Energizer bunny." The Coors ad would create "a false association" of the bunny with Coors beer, he added.[63] Coors's lawyers argued that the bunny itself was the product of parodying other commercials and that there was no real association between Nielsen and the bunny. Coors took the position that they chose to do this ad not to appropriate the bunny as their sign, but to appropriate the sign of parody. They argued in court that Nielsen was selected for the part because they wanted the ad to be "instantly recognizable as parody."[64]

Did Coors appropriate the sign of parody or did they swipe a sign value?

The court ruled against Eveready's petition to stop the Coors ad from airing. Despite the fact that this case was about measuring the commodity value (or conversely, the question of damages) of a symbol, the judge took a literal rather than a symbolic approach in making his judgment. He ruled that Eveready's copyright and trademark rights to the drum-beating mechanical pink bunny were not violated by the Coors commercial in which Nielsen wears a business suit, white rabbit ears, and a puffy white tail. "Although Mr. Nielsen dons rabbit ears, tail and feet, he by no means copies the majority of the Energizer bunny's 'look,'" the judge said.

The Anti-sign

Today we frequently define ourselves in terms of who or what we are not. The *not* category defines much of what passes for sign/status currency. The latest breed of signs to emerge from sign contests are those positioned as not-signs and those positioned as anti-signs. Let's start with the not-sign category. With a relatively small share of the mass-production beer market, but with a reputation as a "European" beer, Heineken has opted to position themselves as the beer without a commodity sign. Their rhetoric is, "Hey, we're just a product—in fact, our quality is so high that we are unconcerned about throwing aside the masks of signs." Heineken positions itself as the beer that has no celebrities, no bullshit, no beach scenes, and no flying bottles. This radio ad conveys the flavor of the campaign:

"You won't see women in bikinis in Heineken ads . . . You won't see paid celebrities in Heineken ads . . . You won't hear catchy jingles in Heineken ads . . . You see we know that no amount of clever advertising will make you drink a beer if you don't like the taste . . . a little less glitz . . . I mean you don't drink a commercial."

Heineken presents itself under the sign of "no glitz." In so doing, they appellate viewers as too smart to be taken in by the ruse of arbitrary images anyhow. Asics and New Balance have deployed the same approach to call attention to the marketing practices of the fast shoe industry goliaths, while appealing to athletes who would like to see themselves as interested in pure performance.

Not too many decades past, cultural identity was securely anchored in one's producer status, one's religion, or one's class. While consumption has not totally displaced production as a locus of identity, and while race, gender, and income remain potent forces in people's lives, none of these forces has been able to block the forces of commodity culture. Today our capacity for garnering status and identity is far less connected to our occupations and far more connected to how we act as consumers. Today we talk about race and gender mediating the individuated lifestyle categories offered by commodity culture. In a culture where personal identity in an impersonal urban society is usually constituted by the signs one wears, it is hardly surprising that the not-category would emerge as a methodology for differentiating the self. This not-category is also a historical product of alienated spectators and consumers, a subject we'll return to in chapter three. Perhaps the not-stance (the negative stance) is a defensive stance for coping with the avalanche of signs and images and the overstimulation of desires?

Subaru as the Anti-sign?

In yet another parity market, Subaru presents authenticity as someone who doesn't believe in signs at all. Does this signal the end of sign wars? Hardly. Subaru positioned itself against the excess and extravagance of 1980s car ads with a slogan that calls for an end to the hype: "A car is just a car." Self-conscious reflexivity about the semiotics of status is a higher category of consciousness than mere selling. In a social world where commodity signs reign, the denial of such a world can become a commodity sign itself. Subaru's 1991 campaign foregrounded a deliberate and intentionally heavy-handed critique of commodity sign promotions. These ads remind viewers that cars are made of steel and plastic: "A car is just a car. It won't make you handsome or prettier, and if it improves your standing with your neighbors, then you live among snobs." One ad contrasted the functional value of their car with the claims of sign values made by others. The Subaru won't say who you are, in contrast to a series of satiric portraits of people stating, "Mine says I'm handsome. Mine says I'm cosmopolitan . . . sexy, energetic, powerful . . . that I have a better gene pool . . . that I'm another pathetic sheep following the herd. . . . When you buy a Subaru all it says is you bought a stylish car and can still pay your mortgage." The Subaru ad hails you as someone who already has a firm sense of self-identity—you are not buy-

Commodity identity?

ing a car to find your identity because you already have one. The Subaru campaign offers the viewer a choice between being a poseur (dependent on spurious commodity signs) and being someone who can keep commodities in proper perspective in their lifestyle. After all, the function of a car is to transport. This ad campaign appellates the viewer as unconcerned about his or her presentation of self to others, with the voiceover in one ad dryly stating, "I don't care what my neighbors think . . . I don't even like them that much." It metacommunicates by criticizing the system of commodity signs itself. It denies self-construction as self-presentation. It is another version of the critique of conformity, and the celebration of inner-directedness that lies deeply embedded in American culture.

Subaru invites viewers to join in a small refusal to be caught up in the constant circulation of signs. The refusal to submit to the hegemony of consumption is often taken to indicate a core of identity—just as embracing the negative sign can be seen as an attempt to indicate strength of character. Defining oneself against a whole complex or ensemble of signs is a way in which we daily confirm our own ideological identity independent of the amorphous forces that we sense regulating our cultural lives. Hence, in the beachwear market, Gotcha sportswear adopted the strategy of positioning themselves as the antitotem group. At a time when nostalgia was flowing like syrup, Gotcha chose antinostalgia as a method of hailing their viewers: "We had to talk to a surfer's feeling of 'I don't want to be part of your tribe.' "[65]

Benetton: Differentiation via Code Violations

Benetton has shown itself to be a company that understands the limits of signs and then tries to go beyond the limits of the field. Benetton first gained attention by edging beyond the traditional boundaries of advertising and addressing the subject of racial politics. Whereas advertisements ordinarily deny that they are tainted by any ideological mark, Benetton recognized it could make a distinctive impression with its target audience by facing up to bothersome political issues that surround the world of privileged consumption. Graham discusses this particular campaign:

> Benetton is testing the boundaries between advertising and politics in a provocative new campaign that's touched a nerve in Europe and the U.S. . . . Two of the campaign's eight executions make an unmistakable visual statement on the races. One shows a black woman with a red sweater loosely draped about her shoulders, nursing a white baby. Another shows a black man's and a white man's hands in handcuffs; both are wearing jeans jackets. "We believe our advertising needs to shock—otherwise people will not remember it," said Vittoria Rava, Benetton's worldwide advertising and licensing manager of the retailer, which operates 5,000 stores in 79 countries.[66]

The key to Benetton's campaigns has been their shock value, their willingness to provoke by juxtaposing images that rub connotations the wrong way. Their early campaigns used the tag line "United Colors of Benetton" to focus on race-mixing imagery—drawing parallels between the colorful Benetton sweaters and the skin tones of the world's many ethnic groups. These ads established a nonracist aesthetic, more global in sensibility than strictly American. Provocative in-your-face political statements on the subject of racist culture such as the one showing a black woman breastfeeding a white infant prompted critics to observe that "the black models are there for shock value, to make the viewer feel how risqué, of Benetton."[67] Responding to criticism that Benetton was simply exploiting notoriety gained from making such a public scene to spur their marketing interests, Benetton spokesman Peter Fressola said: "People can be cynical and say, 'Oh, that's just Benetton doing its one-world lovefest thing.' But we've found a way to create a desire for our products that's much more subtle and caring than showing an attractive model in a sweater."[68] Benetton understands that their target audience may be more effectively hailed this way than with the conventional model in a mirror. We shall pursue this point in Chapter 3 because we believe ads like these are really about the subject who is deciphering them. These ads offer viewers a sign, a sign that designates the kind of person you are, or might become. Benetton establishes itself here as both humanitarian and willing to defy convention. It has, at any rate, been debatable whether Benetton's advertising philosophy is accurately reflected in an ad decorated with a variation of its infamous safe-sex ad (a field of unrolled, colored condoms): "We believe that advertising can do more than sell products. It can broaden minds."[69] Perhaps, but more likely these ads speak to the choir—they organize a form of flattery—a method of hailing that establishes an economy of gratitude between individual spectator and corporate logo. Indeed, the real issue, as Fressola pointed out, is *creating desire for commodities.*

Benetton has since continued to execute controversial campaigns, always associating itself with that which is not permissible (in advertising). This means violating sacred cultural boundaries, for example, with ads featuring a priest kissing a nun, a new born baby still covered with the placenta, the aftermath of a car bomb, an electric chair, and desperate refugees hanging from the sides of a ship. Such images violate bourgeois (middle-class) sensibilities and the legacy of bourgeois morality. They derogate the hegemony of the Catholic Church and its vision of morality. Benetton's originality lies in placing images normally confined to the news into a sphere of discourse where they are normally excluded. The infamous Benetton ad of the dying AIDS patient surrounded by his family was originally shot by a *Life* magazine photographer.

Without captions to direct or guide interpretation, and placed in a framework normally devoted to the currency exchange of consumption values and to making aesthetic distinctions and associations, these scenes are opened to a wide range of interpretations. The Benetton ads seem to embrace what John Berger calls the "abyss of discontinuity."[70] Photographic decontextualization of images in ads is usually masked by the work of captions that renaturalize the image in a commodity setting. The Benetton ads do not demystify this process. The ads push the viewer to interrogate the decontextualized images according to the discursive logic of ads—the disjuncture between subject matter and the motivation of the ad is a shock delivered to the advertising form itself. Savan analyzes the Benetton approach:

> With this latest campaign, however, it's not the images that shock, but, as Fressola says, the "recontextualization of the image." The idea may be to generate discussion about AIDS or racism, but the ads do it only by ripping up your response to advertising itself. "Fashion magazine readers are in a narcotized fantasy world. I think it's much more insidious for Jewish children, for instance, to be hit with ads from Ralph Lauren, who is Jewish, and his images of Aryan perfection. But nobody's upset with that because it's fantasy. Our AIDS ad took AIDS out of the realm of abstraction and into the realm of the real."[71]

Or did it? Here is the ultimate hyperrealism—dying of AIDS! Quite apart from Benetton's intent, this depiction thrusts the viewer into an awkward cultural tension. Like most ads, this ad positions the viewer as a voyeur who may find pleasure enacting the role of unobserved observer. There is an aestheticization in the AIDS ad—the style of the image becomes as important as the subject matter it represents. Benetton mixes the pleasure of viewing with the subject of the ad to evoke a powerful emotional response. Olivieri Toscani, who usually does the Benetton photography, called the image of the AIDS deathbed a "modern *Pieta*."[72] A bit exaggerated perhaps, but this remark points to the aesthetic pleasure of the image as art with connotations of religious devotion and reverence.

Benetton differentiates itself as a company that violates the boundary rules of advertising discourse. Ordinarily, advertising presents a world of consumption sheltered and removed from the nitty-gritty of the workaday world. Boundary rules are set in advertising according to the logic of personal desire and the rules of value associated with the exchange of desired goods. In contrast to the prosaic beauty and glamour images that characterize the ads that appear before and after them in the fashion magazines, Benetton has taken images of human suffering and placed them within their advertising page, at least structurally linking them with issues of personal consumption and desire. This poses a jarring opposition that has offended bourgeois public sensibilities along with those of the Christian Right.

Advertisers normally seek to appropriate cultural meanings that they think have positive value for their target audience. But here, in order to differentiate themselves, Benetton has gone to the refuse heap of pestilence, war, and famine, and taken cultural meanings that have antivalue—moments we ordinarily shun and repress (we shun the moment, but the image is not shunned). Through the process of advertising alchemy Benetton turns these advertising taboos into a sign that represents difference. Their value is constituted by the mere fact of being different: images on the margins of what is socially acceptable have not previously been seen in advertising. By 1990, the spectacle had evolved so that it no longer excludes harsh lived reality, but integrates it (fuses it) into its stream of images. Why deny lived reality when it can be aestheticized, its meanings turned into second-order signifiers as servants to commodities? According to Debord, "in a world which really is topsy-turvy, the true is a moment of the false."[73]

To repeat: this kind of differentiation is a way of hailing individual spectators about their own identities as sign wearers. Benetton's ads are exercises in advertising metacommunication. One potential signified of this ad is heightened political consciousness: "I am aware of suffering and hardship. When I wear Benetton clothing, I signify to others my cosmopolitan political consciousness." The action in these ads takes place at the level of the subtext.

Benetton ads try to turn shock value into sign value.

Placing the familiar green-and-white frame and logo associated with the United Colors of Benetton over and around these images challenges all of our usual interpretive assumptions about reading ads. These assumptions are part of the advertisement's "metacommunication," the tacit and typically unspoken assumptions that guide interpretation. When Benetton shows scenes of death, poverty, and misery inside the field governed by their logo, there occurs what Leslie Savan called "the shock of the logo." This calls our attention to the metacommunicative level of ads. "The presence of a logo when unexpected (or its absence when expected) acts as a flash of consciousness—not good or bad consciousness—but as a commenter, an interlocutor, a readjuster of the usual."[74]

> When you see the green and white "United Colors of Benetton" slapped on the pictures, there are several possible responses: (1) You see only the logo; the picture recedes because the logo becomes a kind of lens, colorizing the picture with the whole history of ad exploitation; (2) You cease to be bothered by the logo, since you expect a tag on every tale nowadays; or (3) You see the logo as a sardonic caption: Poverty-stricken Third World girl with white doll from trash can—*United Colors of Benetton*, ha![75]

Benetton's metacommunicative exchange with viewers sounds something like this to us: "We know you know that the world we live in is not neatly packaged and cleansed as most ads depict it. We know that such representations are not just a lie but a gross distortion of the relationship between consumption and life. At Benetton, we no longer want to participate in such commodity fictions. We know consumption won't make for a perfect world and we are not even remotely suggesting that. So, if you are the kind of person who feels the same, then you might want to wear Benetton because we are candid and because you will be wearing a sign of authenticity and honesty. You can engage in consumption without being dishonest and immoral because we have bridged the gap by not ignoring the reality of a world where misery and suffering still exist. How can we deny AIDS? How can we repress it from our discourse when human beings are dying? The discourse of advertising is ordinarily about indifference to these issues, turning a blind eye, encouraging depoliticized stances—but at Benetton we are not like others, we have vision. Come be part of our Benetton family—the Benetton tribe."

Does Benetton actually associate suffering and death with consumption? Or is this discourse calculated to appeal to a world of jaded, cynical viewers who want something, anything, to spice up desire? Or does it conjure up a higher order of authenticity—not fake? Or is there an economy of gratitude here that offers the hip young viewer a sense of moral superiority? As Savan remarks, "By deciding to appreciate—if not necessarily *like*—their ads, I get a little payoff of feeling quite the radical—a prize in the Cracker Jacks that's also a piece of their marketing."[76]

Rereading Image Disputes

When big corporations attack each other in their ads it may become a topic of discussion on TV news and entertainment shows. Yet media discussions usually skirt the systematic analysis of sign value. Sign value competitions have grown so ubiquitous that the evening news can report an intensifying TV ad competition between vacation amusement parks (Disney World and Six Flags), and yet fail to notice that competition is being conducted between the signifiers of Mickey Mouse and Bugs Bunny.

Accidents, scandals, and controversy, however, can draw out the subject of sign value, making it visible. Each case the media defines as controversial points inadvertently to how the political economy of sign values impacts everyday life. Reebok's bungee-jumping ad went to extremes to establish a differentiated sign for Reebok. It momentarily succeeded, at the expense of vigorous moral condemnation and banning because it overstepped a middle-class moral line by ostensibly encouraging impressionable youth to try dangerous thrill-seeking activities.

The "social problems" attendant to the dissemination of sign values are most evident in cases related to the black community, for example, the marketing of basketball shoes in relation to inner-city violence. After incidents of youths being killed by other youths for their sneakers, black community leaders such as Jesse Jackson charged that marketers were exploiting the black community by drawing on the value of black athletic images to make profits. Though firms like Nike and Reebok have denied such charges, we cannot resist asking whether or not advertising efforts to elevate the sign value currency of sneakers have

Banned in Oregon: Appropriating the hot sign of the moment can sometimes offend predominant middle-class morality.

been far too efficient? This points to the materiality of signs, and yet oddly signs can displace the materiality of the objects they become associated with. Malt liquor advertising plays a more prominent role in contributing to its value than the material production of it and—no surprise—the new prohibition takes place at the level of signs when the signifier in question is rapper Ice Cube. Oregon authorities banned a poster for St. Ides malt liquor that featured the rapper Ice Cube holding the product in one hand and gesturing "a gang sign with the other. The sign is the identifier of the Black-P-Stone Bloods gang of Compton, Calif."[77]

A developing contradiction of sign wars is that the importance of the image has begun to eclipse the commodity associated with it. This presents a risk insofar as people might rather consume the sign than its commodity. It also opens up the terrain of sign wars even further because it encourages other competitors to reproduce the hot sign. As this process continues we have begun to see campaigns that self-consciously address the semiotics of style as a means of articulating a sign that stands out from the crowd—the sign of the savvy lay semiotician.

2 *Advertising in the Age of Hypersignification*

$P_{RIMITIVE}$ as it seems now, television advertising in the 1950s aimed mainly at promoting product recall. From the 1950s through the 1970s, TV advertising established the appearance of a seamless web of commodities. In the 1950s, commodities or their representatives sang and danced their way into our hearts and minds with jingles based on the logic of memorization and recall. Jingles, short musical rhyming phrases repeated over and over—for example, "You'll wonder where the yellow went, when you brush your teeth with Pepsodent"—were associated with the most heavily commodified forms of advertising. During the 1960s and 1970s advertisers refined and polished the formats into which they plugged product names and images. Streamlined and rationalized formulas for assembling and delivering commodity signs repeatedly built on a trinity of interpretive procedures: abstraction, equivalency, and reification.[1] As this advertising style grew slicker and more colorful, advertisers competed at capturing the look of perfection. Bright colors and seamless editing practices filled the formulaic and overdetermined frameworks. Advertisers selected only positive moments for inclusion within these frameworks in order to promote unambivalent correlations between their commodities and images of desire and pleasure. From 1946 through 1980, advertising thus painted a social world that was primarily consensual and nonconflictual, a sphere separated from daily life, but supposedly representative of it.

Critical theorists from the 1940s through the 1960s spoke of a "culture industry" that conditioned an ideologically one-dimensional universe of cultural discourse.[2] They described this as a hegemonic stage of commodity culture during which "space outside the world of consumption" inexorably disappeared.[3] Yet by the

In television advertising semiotics, things are often cast in terms of what they are not. This image from a 1993 campaign for a new product launch named Crystal Pepsi positioned itself as "clear" and natural by framing this scene of Hollywood kitsch (the signifier of blatant commodity imagery) with the words *"right now artificial does not feel right."* Pepsi framed this image as artifice, as souvenir kitsch—the iconic tableaux of living large in Hollywood amid the convertible and the palm trees. The now bygone commercial hegemony of Hollywood's glamorous lifestyle is turned into a marker of the inauthentic, and hence, the less desirable way of life. While Pepsi has reframed this signifier as artifice, we will not be surprised when we also see the pink Cadillac framed as an emblem of metakitsch, that is, as a marker of a higher level of the ability to recognize authenticity.

early 1980s audiences identified the jingle—such a familiar marker of conformist consumerism—as artifice and the jingle's marketing efficacy limped to a halt. Actually, the crisis of advertising went considerably deeper than the failure of jingles. Advertising, and commodity culture in general, had glamorized itself into crisis by continuously painting an unreal world, relentlessly trying to top one set of unattainable promises with yet another.

The genesis of "new" advertising in the 1980s was located in the maturation of this dominant advertising form and the cultural toll it took on spectator-buyers. After nearly 40 years of watching TV ads, viewers had grown too acclimated to advertising's routinized messages and reading rules. Continual consumer positioning provoked viewer resentment and hostility. Savvy, media-literate viewers now present advertisers with a challenge. Bored and fatigued, these viewers restlessly flip around the channels in search of something that will momentarily arrest their attention and fascination. Viewers belonging to the baby-boom generation have also adopted stances of indifference toward advertisements' mode of address, both for purposes of negotiating the meaning of ads and for defending themselves. Other defensive reading postures include cynicism, skepticism, belligerence, and intentionally twisted ("off-the-wall") interpretations. Skeptical viewers have grown wary about "what's real and what's not," while belligerent viewers refuse to participate in the interpretation process or willfully undermine it. The constant process of simulation on TV eventually contributes to widespread doubts about the credibility or sincerity of media representations.

Ironically, the trends in 1980s TV advertising parallel the theoretical critiques of mass culture dating from the late 1940s. Some advertising campaigns from 1986 to 1989 tried to reverse the critiques leveled against advertising by incorporating those critiques. Advertising strategies such as hyperreal encoding, reflexivity, and the use of hypersignifiers have been motivated by intertwined crises in the political economy of sign value. Advertisers not only confronted disaffected, alienated viewers armed to foil ads with their remote control zappers, they also faced the problem of differentiating their commodity signs from the clutter of formulaic advertising. Further, advertisers in the 1980s felt the sting of criticisms that ads promoted an unreal world that showed only the positive side of life and cut off all conflict, negativity, and tension; glamorized commodities by separating them from daily life; and manufactured "false needs." Critics in recent decades have found ads overemphasizing social appearances—superficial sign values—and eclipsing the actual use and exchange values of products. By the late 1980s advertising agencies such as Foote, Cone, and Belding, Chiat/Day, and Weiden & Kennedy were responding to the cultural crisis tendencies spawned by an advertising industry dedicated to hyping sign values and commodity aesthetics. As it grew more difficult to sustain product and image differentiation, this leading edge of advertisers sought to take advantage of viewer antipathy toward advertising by turning criticisms into positioning concepts. Criticism has thus been converted into a series of competing stylistic differences.

Accused of cultivating an unreal world, advertisers have turned again to the shadowy world of "hyperreality" in which encodings of reality seem to simulate reality itself.[4] Self-consciously hyperreal advertising critically "acknowledges" the generic field of "hyperreality" by technically modifying the encodings of realism and drawing attention to the codes of media realism. Through these encoding strategies, this form of advertising embraces critiques of consumerism as a means of disguising questions about needs and their means of satisfaction. Reflexively confronting criticisms has enabled advertisers "to say" to viewers that they recognize them as savvy consumers capable of both making their own choices and of recognizing a ruse when they see one.

Advertising has entered a stage based on hypersignification, a stage in which "semiotics gets increasingly annexed by the advertising and marketing industries."[5] Signification practices themselves become the currency with which advertisers negotiate a market cluttered by simulated reproductions, and an audience populated by recalcitrant viewers who no longer compliantly complete the meanings of ads. Advertising in the age of hypersignification no longer tries to conceal the code—the metalanguage—of the commodity aesthetic, but instead tries to turn the "code" itself into a sign. This kind of advertising in the 1980s symbolized a shifting stage of hegemony that left open more space not just for interpretation, but for presenting a series of claims about stylized individuality that emphasized individuals making choices in their consumption and using products as they see fit. This approach promotes the appearance of individuals playfully adapting corporate signs to their own needs. Artsy print ads in the 1980s stressed the role of individual viewers in the assembly of meaning. Nonconventional narrative forms, editing techniques, and photographic styles have been designed to deny the existence of predigested meanings and to create a hunt for meaning. In the effort to deny the hegemonic content of commodity culture, advertising reroutes and reconstitutes it.[6]

Realist Conventions

Questions of realism in TV are always a matter of codes. As Fiske remarks, "Realism does not just reproduce reality, it makes sense of it—the essence of realism is that it reproduces reality in such a form as to make it easily understandable."[7] In the mid-1980s the slick polish of realist color photography gave way to an eruption of exaggerated realist conventions meant to convey the idea that realism does not equal perfection. Color photorealism emphasized the perfection and allure of commodities. Aided by glossy graphics, this style of color photography located the material desirability of objects on the page or screen itself; the commodity and the image merged and could no longer be easily distinguished. The ideal in commercial photography from the 1950s through the early 1980s was to flawlessly simulate material objects; thanks to the airbrush, commodity images were made to appear perfect. The closer such photography got to its goal, the smoother it became, paradoxically, the less "real" it seemed. Television ads suffered a loss of texture: they seemed too shiny, polished, glossy, and smooth. Prompted by popular criticism of advertising for falsifying the conditions of daily life, advertisers sought a signification style that would reintroduce a sense of "everydayness." Advertisers moved to regain a sense of texture—a visually tactile roughness—that could be juxtaposed in semiotic opposition to "glossy." This is what motivated the recovery of graininess in photography.

Advertisers began venturing outside their studios to select subject matter that connoted everyday life. Levi's pioneered this movement by presenting "nonmodels" in urban street settings. Levi's thus distanced themselves from what spectator-buyers had come to regard as the unattainable perfection of *GQ* and *Glamour* models. Esprit simi-

In 1994 Citibank Visa jumped on the real-people bandwagon because "real-people ads give authenticity."

Circa 1990, Nissan presented trace fragments (blips and particles) of real-life moments spent in the car. This ad combined very grainy color video, swish pans, and jump cuts with odd camera tilts to stress the perceptual experience of everydayness.

larly invited real consumers to apply to become models for a day. "Real" people have since become an "industry" in and of themselves, appearing in ads for cars, soda, burgers, detergent, beer, and—most recently—ads for investment banking and home pregnancy tests.[8] A second signifying strategy pictured everyday situations and "unreconstructed" real-life situations (e.g., a Nissan ad shows children bickering and screaming in the backseat of a car) that viewers can readily identify as fleeting moments that occur spontaneously (unglamorously) in daily life. A related method represented scenes of minor conflict, for example, a woman aggressively pushing a male suitor away, or persons exhibiting anger, tension, or anxiety. These moments of conflict become abstracted and isolated in the form of abbreviated signifiers (e.g., a female shoving away a male). Such decontextualized signifiers represented a difference from previous styles that depicted a world of commodity signs that apparently insulated wearers from the conflicts of daily life. Advertisers next discovered that breaking the narrative flow permitted them to signify a different sort of realism. Ads for Lee jeans and Suave shampoo fractured and fragmented pieces of conversation and placed them against the background noises of daily life—for example, a Suave ad takes place in a cafeteria amid the clatter of trays and glasses. Advertisers isolated phrases from actual conversations and turned them into hypersignifiers of "real conversations."

The word "real" in lyrics and tag lines has become so pervasive that its referent has grown uncertain. Miller beer was a familiar brand name that tried to draw on narrative and photographic codes of realism. Linguistically and visually, they positioned themselves as "real," offering real draft beer and real social relationships. Their "It's Real" ad campaign featured an ethnic wedding party. Pulsing music and video cuts raced along at a frenetic pace, hurling viewers through a collage of images that connoted real life and the authentic moment of male bonding as opposed to the "hokey" and "staged" male bonding scenes that previous Miller campaigns had been media-lampooned for creating. Miller subsequently abandoned "It's Real" in favor of "Buy that Man a Miller," a campaign that restaged valiant moments of "everyday heroes." In their quest for authenticity, the Miller campaign was further revised to salute everyday heroes in ads about their own acts of bravery or honesty. The "Real Heroes" campaign

Miller Brewing Company sought to construct an atmosphere of everydayness by relying on an exaggerated realist photographic code. Again and again in the late 1980s, as in this imagery of guys casually chatting on the front stoop, advertisers sought to encode a reality that emerged from the fabric of people's actual lives.

reenacted dramatizations like that of Eddie Turner of Catawba, North Carolina, who risked his life while parachuting to dive down and pull the cord of an unconscious fellow parachutist. The ads chronicle the heroic act in the photographic codes of scratched and grainy video, but switch to the smooth color video of television to salute the heroism and pay tribute with the beer.

Going Backstage: The Spatial Coordinates of Realism and Reflexivity

Tying together "realism" and "reflexivity" is a visual concentration on back regions. Goffman distinguished between frontstages where performances are presented and "a back region or backstage . . . as a place, relative to a given performance, where the impression fostered by the performance is knowingly contradicted as a matter of course."[9] In the back region actors need not maintain a front as they prepare for performances. From 1986 to 1988 numerous ads featured the backstage region, making viewers privy to the process of producing the ad (e.g., K-Mart; Le Tigre). These ads proposed that the finished text is secondary to the process of its construction; they exposed the ads as constructed artifacts whose polished appearance is contrived. Such ads accept the premise that presentation of self is a deception that corresponds to the commodification of daily life. In a world dominated by appearances, Le Tigre purported to reveal the backstage arena where appearances are constructed. By showing us their dancers getting dressed in a restroom, they confide in us, and thereby discredit arguments about their own involvement in promoting pseudoindividuality.[10] "Don't be fooled," they say. Appearances are usually not what they seem, but because they have shared this with you, you can trust that their motives are not contrived. K-Mart ads likewise contrived to show models who are really just like us—insecure regular people who may be no more talented, no less self-conscious, just on stage. Stylistically, these ads resemble Frederick Wiseman's film *Model* (1982) which spelled out the tedium that goes into making ads, a tedium that is concealed in the finished product. But whereas Wiseman showed cultural production as work and thereby exposed the fetishism of commodities, the Le Tigre campaign turned the exposure of the ad's production into its own sign—le cool tigre is wise to the manufacture of cooked texts. Advertisers in the late 1980s tried stripping ads of their ideological masks as a means of preempting criticism.

A few ad campaigns actually let viewers in on the preproduction design process of the product itself (e.g., Nissan took us behind the scenes to ostensibly listen in on their automotive design process). Television ads rarely concern themselves with questions of workplace production relations. When they do, they normally depict the work group in a ritualized way (e.g., Ford, McDonald's). Just as important, since "back regions are typically out of bounds to members of the audience, it is here that we may expect reciprocal familiarity to determine the tone of social intercourse."[11] The Nissan ad's photographic style attempted to humanize the work group by connotatively locating it in everyday life: we recognize the room and its arrangement as presented in the ad as representing the phenomenology of daily experience. The soundtrack included raw background sounds rather than the pure, cleansed sounds generated by skilled technicians in studios. And, what is more, these workers do not sing to us. The Nissan ad emphasized the informal nature of the work group, an informality conveyed via their casualness, the absence of hierarchy, the humorous put-downs, references to family life, spontaneous interaction, and brainstorming.

Ad campaigns examined questions of social performance and social identity by literally taking us backstage to see the unpolished/authentic side of performing. A Miller beer ad pulls us behind the scenes to visit a standup comic preparing to perform. He acknowledges his anxiety to a select coterie of friends who are drinking Miller beers. We are made a part of that coterie, admitted to the inner circle to participate in a male-bonding ritual. Making us a team member, and letting us in on team secrets, boosts the ad's sense of authenticity. The campaign tag line, "As real as it gets," suggests that Miller beer possesses an authenticity and value that corresponds to the authenticity of the relationships seen in the ad. At least superficially, this ad positioned Miller against a previous procession of ads that made the commodity the ventriloquist. Here, the beer named Miller does not claim to speak or perform, except insofar as it functions as a signifying correlative for the experience of authentic comradeship. In a more glamorous vein, the technique of exposing the backstage shapes a Michelob ad featuring the "real" Eric Clapton (not the arena performer, but the artist playing for his own aesthetic enjoyment). A sequence of images portrays Clapton finishing a concert performance before ambling down a night street to an intimate bar closed for the evening. Clapton straps on his guitar and jams with a few musician friends. An alluring, unattached, female is seen watching and enjoying his play. Clapton plays music, it would seem, not for money or fame, but for simple aesthetic enjoyment. Ironically, though Clapton sold out to Michelob, he was presented as an authentic, genuine artist.[12]

The Miller and Michelob ads encouraged viewers to distance themselves from the viewing masses, positioning each viewer as a privileged person who is one up on the rest of the audience. These ads hailed the viewer as not just another spectator but as part of the performance and its preparation. The backstage emphasis also gave a sense of depth to the experiences of daily life. Between 1950 and 1980, advertisements addressed viewers about their personal leisure lives, but rarely in the vernacular of the mundane routine of daily life. Daily life, according to advertisements, paled in comparison to the glamorous world of the spectacle. Going backstage offered 1980s advertisers a method for responding to the cynical and savvy viewers who declare ads "insulting." The disparity between the spectacular ideal and everyday reality has always bred a certain resistance and doubt about what "authenticity" meant. The first round of ads that "went backstage" stood out from other ads because they seemed to present social relations that were not fabricated. After all, to go backstage is to see that the surface appearance of the performance is not the performance itself and does not take place by magic. However, the backstage region is not shown as work, but is represented as "fun." Once again, negation is so carefully contrived that representations of production, tension, and anxiety are turned to become signs of personal authenticity.

Many contemporary ads are predicated on the notion that viewers have become alienated from the appearances they consume. These ad campaigns are constructed to convey a sense of greater depth, but this is merely the appearance of depth, itself constructed. Meanwhile, during the same time period, another body of advertising intermittently played on a postmodern cultural theme that everything is surface—that there is no deeper layer—and that all texts are therefore equivalent. It is easy to point to MTV-style ads and their flattened voice, but this style does not require an MTV audience. A recent ad for Chevy trucks featured small-town rural folks in Iowa reciting a copywriter's words in obviously flattened monotones. In this ad grizzled oldtimers in a local diner comment on the aesthetics of the new Chevy truck: one man speaks of the "Bauhaus influence," while another mentions the "overstated simplicity" of its lines. A moment later, the entire group chimes in with "Form follows function." Chevy's version of postmodernism for Middle America is a bunch of rubes reciting the theoretical clichés of high modernist design and making fun of urbane talk.

Hyperreal Encoding

We use the term "hyperreal" to refer to video techniques that encode a heightened awareness of reality as mediated by the television world. Hyperreal encoding points to efforts to connote a sense of unmediated reality, but always via a coding system that is mediated. Technique overwhelms substance as a semiotic system. The semiotics of technique dominate the reading of these advertising texts. Seamless technicolor realism, so popular from the 1950s through the 1970s, backgrounded technique and disguised the camera's presence. By contrast, hyperrealist encoding techniques tacitly acknowledge the insurmountable gap between photographs and that which they represent. Hyperrealism acknowledges the presence of the camera, although once the technique gets routinized, reflexivity about the camera's presence fades.[13]

A familiar technique of hyperreal encoding is the use of the jerky or shaky camera and the searching camera. The searching, wandering camera does the looking for us; when once there was a fixed object of focus, now the camera leads us in a fidgety search. This has an oddly decentering effect because there is no central object. It mimics the decentering of the self and metacommunicates the claim that there is a new relationship between the viewing subject and the product. The camera technique draws on Jean Rouch's cinema verité method that acknowledges the camera's presence.[14] Cinema verité is variously known as "truthful," unplanned, or spontaneous cinema because the movements of the actor are not determined by the camera; rather, the camera's movements are determined by actors or objects in the frame. This strategy is often associated with AT&T's "Ball-Buster" or "Slice-of-Death" campaign.[15]

Increasingly, ads use photographic techniques that literally decenter products by displaying them along the margin of the screen rather than in the center. Or commodities are shown blurred and unfocused, or camouflaged in ensembles of other objects. The product is given no apparent priority as a signifier/signified within the narrative; neither does it serve as the motive force of the narrative. This technique may tacitly permit a debunking of criticism that American advertising exclusively caters to shallow materialism, but it is more likely a technique for holding the interest of restless viewers. For example, an ad for Honda motor scooters sent a restless and wandering camera surveying the surfaces of objects, but never for very long or directly. Indeed, this wandering camera keeps viewers guessing what the ad is for as the camera lands on a coffee maker, before flitting across drapes, wood floors, and upscale bedding. Comparable photographic techniques also decenter subjects as well as objects (see next section). Though such decentering subtly denies that the subjects must become part of the totem group before they can realize their subjectivity—that is, they claim to privilege the subject over the product—taken together, the hypersignifiers soon comprise a lifestyle ensemble of stylized objects.

Using telephoto lenses magnifies the grainy and hazy quality of images, and also permits a heightened emphasis on hypersignifiers (see next section). Levi's popularized this photographic style by shooting their subjects from two blocks away in order to capture actors in unrehearsed and natural actions. Advertisers have also used the telephoto lens to create a sharpened sense of realism by allowing objects or persons to pass in front of and between the viewer/camera and the object of vision. Disrupting the frame in this way conveys the perception of an unstaged reality.

Frames may also be disrupted by discontinuous editing practices that create uneven and unpredictable rhythms and emphasize the rapidity of movement between images. Perceptual discontinuity is generated by increasing the sheer number and speed of edits, along with violations of continuity codes—that is, edits are made to violate expectations about coherence, connection, and flow. Specific methods of disrupting the rules of continuity include: (1) not matching consecutive actions; (2) radical change in image sizes; (3) use of oblique angles; (4) failure to preserve a sense of direction (a person or object entering from opposite directions in consecutive shots); (5) failure to match tone in terms of graininess, film stock, lighting; (6) temporal discontinuity through jumpcuts or overlapping action (duplication); (7) cutting on movement instead of on a rest; and (8) violating the content curve, that is, the amount of time necessary for a viewer to recognize what is going on in a shot.[16] Discontinuity is further enhanced by using camera techniques such as swish zooms and swish pans that create perceptual disorientation, or tilts that throw the frame out of balance and violate media codes of symmetry, correspondence, harmony, order, and proportion.

Miller's "It's Real" campaign took the kitchen-sink approach of using film code violations to encode "hyperrealism"—this sequence includes swish pans, overexposure, and objects passing in front of the scene.

Exposing the graininess of photographic images is a common encoding technique used to signify "reality." Graininess has become a primary signifier in the system of ads: the grainier the image, the more it signifies reality. Historically, the semiotics of graininess and film color derive from the time when black and white film stocks were faster than color. Until the mid-1970s color was associated with the studio, where lighting could be controlled. Thus color is identified with the musical and fantasy: the more saturated the color the more fantastic the signification. Conversely,

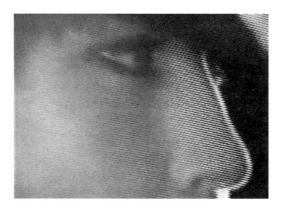

When Michelob used this hypergrainy photographic look in 1988 it seemed novel; today it is so common it almost seems "natural."

black and white was associated with documentaries because these were traditionally shot under natural light conditions. The hyperreal use of grain often exaggerates the code of graininess until it draws attention to itself as a signifier of realism. Drawing out the grain in ads offered a differentiated look or style in the mid-1980s. But just as importantly it functions as a metamessage about how to interpret the commodity narrative, because tacitly embedded in the use of graininess as an encoding technique is the semiotic history noted above.

Once the value of technically clean images was called into question and made transparent, it became susceptible to a variety of intentional code violations used to differentiate product images. Media code violations multiplied in ads between 1986 and 1989, and gave rise to a revised code. The hypergrainy look of Nissan or Michelob ads soon gave way to framing the video screen within the text so that different levels of graininess are juxtaposed (e.g., Michelob, "Into the Night"). The viewer is thus positioned to decipher different levels of reality and mediation, different levels of glamour. Other ad campaigns mixed color video with black and white so that the grain establishes a semiotic distinction—for

Michelob: The flicker lines of a screen within the screen serve as a reminder of multiple levels of mediation.

example, in a Nuprin ad the yellow Nuprin Tablet that will provide relief is contrasted with the black and white headache. Chic jeans juxtaposed the narrative of an unsettling date, shot in severely grainy black and white, against the less jangled and clearer images of changing into Chic jeans, signifying that you may not be able to count on men as your source of satisfaction, but Chic jeans are always there waiting to please you.

These techniques are finally reduced to the home-video, amateur style, where ads claim to signify the space of real life by recapturing the noise that "naturally" marks reality, but has been artificially cleansed away by professional studio tricks. Campaigns for 7-Eleven convenience stores, Surf detergent, and Sprite soft drink exemplify campaigns designed to look nonprofessional and reveal the constructedness of the video. When texts are made increasingly writerly, the final step is to permit the readers/viewers to produce their own texts, as with the Sprite campaign that placed a video camera in the hands of black inner-city high school students.

In addition to radical camera tilts, this 7-Eleven campaign used all the techniques of hypersignification to capture the "unmediated" noise of real life.

Another encoding method associated with the hyperreal involves a form of ellipsis in which the diegetic structure of conventional narrative forms is fractured, so that the narrative process of making sense has to be constructed by viewers. The typical advertising narrative implies a past, a present, and a future, but compresses time by leaving out the unessential elements of the story. Ironically, by erasing the familiar commodity narrative markers and replacing them with an apparently discontinuous array of images, ad creators give viewers a more immediate sense of the phenomenology of lived experience captured in "real time." Ad campaigns such as that for Lee's jeans attack classic commodity realism by redefining realism by letting reality break into the text unencumbered by the narrative. The text is littered with ambiguous dangling signifiers, so viewers must supply a narrative based on their knowledge of the connotative and denotative associations of a signifier. Viewers must now retrieve a narrative relationship from the signifier itself. The question of what motivates the sequenced inclusion of particular signifiers is made enigmatic—and again demands that viewers supply a meaningful relationship that connects the apparently unordered markers of real life. There is no longer a guarantee that everything that appears within the advertisement is there to advance the narrative. Though title cards sometimes provide clues to meaning, they may also mislead, thereby violating the viewer's expectation that written text on the screen clarifies the meaning of images. In Lee's 1989 ads, title cards introduce additional ambiguity rather than solving the mystery of the sequencing of images. Traditional narrative sequences are violated by having images apparently jerking back and forth between time and place.

Every new generation of ads introduces forms of ellipsis based on the abbreviation of encoding rules. TV ads begin by tacitly positioning viewers to bring up their knowledge about the reading conventions of ads without foregrounding those reading rules. This form of ellipsis reached a kind of stark minimalism in recent years when advertisers found that they could presume that because of previous exposure to ads, viewers no longer require an explicit commodity narrative. As a result, the commodity narrative is now embedded in the code itself. A related form of ellipsis involves the disappearance of the product. A third form of ellipsis creates enigmatic ambiguity, challenging viewers to act as self-conscious semioticians. Here advertisers rely upon viewer expectations that images mean something, but they throw viewers a curve by leaving out critical elements of the meaning process.

Hypersignification

Advertisers in the 1980s introduced two fundamental changes in the way they framed photographic images. First, advertisers now commonly included shots that we call "denotative danglers." These close-up shots of signifiers emphasize the detailed contours of material objects and human gestures in "the world of directly-experienced social reality."[18] Stringing together closeup shots of objects and gestures telescopes these things into hypersignifiers. A second change incorporates violations of photographic conventions about centering images. In the new realism (e.g., AT&T, Levi's, Michelob, and Clearasil ads) faces and objects are dispersed asymmetrically along the edges of the screen, or sometimes the primary signifier on screen consists of an oversized and off-center body part or

Levi's "Wildman" (1987) and the hypersignifying eye.

object. The new "realism" materially decenters human subjects within the frame of the screen. Joined to the practice of photographically decentering people are extremely tight close-ups of their body parts, with an eye here, a hand there, a foot, a partial face. Levi's "Wildman" ad featured 22 shots of hands and 26 shots of eyes and/or facial expressions. Hypersignification and photographic decentering depend on the extreme abstraction of body parts from the human subject.

The shift to hypersignifiers has been motivated by the need to stand out and break through

By 1993, Levi's routinely decentered models on the screen.

the advertising clutter. When Johnson and Johnson wanted a campaign that would break rules for baby advertising, their advertising agency, Lintas, tried to be "impactful" by concentrating on tight blowups of babies' legs or arms.[19] Pepsi pioneered the use of hypersignifiers with a campaign featuring vignettes of interaction focused exclusively on close-up shots of hands and feet in social encounters. These were slowly paced narratives, but over the years the pace has quickened and the abstracted signifiers have been thrown together in ways that sometimes appear nonnarrative. Accustomed as viewers are to recognizing media codes and to seeking out and identifying stories (seeking closure), commercials such as Levi's "Wildman" represent startlingly opaque texts.

In the 1970s, advertisers perfected the art of depicting the self in terms of its constituent body parts, fetishizing each body part so it corresponded to appropriate commodities. Typically, advertising fetishism was defined by linear editing practices that set up assumptions of causality between properly commodified body parts and desirable social outcomes. In contrast, 1980s campaigns like those by Pepsi or Johnson & Johnson dwelt on the textured detail of a hand or a foot in relation to a trace of a surrounding material reality. These ad campaigns treat the part as an indicator of a subjective moment; indeed, the personality seems to express itself via the body part. In contrast to ads that abstract a perfect hand and represent it as the idealized and perfect hand, ad campaigns that rely on the "realism" of hypersignifiers seek to convey an existential quality by emphasizing its gestural significance rather than its form. Whereas the conventional ad as commodity mirror asks that we collapse our ego ideal with commodity abstraction, campaigns that rely on apparently nonmediated hypersignifiers "claim" to leave your existence intact but "merely suggest" that you can integrate the commodity sign into your own authenticity in ways you deem fit. As an alternative to ads that steal your self and offer it back in new and improved forms, hypersignifier-based ads appear instead to offer you back a momentary glimpse of yourself as you really are.

And yet the very form of advertisements subverts this kind of humanist, existential claim since every ad demands that we interpretively abstract and universalize the object, sign, or gesture as corresponding to what we might potentially have if we used the commodity in question. Hypersignifiers may be organized to deny the fiction of reproducibility, but they actually reproduce that condition.

Intertextuality

The code violations we have discussed thus far are based on extensive familiarity with television codes and texts. A growing proportion of ads in the 1980s presumed this media literacy by recirculating the form and content of previous ads and transforming these into signifiers of media reflexivity and commodity difference. Self-referential intertextuality in TV advertising is a function of 4 decades of television history and the ubiquitous presence of television and advertising in our lives. Television has become the hegemonic medium in the United States: 99% of all households have a television and it's on an average of 7 hours a day per household. We live in a sea of signs in which it is ever more difficult to differentiate one sign from another. Viewers who have a history of media consumption also have a history of negotiating the positioning strategies used by advertisers; this dual history permits advertisers to call on viewers' memories, as well as their hostility toward the most formulaic and invasive advertising strategies of the past.

Textual allusion relies on a banking approach to knowledge: it requires that we collect and recognize discrete units of information (as in the game Trivial Pursuit). Ads that rely on self-referential intertextuality demand a degree of reflexivity about the system of advertising; they thus speak to a higher form of media literacy where viewers are asked to abstract and generalize from specific texts. Contemporary culture is turned into a giant mine for intertextual references. Any text can be carved up into component signifiers, with its parts appropriated to augment the symbolic exchange value of commodities. Appropriating narrative moments or scenes from films (e.g., 9 1/2 Weeks in GM's, "We Build Excitement" campaign or the Dairy Board's unabashed rip-off of Risky Business) turns the meaning of any text into a floating signifier. Under these circumstances, the game for viewers becomes "name that sign": How abbreviated can a signifier become before they can no longer recognize its source? Viewers who possess more comprehensive familiarity with popular culture can better recognize the twists and ironic nuances available in ads these days. In this sense, advertisers have tried to restore the pleasure in reading texts. To recognize the ad text is to feel literate and may be a source of ego enhancement; or it may make us feel a part of an "in crowd" privy to a full understanding of the multiple layers of meaning (note the similarity to going backstage).

Media intertextuality is certainly not new to advertising. Historically, the most common and vulgar form is the celebrity spokesperson whose presence summons forth the value he or she has accumulated as a star and attempts to transfer it to a product. Equally pervasive is the use of the celebrity as character, where the celebrity's best known role is referred to in the commercial (e.g., Karl Malden as the all-knowing ex-television cop who warns tourists on behalf of American Express Traveler's Checks). But this form of intertextuality requires no reflexivity. In the late 1980s, however, the use of celebrities has become mixed with media reflexivity. Karl Malden now appears on the television screen in the tourist hotel room, and Michael Jordan and Spike Lee self-reflexively play with mixing multiple referent systems for

This Nike ad joined cinema and basketball referent systems as Spike Lee reprised his character of Mars Blackman, along with Nola Darling, from his film *She's Gotta Have It.*

Nike. These ads rely upon our knowledge of celebrity-ness, ad-ness, and the reputed powers of commodities as the basis for spoofing all of the above.

Intertextual references work as a hook to anchor the association of the commodity with the consumer's memories. One way to do this is through musical referents. In the early 1980s, advertising jingles gave way to the nonjingle. Jingles were short musical phrases repeated over and over; they were commissioned specifically for the advertiser's purpose and were keyed to memorization. In the nonjingle, the music no longer seems to emanate from the commodity; indeed, now the latter must draw on (import) an outside referent system. Whereas the jingle aimed to elicit name recall, ads now aim to transfer or exchange value from the music to the product. This manifests the same tendency in music that we have already observed with images: the tendency toward creating purer forms of sign value. Music, like images, has been broken down into signifiers and signifieds. Any musical style can be chosen for the currency its signified can lend to the commodity in question. Advertisers in the 1980s recognized that rock and pop constitute independent referent systems that already have value. TV ads began to draw on previous mass media musical hits as a method of hailing various target audiences. Thus, to address so-called yuppie target audiences, advertisers pulled out pop–rock classics from the 1960s.[20] Since the music of that generation had mixed with the phenomenology of everyday experience, its use as a signifier evoked nostalgia as well as a sense of collective aesthetic identity. Now advertisers were playing our totem group.

The nostalgia boom in musical intertextuality convinced many advertisers that the rock 'n' roll generation of the postwar period perceived a vast difference between synthetic music (nonauthentic) and rock (authentic). Soon, Michelob ads began to tap the meaning of rock 'n' roll—as defined by Phil Collins, Eric Clapton, and Stevie Winwood—and the meaning of MTV videos. Whatever else we might say of Robert Plant's Coke ad or Robert Palmer's deadpanned-sex video for Pepsi, the sponsors obviously sought to sim-

Pepsi adapted Robert Palmer's music video.

ulate state-of-the-art rock videos. However, audience members who invest part of their aesthetic identity in a particular song or performer may deeply resent exploitation of what they have defined as the "authenticity" of the "original" text.

Advertisers tap into rock because it already has value—which is particularly important in the transfer of value to a product. Whereas the jingle allowed maximum recall, the critical issue today is the transfer or exchange of value from the cultural referent system (e.g., Eric Clapton) to the product name. The jingle hailed a less sophisticated television viewing audience. Though the agenda for moving from the jingle to "real music" was to signify a departure from overpackaged artifice, the movement also represents a more highly developed stage of commodification, rather than a move away from it. As the average life of ad campaigns has shortened to 13 weeks, the jingle no longer fits the demands of the marketplace because it requires a longer period of time to establish its value by implanting itself in the collective memory of the viewing audience.

Each form of intertextuality is based on abstracting a slice or even a particle of a musical text, a photographic style, or a scene from a film or TV production. The signifier is the bracketed text and the signified becomes the "appreciation of American pop culture" attached to the commodity in question. For instance, Coors and Hershey's ad campaigns hurled myriad abstracted signifiers at viewers to a staccato beat. Each signifier is a reminder of a previous cultural production or a star or an event, now reframed as an "American Original" (Elvis, Marilyn Monroe, Sugar Ray Leonard, Neal Armstrong on the Moon). Each discrete signifier (e.g., Marilyn) is also made to stand for something larger: American pop culture history. Coors attempts to cumulate the value of these icons and thereby transfer to itself the meaning of an "American Original." Coors thus identifies itself as both an essential moment in this cultural formation and a means to sharing in it.

This constant process of remythologizing pop culture is grounded in a pervasive process of intertextual circularity. Ads increasingly depend on viewer recognition of previous media texts in order to establish marginally differentiated meanings. As people spend a greater proportion of their time consuming texts, textual consumption replaces everyday experience as the social capital necessary for transacting social relationships.[21] "I saw" replaces "I did" in the society of the spectacle.[22] But intertextuality does not just refer to other texts, it ransacks and devours them in the relentless search for sign values. As a result, collective memory is no longer grounded entirely in history or social context, but also draws on the perpetual process of abstracting and rerouting meanings. This process of recycling and rerouting cultural fragments in search of new exchange values ironically contributes to a collapse in the hierarchy of cultural value. As Marx prophesied, "All that is solid melts into air."[23]

We cannot underestimate the cultural impact of the constant process of decontextualizing signifieds, turning them into signifiers, and redirecting them toward other signifieds. Our desensitization to this fact makes it possible for a huge conglomerate like ITT to appropriate the modestly populist lyrics of the Jefferson Starship's song "We Built This City," and then convert them into a corporate musical slogan: "We Built This Business." Since history has little meaning within mass culture, even the texts banned in one historical period can find their way back when textual fragments are retrieved in the context of an ad. Although blacklisted by the FCC as a drug song in the 1960s, Donovan's "Mellow Yellow" served as the background wallpaper for margarine ads in the 1980s.

The Inbreeding of Ads

But the advertising industry can no longer content itself with merely appropriating bits and pieces of culture from other fields. In order to one-up themselves and their competitors, advertisers have tapped into our store of knowledge about advertisements themselves. Some campaigns are now predicated on viewer familiarity with previous ads in a campaign, such as the Bo Jackson ads for Nike. Initially, this campaign merely demanded that viewers know about Jackson as a sports figure who plays more than one professional sport. But as the campaign unfolded, the narrative of each successive ad made the content of the previous ads the referent for a new joke about the "Bo Jackson legend."

Sign wars are direct attacks on the sign of an immediate competitor, and presume viewer recognition of the sign values generated by other advertisements. For example, Stroh's attacked the signifier of Bud Light (Spuds Mackenzie) by having a dog named "Alex" do dog imitations; Converse attacked Michael Jordan, the sign of Nike, with an ad showing Isiah Thomas driving past Jordan; Macintosh one-upped IBM by using the cane of Charlie Chaplin to "hook" the IBM off stage. Contemporary attacks on competitors differ substantially from previous rounds of advertising where, for example, Avis would attack Hertz by positioning themselves as trying harder to serve the customer, whereas the more recent struggles between Pepsi and Coke concentrate on who has the more powerful sign. With greater frequency, the attacks are aimed against the competitor's sign, not its product or service. This is a potent reminder that today the sign value of commodities tends to outweigh even the use value of the product—or put another way, the sign value may now be the use value.[24]

When the unit of intertextuality becomes the sign value itself, advertisers try to siphon off the value of a competitor's advertising (we will discuss examples of this in the next chapter). Another approach used in recent ad campaigns relies on viewers' prior knowledge of a media genre and its codes, conventions, and reading rules. By exaggerating or otherwise violating those conventions, they poke fun at the genre and at advertising. A 1988 Ragu ad campaign coyly played at disguising its ad-ness by appropriating and foregrounding the structural codes of the situation comedy genre (including the laugh track, the lighting, and the character interactions). The texture of the images and the presence of sitcom codes momentarily disguises the boundary of the ad. The Ragu ad asked viewers to deconstruct the genre that it mimics. The first viewing alerts the viewer, toward the end, that he or she is really watching an ad. On subsequent viewings the viewer is able to dwell on the joke of an ad presented as if it were a sitcom, while also reflecting on the difference of this ad from advertising in general.

Intragenre knowledge of the advertising form has also been invoked as the very condition on which interpretation of specific ad campaigns hinge. Energizer and Bugle Boy have produced attention-getting campaigns that turn the usually unspoken grammar and syntax of ads into part of their narratives. The Energizer battery campaign features a drum-pounding bunny who wears sunglasses and "keeps going and going . . . and going."

The Energizer campaign started with an ad in which the bunny is seen going (and going) literally out of the studio, as the ad apparently ends. At this juncture, the familiar codes of television would seem to indicate the beginning of a separate ad, in this case for a mannered wine called "Chateau Marmoset," with a dinner party setting full of aristocratic ambiance. But suddenly bursting through the scene and disrupting it by knocking over glasses is that damned Energizer bunny, still "going and going." In this ad, the pleasure of the text is two-fold: it comes first from poking fun at pretentious art and the upper social class (the bunny becomes something of a masked avenger for the working class). The pleasure of the text also comes from poking fun at formulaic ads: the bunny transgresses and violates the boundary markers that separate the reading of each ad.[25] This occurs by momentarily fooling the viewer that the ad is legitimate before allowing the viewer to recognize it as a parody.

Bugle Boy ads poke fun at the narrative of the commodity self that predominates in jeans ads, and the usual message that if you put the jeans on the self stands out. The right jeans, so the narrative usually goes, make you popular, attractive, and desirable. The constant equation between subject and commodity not only drives up the narcissistic ante, it has also gradually, and paradoxically, led to a displacement of the subject by the commodity. Now, the commodity stands center-stage, casting subjects in its likeness. This is the wry focus of the award-winning Bugle Boy ad. A young Adonis stands alongside a deserted western highway, trying to hitch a ride. A fast car zooms past. It suddenly screeches to a halt and backs up. The power window whirrs

Not you, but the jeans, capture the look of desire in this Bugle Boy ad.

down and a beautiful young woman is revealed. Boom! The male gaze flashes into operation. The young man cockily inquires, "Yes?" The camera focuses on the woman's face as she replies, "Are those Bugle Boy jeans you're wearing?" Smiling self-confidently, the male answers, "Why yes, yes, they are." To which she smiles and says "Thank you." The electric window rolls up and she drives off, and he is left standing alone. The ad's ironic twist is that she is attracted to the aesthetics of his jeans, not to him. What once was the logic of the commodity self has created its own cultural contradiction; the message is one about the decentering logic of commodity consumption—put the jeans on and they steal the show and the subject becomes background.

Reflexivity

In a different context, Bertoldt Brecht once argued that calling attention to the constructed nature of texts would open those texts to audience dialogue and criticism. Reflexivity in advertising, however, has emerged as a strategy to reroute viewer criticism. How has reflexivity as a critical method been absorbed and used against the intention of critics? Advertising has shifted reflexivity to the plane of metacommunication. It now attempts to create an empathetic relationship with the viewer by foregrounding the constructed nature of the text. Such positioning gives the viewer status, by recognizing the viewer as a holder of cultural capital, someone who has knowledge of the codes. By positioning the viewer in this way the advertiser appears to speak to the viewer as a peer. Reflexivity exposes the metalanguage that composes the underlying code of advertising. Cosmopolitan viewers can then consume the sign of someone conversant with both the content and the metalanguage of ads. Current advertising practices try to turn self-reflexive awareness of advertising codes into an object of consumption, into a sign the viewer can clothe herself in and thereby use to indicate a certain immunity from the manipulative effects of swallowing too much code.

Reflexivity has been encoded in a variety of ways. A character in an ad may call attention to the nature of the ad itself by stepping out of character to address the audience, for example, by making a knowing wink or an aside. This was done with an ironic inflection in a Sunlight dishwashing soap ad that features cartoon bubbles of dialogue that mock the absurd notion that clean plates could be the key to a romantic relationship. Another familiar instance of advertising reflexivity was the campaign constructed around "Joe Isuzu." These ads build on the humorous discrepancy

Sunlight: A self-mocking ad.

between the huckster's statements and the advertiser's superimposed commentary on the screen to call attention to the commonly shared view that car salesmen and car ads are dishonest. The commentary thus allows the advertiser to satirize Joe Isuzu, and unite with viewers in exposing the hype behind selling cars. The ad exposed the excess and exaggeration of the system of advertising and thereby absolved Isuzu from charges of complicity in this mendacious system.

Another method of encoding reflexivity uses camera techniques that call attention to themselves. These include cinema verité techniques that do not try to disguise the presence of the camera. Similarly, pointing to the television screen within the screen of our own television frame draws awareness to the constructed nature of the advertisement. Several years ago, a Le Tigre TV campaign consisted of revealing the actual video construction of the ad. The screen within the screen ostensibly calls into question both the relationship between image and reality and the relationship between the image maker and the viewer. When the screen breaks up or rolls within an ad, does it remind viewers that a form of self-interested production has taken place? Scratches, defects, and glitches in the video are not only techniques for encoding "realism," paradoxically they also draw attention to the mediated character of the advertisement.

MTV and Jonathan Demme call attention to their self-reflexivity by using hyperreal encoding techniques such as exaggerated tilts and decentering.

When Sprite featured ads made by inner-city high school students and Surf detergent featured "genuine" American families constructing their own ads, they did so because obviously amateur production violated the familiar codes of slickness that define most advertising.[26] By offering viewers ostensibly unfiltered cultural production, advertisers demonstrate their support for "populist" criticisms of the corporate manufacture of culture.

Home video as unmediated reality: here the O'Sullivan family makes an ad for Surf laundry detergent.

Max Headroom was a product of the age of media reflexivity, and his appropriation as an advertising icon of cynically aware media reflexivity by Coke is the archetype of how easy it is to absorb and reroute critique into the cult of personality. Max Headroom began as a dialectical vision of a futuristic capitalist media system that presides over a "total simulacrum" packed with "blipverts," intensely concentrated ads that viewers cannot zap. As the first computerized and totally simulated talking head—unconcerned about feeding or keeping safe a material body—Max has no misgivings about bursting the mirage of the media bubble. Coke expropriated the image of the video-stuttering, truth-exposing Max housed in the electronic body of the television screen to debunk the P-word: Pepsi.

Like the Nike "Bo Knows" campaign, the Diet Pepsi campaign featuring Ray Charles joined intertextuality with reflexivity to lure viewers back into the appellation box where we are hailed by unusual narrative strategies. The first Ray Charles ads played off jokes based on knowledge of his blindness. As he prepares to taste a Diet Pepsi, someone switches a Diet Coke for the Diet Pepsi. He takes a sip and frowns as we hear a stagehand laughing off-camera at the practical joke. In the post-Levi's age of individuality, jokes based on a handicap are acceptable. The handicap is a badge of recognition and achievement: here is the true taste test and the true blindfold. Diet Pepsi was referring back to its own campaign of many years featuring the blind taste test as the proof of its pudding. Both Ray Charles and Diet Pepsi have one thing in common: they are both "the Right One, Baby!" A subsequent ad featured a blindfolded Joe Montana taking "the Pepsi Challenge." In front of Montana sit two Diet Cokes, but he's not fooled. As he pulls away the blindfold, he, and we, see Ray Charles sipping a Diet Pepsi and then having a good horselaugh. Isn't making commercials fun? These ads appellate viewers as media-(content) literate, familiar with the referent systems of Ray Charles and cola wars taste tests. Foregrounding Ray Charles and Joe Montana as discriminating connoisseurs of diet colas tacitly addresses viewers in terms of the popular criticism generated by their previous use of celebrities such as Michael Jackson who did not drink the product. Like the Nike "Bo Knows" series, each successive Diet Pepsi ad refers back to previous ads. Getting the jokes depends on recognizing the references, and this insider knowledge puts the viewer backstage, positioned as the commercial's director. Thus privileged, viewers may share the camaraderie of the practical joke, and thereby feel as if they participate in constructing the ad: this is Diet Pepsi's means of reflexively denying deception.

The 1989 Infiniti ad campaign exemplified a self-reflexive attitude toward the categories of "desire" and "need" in relation to the semiotic meanings of objects.[27] These ads gained media notoriety for their Zen-like commentary on the simplicity and beauty of nature along with the photographic absence of any apparent commodity referent. A typical ad showed waves breaking against a shoreline or the symmetry of birds flying in formation, while a male voiceover tranquilly discoursed about the meanings of consumption and needs. The campaign included self-conscious dialogues about the relationship between status and commodities. One ad featured an older man quizzing a younger man about why the latter wears an older man's wristwatch. He engages the younger man in a semiotics of wristwatches: "What does that watch on your wrist say about you?" Has the younger man accomplished something that would merit wearing a watch that "makes this kind of statement"? "Are you at the top of your profession?" "Do you make a million dollars?" Responding "No" to each query, the younger man subtly negates and redefines previous value structures. Do commodities make a decisive statement about your station in social life? In tone and content, the Infiniti ad campaign suggests a critical attack upon status semiotics, but this attack is actually aimed at outmoded notions of deferring gratification on major-ticket items. With a tone of quiet defiance, the younger man asserts that one wears the watch (owns the car) because he (you) recognizes quality and wants to experience the aesthetically most pleasing watch (use value) right now, regardless of any social signals it may give off.

Hyperactivity

Advertisers compete at differentiating their images to stand out in the marketplace. In saturated consumer markets, positioning is geared toward effectively differentiating the signs of commodities. Confronted by the 1980s pincers of bored, jaded viewers and the constant requisite of maintaining market share, many advertisers opted for a rapid-fire barrage of images. The result was a stylized form of cultural noise consisting of an arresting visual and aural array of signifiers strewn together in a fused stream. All the signifying techniques discussed above have been thrown into the pot of hyperactivity: the screen within the screen; hyperrealist encoding; scratchy, grainy images; off-center and crooked camera tilts. These combinations appear most often for leisure-time goods, such as sodas and beers; goods associated with the body, such as shoes and jeans; cars and motorscooters. Hyperactive ads such as those for Michelob Light, Diet Coke, and McDonald's, and more recently Coors Light, offer energy fixes, or rather, the sign of energy. The intense style of superabstracted editing established an urgency satisfied only by the whirl of excitement that comes from the world of the product.

Ads that utilize the codes of magnified realism have quickened the pace of cuts and images. Obviously, the popularity of MTV in cutting images to fast-paced music demands a comparable speed of editing, and constitutes a prerequisite to being able to decipher hyperactive texts. There is little doubt that MTV styles also contribute to declining attention spans, and thus set the stage for hyperactive ads. Other factors re-inforced this tendency toward hyperactivity. First, the constantly rising cost of buying TV time has motivated advertisers to compress their messages and squeeze more into less time. Second, the field of television advertisements has become so saturated with competing images and signifiers that it becomes increasingly difficult to differentiate them. As a result, the effective commercial half-life of sign values becomes shorter and shorter. Combine these realities with bored and jaded viewers, and advertisers find themselves constantly upping the ante in their efforts to grab the ever dwindling attention spans of viewers. Hyperness is another method of commanding "Hey look at us, we stand out."

The Contradictions of Sign Values

We have examined changing advertising styles in the late 1980s in the context of the self-contradictory dynamics of a political economy of sign values. The constant pressure to reproduce differentiated sign values has motivated a growing number of advertisers to rely on conventions of interpretive reflexivity in their ads. Ads based on reflexivity ask viewers to dwell on the form or structure of ads. Advertisers also pursued this strategy to "cool-out" viewer unhappiness about being positioned by ads. Positioning may be the most rationally efficient and superior method for gaining and maintaining sign value in the marketplace, but the repeated positioning of viewers breeds a sense of alienation and resentment.[28]

In the production of commodity signs, the origin of surplus value lies in the structure of the fetishized communicative exchange set up by ads. Viewers habitually perform this exchange as an unequal exchange, giving value to the signs when they permit themselves to be positioned in the advertising mirror as potential subjects of the discourse. Judith Williamson has detailed the mechanics of how ads appellate viewers by hailing viewers and inviting them to step into the mirror of the ad. Viewers who do not gracefully participate in this mode of address—who do not step into the appellation box—are less likely to execute the interpretive labor necessary to assembling sign values, and then the possibility of surplus value diminishes.

Every communicative exchange consists of both a report and a command.[29] When ads position viewing subjects, a power relation is present. At the same time, an ideology of freedom of choice is embedded in the very substructure of consumer ads. It is therefore imperative to make the command portion of ad messages appear congruent with the notion of free choice, even though the very act of positioning a viewing subject involves the exercise of power. In years past, ads worked best when they worked as if they were transparent bearers of messages; power relations were invisible. This continuous consumer positioning of viewers eventually took its toll as viewers grew irritated about being positioned. Mistrustful viewers contest the efforts to position them vis-à-vis the advertising discourse by adopting cynical stances or even by withholding the good-faith interpretive labor necessary to give value to signs.

Advertisers have responded to this shift in the winds by resorting to methods of structuring ads that strategically employ what Gregory Bateson referred to as "falsified metacommunication." This means that advertisers have adopted a form of address that acknowledges the relationship between advertiser and viewer, but just as important, acknowledges the relationship between the viewer and the code. By taking a self-reflexive stance about the power dimension of positioning, these ads now misdirect viewers to a kinder, gentler, more honest political economy of sign values. Toward this end, some ads now acknowledge the command portion of the ad in order to misdirect viewers about the commodity agenda of the ad. Reflexively positioning the subject is an attempt to borrow legitimacy from the subject's everyday life. Self-reflexive modes of address also admit that ads normally operate on the basis of false assumptions. This allows an advertiser to apparently take the side of the viewer: advertisers thus seek to regain viewers' confidence and interpretive cooperation by exposing the false assumptions of other folks' ads, and claiming that they (as opposed to competitors) do not appellate viewers with distorted communications models. Viewers are thus ostensibly armed.

These developments mark a crisis in the system of producing sign value. We witness this crisis when particular ads discredit the ideology of advertising to validate their own particular sign. However, it should be added that advertising contributes to a still deeper crisis of meaning in our society. Collapsing opposing signifiers onto each other disrupts the relationship between the signifier and signified in the sense that it disintegrates the signifier–signified category. Advertising has instrumentally reduced both the signifier and signified to semes: these units of meaning become meaningful only insofar as they are understood to mean at all. What happens when the signifier and the signified become indistinguishable in the whirling vortex of the advertising form? The integrity of the signifier–signified relationship is defeated when the difference between them is undermined. The contextualizing factors responsible for determining what signifies what, that is, the chain of signification as a whole, are cut off. Meaning becomes a floating point, a search for narrative where advertisers confuse the identity of signifier and signified. Uniquely privatized meanings must surely abound under such circumstances.

The repository of relevant cultural meaning necessary to interpret ads is drawn more and more from the world of previous media images. Even this intertextuality is, however, undermined by both the shallow appropriation of stylized surfaces and the constantly shifting change of contexts that places them in opposition to other equally abstract signs. Thus the chain of signification tends inward rather than outward. In such contexts, signs are transmuted in their social meanings in the instant they are fused with their opposites. Shaped by the internal structure of the ad, decontextualized signs become the internal world of an almost solipsistic ad space, and whatever meaning they may previously have had is shed like a skin.

The streamlined structure of advertisements has abolished the ability to tell which end is signifier and which end is signified. Ads as a whole, and every sign in them, have become meaningful only in that they mean at all (i.e., that they are intended to be interpreted). This is the consequence of structurally reducing any, and every, meaning system to the status of a signifier, forced to serve as a means to the goal of commodity realization. We contend that the very logic of producing commodity signs demands that all meaning systems be reduced to the status of mere signifier. The velocity of this process increases as the sign value market matures and it becomes more and more difficult to sustain a differentiated sign position. There is a constant tendency for the exchange value of a sign to depreciate because of the dialectic of saturation and redifferentiation. In its drive to reproduce a system of sign values, advertising has contributed to a corruption of the signifier–signified circuit. Ironically, in this regard, in the long run, advertising undermines the system of commodity signs, because it erodes the bread and butter of the commodity sign business: the desire to pin down and possess the mighty signified. What happens when the signified gets replaced by the mere fact of signification?

Aggravating these mutations of the signifier–signified relationship is the relentless hyperreal encoding prompted by the collapse of sustainable distinctions between the "real" and the "simulated" in the world of representations.[30] Baudrillard's notion of the "hyperreal" points to an everyday life world where technologically mediated simulations of reality have made indistinct what is representation and what is referent. In an image-world dominated by self-referential signs, we must further emphasize "hyperreal" encoding as a style of representation that acknowledges both the history of media simulation and the distinction between a "world-out-there" versus media representations. This encoding style permits the voice of a brand-name commodity to relegitimate itself as more authentic, for example, as the new improved version, "more real than real." Positioning their ads as realist texts in relation to previous "unreal" media texts, advertisers ironically displace everyday life as a reference point. Questions of realness now lie in the encoding strategies rather than with referents. The media have become unremittingly self-referential.

What, then, is the relationship between the crisis of meaning in the ad, and the crisis in the economy of the sign as a whole? The trend toward turning the relationships that make signs meaningful into signs themselves may have something to do with this crisis of meaning. There is a certain paradox to having the structure of meaning as the particular meaning of a sign. When ad campaigns bring the structure of meaning to the surface in order to stylistically differentiate themselves from other ads, this "structure of meaning" becomes both signifier and signified of the ad. As viewers sift through the debris of signifiers cut off from both their cultural referent systems and the security of narrative structures, the only overarching signified to be found in such ads is calculated "ambiguity." With no difference between signifier and signified, differential meaning is forfeited and the sign is reduced to its own instrumentality so that it only means that it means. This seems to be an inclination in postmodernism as a whole, too, where the claim to discarding unitary desires and concepts is in fact an attempt to elevate the sign and structure of difference into the grand unified cultural meaning; the transcendental signified becomes nothing more than the fleeting moment of signification. By stressing difference, the postmodern does not ensure difference, but instead moves to abolish it. The sign of difference replaces difference. The fact of "interpretive freedom" replaces interpretive community.

Though bringing the structure of meaning to the surface could potentially promote an interpretive community based on reflexivity, the greater probability is a fractured and privatized fascination with the isolated and fleeting moment of signification. When every moment of signification is encapsulated in a sea of roughly equivalent video texts, the substance of any single signified tends to be eclipsed by its temporal video successors: its significance is lost in a stream of video matter. When this is compounded by the heavily privatized social relations of reception, we must wonder what kind of discursive rationality can grow in such a climate.

We have situated contemporary advertising as a political economy of sign value subject to its own self-contradictory tendencies. Still, there remains the difficulty of how we conceptualize the economy of the sign. David Ogilvy's famous commandment about the principle of sign value—that every advertisement is an investment in the image of the brand—speaks only to one side of the coin. A sign's exchange value can be diminished in the same ways that any other commodity's value is subject to devaluation. The advertising industry endeavors to transform meaningful images into commodity form, which makes the various signifiers like currency (capital). But the more currency that is imaged to represent the same amount of a commodity (whether it be gold or individuality), the less the currency is worth. And this devaluation of the sign hardly exhausts the crisis of sign value. The crisis of sign value is also a crisis of meaning spurred along by advertisers' constant rearrangement—coupling and uncoupling—of the signifier and the signified. To counter the tendencies toward devaluation and saturation, advertisers increase the temporal velocity at which the process of decomposing and recomposing signifier and signified takes place. We have previously called this the declining half-life of sign value. This speed-up in the circulation of signs and meanings further alienates the viewers whose interpretive labor is necessary to keep the sign circulation process humming along. This is the world of hypersignification, where fetishized signs eclipse their commodity referents precisely as they become ever more arbitrary.

3 *Yo! Hailing the Alienated Spectator*

A SIGNIFICANT portion of contemporary advertising assumes an audience of viewers/readers who are alienated from ads. It assumes spectators who are cynical and disbelieving. Each passing round of advertisements contributes to creating audiences who are increasingly media-literate, cynical, and alienated. A primary force determining the semiotics of advertising today is the advertiser's perception of the alienated spectator.[1]

Repeatedly positioning viewers to complete the recombination of signifiers and signifieds necessary to valorize glamorous sign values has borne an unintended consequence. By the 1980s, the formulaic nature of deciphering ads had provoked viewers to boredom, anger, and cynicism. Viewers grew scornful of advertisers' motives and resistant to performing the task of joining disconnected signs by accepting the guidance of advertising formulas. Viewers responded by using their remote control devices to "zap" ads. Psychologists use the concept of "reciprocal inhibition" to describe what happens when individuals are asked to respond to different cues that call for radically different emotional responses in a quick successive manner, and thus defend themselves by becoming affectless, by shutting down response. Because advertisements demand exaggerated responses, because the format is shrinking (to as little as 15 seconds), and because the number of ads continues to increase (clutter), advertising has undermined its own effectiveness by unintentionally negating the ability and the desire of viewers to respond. The challenge of holding the viewer's attention combined with the problems of product-image differentiation and rising media costs has led to changes in the method of address and in coding practices. A series of closely interconnected coding practices have emerged as a methodology for holding the interest of jaded viewers. This chapter examines these practices: *negative appellation, the knowing wink, reflexivity, death of affect, and a reliance on falsified metacommunication.*

Scenes from a 1990 TV ad for Wayfarer Ray-Ban sunglasses exemplify the glamorized fetish form (and the male gaze) of advertising. This formula of abstraction, equivalence, and reification, though still a predominant advertising paradigm, also provokes viewer resentment. This ad constructed a montage of pulsing scenes set to a rhythmic soundtrack, flashing back and forth between sharply edited shots of models' faces and product shots. This ad hailed an audience that had no need for a voiceover offering interpretive instructions to make sense of these fleeting glimpses of objects of desire—to either look like her or have her. Indeed, the codes of this ad are so thoroughly presumed that the only thing necessary to turn it into a completed commodity narrative is the punctuation mark of the brand name over the final image.

As advertisers develop and refine more rationalized tools for dividing, targeting, and addressing audiences as "lifestyle clusters," there has been a corresponding shift from mass marketing to segmented and target marketing.[2] The segmentation of national network television along with the fragmentation of lifestyle and demographic categories and the emergence of data-base marketing have placed a premium on pinpointing the preferences of privatized viewers. Tracking and targeting audiences has led some advertisers to devote more attention to how they address their viewer, especially in their competition for the attention of jaded baby-boomer and Generation X viewers. Better use of demographic data to target these audiences has, however, had a significant drawback as well: it contributes to competitive clutter, and hence to a rising tide of viewer indifference.[3] For these audience segments, advertisers have altered their mode of address to reflexively acknowledge advertising codes because advertising executives have learned that "it's incredibly difficult to get under their [young viewers'] radar. They've been so saturated with ads that they almost tune out to everything. They know they're being sold to, and most want nothing to do with it."[4]

Beginning in the 1980s, advertisers were confronted by viewers who had grown recalcitrant about doing their part in completing advertising narratives. Efforts to cope with such viewer alienation led advertisers to include meaning systems former-ly excluded from the sanitized world of advertising. Cultural analysts have long noted the absence of conflict from ads, as well as the absence of class and race differences. Likewise absent from ads was the seamy side of daily life: for example, poverty, abuse, despair, and urban decay. Beginning with the Levi's campaign of the mid-1980s, ad-vertisers edged tentatively toward differentiating themselves from competitors by in-cluding references to conflict, alienation, and yes, even race and class differences. A legion of imitators fol-lowed with attempts to signify "realism," al-though as Bob Garfield correctly points out, the aim was never reality, but "verisimilitude"— the appearance of being real. By the early 1990s, "dark ads" had cast their shadow across the televi-sion screen in the form of "commercials calcu-lated to be resonant and credible amid social and economic hardship."[5] In the 1960s, Marcuse per-ceived a *one-dimensional society* that reincorpo-rated within the com-

Sign wars and the pissed-off spectator. This MCI ad in the "Proof-Positive" se-ries is a sign wars ad aimed at AT&T's "Please Come Back" series in which disaffected MCI customers return to the fold. MCI shows a view-er who has finally had enough of the repetitive mantra of parodied AT&T ads. He raises his hand as if to take imaginative aim at the television and then "shoots," blowing it away.

modity system those differences that might imperil commodity reproduction.[6] Today advertisers no longer exclude negations, but rather seek to place negations within the framework of commodification. Still, it is undeniable that images and representa-tions formerly banished from the ideological world of commodity consumption have finally infiltrated that world. Circa 1990, the conditions that surround the processes of ideological incorporation have changed only insofar as the motivation to address oppositional meaning systems is spurred primarily by marketing considerations. Viewers are hailed now in terms of market niches so that ideological agendas have become significant to the extent that they can be converted into profitable signifiers or positioning devices.

Absent in most contemporary advertising representations—or rather, in its nonrepresentations, of class and inequality—is direct reference to the alienation so characteristic of late 20th century social, economic, and political life. Advertising in the first half of the 20th century presented consumption as an explicit alternative to alienated labor. Commodity consumption was depicted as the reward for alienated labor: if freedom was not available through one's work, at least it could be purchased during one's nonwork time.[7] As the decades passed, this theme became so well understood as a tacit part of the advertising message that explicit mention of alienated labor became unnecessary. To be sure, in the late 1980s a few advertisers, most notably AT&T, adopted a style known as "slice of death" advertising to chillingly depict the corporate work world as a vicious and unforgiving environment. And in the spirit of realism, headache relief ads revisited the strains suffered by isolated workers. But it's now the 1990s and relatively few ads any longer address the alienation of work; those that do tend to treat it in a joking fashion divorced from realist imagery of the workplace. A 1993 GI Joe's department stores commercial encourages us to laugh about the programmed character of white-collar work by featuring a man (not a recording machine) whose work consists of endlessly repeating the phrase "No loading in the white zone . . . " The ad's tag line, "Seize the Weekend," still suggests that commodity consumption (e.g., buying fishing equipment) is a way of compensating for a life of boring work, but it does so by winking at the nature of work as inevitably alienating and without meaning. Another offbeat take on the meaning of work in our lives appears in a recent Bud Light campaign that assumes a distinctively postmodern tone. Against a musical soundtrack appropriated from the Dream Warriors, a Canadian rap band that relies on jazz samples, workers are portrayed as contented automatons in an almond blanching factory. Theirs is an oddly tinted, oddly angled, precision-oriented space. The concocted narrative has a mock-childish tone: "Some men work all day in a nut house/It is an almond factory and they are the almond blanchers/In go the cold raw almonds, out come the blanched white almonds/After their long day's work is done, the men see the truck. It is white like their almonds/'How can this be?' the men wonder/This is a burning question/But once they have had such a most refreshing beer it does not seem so important/The men may work with nuts, but they are not crazy." Work ap-

White-collar work depicted in a deadpan joking fashion by GI Joe's.

pears neither alienating nor satisfying, neither authoritarian nor free, but instead idiosyncratic. Bud Light offers a space where the pleasure of the men's senses can intermingle with their analytic fascination with beer as an object of desire. Just as the men obsessively measure the size of their almonds with calipers, likewise they are preoccupied with measuring the foam head on a Bud Light with their ubiquitous calipers.

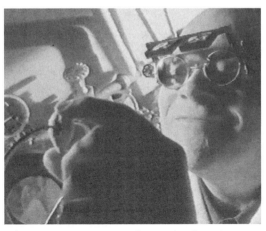

Obsessive measuring replaces manifest desire in this Bud Light series.

While there is little serious acknowledgment of alienation on the production/labor side of the coin, on the consumption side of the coin there most assuredly is a form of alienation represented in advertising today: our alienation from advertising itself as a cultural form. The alienation acknowledged in ads like those for Toyota's Paseo, U.S. Bank, Nike (in its Denis Leary series), and Subaru Impreza is our alienation as viewers, as spectator-buyers.

Today, when advertisers play to our alienation as viewers, the economic vitality of commodity culture literally requires subcultural challenge and opposition. Representations of subcultural resistance give the cutting edge of sign-value production something to push against; it provides new surfaces of differentiation. Images of cultural alienation provide those crucial *appearances* of difference with which the alienated consumer can claim to distance himself/herself from mainstream consumer culture. In contrast to postwar advertising from the late 1940s to the early 1980s, advertising is no longer monolithic in its efforts to repress the alienation of everyday life from its representations. The representation of alienation has emerged as a source of new sign value: people now wear signs of alienation as status markers. Paradoxically, capitalism today depends on signs of cultural alienation; should such signs ever lapse, capital would have to invent its own.

Addressing the Savvy Spectator

Discussions of the circuit of producing sign value have shown how the viewer must perform as an interpretive laborer. This means that the viewer supplies the interpretive energy necessary to fire a connection between social images and products.[8] Insofar as the sign value is the rejoining of signifier and signified to boost the commodity, the viewer must complete the sign value. The dilemma for advertisers is that the very process of executing these connections (i.e., continuously reproducing a field of sign value) can alienate both interpretive labor and consumption. This problem of spectator alienation tends to be aggravated by the imperative of reducing the total circulation time of capital—a requirement that intensifies under the conditions of so-called flexible accumulation and electronic currency exchanges. The result is not unlike a "speedup" on the old production assembly line: the speedup may churn out more units of production, but it also feeds worker alienation and resistance.

Viewer alienation has subsequently become embedded in the form of address, that is, in how ads hail viewers. The application of semiotics to encoding ads emerges as a methodology for regaining the interpretive participation of jaded and alienated viewers. The MTV style of advertising, with its sardonic visual commentary on television as an advertising culture, is the prototype of alienated encoding. MTV has positioned itself as the channel of the cynical and the media-literate, employing a bag full of self-effacing techniques that it uses to promote itself. Assembled as pastiche and collage, MTV spots often play at "deconstructing" commercial television texts, while steadfastly refusing to acknowledge the political economy that contextualizes the world of television ideology. The alienated sensibility that informs MTV's persona is illustrated by an MTV promo featuring a brief animated sequence of two men (drawn after the grotesque style of the dada artist George Grosz) shown straining from the neck up before revealing that they are crapping MTV logos. Shock value (à la Benetton or Diesel jeans) is another method of grabbing the spec-

Straining-to-shit MTV logos.

tator's attention that turns alienation into both the subject and the framework of discourse. The approach pursued by firms such as Subaru and Nike seeks to engage the spectator in a candid discourse of reflexivity: reflexivity about ads and their underlying assumptions, reflexivity about commodity fetishism and the norms of consumption, and reflexivity about the arbitrary character of commodity signs. As one advertiser put it: "Advertising that tries to disguise its motives doesn't work well anymore. If we tell consumers up-front that we know that the purpose of advertising is to sell them something, we'll have a better chance of convincing them."[9]

To appease viewer resentment about decades of ads that have denied and disguised their motives or promised too much, advertisers have edged toward acknowledging this resentment by joking or kidding about it. To sate the jaded viewer's desire for novelty and difference, advertisers have edged toward irreverence. The "seen-everything" attitude manifests itself in ads that seek to disguise the ad's motives and thereby distract the viewer. Ads like this are the product of advertisers searching for ways to get messages across to savvy viewers while competing for "share of attention" in a cluttered market of signs and images. As Patricia Greenwold noted, "There is an axiom in marketing theory that 'share of mind' has to precede 'share of market.'"[10]

Beginning with the well-known "Joe Isuzu" campaign and continuing with the Energizer bunny a genre of commercials developed based on reflexivity about the nature of advertisements themselves.[11] TV ads began to call attention to the system of codes and clichés that constitute ads. Recall the Sunlight soap ad that reflexively asks

Truth in advertising?

"Who writes this stuff?" as it mocks the typical theme of dishwashing soap ads: that men are attracted to women whose dishes sparkle and shine. The Joe Isuzu commercials skewered car salesman and advertisers in general by featuring Joe as the ultimate, bold-faced prevaricator. With each lie by Joe the salesman, Isuzu placed on the screen a response that corrected the deception, usually "He's lying." By creating humorous discrepancies between the visual and aural channels of the ad, the ads' creators hoped to distance the sponsor from those competitors who engage in the nonsense and deception of advertising by exposing their deceptive practices and by indicating that the people who make Isuzu ads side with the viewer. This kind of campaign has proliferated in recent years; indeed, more and more ads dwell on the process of making advertising images. The practice of including outtakes in the finished commercials registers as a method of drawing attention to the construction of the ad, and hence has become a popular method of signifying "honesty" in ads.[12]

Closely related to this style of reflexivity is what we call "commodity-sign reflexivity." Familiar examples start with the Energizer bunny campaign. When a 1991 Energizer ad lampooned the Merrill-Lynch bull/buffalo, was it coincidence that this ad

Energizer's pink bunny bullies a Wall Street symbol of investing power.

appeared on the heels of recurrent Wall Street scandals? The mechanical Energizer bunny struts through, still cool in his Ray-Ban sunglasses and blue thongs, disrupting the "bull" narrative that is semiotically identified with Merrill Lynch. Indeed, the presence of the devilish (impish) bunny makes the buffalo skittish and it turns tail and runs away. Like Crusader Rabbit, the hero of a 1950s animated cartoon series, this bunny is thus positioned as friend and ally to the alienated spectator. After all, he has the stamina and daring to expose the bogus signs of corporate America. The most explicit exposure of commodity-sign rhetoric may be found in the Subaru commercials discussed in Chapter 1 that dare to mock the logic of status semiotics: "A luxury car SAYS a LOT about its owner." The same ad agency responsible for the Subaru campaign, Wieden & Kennedy, has used a similar technique in their advertising for Nike. In a memorable series of ads that teamed Michael Jordan with Spike Lee (called Mars Blackman in the ad series), Mars plays with advertising conventions concerning the relationship between the product and the traits of the star. One ad features Mars contrasting Jordan's dunking ability with the Nike shoes that bear Jordan's name: "This is something you can buy. This is a patented, vicious, high-flying 360 slam-dunk. This is something you cannot do. Let me re-

Mocking status semiotics: "A car is just a car . . . It won't make you HANDSOME or Prettier or Younger. And if it improves your standing with the neighbors, then you live among Snobs with DISTORTED values."

peat myself. This you can buy [shows shoes]. You cannot do this [shows Jordon dunk]. Can. Can't." In the most famous of these ads, which begins by posing Michael Jordan with Nola (a character from Spike Lee's film *She's Gotta Have It*), Mars insists, tongue-in-cheek, "It's gotta be the shoes." More recently, Charles Barkley can be heard telling kids that if they buy his shoes, all they will get is a good pair of shoes: "They won't make you rich like me. They won't make you rebound like me. They definitely won't make you handsome like me. It'll only make you have shoes like me.[13] Period. Now that's what I wanted to say." Barkley has established his sign as straightforwardness and a refusal to accept the premise that his superstar athlete status automatically makes him a role model.

Still another variant on reflexivity in advertising overlaps these approaches, but with a focus that shades over to reflexivity about the promises associated with commodities per se. Campaigns such as those for Bugle Boy and U.S. Bank acknowledge the shallowness of pure commodity culture. Bugle Boy jeans garnered national attention with its ad that poked fun at the male commodity self, eclipsing the commodity self with the commodity itself. For years viewers have been exposed to ads that stress the theme that one absorbs the characteristics and personality of the commodity being pitched; this ad subverted that theme by suggesting that the commodity far outshines its wearer. The U.S. Bank series explicitly cautioned consumers to be disciplined and discerning consumers of both ads and commodities. Their self-conscious characters were portrayed as being insubstantial as the ether. Although they never have to work or pay bills, you do.

Negative Appellation

In her structural analysis of how ads work, Williamson shows how consumer ads appellate—hail and name—the viewer, inviting the viewer to step into the commodity mirror. Sometimes, ads hail us in terms of what Williamson calls our "already-ness." Sometimes ads hail us in terms of how we "wannabe."[14] Even ads that seem to blatantly address their audience with signs of cultural alienation (e.g., the current Bugle Boy campaign with its images of pierced nipples) hail the viewer in terms of membership in a nonconformist totem group.[15] Rarely do ads ask us not to identify with a product image. Certainly, even a few years ago, it would have seemed ludicrous for an ad to do so; after all, it would be, on the surface, self-defeating. And yet just such an approach offers both a means of sharply differentiating one's advertisements and a possible method of holding the attention of the jaded spectator.

U.S. Bank has run a campaign aimed at boosting consumer confidence with a broader audience than the jaded spectator. Borders, Perrin, and Norrander designed the campaign to differentiate U.S. Bank by hailing viewers skeptical about ad imagery with caricatures of instant consumer gratification. The ads cautioned viewers against abusing credit cards—to this end, they parodied conspicuous consumption with exaggerated characterizations of commodity fetishism. The ads make transparent the practices of conspicuous and indiscriminate consumption, warning that the world typically represented in television commercials is a fantasy world. In one ad a pretty young couple run along a beach in the gauzy slow-motion of television glamour as a voiceover tells us:

HE: *We live in a world of pleasure. . .*

SHE: *A world of romance. . .*

HE: *A world that doesn't exist. . .*

SHE: *Except on television. Which is why U.S. Bank hired us.*

HE: *To say that getting started in life takes more than just running together in slow motion.*

A second later, "Travis," the male companion whose head is turned only toward the ethereal world of beaches and pleasure, disappears because he apparently fails to notice the financial quicksand that claims him. "Brad and Tina," the best known ad in the series, represented the epitome of 1980s excess as the couple pretentiously charged extravagant items for the sake of their badge value. When Brad sees an over-priced sculpture, he exclaims: "It's ridiculous. We'll take it." The characters openly acknowledge that they "get paid to say stuff like this—we're just actors." Scripts like this differentiate U.S. Bank as responsible and committed to limiting unnecessary con-

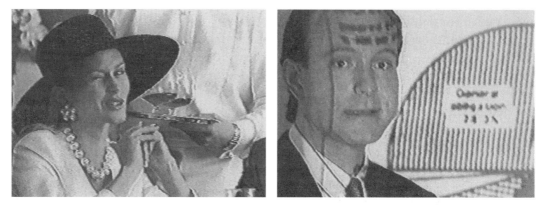

Scenes from two ads in the U.S. Bank campaign. The scene at left from "Brad and Tina" combines the knowing wink with negative appellation. The scene at right from another ad in the U.S. Bank series jacks up the meta-ante. This ad hails a spectator who has by now adopted a jaded attitude toward hyperrealist techniques. Combined with the self- reflexive talk of the actors, scenes like this expose the fetish of hyperreal techniques.

sumer debt.[16] Consumer groups applauded this campaign because it cautioned a practical and down-to-earth approach to credit card use.[17] By exposing advertising clichés, U.S. Bank positioned itself as the consumer's ally. A spokesman for the ad agency remarked: "Our experience is that there is a lot of advertising imagery that people don't believe. They don't respond to it because it's all make-believe. That's the point we are trying to make—that life is not make-believe and we are a bank that understands that."[18]

After Bo Jackson suffered a career-threatening hip injury, observers speculated that Nike would abandon him as one of its celebrity athletes. But Nike chose instead to retain their association with Bo in an ad that featured Denis Leary in a tirade about the fuss being made about "Bo's bad hip." Nike foregrounded Denis Leary's "attitude"—the ad is shot with him literally in the viewer's face—to push their reflexivity quotient higher. A comic, Denis Leary has been described as "the fidgety, Marlboro-smoking, profanity-spewing, red-meat-eating, angry Everyman of the Apocalypse, the pop prophet for a world on the verge of a nervous breakdown, the man who truly says what other people barely dare to think."[19] Leary is familiar to younger viewers

Denis Leary hailed viewers by getting in their face.

from his previous performances in MTV promos. Screaming "Shuttup!" at the viewer, Leary is belligerent, abrasive, and sarcastic. Through Leary, the ad addresses the viewers in an antagonistic tone. Dressed in black, with his leather jacket collar turned up, Leary snarls, growls, and sneers at us through a chain-link fence, derisively jeering viewers for passively watching TV. He loudly insults viewers for watching commercials. The chain-link fence and the toothpick he chews on function as signifiers of alienation and disrespect for the viewer.[20] Leary's monologue sounds like this:

> *"Hey! No more questions about Bo's hip. OK? No more questions about football, baseball, or advertising. SHUTTUP!! You thought it was over. WRONG! It ain't over till the hip socket sinks. OK? So Bo's got a bum hip. So what? Look what he's doin' with it—he's hitting the bike, he's hitting the weights. He's wearing the shoes. As a matter of fact, he's in the pool, wearing the shoes, riding the bike with 120 pounds of weights strapped to his neck. OK? And what are you and your*

"I think you hear me knocking. And I think I'm coming in."

good hip doin' right now? WATCHING COMMER-*CIALS!!!!! I think you hear me knocking. And I think I'm coming in. And I'm bringing Bo and his big bad hip with me.*"

Leary glares at us and mimes rapping his knuckles against the glass screen that separates us. Sound effects supply two sharp knocks. Leary's knocking is an unnerving surprise that punctuates the diatribe much the way he uses OK to close a line of discussion. OK? Leary's knocking signifies an aggressive and threatening attitude, an intention to intrude into *our* ordinarily protected, private, voyeuristic space, rather than respect the usual relation we have with television, which involves imaginatively entering *its* space.

Matching Leary's rapid-fire delivery are background cuts from one TV Bo-image to another. Accentuated and distorted scan lines from TV images stress the image character of Bo's mediation through the apparatus of TV: TV images of Bo playing football, baseball, hawking shoes, pumping iron, working out, working out, working out. In the scene that corresponds to "No more questions about . . . advertising," with Bo

standing posed as a product shill, holding up the shoe with the caption on the screen beside him, Nike mocks themselves and their own advertising. This is a self-mocking cartoon that remarkably encapsulates what we have been calling the "commodity sign." The image of Bo presenting the shoe is flanked on one side by the words

Nike's commodity cartoon.

"Bo Knows" and on the other side by "Nike Is Neat"—shoe advertising is about joining the meaning of a celebrity sign with the meaning of the brand. The remainder of the ad is a caustic assault on the couch potato who consumes commercials. In this way, Nike gets across a message that is consistent with their long-running tag line and sign: "Just do it." The negative appellation actually provides Nike with another method of reinforcing their overarching commodity sign: the swoosh sign.

Gender and Alienation in Sign Wars

Nike hails men and women differently with respect to questions of authenticity and alienation. Their agency, Wieden & Kennedy, has been more likely to address males in terms of their status as alienated spectators. In contrast, Nike competes with Reebok to hail the female audience with expressions of respect for their souls as well as their bodies. In the competition to hail women about questions of authenticity, Nike has chosen to reinstall the mirror of advertising, but with a self-conscious rhetoric about "your" relationship with yourself. The ads caution that one must take care of oneself, rather than being overly self-critical because of unrealistic expectations about pleasing others. One recent Nike ad epitomizes what Lears calls the "therapeutic ethos," the premise that through our enlightened consumption choices we can humanistically minister to our deepest personal needs.[21] This Nike TV ad concludes by speaking of "your [woman's] body" as "a miracle . . . and every move you make is another celebration. Or a prayer." Accompanied by the "Just do it" tag line, this message seems to offer powerful personal counsel: Nike endorses a method of "exercising" the inner self so it can grow in power and self-esteem. Another ad in the Nike series counsels, "Don't rush. The world rushes enough as it is." These ads are about healing long-standing forms of socially coerced self-estrangement. Female authenticity is represented in these television ads as a mode of address that respects women for being whole human beings and not just bodily shells. Empowerment, self-realization, and self-esteem have emerged as the subjects of Maidenform, Nike, and their competitors. "Advertising is generally not awfully good at speaking to women in a way that respects how women actually are. I think women found the ads refreshing and welcome," said Wieden & Kennedy's Charlotte Moore, who wrote the "Empathy" campaign ads with Janet Champ.[22]

Reebok, for its part, has hailed women viewers with explicitly antipatriarchal rhetoric, with a campaign featuring a montage of aerobically fit women working out, spouting soundbites like "I believe 'babe' is a four-letter word" or "I believe high heels are a conspiracy against women." The Reebok ads combine aerobics training with assertiveness training. In the last several years, a stream of advertising has addressed women about their anger regarding both sexual harassment and the general tenor of sexist imagery in the mass media. One Reebok ad humorously depicted a woman's tennis fantasy about getting even with male sexual harassers. There is considerable anger among women viewers about how ads have addressed them throughout their lives, an anger that finally crystallized around the Swedish Bikini Team in the Old Milwaukee beer ads.[23] In focus groups for *Self* magazine, researcher Judith Langer found women had "much less patience" with ads they found demeaning to women. Although Langer observed "a lot more angry women," she also notes that "most advertisers are afraid to reflect that . . . there's a lot of resistance. Advertisers don't want to see women are angry. . . . That's not their image of women. They're supposed to be sweet and nice. Advertisers may not be even aware of it, but it's there in the back of their mind."[24]

Advertisers are learning, however, to speak to women in ways that appease the anger and resistance generated by countless ads marked by male voiceovers counseling female choices. A 1991 ad for the Reebok Fitness Walker shoe features a prominent male voiceover giving a spiel about the shoe's new technological advances while the camera follows a properly outfitted woman striding briskly through a park. He is talking the technical jargon men talk. A brief excerpt conveys its flavor: "the pump accelerator with the dynamic cushioning system. With each step, compression of the heel chamber forces air through a transmission channel. . . ." Finally, the woman in the ad has had enough, and she turns her head to sharply intervene. "Hold it!" she commands, and both the voiceover and the overly serious classical musical soundtrack screech to a halt. "I'll make this real simple. These cushions," she snaps, pointing to her shoes, "take off these cushions," pointing to her buns. Hers is a no-nonsense explanation, terse and to the point. She turns and resumes her vigorous walk. This scene is replaced by a screen with the tag line "Life Is Short. Play Hard." As the screen returns to a shot of her walking away from the camera, the male voiceover returns to protest, "I was getting to that." She dismissively waves him off as if to say "yeah, a likely story" and continues on her rounds. Her intervention has been made

Image is everything. Reebok's construction of the female hardbody shifted from sexual fetishism in their 1989 "Physics of Physique" campaign to a physical self-assertive athlete in their 1993 "I Believe that Babe Is a Four-Letter Word" ad. Commitment is nothing.

to appear as if it is in behalf of the viewer, and against the narrator, whom she opposes not simply at the level of the ad's "report," but also at the level of the ad's command structure. Thus, crucially, she becomes for the sympathetic viewer an ideal object of identification, because she refuses to accede to the authority of advertising's masculine techno-voice.

The shift toward an alienated mode of address in women's TV ads continues with Wieden & Kennedy's 1993 television campaign for *Young Moderns* magazine (formerly *Young Miss*) that hailed young women within an ominous framework signifying an alienated world. A young woman, clutching the magazine to her bosom, walks serenely through an apocalyptic dark blue space, oblivious to the demolition derby of crashing cars all about her. Each car is symbolically identified by labels such as drugs, sex, college, dad, hair, guys, and AIDS. Each represents an anxiety and danger that young women today must learn to navigate past. The tag line on screen at the end of the ad reads, "It's her world. We're just living in it." Presumably the young woman we watch is armed by her status as a reader of *Young Moderns* and thus able to take her life where she wants.

A leading edge of advertisers have responded to women's resistance to being positioned in terms of the classic male gaze with its implications of subordination. Maidenform introduced a campaign in the fall of 1991 that contested the omnipresent male gaze in advertising. The ads contained no explicit product references and were composed as social commentaries on how women have been culturally represented in our society. One 15-second ad entitled "Stereotypes" presented four visual stereotypes of women (a cartoon of a piggish high-society matron; a busty blond sweater girl who throws her chest out, tosses her head back, and pouts; a prudish, severe-looking headmistress; and a bawdy stripper performing in a red corset and blowing kisses) as a female voiceover narrates: "Stereotypes of women. There aren't many women who fit them. A simple truth known by all women, most men, and one lingerie company."

A longer ad was set to the children's nursery song, "Did you ever see a lassie go this way and that way, turn this way and that." As children's voices sing this rhyme, close-up images of women's bodies bound in the fashions of Western history appear serially, sequenced one after another. The sequence of images juxtaposes the exaggerated bodices and bustles of the late 19th century with the exaggerated slinkiness of the 1920s. The predominant visual reference in these images is the clothing costume imposed on Victorian-era women. One need not be a historian to recognize the disabling corset that maximized the display of the bosom and the heavily layered caricature of female receptivity.[25] After 15 seconds, a "knowing" female voiceover intervenes over the children's voices and rhetorically asks: "Isn't it nice to live in a time

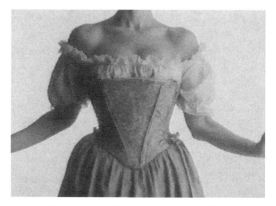

Maidenform featured images such as this, which identify historically defunct stereotypes of feminine submissiveness, to indicate what Maidenform is not.

when women aren't being pushed around so much anymore?" This sets up a binary distinction between a historical past in which women's fashions were dictated by a male-dominated society in contrast with a present where women can now live free of such domination. The tacit inference that viewers may make to complete this narrative is that Maidenform (the product) is domination-free. The voiceover that draws attention to our history of patriarchal domination is both revealing of who the advertiser thinks their audience is, and oddly contradictory, given the fact that Maidenform has clearly chosen not to change its name. Despite the postpatriarchy suggestion of the voiceover, the name "Maiden-form" still carries the worst connotations of an era in which women conformed to definitions of female beauty imposed by a male-dominated social structure.

The subject here is the male gaze, mediated by the logic of commodity relations and the apparent cultural opposition of feminism as a body of discourse. Long before this ad appeared on the horizon, Foucault observed a shift to the interiorization of the gaze whereby the subject takes herself as the object of the gaze, exercising surveillance over herself. Narratives of female control and power in ads have evolved a self-policing gaze, even if it is a narcissistic gaze. In fact, decades of consumer-goods ads targeted at women have been predicated on the narrative assumption that self-fetishization provides a route to social power. If as Foucault, Mulvey, and Berger suggest, the gaze has historically functioned as an "instrument" of objectification and the narrative of fetishized sight has provided a means of reproducing male power, bureaucratic power, and capitalist power, what should we make of Maidenform's self-reflexive account of the fetishized gaze? The Maidenform ad addresses the female spectator-consumer about the male gaze of the spectator-owner. But unlike what happens in the vast majority of ads preceding it, here the viewer is not asked to try on this gaze. She is not asked to interiorize it. She is presumed to already have rejected it in theory, if not also in practice. This ad presumes that the absent spectator-owner is not male, but female. The ad addresses women about the male gaze as a form of alienation. In this light, the gaze of objectification is depicted in the past tense, and condemned as coercive. The Maidenform ad claims to be on the side of the female-spectator who resents being treated as a mechanical object of desire, molded and pushed around.

The goal of commodity reproduction—sustaining market share—motivated this advertiser to dismiss the established patriarchal narrative as outdated. Though the hegemony of the commodity form and patriarchal hegemony have heretofore historically reinforced one another, the continued development of consumer markets has begun to disengage the affinity between these forms of hegemony. Marketers of women's consumer goods are beginning to perceive patriarchal hegemony as an anachronism they can no longer afford. Predictably, other lingerie makers have responded in sign wars style with similar campaigns. Of particular interest is the print campaign for Vanity Fair that engages in ideological self-reflexivity both about the relationship between women's self-images and the mirror of advertising, and the relationship between women's self-conceptions and patriarchal ideology. These are narratives about the domination women experience.

Disguising the Alienated Mode of Address

Advertisers' attempts to differentiate themselves from the crowd have settled into competition to disguise the formula of addressing the viewer as a commodity coefficient. The effort to induce a moment of reflexivity about how ads normally hail and position the viewer comes in multiple flavors. Sugar-coated alienation is exemplified by a 1991 Bugle Boy ad, "Monkey Suit," that featured a chimpanzee dressed in a miniature business suit and a yellow power tie walking along a beach with a young man casually dressed in an outfit from Bugle Boy. The ad features a one-sided conversation in which the young man offers the chimp advice on how to present himself socially:

"Hey man, only a friend is gonna tell you, but, ya know, hangin' out in that monkey suit, well . . . you're attracting the wrong kind of attention—at a party, you got people offering you deals on kiwi farms, instead of plates of hors d'oeuvres. I mean, loosen up. Like, like be yourself. Try changin' your clothes for starters. Then maybe get a dog—a shar-pei, a bouvier . . ."

Dressing a monkey in a business suit makes this ad seem different. But it's not really different at all. Listening to a chat with a chimp in a business suit might reduce viewer defensiveness because the viewer wonders "What's this an ad for?" Only at the end does the sign "BUGLE BOY MEN" appear across the screen. Still, the advice offered

In this ad, the Bugle Boy chimpanzee does the mall scene.

by this ad is to "loosen up . . . be yourself . . . try changin' your clothes for starters." Dressing a chimp as an adult is a way of denying that the ad is based on the conventional advertising mirror that asks us to imagine what it would be like to take the position of the model. Various segments of the audience understand that this advertising mirror of desire is based on distortion. And yet this chimpanzee gimmick does not alter, even by an iota, the underlying structure of this ad. Indeed, here the male who acts the role of the friend and mentor is smuggled into position as the mirror object himself, while sharing with us how you too can "be yourself."

No Advertising Tricks: Nothing Up Our Sleeve

Ads adopt a "tone of voice" and an "attitude" in addressing viewers. Until the late 1980s, most advertisers kept their "tone of voice" tacit. But as viewing segments have grown resistant to being positioned by the command structure of advertisements, some advertisers have countered by bringing metacommunicative assumptions about the relationship between advertiser and viewer to the surface of their advertisements. As Herskovitz notes, "The nature of a relationship must be metacommunicated, but in a power relationship an authority may attempt to falsify the metacommunication."[26] In recent advertising the aim of metacommunication is to disarm the viewer, to convert his or her anger and resistance into a new totem of identification. In television advertising, falsified metacommunication has become routinized and its codes become flashier and flashier.

The presence of a "knowing wink" in the Levi's campaign during the mid-1980s offered the advertiser a way of acknowledging to viewers the bogus character of pseudoindividualism in advertising discourse.[27] The wink was subsequently imitated by other advertisers and modified until it too reached the level of banality. Within a few years, the wink had become overtly self-conscious. The "Joe Isuzu" campaign was perhaps the most noteworthy attempt to self-consciously foreground the issue of falsified messages in advertising and then make jokes about it.[28] This foregrounding of metalanguage speaks to a level of spectator sophistication about codes, to the inability to suspend critical judgment, and to the inability to respond spontaneously (self-consciousness). It seems a bizarre twist that spectators who distrust the simulacrum of television and advertising are offered metadiscourse about the world of ads as a substitute for the authenticity they desire.

To up the ante, Toyota promoted its Paseo by constructing a series of ads based on heavily exaggerated *winking*. Like the Joe Isuzu ads, this ad series created a split discourse that alternated between the voice of moderation and practicality and the voice of fun and excitement. The Toyota Paseo campaign built a double narrative into the ads: one about the commodity and one about the nature of advertising and metacommunication. By naming the metacommunication, and drawing viewer attention to it, the advertiser professes not to engage in the usual positioning games vis-à-vis the viewer. Toyota invented a spectacular subtext solely for the purpose of exposing it, thus raising questions not just about advertising metacommunication, but also about falsified metacommunication. The focus of the ads is the contradiction between the spoken claim that the Toyota product needs no flash and the visual hyperbole of glitz. One channel or voice in the ad emphasizes the practical side of the car: function and performance, nothing sexy. However, at the same time the ad visually contradicts this spoken message by flashing "outrageous" images of sex and excitement between the sedate and straightforward product shots. By foregrounding these blatant intercuts, the Paseo ad *names* these as "subliminals," while reassuring the viewer that "Hey, we're just having some fun with you." The ad pretends to give the subtext primacy over the text by constructing a semiotic opposition between the practical (use value) and the spectacle (sign value). It is the construction of this opposition that becomes the overall sign of the Toyota Paseo ad. Toyota seeks to harness the cynical and savvy viewer's alienation as the energy for turning this semiotic contrast into a sign. The ad continues to cut back and forth between the Paseo and flashes of the Three Stooges, a rocket blastoff, glamorous come-hither women, sensual

A practical, sensible car.   Women dig it.   For people who know their limitations.   Let's party!

passion, electrifying jolts of excitement, and an orgy of hyperactive images and fonts.[29] This extreme winking is the sort that Monty Python indulged in their "wink, wink, nudge, nudge" routines.

Falsified Metacommunication and Resistance

All communication consists of two levels. First, there is "the content level" or report; second, there is the level that Bateson calls metacommunication, where "the subject of discourse is the relationship between the speakers."[30] Metacommunication undergirds our communicative interactions with tacit understandings about the relationship or context in which an utterance is made. We often recognize it in a "tone" of voice or a gesture. Ordinarily, we do not attend to metacommunication unless it seems to contradict the manifest message of a discourse. Usually, the more powerful participant in a communication prefers to keep silent about the metacommunicative assumptions that structure our discourses.

Toyota has done us the favor of producing an ad that clearly illustrates the practice of falsified metacommunication. Auto manufacturers confront the difficult task of maintaining a differentiated advertising look amid the clutter of car commercials. Cable television and VCRs brought the remote control device into a majority of homes. Using remote control devices to "zap" commercials represents an important social response to the intrusiveness and tedium of commercials. This Toyota Celica ad hails the viewer self-reflexively about the subject of zapping by introducing the material practice of channel surfing into the story line of the ad itself. In the battle to stand out and make people pay attention to one's message, Toyota found a nice gimmick. On the one hand, the gimmick permits the advertiser to acknowledge the anger of the viewer, to empathize with it, and in fact to show solidarity. It's also the central plot device for building up the currency of the Toyota sign. This is a significant reversal. Instead of signifying "disinterest," Toyota directs the channel zapping (interrupting) so that it now signifies "interest." Zapping now drives our interest in the Toyota car. The ad suggests that as much as we wish to zap it—as an automatic reflex based on our aversion to more ads—there is something just too damn desirable about this Toyota. Its allure, its value, just keeps drawing us back, because no matter what we turn away to, we keep coming back to the Toyota ad from our excursions across the channels.

The ad begins with a male voiceover: "The Toyota Celica GT extra-value package is so incredible you can't resist it." The channel abruptly switches and then returns to the ad. "See," the voiceover says, "you can't resist popular features like cruise control. . . ." Pop, the channel switches to a generic aerobics scene and back. "Uh huh," says the announcer in a knowing tone, certain that he knows our inner desires, "couldn't stay away from power door locks, could you?" Again the screen cuts away to a scenebite of generic TV golf. Another jolt back through the hyperspace of TV channels and we are brought face to face with a shiny car. "Came back for the savings, huh?" says the cocksure voice of the announcer who can predict our every move. Well, of course, he can predict "our" preconstituted channel jumping because Toyota has predetermined the path. We may never see a better example of an ad that attempts to colonize viewer resistance. We nominally play the role of the zapper, but more than ever Toyota has attempted to usurp our willpower by preconstituting our channel surfing—colonizing our desire and colonizing our resistance.

This ad acknowledges the practice of remote-control zapping as a way of getting viewers re-involved with the ad's other message about the Celica GT, but it comes dangerously close to further antagonizing the alienated viewer once he or she figures out the ad. The announcer's stance toward the viewer is condescending and nearly taunting as he dares us to resist the product's allure. It is interesting that as Toyota addresses viewers about their resistance, Toyota can scarcely repress its own anger.

The Competition in Shock Value

At first glance, Benetton ads over the last 5 years appear to decisively reject the predominant representations of advertising culture. Benetton ads are noteworthy for the ways in which they appear to break with the imperialism of Western culture: they do not privilege blond hair and blue eyes, and they seem to place "otherness" on the same ground as Western representations of identity and appearance. Initially, these campaigns spoke not to conflict, but to visually stylized fashion that relied on the "exotic" to signify "otherness." These ads evoked a sense of one-world-ness, a United Nations of fashion in which difference and conflict can be bridged by how we dress and represent ourselves. Still, ads that broached the topic of racism in society were jarring and controversial, especially when the images touched on mixed-race intimacies. Not surprisingly, Benetton's competitors such as Esprit and Diesel have also tried their hands at shock value.[31]

Benetton ads have continued their penchant for maximizing the burden on the interpreter (the viewer) to find a narrative in the images, but they also depict scenes of terrorist violence, civil war, misery, confusion, disease, and even death. The ads register as the kind of photography found in the news. These images, decontextualized as they are, hint at the violent relations of domination, subordination, and resistance. The Benetton ads are not alone in addressing social conflicts. Liz Claiborne recently undertook a billboard campaign against the "War at home," the violence perpetrated on women in public places and in the home. Like the Benetton images, the Claiborne-sponsored billboard images are "deliberately disturbing—a battered woman looking out from behind chain links; a man's clenched fist ready to strike; a man holding his head in his hands under the words 'She had: a broken nose, a displaced jaw, one black eye, three fractured ribs, a mild concussion and a man who said he was sorry! But sorry didn't do it! You did!' "[32] Yet there is something profoundly different about Benetton's picture of war in Africa from Claiborne's portrait of violence in the home. The Claiborne billboard image speaks with the quiet, but firm, condemnation of an actuality that has been photographically documented. The code of realism used by Benetton also is in the newscode style of *Newsweek* magazine but it lacks the explanatory caption seen there. Indeed, without a written narrative to contextualize the image, the Benetton image demands that the viewer *motivate* the image's agenda. The difference between the Benetton ads and the Liz Claiborne billboards is that the latter do not metacommunicate that "This is an ad." The Benetton ads do! They are still promoting a sign—the sign of the United Colors of Benetton—of a sponsor.

Benetton acknowledges that "We've chosen to appeal to a certain type of person that shares a somewhat iconoclastic view, who questions the status quo, because progressive thinking and fashion go hand in hand."[33] The stark images of violence and misery are aimed, however, at provocation, not rebellion. Do these ads educate consumers to the realities of capitalist production, or to the effects of our consumption upon the third-world workers who produce what we consume? It is ironic, then, that imagery of third-world misery fuels the construction of sign values like those of Benetton.

Benetton, of course, has offended a great many people by assembling images that connote blasphemy. The ads challenge the middle-class expectation that it is inappropriate to dwell on the horrors of this world in the domain of advertising. Another response goes deeper: it perceives falsified metacommunication at work. It sees Benetton's willingness to expose social reality as a calculated and cynical publicity gambit designed to shock and disturb for the purpose of selling more clothes. In the upscale jeans and clothing market, it would be surprising not to see other competitors adopt similar methods of hailing the target audience. True to form, Diesel, an obscure line of pricey Italian-made jeans, struck publicity gold with "irony-laden ads with social messages that make Diesel the first advertiser to at least temporarily out-Benetton Benetton."[34] The ad that caught the most attention foregrounds multiple image reproductions of a young man aiming a handgun point-blank at the viewer. The framing text reads "How to teach your children to *love* and care." Text in a smaller type size below explains:

MODERN CHILDREN need to SOLVE their OWN problems: teaching kids to KILL helps them deal directly with reality—but they learn SO much quicker when you give them a guiding hand! Make them proud and confident! If they never learn to blast the brains out of their neighbors, what kind of damn FUTURE has this COUNTRY of ours got???

The ad's tone of voice drips with sarcasm, and predictably achieved instant notoriety by offending those who were not in their target audience. Interestingly, the folks at Benetton endorsed the effort. "If you are a jeans maker you can't run with the pack and expect to get any attention," said Peter Fressola, spokesman at Benetton. "Jeans are about sex and danger. And the people who are offended by these ads are probably not Diesel customers anyway."[35] Diesel ran a series of social issue ads that satirize everything from environmental degradation to smoking to plastic surgery. Each ad in the series featured a photo of an ultrathin sex doll clad in revealing cutoff jeans. An antismoking ad showed a voluptuous woman mounted on a 5-foot-long cigarette next to the headline "How to smoke 145 (cigarettes) a day." The ad lampooning plastic surgery pictured a razor blade stuck in a slab of red meat, with the headline "How to reach perfection." The ad proposes, "Why be yourself when you can be somebody else?"

The Profane

Even as commodity culture gained hegemonic status in the latter half of the 20th century, resistance to it has also grown. To many who have lived their entire life in the society of the spectacle, alienation seems inescapable in the fiber-optic dystopia of the cult of appearances. Like the siren's song, the spectacle seduces us with commodity images that turn "vulgar" when we get them home. One youth-culture response to the society of the spectacle has been a furious refusal to consent to the hegemony of commodity consumption. The Sex Pistols sought to smash the dreams of everyday life, exposing the falsehoods of consumer ideologies. Singing "No future, no future, no future for you, no future for me," the Sex Pistols in 1977 declared an end of faith in the capitalist dream machine of navigating through labor markets, capped by shopping sprees in the cathedrals of consumption. Punk style was calculated as an affront to mainstream conventions. "The punks wore clothes that were the sartorial equivalent of swear words, and they swore as they dressed—with calculated effect."[36] Punk philosophy held that "the forbidden is permitted, but . . . nothing, not even these forbidden signifiers (bondage, safety pins, chains, hair dye, etc.) is sacred and fixed."[36] The sacred—that which had become ideologically "naturalized"—was renamed by the punk subculture as constipation. The punk subculture scrambled the meanings of commodities as defined through the spectacle to create a new lexicon of profanity.

Greil Marcus describes an event at a punk-rock concert in Los Angeles in the late 1970s that characterized the strident, confrontational attitude of punk at its antihegemonic apex: "A woman strides naked onto the bandstand as Vox Pop plays, collapses into the bass drum, rises, pulls a Tampax from her vagina, and hurls it into the crowd—'grown men, skinheads, turned white and ran away.' That was punk."[38] The flying Tampax wasn't just thrown at a horrified crowd, it was also thrown, like an anarchist's bomb, at a whole hegemonic complex of ideological assumptions.[39]

The task of hailing alienated youth has driven some advertisers to more drastic methods: they too have turned to the profane. The profane has made its way into magazine ads such as the Benetton ads that dwell on images of death, disease, brutality, and sacrilege (a priest kissing a nun); or the explicit visual allusion to a man going down on a woman in oral sex in a Wilkes-Rodriguez clothing ad; or rapper Marky Mark clutching his crotch in Calvin Klein ads. In response to one of Benetton's "disgusting" and "offensive" print campaigns in 1992, angry reactions flooded in to *Advertising Age:*

"They want real life? How about common diarrhea?" said one respondent to *Advertising Age*'s fax survey last week about the retailer's new campaign. "For their next campaign," said another, "they might feature a pile of . . . ! After all, that's real life too!"[40]

Sound advice, wrong campaign. The conventions of bourgeois civility demand that mention of bodily functions be repressed in civilized discourse. On the other hand, maybe a pile of excrement would grab some attention. Sure enough, a Powell-Peralta skateboard ad framed a pile of shit with a fly sitting on it with the ambiguous caption "Quality Doesn't Matter." The pile of shit stands for an attitude or a stance toward commodity culture. It offers a method of hailing. Rap and youth culture frequently position themselves in terms of the profane—for example, the band name Butthole Surfers, self-mutilation, anything that violates and offends the codes of middle-class civility about the body or that transgresses bourgeois aesthetics.[41] Formerly out-of-bounds encodings provide the stylistic energy driving commodity culture:

> The fundamentalists are right to be worried: the images of forbidden and unnatural desire do surround us. They lead all who look at them to consider all the possibilities of who they and their mates might be. From back-room dance bars to gay-ghetto billboards to downtown bus stops, the discourse and disarray of forbidden desire is everywhere.[42]

In advertising we have watched the discourse and practice of forbidden desire mix with the practice of pseudoindividuality in ads such as the 1993 Bugle Boy ad campaign running on MTV. Here Bugle Boy attempted to disguise pseudoindividuality by hailing their totem group with images of body piercing. This may look different, but it is conventional advertising. The ad depicts the brand name as the measuring rod against which you measure your inclusion in this totem group—it's just that in this case it's a group defined in opposition to middle-class codes concerning the body. Bugle Boy's effort aims at unifying your "different statements" by their "common thread." An identity defined by the semiotics of piercing hails the subject about setting oneself apart from poseurs. Here, as elsewhere, in a commodity culture that

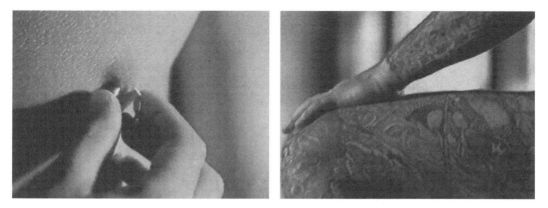

Signs of the profane. The nipple ring and the full-body tatoo have emerged as signifiers of a "different measure" of identity. They are presented here as signs of admission to a nonconformist totem group: young men who belong in spirit to the Bugle Boy nation.

continually looks to appropriate the next hot image from those subcultures that oppose it, alienation itself becomes a pose.

"Before Your Future Gets Here You Know What You Gotta Do"

The openly alienated anti-aesthetic adopted by punk vulgarity has long since been sanitized and domesticated for use by the culture industry. By the time images of bodies out of control (burping, farting, belching, etc.) get refracted through television for popular consumption it looks like a Pepsi ad. Pepsi's 1993 Super Bowl ads sought to appropriate the flavor of this with bodies out of control and a vulgarity of excess. Visible excess would seem to violate most of our inherited moral codes about appropriate consumption. And yet advertisers such as Pepsi, Reebok, and Toyota now foreground images of frantic, frenzied consumption. These advertisers intentionally mark scenes of intensely compressed consumption as "subliminal," still afraid to openly endorse hedonistic bingeing, but willing to suggest it in a winking manner by including scenes shot in exaggerated close-up that distort facial features as they convulse, spasm, and gyrate in apparent excitement and pleasure drawn from their commodity fix.[43] We have come a long, long way from the Protestant ethic.

During the 1993 Superbowl, Pepsi ran an ad we call the "Road to Nowhere, Revisited." Two kids sit on a curb drinking cans of Pepsi in front of a Pepsi vending machine and a sign that reads "Prest-O-Lite Battery Service." One boy asks, "Hey man, whatta you wanna do?" The second kid responds, "I dunno . . . ," pausing to muse about how he envisions his life playing itself out. The ensuing mini-tour of his future is framed by a soundtrack of bugle-dominated chase music from movie serials. "I'm thinking maybe finish high school, then college, wife, kids. . . ." As he begins to narrate his future the first overlay is a fadeover of him with his smiling bride ("wife"). Note that in every scene he is still wearing his baseball cap. The scene cuts to him looking a bit haggard with a paint brush in hand ("house"); cut to him with wife holding baby ("kids"); cut to wife next to a station wagon, he in foreground, his voice now weary, "station wagon"/"riding mower"/"in-laws over for a barbecue" (heavy sigh)/"I guess I'll give up Pepsi and start drinking prune juice" he says mournfully/"rewire the attic"/"join the lodge"/"bowl on Wednesday"/"work off the old gut" (on a stationary bike)/"kiss a little butt at the office"/"make middle management"/"I hang it up and head on down to Miami"/"buy some white shoes and pants that come up to my chest and complain about the government full time!" "No," cries

A Pepsi signifier of uninhibited "pleasurable excess."

the first boy, "I mean what do you want to do this afternoon." "Oh," he replies, pausing before screaming, "The Beach!!!!" The final scenes show the lads at the beach, indulging in excess, across them the slogan "Be Young. Have Fun. Drink Pepsi." A youthful voiceover advises, "Hey man, before your future gets here, you know what you gotta do." Every ad in this series ends with a young male gesticulating, shot in distort- edly tight close-up, in socially unregulated paroxysms of overindulgence. Though a comic piece, the vision of adulthood presented here is grim and even fatalistic in its overdetermined attitude. It depicts education, women, and work as forms of entrapment. The completion of education seems to lead to conformity and the compartmentalization of life, not to liberation or even mastery of one's life.

Pepsi claimed these ads spoof America's return to "traditional values" with the simple message: "Do what you love, and live life to the fullest."[44] This spoof indicts the entire middle-class life cycle as boring, empty conformity. Pepsi's spoof on tradi- tional values paints a picture of a grim, vacant life. It suggests little space for choice. There is no heroic individual in this story—instead, he imagines a future already set by the institutions that dominate him: family, private household, and corporate ca- reer. The image of domestic life is one of empty obligation, and the scene from the managerial workplace ("kiss a little butt") offers an unflattering view of meritocracy in the corporate world. These, of course, are not the institutional axes of traditional values; they offer instead a spoof of "modern" values. Despite media hype about a movement back to traditional values in the 1990s, marketers see data that show a continuing drift in the opposite direction. Pepsi addresses a youthful audience unin- terested in defining themselves in terms of values that are boring and oppressive. Pepsi's spoof on traditional values hails the spirit of hedonistic resistance that the re- newal of traditional values seeks to tame.

Beneath the ad's dark comic fatalism that caters to the lowest common denomi- nator of mass culture—namely, unthinking consumption—lurks an oddly Hegelian refrain about the highest stage of freedom existing where freedom and necessity con- verge.[45] Hegel's idealism envisioned freedom depending on neither accident nor con- tingency. True freedom lies in choosing necessity. Updated, this means recognizing and choosing the icon of Pepsi as total necessity. Necessity is freedom—"Gotta Have It"—choosing and doing what you have to do. Looking at it this way, we see that Pepsi's youths in no way reject the dominant culture portrayed. They accept it as necessity, as their destiny. In the meantime, PARTY!!!

The Self-Referential Sign: Grinning at the Annihilation of Everyday Life

In the post-Biff age, advertisers read Roland Barthes.[46]

Since 1988, reliance on self-reflexivity in ads has escalated. During the early 1990s, we have witnessed ads layered in levels of metacommunication, intertextuality, and self-reflexive awareness. No ads are better recognized for this layering than those done for Nike by Wieden & Kennedy. In particular, the "Bo Knows" spectacle ad embraced the contradiction lurking beneath the construction of commodity signs that are supposed to connote authenticity. Opening a big-budget musical extravaganza with orchestra and sequined, costumed dancing girls, Bo appears as the superstar singer/performer. The chorus sings, "Bo knows it's got that air thing," which refers to the "Bo Knows" series of ads and presents itself as a form of Nike self-mockery. After

a few seconds of the number, Bo yells, "Stop." In an aside he states, "This is ridiculous. I'm an athlete, not an actor. Let me out of this thing. I have rehab to do." Suddenly he is climbing through the TV screen into a middle-class family den. As he passes through, he matter-of-factly admonishes the boy not to watch too much TV, while the boy can be heard remarking, "Great shoes." The ensuing montage shows Bo weightlifting, swimming, and bicycling. In the middle of this activity, the big musical production number can once again be heard rising faintly in the background. Bo halts his workout to object: "Hey, where's that music coming from?" The next scene shows Bo scolding a large screen bearing the Nike logo. "You know I don't have time for this." But the final shot completes the joke, as the scene cuts to George Foreman declaring, "But I do! Hit it!" The showgirls resume their song and dance with Big

Bo versus the Spectacle.

George, who happily participates in the spectacle and hype. Bo's role in the narrative is to critique the logic of the spectacle, because it moves him away from his real identity as athlete to an inauthentic self (the entertainer). Nike has executed an ad "analyzing the essence of hype and the inevitable cycle of mega-celebrity: mass adulation, giant commercial deals, overexposure, death and revival as self-parody."[47] Having Bo speak directly at the swoosh sign shows that Nike can laugh at itself and participate in its own self-critique.

A year later, Nike's "Boys in the Barbershop" ad aired during the 1993 Baseball All-Star game and built on references to the "Bo Knows" Las Vegas campaign. The ad opens with the men staring at a Nike "Bo" commercial on the barbershop TV. The music accompanying Bo's workout in this mockup ad refers to the "Bo knows it's got that Air Thing" music from the prior spectacle ad. However, it is reproduced here in an even more repetitive form to both aid recall of the prior ad and to stress the tedium of Bo's everyday routine with its constant repetition. An oldtimer mutters, "This Nike commercial is boring." On screen, Bo is seen doing squat-thrusts as a second man remarks in deadpan tone, "It's just Bo in a gym." A third man allows that "I can do that." In turn, they continue to critique the Nike ad:

MAN 4: *Where are the dancing girls?*

MAN 3: *Where's the singing?*

MAN 1: *I miss the montage style of editing.*

MAN 2: *It's just Bo in a gym.*

Their voices wander from deadpan to flattened numbness and disbelief. The comment, "I miss the montage style of editing," contrasts Bo's exercise and work ethic with the glitz and tricks of the spectacle. Comparing the place of the barbershop with the space of the ad sets up the ad's humor, as the men state their preference for the "entertainment" ads that enliven their otherwise uneventful lives. By calling attention to its own spectacle, Nike calls into question the authenticity of that spectacle and advertising's manipulation of excitement. The ad draws to a close as one oldtimer opines that "only a Nike commercial in a barbershop would be more boring." The barber replies, "Even Nike's not that dumb." The camera scans back to the television screen and the music pauses. Bo looks up from his workout as if he has been listening to the last exchange. His look, an ironic glance toward the audience, suggests that "well, I dunno—Nike could indeed be that dumb." Bo knows. Wink, wink.

Why lament the absence of the montage style? Because it manipulates the codes

This Nike ad used a barbershop setting to deconstruct its own advertising. It ends with Bo both knowing and winking.

of time and space to make the mundane and commonplace seem interesting. Minus the montage style and the decorative presence of dancing girls, Nike ads would be disappointing because they'd merely reproduce the everyday routine of a workout. To the men in the barbershop, the gym workout is as repetitive and routine as their own lives. It does not divert them from their own boredom, but instead reminds them of it. But we as spectators are not invited to identify with these men as spectators, nor are we really invited to identify with Bo. In fact, this ad is not directly about shoes, but about the totalizing image of Nike. The imagery of small-town rubes analyzing the video in the language of film criticism evokes what Hebdige calls a "sensibility attuned to artifice." Nike isn't just a shoe anymore, or even a collection of superstar athletes, it's an attitude—it's an ironic awareness that Barthes called "the second degree."[48]

Nike has cultivated this ironic and reflexive awareness about the role of ads in daily life. Nike's profile of self-awareness has developed over time through a range of ads that all address questions of identity—Nike's identity. Nike advertising has, since the Spike Lee and Michael Jordan ads, been able to consistently distance Nike from their own pure commodity rhetoric—for example, "It must be the shoes." They consistently joke about their slogans, as if to say "our primary message to you is still that the capacity to change and develop as a person must come from you. Hey, we just sell good shoes with an attitude."

The ironic winking encourages reflexivity and constructs Nike as a self-effacing company with a sense of humor. They don't take themselves or their ads too seriously. These are ads about ads and ads about images. In them, the shoe as commodity is absent, but is inferred from our past knowledge of Nike. Instead, these ads sell the corporation as a commodity-sign on the basis of its attitude. They suggest that Nike not only has a philosophy, but also has a philosophical personality—it has a *mystique.*

From the regular viewer's point of view, the Nike scene in the barbershop highlights yet another media-referential dimension of advertising today. There was something immediately familiar about Nike's barbershop scene because, during the preceding year, a corporate image campaign for TCI (a leading cable TV firm) had used a nearly identical scene of a small-town barbershop. But the TCI ad felt like a corporate image ad. It framed a more romantic, emotionally loaded vision of a subdued community barbershop space where men gather and find themselves enlightened by what is available to them on cable television. TCI presented television as an important force for integrating a sturdy and informed public body of citizens. Could the Nike ad be mocking this kind of romanticized scene with its utopian depiction of television as the unifying information resource behind democracy and community? Counterpose the TCI's vision of TV as enlightenment with the imagery of benignly narcotized spectators in Nike's barbershop. Whereas TCI's scenes are self-congratulatory, Nike needles themselves and the cultural relations of the spectacle to which they contribute. And yet, irony of ironies, this Nike ad functions just as much as a legitimation ad as TCI's. This ad does not sell shoes: it sells the Nike mystique. Here is a legitimation ad that works by self-mockery. Nike's interest in cultural legitimation stems from their need to promote their most precious commodity: their sign value. It again boosts their authenticity quotient by establishing Nike as having the capacity for honesty and a willingness not to engage in deception.

Just as in the Denis Leary ad, Nike's attack on the passivity of television watching situates a basic contradiction: on the one hand, Nike depends on celebrity culture and promotes the identification of spectator-consumers with *celebrities as sign-minters.* Nike has had great success in hailing fans by giving celebrities personalities, and reducing those "personalities" to one-dimensional signifiers: for example, Charles Barkley equals strong-willed honesty, or Bo Jackson equals workaholic versatility. On the other hand, Nike's overall sign (their metasign, if you will) depends on self-reflexivity about the game of celebrity construction.

Both Nike and MTV have embarked on a new stage in advertising. They legitimate themselves by engaging in self-deprecation about their own signifying logos, by refusing to treat their own sign as sacred. In a curious way, Nike's advertising has adopted the punk refusal to honor anything as sacred. In its most recent campaign, Nike has run a series of ads featuring Dennis Hopper as a whacked-out, gonzo football referee who "hears the footsteps." Though the media attention to this ad has focused on how it has upset mental health advocacy groups because of Hopper's portrayal of an obsessive character, more interesting to us is the way that Nike has chosen to punctuate these pieces. The conclusion to each of the commercials in this series in-

Nike playfully cast Dennis Hopper as an eccentric ex-football referee obsessed with football and shoes. Here, Hopper indulges his shoe fetish by sniffing Bruce Smith's shoe, before Nike cut to its swoosh symbol on a background of rippling meat.

cludes what appears to be the Nike logo, the swoosh sign, across a slab of rippling, marbled red meat. Why? The creative talents behind this imagery named the campaign "Cool Meat" and indicated that the computer-graphics manipulation of the logo was done to underscore the "weird intensity" of the Hopper spots. Although establishing the precise meaning of the "cool meat" is up to the viewer, we believe that, like the MTV penchant for promos that degrade their own sign-logo (e.g., shitting logos), Nike's approach demonstrates an irreverence toward their own sign that was already apparent in Bo's confrontation with the Nike logo discussed above.

As ads adopt a more cynical tone to appease viewer antipathy, do they move the audience further toward cynicism? We suspect that these maneuvers to counter viewer alienation further contribute to a generalized crisis in the sign-production industry. Surely these ads do nothing to dispel the pervasive climate of cynicism that defines the public sphere. In fact, the cynical attitude becomes a virtual prerequisite to the possibility of gaining interpretive pleasure from these ads. But what comes after cynicism?

4 *The Flip Side of Jadedness: Memory and a Sense of Place*

CAPITALISM and commodification have bred the conditions for nostalgia. The maelstrom of capital disrupts and displaces traditional structures of family, community, and religion that previously buffered—even if in oppressive and mystifying ways—the experience of rapid social change. Compounding this, urban life organized around commodity relations and the television encourages the proliferation of socially disconnected and isolated individuals who live privatized lives. The acceleration of commodities, signs, and people through the circuits of production, distribution, and consumption have contributed to a privatized world of expanding individual freedoms and exhilerations coupled with disorientation, boredom, and insecurity.[1]

Evoking memory is a method of socially positioning viewers. Advertisers turn nostalgia into a talisman to ward off fear of constant upheaval. Since the inception of modern advertising, one dimension of advertising has been aimed at soothing distress about moral and ethical upheaval by speaking to, and about, memories of the past. This kind of advertising substitutes the solace of quieter, simpler times for a present that is represented as a time of social and cultural crises and disintegrating community relations. This reliance on nostalgia as a marketing instrument runs in cycles, with the latest market boom in nostalgia coming in the late 1980s, pegged to an aging generation of baby boomers.[2]

Advertisers have instrumentalized the categories of history and memory as signifiers. By stressing the signification of history and memory as categories, they hitch these categories as signifiers to the signifieds of nostalgia, progress, quality, or legitimacy on a case-by-case basis. By virtue of their increased reliance on formal semiotic technique, advertisers have grown more skillful at reconstituting the appearance of memory and memory traces. Under these circumstances, memory becomes no less a reified object than a pair of jeans or a can of beer or a woman's legs. Images and music from the past are turned into stock signifiers of memory by passing them through film codes. Conventional codes such as soft focus, schmaltzy personal narratives, and slow motion romanticize and reify the past, while hyperreal codes based on jerky camera movements, jump cuts, scratched film, black and white film, and first-person narratives can be made to evoke a perceptual sense of historical realism.

In the sign economy of advertising, the past becomes a storehouse of recyclable exchange values. Advertisers' adoption of nostalgia turns history into a giant pot into which one can reach for disconnected snippets of memory.[3] Meanings rooted in history are thus dislodged and made to join the endless circulation of signs, where they become limitlessly sequenced and resequenced according to the logic (or whim) of the market. This never-ending commodification process relentlessly discards meaning systems to make way for the new or the improved or the different, thus amplifying the conditions for nostalgia. On the one hand, the semiotic engine of sign production collapses meaning systems and disregards the temporality of meaning. On the other hand, capitalist culture draws on images of the past to salvage the appearance of imagined communities.[4]

When contemporary advertising addresses viewers about social relations that are absent from their own lives, memories once located within the local relations of everyday life are taken over signifier by signifier and reconstituted by the mass media as nostalgia. Storytellers, who once functioned as organic intellectuals within community contexts, passing along idiosyncratic local narratives and myths, have been replaced by a monoglot corporate revivalism that refracts all history, all stories, through its panoptic lens.

When memory is translated into photographic replicas available through the TV, it becomes stylized and privatized nostalgia. Transmuting historical reality into images that signify "historicalness" may actually contribute to a dissipating sense of shared history, because as Barthes observes, meaning hemorrhages away when primary signifiers are redirected into second-order signifiers. In the hands of advertisers, memory becomes a second-order signifier: the personal memory is transformed into social myth.[5] Likewise, the historical moment has become a matter of coding decisions. In ads, history is almost always a simulation constructed through the arrangement of conspicuous signifiers that overlap across ads; for example, scratchy black-and-white film becomes a signifier of history per se. The concept of "history" becomes contingent upon recognizing such overlapping signifiers in television ads. History then becomes a signified emptied of specificity; it functions as a generic sign. The substance of history erodes; instead, history is conceived as pure form, a category to be filled by this or that signification. When invoked as a formal category in ads, history is usually represented as a source of value, which when placed in formal equivalence with the corporate name, lends value to the sponsor. Ironically, insofar as we become a culture without historical memory, history seems to have little value in daily life where the "creative destruction" of the market is relentless.

Schmaltzy Gemeinschaft

Advertising turns the absence of communal relations in everyday life into its symbolic opposite, signs of communal rootedness. In the late 1970s and early 1980s, TV ads for consumer goods regularly joined commodity brands to images depicting rural and natural settings to signify a celebration of individual autonomy, nurturant family relations, and the spirit of community. Rural scenes were used not simply to hail rural audiences, but to praise the values of hard work and self-reliance while stressing the emotional vitality of intimate primary relations, what Ferdinand Ton-

Advertisers regularly draw on the handshake as a down-home signifier.

nies once labeled *Gemeinschaft* relations, a "community of blood" (kinship) and a "community of mind" (friendship) vanquished by the advent of market relations. Ironically, the same ads that stress the past virtues of rural life also appear to make available such relations via the consumption of appropriate commodities.[6] Advertising taps into a referent system in which noncontractual, noninstrumental communal relations signify honesty and trust and goodness. Qualities of permanence, tradition, and interdependence are thus translated into meanings of authenticity and honesty. Though these connotations come from our past, ads mundanely construct a spatial nostalgia for a noncommodified and nonurban world, rather than a temporally precommodified world.[7] In an AC-Delco ad, a rural woman describes the inseparable relationship between her husband, his truck, and his dog, and how AC-Delco parts have kept the relationship going. But someday, when the truck does, in fact, as it eventually must, stop running, she imagines it will be parked behind the house and serve as a rural gazebo for husband and dog. Gemeinschaft locales are intended to offer the appearance of down-home country places as the background for portraits of relations among simple, honest people. Think how often we see ads that place grandfathers on country porches or grandmothers in kitchens to hype the authentic qualities of mass-produced foods. People who work honestly for a living apparently have a more grounded, and hence more trustworthy, sense of what is worth valuing. The Delco ad situates the commodity (auto parts) in terms of a long-term relationship defined by durability rather than flighty change, a groundedness in the land, and an unshakeable bond (between a man and his dog) that cannot be influenced by market relations.

Ads also reconstruct Gemeinschaft relations as childhood memories. In a Country Crock Churn Style Margerine commercial a young, blue-eyed, and blonde housewife bites into a blueberry muffin covered with the spread, provoking an involuntary memory of her youth: "The taste reminds me of my mom's butter on the farm. I loved growing up with that sweet butter taste." The camera focuses on the picture on the Country Crock container, which fades away to be replaced by a soft-focus depiction of the woman as a child eating a blueberry muffin served by her mother. A fabricated memory drawn from a mythic preindustrial past, the role of farm mother as a producer of basic products like butter disappeared long before the 1970s when the blond woman in this ad would have been a child. Correlating the product with this image draws on a notion of motherhood as a signifier of purity and goodness. Country Crock is marketed to women who would like to see themselves as a source of warmth, love, and goodness. Women's roles are defined by references to a mythological past and then rerouted into consumption of the signifier. The name, Country Crock Churn Style, suggests the product is made like butter and has a metonymic relationship with the farm mother and these signifieds. But what is this product? It is a butter substitute that goes unnamed, because to name it is to categorize it and differentiate it from butter, and thus bring to the surface the natural/artificial opposition. Spreading Gemeinschaft-tinted images of memory over the product disguises this opposition.

Gemeinschaft memories are no longer confined

Here are the television codes of memory at work. First, she dissolves into an old-timey drawing on the Country Crock container. The meaning of this overlay is reinforced by the woman's voice saying "I remember . . ." As the camera moves in on the image depicted on the packaging, in the drawing comes alive as a scenic reconstruction of a mother–daughter relationship set in a farm household. Notice how the last scene here is shot with soft-focus halo effect to simulate memory itself.

solely to the rural. For the benefit of baby-boomer audiences, advertisers have played on the nostalgia for cultural artifacts of the 1950s and 1960s. A recent Koolaid campaign illustrates this phenomenon, as it invites an audience of baby-boomer parents to glimpse memories of their own childhoods when their moms made and served Koolaid. The ad invites us to think of Koolaid as a "tradition" we can reenact with our own children. Koolaid thus romanticizes the construction of commodity traditions while it traditionalizes the construction of community among contemporary parents around the totem of the Koolaid pitcher. Williamson discusses the relationship between memory and advertisements:

> Proust describes how memory creates consciousness, putting together a "consistent self" out of surrounding chaos, from the symbolic components of the past. Advertisements rely to a great extent on this property of memory; and since it is impossible for them to invoke the actual, individual past of each of their spectators—the past that goes to make up personality—they invoke either an aura of the past, or a common undefined past.[8]

With sepia-toned, gauzy encodings of personal memory, Koolaid hails us with the promise of providing continuity in our lives. Instead of offering Koolaid as a thirst quencher, the ad offers the product as a means to reduce anxiety about the absence of meaningful community in the social world of the 1990s. We need not belabor the multitude of forces that threaten the paradise of civil society pictured in the Koolaid flashbacks to understand the anxiety that might make the Koolaid-sponsored community appealing.

References to the past reaffirm traditional gender roles. While mom is associated with preparing food, dad is associated with his car. In "Dad's Old Corolla," a Toyota commercial, the product substitutes for the person. Standing in his garage, a man addresses us: "I promised my wife I'd sell it when we bought the new one but every time I looked at Dad's old Corolla. . . . Well, I remember the first time he brought it home. 'Well, what do you think?' He was so proud. He said, 'these cars are built to last.' He was right." A narrator's voiceover intervenes to back this statement with quantitative evidence: "The Toyota Corolla: over 15 million happy memories and still counting." The son concludes: "Sell Dad's Corolla? Not for a million bucks." He stands next to the car with his own son, and they touch the car caringly as piano music swells emotionally, and the scene shifts to a memory (signified by a blurred image) of his father driving the once-new Toyota into the driveway. Corolla taps into the psychology of memory, locating the memories of others in the commodities they possessed. Once commodities enter everyday life and are immersed within the context of real social relations they take on new meanings and emotional valences—their sign value is no longer simply that inscribed on them by their advertisers.

Commodities become part of our life histories. Creating a scenic memory requires that advertisers identify and appropriate emotional-charged signifiers that can inspire our personal associations with objects. Corolla took a generic memory (of a man's father and his car), abstracted it, stylized it, and then returned it to viewers as a formula for remembering a loved one. It rerouted the emotion attached to the memory of any actual father to the commodity through the abstracted formula of the generic father. Advertising thus unlocks the emotional power of personal memories as a catalyst for consumption.

In a social world where anything can be reduced to a capsulized sign, the hyper-sign, the model for memory is the captured moment. This abstracted moment is the absolute zero of the signifier–signified relationship. It is the most efficient way of summarizing a relation, a feeling, a biography. Commercials for the photography industry offer inventories for moments worth "capturing" on film that can be recalled at will. A typical Kodak commercial starts with a female voice singing "These are the moments." The warm, caring voice of a male narrator follows: "This baby is going to have a very momentous year, a year of first smiles, first steps, first discoveries, and none of these moments will ever happen again. Now if you were this baby's parents, which film would you choose?" The singer answers "These are the moments, Kodak moments" before the voiceover closes with: "Aren't all your moments worth Kodak film?" Kodak reframes experiences as myth, signifiers of the ideal family, the perfect child, the life defined by the perfect moment. Kodak prescribes a format for organizing memory. Kodak's script, however, empties out real pain and joy and replaces it with formulaic schmaltz. According to Berger and Mohr, "A photograph quotes from appearances, but in quoting simplifies them."[9] The concrete and the substantive are transformed into pure form, an essence, an ideal type available to everyone who consumes the abstract sign of Kodak. It seems doubly ironic, then, that this generic and abstracted past is invariably pictured as white and middle class—the class that more than any other has tried to deny its own history by sloughing off its ethnicity to lead privatized lives in mass-produced "model" communities.

Kodak encourages viewers to place their personal memories into this generic formula.

These hegemonic moments are replayed by millions of families. Kodak's formula replaces concrete particular history with a universal sign, the face of *the* infant. Everyday life is spectacularized, frozen into ideal forms that can be saved in an album. Such privatized memories may be less personal than they appear. They are organized in an abstracted and generic form. Photography lends itself to such an endeavor. Susan Sontag perceptively remarks, "As photographs give people an imaginary possession of a past that is unreal, they also help people to take possession of space in which they are insecure."[10] As family members become spatially separated from one another and as media invades family life, photography functions as the storehouse of personal memories. Obviously, reified baby pictures have a cultural history that precedes Kodak, but Kodak's model of reified family memory turns memory into a commodity category, one that is abstract and interchangeable.

When identity becomes disconnected from a community of memory all that is left of our past are discrete abstracted moments. The photograph itself becomes a signifier for care and concern. Photographs can validate the relationship, giving it a weight and permanence. In the film *Blade Runner*, cyborgs called "replicants" are supplied with simulated memories. Their creators even supply them with photographs of their childhood homes, their now-dead parents, and so on, to validate the replicants' "memories." These fictitious constructions served as reference points on which to build identities.

> The problem that the replicants, like the postmodern subject, have to confront, is how to produce themselves and to give substantiality to their lives when history and in particular the means of self-historicizing, documenting or narrating the self have lost any credibility—when they too take on the depthlessness of simulation.[11]

In *Blade Runner*, photographs supplied the replicants with a personal history to fill an absence. How different are the photographs in our lives? While photographs may speak of real events, they are depicted via the categories supplied by Kodak's perfect moment and immaculate family. Experiential memories mix with mediated memories. Like the use of photographs in *Blade Runner*, these images speak to an imagined past filled by the myth of the loving family. Lipsitz calls this replacement of experiential memories with mediated memories "memory as managed misappropriation." Media constructions such as sitcom families become woven into our own memories to construct "the past as people wish it had been rather than the past as they actually experienced it."[12] How, then, do our actual pasts serve as moral guides, if real memories do not matter and we can appropriate a past we never participated in? Whenever history is appropriated, "worked over," and re-presented back to us as ours, then the power of the past as a source of meaning in animating "who we are" is altered significantly.

The social construction of Gemeinschaft is not necessarily restricted to a specific time or place. In a mellow and unhurried voiceover, the narration for Mazda Miata conjures up a mood of innocence: "It was a simple time/a time of hope and faith in the future/blue jeans and white T-shirts were in/and people fell in love with the Mazda Miata/it not only gives you a glimpse of the Nineties/it takes you back as well." The ad is a montage of shots taken from a slow-moving car: a basketball game in the driveway, a sprinkler on the lawn, a child pretending to fly, teenage cheerleaders. Each shot fades to white. The ad differentiates itself from other automobile commercials that use quick cuts and fast-paced music to stress performance and excitement. Mazda constructs a tone of nostalgia by linking stock signifiers of stability and continuity separated by the fades-to-white and underscored by peaceful piano music and a comforting narrative tone. Nostalgia is constructed and experienced as a covering aura defined as standing for a time when the world moved slowly enough to be understandable and anxiety-free. The actual spatial–temporal location of "the past" is undefined. *The past is represented in the present, or rather, the present is represented as the past.* Unlike fades-to-black which signify self-contained images, separated by time and in meaning, fades-to-white convey a utopian undertone, a sunny underglow associated with "days of heaven." This is significant in that the only way the present can plausibly be made to appear desirable is to pose it as the past. It is made idyllic by means of an aesthetic device (the montage style sequenced by fades-to-white) in conjunction with a reference to a past, "It was a simple time."

Mazda Miata strung together signifiers such as these to connote "a simple time."

What are the implications of confusing past with present? We need not be nostalgic for the past anymore when we can be nostalgic for the present. The past as a referent system becomes indistinct and almost irrelevant. The past, as such, pales in significance relative to the simulacrum of *past-ness.* The past becomes nothing more than a construct that can serve as a handy filter through which to "see" the present. The ad imagines the Mazda Miata as embodying the aura of the past, and the means of transporting that imaginary aura into the present. The presence of the Miata explains why we might experience the present as simpler times. However, this deliberate confusion of past and present rests on a perception of a society without an adequate present.

The Mazda ad confuses the memory of perception with the perception of memory. In part, this is because the Mazda ad collapses space and time relationships.

Space becomes a mere backdrop to the memory (appearance) of a "sense of place." Once again, ads can be made to speak a fundamental social truth, even as they mystify social relations—they actually provide vivid reminders of the transcendence of spatial barriers. Indeed, it is only by means of the ad's aesthetic demolition of time and space that the social relations that are absent in our lives, but present in our desire, can be re-visioned.

Whereas the Mazda Miata ad locates a sense of place in a set of codes, the Stanley tools ad locates it geographically. The voiceover for their ad begins:

> *"New Britain, Connecticut, is 119 miles from New York City. It only seems far-ther than that. People here live in the same houses their parents lived in, worship in churches where their grandparents worshipped, and work for a company their great grandfathers built, the Stanley Works. So it's not surprising Stanley tools are made to last. It would only be surprising if they weren't."*

Old New England houses and churches define the landscape. The supporting images are predictable signifiers of an enduring and stable community characterized by care and concern: a boy on his bicycle delivers newspapers, a man roofs his house, an-other rakes a pitcher's mound, a boy helps a minister fix a church door, a young girl works with a saw. In the midst of these vignettes, the ad also shows us the Stanley plant. Though identified as traces of the actual lives of New Britain residents, these images function as generic signifiers of "community." Sociologist Robert Bellah observes that "we can speak of a real community as a 'community of memory,' one that does not for-get its past. In order not to forget that past, a community is involved in retelling its sto-ry, its constitutive narrative."[13] However, in its ad, Stanley assumes the role of commu-nal storyteller, forging a "constitutive narrative" in which capital and community coex-ist as one, so that Stanley's corporate name becomes equivalent to the series of signifiers in which it situates itself. Historical reality is "emptied out" and represented as a "har-monious display of essences," as relations of production become reduced to a commu-nity defined by a unitary interest.[14] In this retelling, Stanley products are defined by a sense of place; market considerations (Stanley tools as commodities) do not supplant a sense of place. Underscored by the metalanguage of music and narrative tone, the qual-ity of Stanley tools draws on the sign value of Gemeinschaft traditions: permanence and quality.

Maxwell House coffee ads (1990) are representative of campaigns that strain too hard to re-create Gemeinschaft-tinted relations. One ad begins by depicting the ritual of the veteran's parade circa the end of World War II. Here Maxwell House as-sociates itself with patriotism, community, and national pride. While watching the parade through the window of the archetypical mainstreet diner, the narrator hails us:

> *"You know, even the coffee tasted somehow better back then. I guess that's why those Maxwell House folks slow-roast their 1892 coffee. Didn't even change the way they used to make it. Introducing Maxwell House 1892 coffee. Made with the old-fashioned pride. The way things used to be."*

This lump-in-the-throat advertising mystifies both past and present in its quest to distill a reified signifier of the past as a commodity sign for Maxwell House. Here, utopia is situated in the past, based on a one-sided recollection that omits negation and conflict while yearning for those days when "old-fashioned values" united us, and blacks and other minorities knew their place.[15] In fact, the Maxwell House "memories" are themselves a product of a media history whose images were precisely this one-sided. The absence of negation and conflict in these images is a media product of an era that resolutely denied the domination of racism and sexism.

Under the guise of memory, such mystifications prompt a form of forgetting. What has been left out is as important as the signifier that is present. Sara Lee's effort to internationalize "a very locally determined product," coffee, illustrates how a historically specific signifier can be abstracted from context and made to signify its opposite. Concerned about "how to unify the country brands without making customers feel that they were buying a bland 'Euro-coffee' . . . an internal Sara Lee development team came upon an old 'Friesian Lady' packaging design," an 18th-century Netherlands design portraying a woman in simple dress pouring coffee. "Sara Lee felt the symbol conveyed a soothing message, full of 'authenticity' and 'quality.'" Thus a culturally specific image is transformed into a generic sign of history and tradition. As firms globalize their production and marketing processes, the challenge is to do so without closing off space for local interpretation and losing consumer support rooted in disparate cultures. The domain of commodity relations is extended while renaming it as its opposite. The "Friesian Lady" now signifies the general historical sign, which when correlated with the coffee, denies its commodified form. As Ewen remarks, "History becomes incomprehensible as people's own collective past comes back to them in the hollow, if appealing, form of a sales pitch."[17]

Reestablishing Relations with Our Past

As stylized memories colonize collective memory, the commodification of the collective past disempowers everyday life as the site of historical production. When stylized, historical signifiers are politically cleansed and substantively aestheticized, distanced from either the experience or language of daily life. Personal memories are now validated by media representations of the past. Debord called the product of this process "the false spectacular memory of the unmemorable." When Debord wrote *Society of the Spectacle*, he drew attention to the semiotic ransacking of everyday life to construct "the pseudo-events which rush by in spectacular dramatizations [that] have not been lived by those informed of them."[18] What remained of daily life after this process was "noise" or "chaff"—that part of everydayness that is the antithesis of commodified desire. But recently, advertisers themselves have become aware of the pitfalls of eclipsing everyday life with the inflationary rhetoric and relentless amnesia of the spectacle. To combat this tendency, advertisers have attempted to appropriate the "noise" of daily life into their narratives of desire. The methodology of mining "noise" as a means of salvaging the authenticity of the spectacle involves what we have referred to as hyperreal encoding strategies. These are strategies that literally attempt to visualize the "noise" of dailyness in terms of signifiers such as very grainy film, overexposure, underexposure, swish pans, and unintelligible cuts, since as we all know, in daily life there is no one neatly directing the potential cacophony of perceptual experience that surrounds us.[19]

MCI's ads for its "Friends and Family" campaign simulated both personal and generic narratives constructed out of hyperreal codes and biographical content. Spliced-together clips from home movies depict "significant others" at weddings, parties, and reunions, as well as the mundane but personally significant footage from neighborhood life, such as clips of children at a swimming hole or playing in the snow. Addressing us as persons whose lives have become privatized, MCI proposes to put us back in touch with our past, when we were embedded in webs of personal and

Decontextualized images taken from home movies speak to us about our past relationships. Just as important, they hail viewers in terms of an imagistic vernacular that feels "authentic" and "real." MCI is responsible for appropriating these home movie images, but they do not hold exclusive advertising title to them. Comparable strings of images may be found in ads for Parker Brothers, Coors, Saturn, and United Airlines, to name but a few.

neighborhood relations. Realness is constructed from signifiers that range from iconic markers of the period (beehive hairdos) to film codes (jumpy camera, scratchy film, poor quality development, washed-out color, grainy film). MCI constructs an alternative to Kodak's formulaic technique:

> *"Each of us has a circle of friends, don't we? That we must, absolutely must, stay in touch with no matter how many years go by, no matter how many miles eventually separates us. 'Do you still talk to Joan?' the question goes. 'Once a week, sometimes twice a week,' goes the answer. It's for those lifelong friends, not to mention close-knit family, that MCI announces the newest idea in long distance saving sense . . ."*

Williamson notes that "we are shown a hazy, nostalgic picture and asked to 're-member' it as *our* past, and simultaneously, to construct it through buying/consuming the product."[20] MCI hails us with "real" people with real biographies located in real times and places. Another ad in this series presents just such a personalized account. Constructed through hyperreal codes, the narrator's biography is assembled out of cuts of "dated" photographs and home movies of college days, weddings, reunions. The voiceover offers the following narrative:

> *"We did everything together in college. We even dated the same girl. And the day I got married it was his jacket I was wearing. Funny how time moves you in different directions and then lets you forget. I might have never talked to Nick again if it weren't for this letter I got from MCI. They asked my wife and me to name the people closest to us, the ones we talked to the most. And whenever we call each other, we'll all save an extra 20%. It's a thing they call 'Friends and Family.' Well, we listed the kids, Melanie's folks, my mother and brother, Tony and Salina. 'There's got to be more than eight people out there we're close to? Didn't you have any friends in college?' Melanie said. 'One,' I said. We sent our list to MCI. And a week later the phone rang. It was a familiar voice. 'I got a date this weekend,' he said. 'Do you think I can have my jacket back?'"*

The ad ends with the two friends reunited on a boardwalk. MCI positions itself as a conduit through which an atrophied relationship can be reestablished and revitalized. Just fill out the names and MCI will contact them. Writing someone's name on MCI's list validates their significance to you. In an odd way, MCI touches on a tragedy of contemporary social life: privatism and labor-market-driven mobility reduce our friends to a tiny few. The ad positions MCI as the company whose service plan fights the erosion of personal relationships.

In a society where communities of memory continue to decay, methods of hailing become proportionately dependent on media texts (intertextuality) because these have common salience to a target audience (for yuppies, music from the 1960s).[21] Fred Davis has observed:

> Where nostalgia once would have focused on specific places—homes and so forth—the objects of nostalgia are increasingly celebrities of the past, of music, films, et cetera. This makes it easier for the media to capitalize on it because the material is in their archives. Nostalgia today is of the media, by the media and for the media.[22]

Advertisers appropriate isolated signifiers to try to tap into our meaningful associations with past media texts. The signifier might be four bars from a Four Tops tune or the tailfins on a '57 Chevy. When such signifiers have been deployed by advertisers as memory triggers, they inflate the moment of the signifier into an imaginary way of life. Such intertextual memory signifiers are almost always conflict-free. Adopting the same photographic styles and techniques as MCI, Coors's "Route 66" commercial depicts the 1960s as a time when college students drove to Colorado to buy Coors beer (then distributed only locally). California Cooler's "Malibu 1964" commercial re-creates its history in simulated images of Malibu beach parties. These names are the reference points that connect product history with biography and youthful memories. A viewer need never have driven a woodie to Malibu beach or a VW bug cross country in order to participate in these memories. The flip side of wanna-bes is *wish-we-weres.* One only has to recognize the reference so that an association between the commodity and a "cherry" past can be fashioned. This is how memory becomes a resource in commodity-sign production.

Coors: Reminiscing about the spontaneity and fun of our youth.

Blasts from Our Past

The recycling bin of mass cultural texts has emerged as a primary resource for narrating our collective past as memory. Music provides the most frequently appropriated signifiers for referencing the past. Music works as a trigger of memory and supplies a mediating bridge between personal memory and collective memory. Memory is not necessarily voluntary: the deepest and most powerful memories are beyond attentiveness. Just as memories are often triggered by a serendipitous sensation—a smell, a sound, a texture, a color—so too music can instantly spark a personal memory.[23] Memories of song may be associated with a specific place, person, and experience in one's life. Advertisers recognize, and draw on the power of music as an instant marker of memory and a catalyst of emotion, as the following quotation demonstrates:

> Music is a powerful medium for stirring the emotions. With a compelling melody and memorable lyrics, the newest Hoover television commercials are sure to tug at the heartstrings and linger in the minds of American consumers. The point is not only to capture viewers' attention but to jog their memories, encouraging them to call to mind that Hoover is an American institution that has been an important helpmate in the home for more than eight decades. "Hoover is not just a vacuum cleaner or a collection of nuts and bolts, it's a part of peoples' lives," said Hoover marketing vice president Dave Gault.[24]

Over the years, music produced by the culture industry has become integrated into everyday life, where particular songs may become associated with personal experience. This primary association between music and phenomenological experiences yields a first-order memory. When advertisers hail their audience with a musical referent, they position the viewer to insert their own first-order memory alongside the musical signifier.

When a piece of music is attached to a commodity in order to appellate an audience, it generates a second-order, or mediated, memory. In this way, music is positioned to signify subjective identity. It draws on the correspondence between the music and a memory and attempts to attach that correspondence to a commodity. The everyday is invaded twice. The music is appropriated because it has the potential to stimulate exchange value, but the music cannot generate new value until the viewer supplies the value of his or her own memory.

Because it is electronically mass-reproduced, music is associated with the memories of "imagined communities" composed of people who have never actually met one another but nonetheless share a body of mass-culture preferences. In the Reagan–Bush era dominated by the discourses of greed and conspicuous consumption, advertisers discovered that baby boomers (a community imagined by marketers) were ripe for nostalgia ad campaigns. For example, the Mercury ad campaign tapped into the success of the film *The Big Chill* and its creative use of "oldies" music as its soundtrack. Music is popularly associated with the decade of one's youth. Since music is deeply embedded in the experiences of American youth, popular songs can functionally link the nostalgic pleasures of youth to a wide range of commodities. Advertising appropriates collective, generational memories that are received and interpreted under privatized social circumstances. While the music may speak to a generation in general, it is hooked to unique individual experiences.

Ironically, in order for music to signify "history" and our collective past, it must be decontextualized, dehistoricized, and depoliticized. Because music preferences demarcate intense personal choices and because primary associations with musical pieces are so strongly held, the advertising appropriation of music can either work very well, or it can backfire by alienating the viewer.[25] Still, when Mercury seemed to strike gold with their appropriation of 1960s oldies, a bandwagon effect ensued. A recent instance of dehistoricizing music to make it signify our imagined collective past is the 1993 Chevy Camaro ad campaign's appropriation of Jimi Hendrix, rock legend of the 1960s. Chevy frames the scene with this narrative voiceover: "If America never invented rock 'n' roll, it would be something like this." Chevy's time-warp version of 1950s suburban America extended into the 1990s constructs a speculative futuristic landscape of 1950s artifice based on technology minus passion (a future of automotonlike existence without the spirit of rock 'n' roll). Modeled visually after *True Stories* or the opening sequence of *Blue Velvet,* the Chevy ad offers a landscape predicated on signifiers of 1950s overconformity: mechanical gestures, flat suburban lawns, lounge chairs, and gadgets. In the language of the 1950s, this is "Dullsville." But wait, this stagnant boredom is

Thanks to Chevy and rock 'n' roll this past—a stereotyped image of the 1950s *volkgeist* projected into the 1990s—never happened.

decisively transcended when the announcer cuts in with "Fortunately, it did!" and then the distinctive voice of Jimi Hendrix abruptly transforms this landscape into one of vibrancy and excitement: "Now dig this baby. . . ." Chevrolet choreographs a montage of quick cuts of Camaros and the energized young couples who drive them to Hendrix's classic refrain, "Let me stand next to your fire." Rock 'n' roll à la Hendrix and the Chevrolet Camaro are turned into an equivalency: "The new Camaro. What else would you expect from the country that invented rock 'n' roll?" Does Chevy signify excitement and nonconformity by virtue of sharing the same advertising stage with Hendrix's music? In the 1960s, Hendrix represented everything that was culturally alien, critical of, and threatening to mainstream America; today his music has been recast as representative of all that is culturally vibrant about America. In the early 1960s, Marcuse already recognized the capacity of commodity culture to accommodate contradiction: "In the realm of culture, the new totalitarian manifests itself precisely in a harmonizing pluralism, where the most contradictory works and truths peacefully coexist in indifference."[26] In the process of appropriating, decontextualizing, and restyling musical texts, a new object (the image of the commodity) becomes hooked to the memory–music circuit.

Commodity revisionism of this sort not only flattens cultural critique, it takes our memories and uses them against us as a positioning tactic. Furthermore, if after seeing the Camaro ad, listening to Hendrix forcibly brings up Chevy's imagery, the pleasure of the original text may be depreciated. In this regard, we can appreciate those musical genres such as punk that strive to destroy the pleasure of the music as a stylistic strategy against appropriation and recommodification. Still, the passage of time along with the helter-skelter logic of commodity restylization erodes the critical moment of most texts, so that the radical styles of the present will become the essential memory correlate for the commodity signs of the future.

Saturn: A Moment in the Hegemony of Memory

There is nothing new in the way ads simultaneously hail us as a collectivity (America) and as individuals (you). Viewers have become acclimated to being addressed this way within the space of a single ad, and tend to gloss over the obvious confusion contained in such forms of address. Though we can identify a continuum, most ads that mobilize images of memory do so by hailing viewers as a collectivity, but string together signifiers of memory as if they constitute personalized narratives. These ads collapse together personal and public memories. The Saturn campaign illustrates the use of "we" to designate the peer group, an entire generation, as well as the "imagined community" of our nation. While these ads claim to integrate the individual's personal (subjective) narrative with the telos of a corporate presence that marks their commodity, they depoliticize decisions about production, consumption, and distribution by dissolving such matters into personal narrative.

". . . or how you'd sit in your grandfather's lap in the driveway and pretended to steer."

In late 1991, Saturn aired an ad we call "Our Romance with Cars." It presented a narrative constructed around memories rooted in a generational phenomenology of perception. Like other Saturn ads, this one relied on a pronounced effort to simulate home movie footage from the 1950s and early 1960s. The ad's narrator hails viewers with personal memories of the automobile in the days of their youth, when their parents were young and they themselves were children: "Maybe it was how it looked to see your reflection in a hubcap . . . whatever it was, it began our romance with [American] cars." The ersatz "home movie" gives the text an aura of authenticity by suggesting that this is our culture that we want to regain, not theirs. The ad is visually constructed by editing together period footage (identifiable because it is in black and white) with simulated period home movies that are shot in grainy color.

Accompanying this sequence of home movie clips is a background song about "The object of my affection." It sounds a lot like Pat Boone. We quickly realize that Hal Riney and Saturn have appropriated the film style made popular in *Roger & Me*, a low-budget documentary film by Michael Moore that used humor to address the impact of GM's deindustrialization strategies on Flint, Michigan. The irony here cannot be ignored. Saturn, GM's new age spin-off effort at producing small high-quality cars to compete with Japanese imports, inflates its stature by stealing the film style invented to critique GM's impersonal and unfeeling treatment of their Flint workforce, and the social disaster of what GM left behind in Flint.

Situating the Saturn ad campaign in relation to Moore's *Roger & Me* exemplifies what it means to talk about the dialectical character of hegemony. Moore's populist cultural style emerged out of a low-budget effort to contest culturally what workers and their organizations could no longer effectively contest at the political–economic level. The movie is structured around the working person's fantasy of confronting the "fat cats" whose decisions so acutely affect the lives of working people. Moore's film documents his quest to speak with Roger Smith, then GM's CEO, about the public ramifications of GM plant closings. This quest was thwarted in the film by GM's strategy of refusing to comment by hiding behind power, privilege, and the shield of private property. Neither GM nor any of its representatives acknowledged responsibility to the community that was "the birthplace of General Motors." As a female worker put it, "He [Roger Smith] can't look an autoworker in the eye."

Moore offers this account of GM's plant closings: "So this was GM chairman Roger Smith. He appeared to have a brilliant plan. First, close 11 factories in the U.S., then open 11 in Mexico where you pay the worker 70¢ an hour, then use the money you've saved by building cars in Mexico to take over other companies, preferably high-tech firms and weapons manufacturers. Next tell the union you're broke, and they happily give back a couple billion dollars in wage cuts. You then take that money from the workers and eliminate their jobs by building more foreign factories." GM's deindustrialization strategy, in Moore's estimate, puts profits before people.

Moore opens the film with a sequence of personal photographs and old home movie footage while he talks about his childhood. This sequence segues into footage of Pat Boone, as Moore recalls that "when I was a kid I thought only three people worked for General Motors: Pat Boone, Dinah Shore, and my Dad." The music behind the scenes of Flint in those glory years is light, like that from a movie musical, while the images are the stock signifiers of an era of unquestioned material abundance "where every day was a great day" and "a salute to Mr. and Mrs. America" was the product of glorious "teamwork." In the wake of the Flint plant closings, the job layoffs, the evictions of families from their homes, and soaring crime rates, Pat Boone, GM's pitchman in the late 1950s, returns to town to perform and extol the virtues of the free enterprise system. Says Moore, "It was like I was reliving my childhood." Moore's strategy in the film is to juxtapose corporate mass culture (Pat Boone, Anita Bryant, Miss Michigan) and its philosophy of exuberant do-it-for-yourself American individualism, with the reality of class inequality in a city dependent on the private capital of GM. Moore shows how religion and entertainment were

The roller-skating carhop has become a nostalgia marker for an earlier stage of consumer culture.

deployed in Flint to ideologically avoid the central issues, that is, to offer distractions and mystify power relations. By reframing the images of mass culture, Moore redirects their narrative to reveal their own ideological absurdity.

But the Saturn ads deftly turn the tables again by lifting the surface of Moore's style and using an old Pat Boone song to wrap their collage of images, an amalgam of authentic and simulated shots of the 1950s. But the ironic and sarcastic tone of Moore's narration has been dropped in favor of the warm, cozy, down-home narration of Hal Riney. Here, once again, the commodity form can be seen reabsorbing dissent, turning the cultural power of dissent into new commodity currency, turning dissent back into the imagery of Americana.

The first five scenes appellate and hail the viewer, as the narrator addresses us and identifies these scenes as representations of our memories. The narrator hails the viewer as "you" 12 times. The ad never stops hailing us, inviting us to join in accepting this as *our* history: a consumer history marked by memories of objects and tactile sensations, transformed into simulated memories that draw on our phenomenology of perception. A distinctive framing device of this ad is the soundtrack it brings to the images. The music is light, almost lilting at moments. The soothing narration begins:

> *"Maybe it was how it looked to see your reflection in a hubcap or how you'd sit in your grandfather's lap in the driveway and pretended to steer. Whatever it was for each of us, it began our romance with cars. You'd wash it, you'd wax it, and polish it until it would shine like a jewel. And when you were done you'd do it all over again.* [The narrative is then briefly interrupted by a musical swell and lyric overlay: *"The object of my affection can change my complexion from white to rosy red . . . ,"* which fades, but continues faintly in the background.] *What was meant to be a hunk of metal to get you from point A to point B, had become a refuge, almost family. Because you trusted what it was, how it was made, and deep down you still believed that some things would last forever. You had something special, almost magical. Isn't it time you felt that way again?"* [The song overlay reemerges to wrap up the ad: *"I know I'll never rest until she says she's mine."*]

The ad is constructed out of a montage of shots of 1950s GM automobiles embedded in scenes from everyday life. The montage fades to a color sunset (yellow, orange, and purple) in a nonurban area, out of which emerges a scene of a new bright red Saturn cruising along a highway while the voiceover invites, "Isn't it time you felt that way again?" On a black screen appear the words: "A Different Kind of Company" followed by "A Different Kind of Car" and the orange Saturn logo. Images of the 1950s not only evoke personal memories but also a period when both GM and America were political powers. Together the narrative and imagery position Saturn as not just a vehicle but the incarnation of a vague but *new* economic philosophy that will enable the mythologized political, economic, and cultural climate of an innocent America to be recovered.

These simulated memories justify GM's corporate strategies as benevolently reinventing our sense of cultural identity and purpose. By tugging on this simulated aura of everyday life in a world gone by, advertisers position themselves as our neighbors, therapists, stewards, historians, and storytellers—in this case even offering to restore the feeling of that "special, almost magical," aura.[27]

A second Saturn ad recounts the historical trajectory of the 1960s working-class generation. The story is told in the first person. The narrator's biography is important here insofar as it is made representative of a generation of workers who grew up in the glory days of American industrial might:

> "*. . . We grew up some. Went away. But we came back to build Mustangs, Corvettes, and GTO's, among other things. It was the 60s. And of all the things we could be thinking about, we still mostly just thought about cars. Life was good. Work was good. But then the oil dried up and it seemed like overnight something happened to the way people thought about cars. It got frustrating. Then I decided to go to work for a company called Saturn and build cars again, but in a brand-new way. There were some things I knew I'd miss, but there were certain things I wanted to remember.*"

Visually, the ad opens with home movie images of childhood—family and friends, a wedding, people in uniform—assembled into a hyperreal montage. In the real social life of families, the 8mm film reels of family leisure relations shot by amateurish and overeager parents are not montage at all; rather, they are simply the stop and start of a parent trying to find a good photogenic moment "to capture the memory." When we view our own actual family home movies we often supply conflicting narratives among ourselves depending on the vantage point we occupied within the family. But the Saturn ads take away our *point-of-memory* when they use our "meaning system" of home movies. They narrate for us, and steer our meanings in a particular direction.

Corresponding to the '60s reference, swish pans and rapid cuts mimic the imagery of antiwar protests, pausing long enough to allow the peace insignia to register in focus. As the narrative continues, images of friends convivially walking to work are followed by images of leisure fun: three buddies hamming it up for a camera in their convertible. But suddenly "the oil dried up" and there is a swift change of tone. Long lines of cars at gas pumps symbolize the 1974 Arab Oil Embargo and gray skies replace sunny skies (the scene's color is literally drained away, to be replaced by a somber grayness). Economic prosperity symbolically vanishes in a cold, gray, and apparently barren industrial setting as our narrator and his wife grimly converse while trying to stay warm. The next scene of an unemployed man drinking coffee at a lonely diner counter, his shoulders slumped, symbolizes the bleak prospects of the auto industry in the 1970s and 1980s. Keyed to the phrase, "Then I decided to go to work," the ensuing scene shows the man we presume to be the narrator speaking to his worried wife. He has decided to move to Tennessee to work for Saturn, because they are forward-looking. She listens, staring emotionlessly ahead: the decision to move in search of work also means abandoning the place where they grew up and where their family and friends reside. He touches her hair and puts his hand on her shoulder to comfort her. (Not to worry: there is always MCI out there, and they espouse the same aesthetic expression of family life. They will keep us in touch.)

The visual narrative shifts to a scenic countryside as a station wagon pulling a U-Haul trailer drives past a sign that reads, "Spring Hill: Population 1200." This feels like a reawakening: sunlight and green earth frame the Spring Hill city limits marker. These are the symbolic landscapes of our political economy: goodbye old Detroit, hello new postindustrial South. The hyperreal photographic technique disappears here, to be replaced by a slow fadeover from the car driving toward Spring Hill to a memorabilia photo of the earlier scene of young friends at a wedding. The narrator admits that while he'll miss the friends he's left behind, at least he can hold on to his memories of their childhood (a black and white photograph of the boys when they were the "Tigers" Little League team). A final fadeover layers the tag line, "A Different Kind of Company," over the icon of personal significance.

How does Saturn's respect for the subjective significance of its workers' childhood memories make it a "Different Kind of Company?"

Now, what does a "Different Kind of Car Company" signify? Are they different because they are going to "build cars again, but in a brand-new way"? Or are they different because they care enough about average folks to do ads about their meaningful personal lives? Saturn, of course, was a wholly independent spin-off of GM, although there is nothing in the ad that might alert us to this relationship. Notice that the oral narrative includes references not just to the glory days of GM cars—Corvettes and GTO's—but also to the Ford Mustang. The ad represents the generalized glory days of the U.S. auto industry and its downfall, not GM's, as a prelude to the birth of Saturn. Why deny this relationship?

Certainly, GM's involvement in the crisis resulting in layoffs and unemployment disappears from view. The demise of an old way of life is explained here by "the oil dried up" as a crisis created by Arabs (foreigners), not by GM (capital). Whereas the nostalgia of youth framed by the vibrancy of color and action is defined by the tacit, symbolic guiding hand of capital, difficult times are attributed to Arabs or to the otherwise curiously timed image of a Japanese flag that flashes across the screen. As in the vast majority of consumer ads,

> the role of labor is elided by jumping the gap from resources in their natural state straight to their delivery to consumers as commodities. . . . The mode of commodity fetishism ties in with certain attitudes toward time, history, and nature: all the contingent, contestable processes of production and historical direction are collapsed into a view of the capitalist order as an immutable natural essence.[28]

Obviously, there are other ways to tell the story of deindustrialization, and equally obvious, every way of telling carries with it some ideological message. Saturn's narrative purports to be that of the working class, when in fact it is concocted in terms of capital's "autobiography" as an "immutable natural essence" serving the interests of all who adhere to the proper values.

If we shift the frame slightly, what we have in this ad is an alternative story of deindustrialization. This is GM's plan for America's deindustrialized worker. Abandon the spent urban environment and infrastructure of Detroit in favor of starting over in pristine rural America. When it does not relocate production in the Third World, this streamlined corporate capitalism locates itself in rural America where nature has not yet been depleted and community (not unions) prospers. The question, of course, remains: How can this nebulous, newly emergent industrial formation provide the foundation for a new Gemeinschaft landscape?

Advertising links biography, personal and corporate, to images of history and memory selected and steered by the logic of the commodity and the spectacle. Saturn's linkage between biography and history depends on the credibility of the first-person narrative. The narrator's voice frames how the viewer reads the images that support his personal narrative. Saturn's application of realist techniques disguises the constructed nature of this commercial. What constitutes real footage? Are these really home movies? How many shots were simulations used to fill in gaps, to make the narrative run smoothly? The personal narrative is given an occasional collective reference (documentary footage) to ensure credibility. Using realist texts and the "having-been-thereness" of the photograph, GM's constructed history appears to be real. The footage looks historical enough, and we naturally assume the events took place in the way in which they are presented. Barthes calls the photograph "a message without a code . . . for in a photograph there is always the stupefying evidence of this is how it is, giving us, by a precious miracle, a reality from which we are sheltered."[29]

The "having-been-thereness" of photographic realism makes the reading seem natural and self-evident. For Berger and Mohr, photography has no language of its own: "The camera does not lie even when it is used to quote a lie. And so this makes the lie *appear* more truthful." Nevertheless, "between the moment recorded and the present moment of looking at the photograph, there is an abyss." This temporal "discontinuity always produces ambiguity."[30] To give a photograph meaning is to give it a past and a future through narrative. In the Saturn ads, GM's narrative fills the abyss attaching the present to the past and constructs a mirage of historical continuity that justifies present corporate practices as extensions of those historical practices documented by the photographic realism of the footage.

Corporate Revisionism: The Sign Wars Version

When corporations reconstruct their own history and capsulize it as a 30- or 60-second spot, history is replaced by spectacle. According to Debord, "The spectacle is the existing order's uninterrupted discourse about itself, its laudatory monologue. It is the self-portrait of power in the epoch of its totalitarian management of the conditions of existence."[31] Corporate history is often linked with technological history, with corporations positioning themselves as the innovating force behind technological progress. Forget political economy: ads depict corporate histories around the organizing principles of vision and innovation. Advertisers frequently employ archival film footage of "modern" technology being tested in the past to indicate the durability of their corporate sponsor, but also to point to a history of technological leadership and the willingness to always go "the extra mile." Archival black and white film has become a primary chip played in the sign wars between upscale automakers such as Audi, Mercedes, and BMW. When affluent baby boomers demanded safety in their cars, Audi, Mercedes and BMW raided their respective film libraries to signify their "early days" in which their forward-looking engineers scientifically tested collision safety equipment. Such scenes are presented on the assumption that they provide historical evidence leading to the conclusion that Audi, or Mercedes, or BMW is still a safety features innovator today. For example, in one Mercedes ad an older engineer reminisces after seeing dated images of crash testing that "we had no idea we were inventing safety science."

Corporations draw value from historical events by positioning themselves at the center of public memories sparked by images of events. In the climate of stock market scandals in the late 1980s, Wall Street investment firms engaged in sign wars structured around competing significations of historical imagery. Merrill Lynch created scenic reenactments of going off to World War I and coming back from World War II to in-

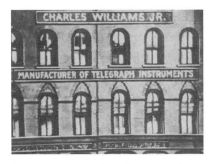

Many corporate firms have sought to legitimate their power via the authority of history. This AT&T ad extols the virtues of small enterprises by recalling when it too was small.

ject itself at the core of American patriotism. The WWI ad provides a narrative backdrop to signify not only how Americans can count on this firm during times of conflict and difficulty, but also to signify how America and Merrill Lynch have grown up together through the 20th century. Just as Chevrolet identified itself as one with a transcendent cultural *volkgeist*, Merrill Lynch positions itself as one with the nation-state. Each story includes a substory about "Charlie Merrill" the man—the guy who preceded the faceless corporate giant, Merrill Lynch. "Charlie" is patriotic, enthusiastic, and above all else committed to the ideology that if you devote yourself heart and soul to a task (a task done well is its own reward) you can also be optimistic in the greatest of all courts: the marketplace. The ad is packed with the iconography of American symbols, with each historical moment romanticized by the cinematography, musical background, and the narrator's intonation. Such references to historical images legitimize corporate practice as patriotic, as serving the national interest.

Not to be outdone, Dean Witter, another investment firm, composed ads that visit successful personal narratives made possible because the firm has remained true to the vision of its founder, Dean Witter. An aura of history is thrown into the mix in the form of the tag line when Dean Witter himself appears, speaking from a distant past. He enunciates the company's slogan, "We measure success one investor at a time," in an electronically whispered voice as he apparently speaks to employees (outside the frame) in a fireside chat reminiscent of President Franklin Roosevelt. We read this scene as authentically representing the past because of two signifiers: the scratched black and white film and the early 20th century eyeglasses he wears. The film looks as if it was pulled from company archives, and it is framed as an enduring inspirational moment. The firm presents itself as following its calling. Boiled down to basics, the Dean Witter ads use scratchy film to signify that they've been around a long time, and that they are responsible, solid citizens who deserve our trust

Bogus history or darn good simulation?

and business. In the spectacle, history has become a matter of frames and framing devices. The gentleman who speaks to us as Dean Witter is a contemporary actor.[32] He is a simulation, though this ad's claim to sign value depends on the viewer accepting the premise of historical authenticity.

Collective Amnesia?

The discourse of advertising erodes both private memories and public history. It does this in two ways: it replaces personal memory with generic memories and it dislodges historical facts and narratives from their contexts and circulates them at ever increasing velocities. This seems such a bizarre concept that we must dwell on it for a moment. What can it possibly mean to say that historical sensibilities now float about, free to circulate at an increasing velocity? When meaning is routinely decontextualized, the association between signifier and signified becomes unbound and eventually goes slack. As the velocity of appropriation increases, history as a self-contradictary process disappears and becomes little more than a "signifier" in a universe of "homogeneous, empty time."[33] History thus becomes an ahistorical intertextual pastiche, where, like hypertext, one can move in any direction without being bound by the unified conditions of space and time. As Fredric Jameson notes, "We are now, in other words, in 'intertextuality' as a deliberate, built-in feature of the aesthetic effect and as the operator of a new connotation of 'pastness' and pseudo-historical depth, in which the history of aesthetic styles displaces 'real' history."[34] Historical weight is replaced by weightlessness, depth by surface, meaning by the superficiality of equivalence. This is Baudrillard's universe:

> Each fact, each political, historical, cultural act is endowed, by its power of media diffusion, with a kinetic energy which flings it out of its own space forever, propels it into hyperspace where it loses all meaning, since it can never return. . . . As regards history, the consequences are clear. Its "recitation" has become impossible, since it is by definition (re-citatum) the possible recurrence of a sequence of meaning. Today each fact, each event, through the momentum of diffusion, through the imperative of circulation, of total communication, is freed on its own—each fact becomes atomic, nuclear, and pursues its trajectory into the void. To be infinitely diffused, it must be fragmented like a particle. This is why it can reach a velocity of no return, which definitely removes it from history.[35]

The logic of commodity sign production drives an accelerating circuit of cultural appropriation and waste. Once the historical enters advertising discourse it ceases to be historical. "History" is uprooted, decontextualized, washed in a bath of aesthetics, stylized, and spectacularized as it becomes the sign value for a commodity. Lacking solid ground and existing within a volatile cultural economy, sign value is inflationary, fleeting, and unstable. The value of any historical signifier is quickly used up and turned into a waste by-product of commodity culture, further contributing to a culture composed of shifting surfaces. While capital risks cultural implosion to keep the engines of sign value running, the same process compels capital to draw from images of a past to bolster collapsing meaning systems.[36] Faced with increasing demands for both legitimacy and commodity circulation, the process becomes ever more manic. We have entered a new phase in the historical relationship between culture and the relations of production. Never before has culture been so thoroughly constituted by the sum of choices made in markets: the remixing of signs is now as defining a feature of a market culture as exchange itself. And the circuit of sign transformation still seems to be accelerating.

Advertising feeds postmodern cultural tendencies: fragmented meaning, the celebration of surface, the substitution of fascination for meaning, cynicism, the breakdown of narrative. Cultural appropriation fuels both the commodity form and its current mode of production: global capitalism. History takes its place alongside other referent systems (nature, politics, youth cultures) as a source of signifiers to be used to direct desire toward the commodity form and to legitimize production practices. Once a signifier is removed from its context, it joins in the circulation of signifiers; its power is derived from a fascination for difference and the spectacle:

> As this happens, history disintegrates as a way of comprehending the world: it becomes an incomprehensible catalog display. It shifts from the realm of human subjects engaged in social relations, motivated by interest, circumstance, and experience, to the realm of objects, discrete commodities to be bought and sold.[37]

Christopher Lasch once remarked, "There is history that remembers and history that originates in a need to forget."[38] We have argued here that the history told in ads more often than not represses our past. Because it is a history fixated on signifiers, it is a history of discontinuity. The memory constituted by advertisements is a history composed of atomized particles (signifiers) renarrativized by commodity interests and by corporate interests. The way contemporary ads invite us to remember the past does not simply divert us from the problems of the present, it also accustoms us to forgetting the links between past and present.

5 *Authenticity in the Age of the Poseur*

WHILE postmodern critics pronounce the demise of authenticity, advertisers continue to turn the sign of authenticity into one of the most pervasive styles and motifs of our contemporary sign culture. Music, food, clothing, automobiles, and advertising itself—all are represented under the banner of authenticity. Advertising has always struggled with issues of authenticity because advertising has frequently been associated with hype. Questions of authenticity and truth seem improbable companions of advertisements, and yet meanings associated with authenticity pervade ads.

Because advertising effectively promotes styles and images (sign values) as integral to the presentation of self in daily life, it should come as no surprise that "posing" (putting on appearances) has become part of the language of daily life. "Poseur" and "wannabe" are put-downs that presume authenticity to be a superior expression of self-identity. Distinctions between surface and depth, or artifice versus the sincerity of true self, mark an important legacy of bourgeois thought. Recent advertising sways back and forth between commodity narratives that cultivate posing by promoting a commodity culture dedicated to impression management and other narratives that counsel us to choose wisely from among the constant recirculation of surface appearances to be "who we really are."

Advertising's obsession with authenticity is driven by a basic cultural contradiction of corporate capitalism. Signs of authenticity in ads reflect a social world in which concerns about the self, identity, and personhood have become paramount. By the early 20th century, "Americans began to imagine a self that was neither simple nor genuine, but fragmented and socially constructed."[1] The quest for an authentic self has become our moral equivalent to searching for the Holy Grail. In a commodity culture structured by the circulation of detached signifiers, this quest for authenticity twists through labyrinths of commodity consumption. Can authentic selves be constituted by assembling chains of commodity signifiers—especially when the meanings of those signifiers are themselves subject to constant recommodification?

Authenticity carries sometimes contradictory connotations in our culture, all linked to a hierarchy of judgments. Questions of authenticity revolve around what is real, honest, pure, and true, whether it be the individual subject, or an object, or even a matter of representation. Bourgeois definitions of authenticity stress a self able to project unmediated, spontaneous expressions of personal identity, a self grounded in the intensity of experience. When the bourgeois subject was defined as a producer, this seemed a reasonable expectation, but defining self in terms of consumption has made the terrain of authenticity more slippery.

As our social world has become electronically mediated by abstracted signifiers and surface appearances of experiences, bourgeois definitions have become imperiled. Today authenticity represents the search for individuated space outside the commodity form and outside the spectacle. The tension between the commodity form and authenticity is as old as the bourgeoisie themselves: we still find something fundamentally inauthentic about trying to buy authenticity. And yet we structure so much around the principle of exchange value. *Authenticity represents the struggle between the will of the individual and the determinism of the commodity structure.* The last half century has compounded this dilemma as experiences—or at least, the images of those experiences—became fodder for commodity signs. Consuming social relations in the form of signs does not automatically rule out authenticity, but any definition of authenticity that surfaces as fashion must bear the stigmata of preconstituted sociality.[2]

Apprehension about commodification also colors our attitudes toward what constitute authentic objects. Concerns about product authenticity are an extension of questions about the self, since we often presuppose that the products we select reflect on our character and our identity. These are status distinction issues, with higher status linked to those who consume the most authentic objects. Our love–hate relationship with commodification also permeates issues of representation as authenticity. In today's highly competitive market, each brand struggles to find a representational niche. Signs must appear truthful and honest in a marketplace that demands the continuous development of new and ever more spectacular signs in order to differentiate brandname products from one another.

Like Roland Barthes definition of myth,[3] *advertising is less about lies than about inflection—the bending and redirecting—of social and cultural meanings to serve commodity brand names.* The dilemma advertisers face is how to design new sign values and yet remain credible in an increasingly cynical world cluttered with their own stream of images and previous truth claims. Needless to say, viewers have real doubts about authenticity, and they have reason to be skeptical because image culture constantly works to confuse the meaning of authenticity.

The dilemma of authenticity in the age of commodity sign is that no sooner does something become recognized as a mark of authenticity than it gets appropriated and transformed into a popular sign. As soon as it becomes a hot sign, however, its authenticity is dissipated and lost for those who gave meaning to the sign prior to its mass commodification. Take the example of Dr. Martens boots. These boots, initially associated with punk working-class bands in Britain, slowly became an underground antifashion statement embraced by rebellious teens and outsiders. Measures of personal transcendence can be found in objectified icons of authenticity—a pair of bruised and battered Dr. Martens, a pair of faded and torn Levi's. But gradually Dr. Martens became more and more fashionable, such that L.A. Gear has announced their own line of knockoff boots to be called "Kombat." Being able to distinguish the authentic from the bogus boosts one's status in the social hierarchy. When an aesthetic preference or style becomes popular, it is converted into a brand signifier. But if too many people adopt your style, it isn't special anymore.[4] Consumers who invest psychologically in displaying their anticommodity sensibilities feel betrayed and compelled to distance themselves from their signifier when it becomes commodified, because it no longer feels authentic to them.[5]

Finding Yourself in a World of Commodity Relations

A 1993 MasterCard commercial addresses this tension between the desire for authenticity and the extension of commodity relations. The ad simultaneously expresses and denies the irony of the historical relationship between the bourgeoisie and capitalism. The bourgeoisie benefitted from extending markets that chewed up nature and society in search of profits, but meanwhile the bourgeoisie insists on having pristine and undisturbed sites for pursuing their own development. This ad opens with a tight close-up of a male baby boomer sitting on a hillside overlooking a picturesque Mediterranean town. He gazes quietly, contemplatively, in this tranquil landscape. As the ad crosscuts between the tourist and a waiter carrying a tray with bottled water, Rob Morrow's voice hails the wannabe bourgeoisie:

"Alright, brace yourselves. Your credit line has nothing to do with your value as a person, OK? You could have a shiny Gold MasterCard with a credit line of at least $5000, I don't care. It doesn't make you a better person. [He pauses, and shifting his tone of voice he wonders aloud:] Well, I don't know, maybe it

does? I mean if knowing that the Master Assist Plan can refer you to a good doctor or lawyer anywhere in the world, let you relax and stop being so uptight and just have fun and be yourself—then, yeah, I suppose a Gold MasterCard could have some effect. What could really help is if you go somewhere really placid, where they tend sheep and play pan-flute for a little introspection, because now, no gold card is more accepted on the planet than Gold Master-Card. And you can use it at cash machines all over the world. So if you're smart enough to take it with you wherever you go, you can get money in drachmas, lira, or krona, or seashells or whatever they use there, so you can tip generously, which as any waiter will tell you is the true measure of how good a person you are."

Narration and scene signify a down-to-earth quality, a state of well-being, minus the luxury and frantic self-indulgence of the 1980s credit card ads.[6] We witness here a *bourgeois gaze* that expresses distance between the self and the social world. This moment of self-reflection can make you a better person, a person at peace with yourself. Why does the narrator begin by questioning whether the quality of self is contingent on one's exchange value? The ad teases us, dangling a critique of commodity fetishism in front of us: Will this be a critique of money, status, and inauthenticity? No, the issue is raised for the sole purpose of denying it. The narrator's ironic tone coupled with the list of Gold MasterCard benefits, and the visual evidence of a man at ease with himself, confirms that his initial question was not serious, but instead a playful method of hailing us.

MasterCard offers a safety net (lists of doctors and lawyers) to protect those who explore the world of otherness and nature on the periphery of the world capitalist system. It sells security for a world that has grown all the less civil the more thoroughly it approximates a total commodity world-system; it simultaneously sells the space for authentic experience beyond the world of crass commercialism. Further-

The contemplative tourist gaze, courtesy of MasterCard, enables introspection. The clasped hands at center signify introspection—these hands signify a self-reflexive person, a person relaxed and comfortable with a "true" self.

more, this card permits you to escape the repressive confines of society—apparently, it is hard to find your true identity in a fully commodified world. Yet, here, in the pastoral setting of the panflute, MasterCard locates the undeveloped space *where you can "be yourself"* as a tourist without giving up the creature comforts available thanks to a universal commodity exchange card. The premise here is that the more experiences one accumulates, the more self-actualized one will become.

We are invited to participate in a "status cycle" by playing upper class for a week.[7] The ad acknowledges the waiter's role in a commodity-structured relationship, but it respeaks the language of class as if it was the language of the individual. The true measure of status is how "you can tip generously" for class support. The voices of the two classes literally become unified through the visual gimmick of the waiter mouthing the narrator's voiceover. You are allowed to experience deference, and to be at ease with privilege. Authenticity is expressed as an attitude toward the world, and—perhaps more important—toward oneself.

This narrative of authenticity is reminiscent of the Enlightenment worldview that sparked our obsessive concern for authenticity. Summarizing the origins of the concept, Berman writes, "Out of the antithesis of nature and compulsion the idea of authenticity develops."[8] Authenticity was conceived as the gap between the natural self and the social self. Enlightenment thinkers such as Montesquieu, Voltaire, and Rousseau perceived social institutions as repressive. A good society would allow the self to develop freely. Berman recounts Montequieu's idea that "No social system can provide human happiness, unless it posits, and its government guarantees, a basic human right: the right of every man *to be* himself."[9] Within this conception of human nature, nakedness became the archetypal metaphor for authenticity. The self is authentic in a state of nature, but corrupted by society which muddies the expression of the self's deepest impulses. To live authentically is to experience the self as coherent, whole, and integrated.

As market forces grew ascendant, modernism freed the individual self from oppressive traditions and left in its wake the social debris of family, community, and religion. The modern individual was both freed to make history and subject to the irony of historical fate.[10] Modernity celebrates the primacy of a self driven by perpetual desire for achieving self-realization.

Authenticity and the Bourgeoisie

The bourgeois worldview has evolved with each generation as corporate capitalism has continued to unfold. As seen in ads today this worldview has been modified and muddied by decades of refraction through the lens of the mass media. Indeed, the bourgeois worldview seen on TV is one that viewers learn to recognize without having to articulate the concept of "class relations." In TV ads, the aesthetic dimension that Bourdieu sees as the axis of distinction has been thoroughly separated from social class. But it wasn't always so.

Beckoned by the lure of accumulating capital, the bourgeoisie set about to harness and convert the power of nature and the labor power of other people into surplus value. The unconstrained marketplace was, per Hobbes's vision, indeed a war of all against all. Freed from traditional social prescriptions and from the master–slave relationship and its method of ascribed privilege, the bourgeois individual stood as the primary unit around which culture and ideology formed. Possessive individualism built on the premise that individuals owned their bodies and everything that accrued from the exercise of their bodies. This proprietary relationship to the self was consistent with the Protestant search for signs of religious salvation in markers of economic success. In both the marketplace and before God, the early bourgeoisie stood alone and naked (revealed). As a class, they sought to conquer and master both outer and inner nature. Status and self-worth were calculated by leaving one's mark on the world—tallied in terms of economic achievement, cultural capital, and even religious fulfillment. The bourgeoisie unleashed creativity and directed it toward restless development, paralleling the volatility of capitalist relations based on competition, innovation, and "perpetual upheaval and renewal."[11]

To maintain its economic advantage and social privilege, the bourgeoisie constructed moral codes and social rituals that set themselves apart from less successful people. Ironically, as the forces of capital multiplied and expanded, bringing new levels of economic success, new social formations made the Protestant moral codes seem irrelevant. The Protestant ethos and its pursuit of salvation through ascetic self-denial gave way to a concern for self-fulfillment that demanded a therapeutic ethos.[12] This ethos corresponded to the rise of medical authority (including psychology), the weakening of repressive religions, and the expanding urbanization and bureaucratic regulation that fostered feelings of overcivilization, artificiality, and loss of autonomy. The price of capitalist civilization and the bourgeoisie's relentless pursuit of progress was the loss of intensity and "real" experience. The bourgeoisie ventured into nature, into other cultures, even into their own unconscious, in search of their lost authenticity.

By the 1920s, mass-produced commodities circulated widely throughout the marketplace, fully abstracted from their relations of production. This played havoc with the meaning of objects. Mass-produced commodities lacked the sociohistorical referents of objects produced within localized communities bounded by a traditional culture. This loss could be amended, however, by manufacturing meanings and joining them to the commodities. Advertising during the 1920s and 1930s played the role of socializing people into modernity by translating elements of a traditional value system into commodity styles.

After World War II, bourgeois cultural and social hegemony expanded with the new suburban middle class, molding social spaces around commodity relations and administrative logic. Government and market forces reshaped, and seemed to domesticate, the majority of social spaces. The culture industry threw kitsch together with bourgeois values, diluting the bourgeois value system, undermining it by the very market forces that empowered the corporate bourgeoisie. From shopping malls to manicured front lawns, no part of social life was immune from the calculating and controlling logics of rationalization and commodification. The resulting "one-dimensionality," as Marcuse put it, bothered the middle class more than the working class. Tourism packaged nature and otherness into standardized and listless experiences; psychology and its therapies rationalized ventures into our inner psyche; department stores trafficked in a steady stream of exotic commodities divorced from everyday referents. Authentic experiences—those that were unmediated and spontaneous—were pushed further to the periphery while middle-class notions of self and identity grew more dependent on accumulating those experiences that serve as signifiers of self-worth.

Today's bourgeoisie experience a contradiction between a social world structured by their own market practices and their desire for cultural space that privileges and celebrates the individual as a privatized, autonomous being. While corporate economic and social power depends on extending an organizational grid over all activities and spaces, bourgeois status and prestige are still ideologically dictated by appearing to transcend the constraints of a commodified and rationalized world.

Standing between material social conditions and the ideology of transcendence in capitalist society is alienated labor. Advertising has historically glossed over the experience of alienated labor by substituting commodity signs for alienated labor. In turn, the pursuit of individual transcendence through commodity signs has acquired its own history, prompting its own legacy of consumer resistance to the alienating character of commodity signs. Consumers have learned that authenticity packaged in commodity form quickly becomes fetishized and devalued. Though advertisers still repress the ways that social and political–economic conditions structure our lives, they cannot avoid addressing the relationship between authenticity and the consumption of commodity signs. Brand legitimacy and exchange value become intertwined, making authenticity an unavoidable subject.

Commodifying Signs of the Organic

Claims of authenticity are usually made against the backdrop of universal commodity relations. This is reflected, for example, in definitions of "folk culture" as spaces for the preservation of traditions. "Folk" has come to define the importance of localized, indigenous activity that remains valued precisely because it stands outside the realm of commodity relations. "Folk culture" offers a comforting mythology set against the cold, impersonal, and relentlessly deterministic forces of commodity relations and government. Tonnies, the early sociologist concerned with the demise of Gemeinschaft relations, spoke of the "organic" and "the real" as grounded in the "totality of reality."[13] He gave authenticity (the real) weight by the specificity, the history, and the traditions of communities. Market relations transformed Gemeinschaft relations as the logic of capital invaded community relations, eliminating communally organized production, turning consumption into private activities. Wage labor pressed the commodity relationship forward, transforming the particular act of labor into abstract labor time, the unique into the standardized, the excessive into the efficient. Wage labor and private property privilege the *exchange value* of an act or an object over its *use value*. The logic of commodities entails a process of abstraction and decontextualization by which products are divorced from their creators and their social coordinates. Hence, individuals and objects circulate freely through the marketplace, but minus the social and material referents that accompanied their production, thanks to the chain of money and commodity exchanges that move commodities to the point of consumption. If consumers encountered these commodities without the benefit of a system of sign value, they would encounter just this. Freely circulating commodities are therefore reinvested with social meanings to stimulate consumption.

Paradoxically, when advertising appropriates a signifier, the content of the signifier is ripped from its context, the source of the authentic. The appropriated signifier reduces the authentic to an empty sign. Commodification hollows out the once-authentic signifier, and a new sign must be located and appropriated. Signifiers of authenticity are thus continually circulated and burnt out only to be replaced by new signifiers. Searching for authenticity within commodity culture results in an endless sign chase. The more that authenticity is signified and attached to products, the more those sources of authenticity become calculated as appearances. Consumers search for authenticity to escape the logic of commodities—always preplanned and preconstituted—but usually return disappointed because the signs of authenticity turn out to be no less calculated and preconstituted.

Television ads expend considerable effort at reconstructing a hierarchy of authenticity in objects. For instance, while ethnicity is not necessarily promoted as a signifier of a desirable self, it is heavily used to connote authenticity in food products. Recognizing the authentic brings status, or as Bourdieu puts it, "taste classifies and classifies the classifier."[14] Recognition of *real* ethnic food is a badge of distinction: it indicates you have taste. Ads deploy signifiers of ethnicity to portray an authentic—that is, precommodified—past. The past, whether ethnic or rural, is remembered as a

To signify the authentic quality of a food product, advertisers often resort to throwing in cheesy signifiers of ethnic precursors. This local commercial for an eatery called "Santa Fe Taqueria" ends by literally instructing viewers to "Join the tribe."

time when people cared about making quality products. Ethnicity has been transformed into a signifier of production that guarantees the authenticity of the object, even though abstracting signifiers from contexts produces fictionalized definitions of the "organic."

The Authenticity of Nonalienated Relations

Authentic production has long been associated with craft production. Since the advent of the Industrial Revolution, pre-commodity production has been romanticized as a time of unalienated labor. The common assumption is that when labor is self-directed and uncoerced, the worker cares about the product he or she makes. Unalienated labor supposedly allows genuine human sensibilities to be communicated and shared.[15] Labor is nonstandardized and the objects produced are one-of-a-kind (this is why handmade objects connote greater authenticity). Buying a handmade object permits us to celebrate our own individuality.

Hal Riney, whose agency is responsible for Saturn advertising, specializes in ads that carry the ring of authenticity. Speaking to Saturn dealers about the opening ad campaign, Riney explained that there would be no jingles because "We have a lot to say, especially the truth, which doesn't sing too well."[16] The Saturn ads emphasize the authenticity of the place (Spring Hill, Tennessee) where the car is made; the authenticity of the people who make it; and the authenticity of those who buy and drive it. Saturn emphasizes the authenticity of the production process designed in partnership with workers to replace the automated mass production line. Perhaps most importantly, Saturn emphasizes authenticity as a nostalgic zeitgeist that corresponds to an earlier era when America and its middle class were dominant. Saturn ads focus on the personal relationship between consumer and producer. One ad features a schoolteacher's letter to Saturn. A female voiceover reads the letter against a montage of shots that mix her relationship with students at Wood Acres School with production at the Saturn assembly plant:

> *"Dear Saturn Team members who are building my car: My name is Judith Reusswig and I'm a third grade teacher. Last week I placed an order for a Saturn SL2. After reading the* Time *magazine article and seeing them around town, I decided my new car would be a Saturn. I liked the whole idea of what Saturn was about. It is one of those things I try to instill in my kids, so I hope it is true. It reminded me a little bit of a mom-and-pop operation in the old days where you made a car for this person and this person was happy with the car they got. I just wanted you to know that you were building that Saturn with the blue–green exterior and gray interior for me. So you know who I am, I am enclosing my school picture. I'm looking forward to my new car. I'm sure if everything I read is true, I won't be disappointed."*

This Saturn ad positions Judith Reusswig as an authentic consumer. Saturn drew on her "organic" character in order to lend authenticity to their car. Saturn depicts Judith Reusswig as a caring grade-school teacher who gives personalized attention to her students. It seems Saturn workers devoted the same personalized attention to the car they made for her. Notice her letter with picture pinned to the car as it moves along the assembly line.

The ad structures a correspondence between the teacher and her students and the workers who comprise the Saturn production team. Each shows care and devotion. She gives her students attention, and the Saturn workers give similar attention to producing cars. Both produce quality products. The teacher is presented as an organic intellectual rooted in a community. Referred to as "team members," abstract impersonal labor at Saturn is reconstituted as a community of laborers characterized by organic relations. The sepia-toned ad and its classical score evoke a quiet certitude signifying tradition and heritage, as the letter compares Saturn's production to a "mom-and-pop operation in the old days where you made a car for this person." This historical reference is a total fabrication, created to wrap Saturn in the legitimacy of a romantic past. Abstract labor is personalized and so is the abstract consumer. Saturn is no longer a commodity but a personally produced automobile. The consumer is no longer an abstraction but a warm, honest woman with roots deep in her community. Commodity and market relations disappear in Saturn's narrative. The ad ends with a worker reading her letter, looking at the enclosed photograph, and smiling with pleasure because he knows that he participated in making a quality product for a quality person.[17] All the elements of the commodity form (abstract labor, market relations, impersonalism, exchange value, standardization) have been replaced by communalism and personalism.

The Auteur as a Model of Bourgeois Authenticity

Valuing objects as authentic comes from valuing the accomplishments of the producing subject, that is, stamping the product by its creator's spirit. Bourgeois legend pictures the crucial relationship as that between the creative subject and the artwork. The artist is the person who is willing to alienate herself or himself socially from the codes and rules of society, in order to create in a nonalienated way. To the consumer, art furnishes an indexical status sign that points to the capacity to appreciate the authentic nonalienated object.

Historically, the auteur has been a male social construction (or contrivance), signifying the integration of creativity, autonomy, and achievement. The auteur represents an ideal bourgeois self, able to achieve recognition by projecting himself into the world and transcending the limits of the commodity form. His power rises from the innermost depth of private being. His product or achievement carries his mark, his soul, his vision, his signature. More than a technician, more than a craftsman, the auteur, no matter what profession, is an artist. Ironically, the commodification of the auteur has made it a more gender-inclusive category in recent decades.

The artistic text is viewed as a reflection of the auteur's inner self. Cultural production, however, takes place within the context of history and is conditioned by social forces. Discussing the original, Baudrillard writes about this relationship and the dilemma that results in market capitalism when commodification is the driving force. The premodern artist aimed to replicate the world, and may even have employed specialists who painted certain elements (trees, rivers, etc.). Since the original inspired copies, forgery did not exist. In modern art, however, signature has grown all important: "The painted oeuvre becomes a cultural object by means of the signature."[18] Signature speaks to the special charismatic quality that differentiates the subject-creator. Signature became equivalent to personal style. Authenticity is a function of the oeuvre itself, stamped upon the work by the artist's signature. If the series is ruptured by any element that does not fit the artist's presentation of self as style, the whole series is called into question. Ironically, the artist is condemned to copy himself or herself, in order to maintain the signature. Further, the signature has the weight of authenticity because it signifies the self as a transcendent force. Market forces, however, determine the signature. The commodification of the signature must be disguised while the signature supplies the sign value and the exchange value. Obvious commodification will rupture the series and call the authentic sign into question.

The relation of advertising to the auteur (the creator of the original) is ambivalent. Since auteur status is based on noncommodification ("I don't do it for the money," or "I'd do it for nothing"), commodification always creates risks for the auteur. Since the auteur has a reputation as an artist, involvement in advertising generally portends a rupture in authenticity. But the lure of the auteur's celebrity value is tempting to advertisers. The dilemma was evidenced in a 1988 Michelob ad campaign that depicted Eric Clapton in an after-hours bar. Clapton, the auteur, is shown being himself, playing out of his love of music, not of money. When the viewer watches Clapton launch into "After Midnight" interspersed with cuts to Michelob, she or he is being guided to think: Drink Michelob and gain access to its sign of authenticity as represented by Clapton. But this performance inside the Michelob ad—as thoroughly a commodified space as there exists—betrayed its own claims to authenticity. Clapton's aesthetic vision of the world was suddenly problematized. If authenticity is salient to the fan, she or he must now search for new a signifier. Neil Young's song "I Don't Sing for Nobody" expressed this disenchantment with Clapton and other performers who sell out their art. According to Grossberg,

> "Inauthentic rock" is "establishment culture," rock that is dominated by economic interest, rock that has lost its political edge, bubble gum, etc. "Authentic rock" depends on its ability to articulate private but common desires, feelings and experiences into a shared public language. It demands that the performer have a real relationship with his audience, based on their common experiences defined in terms of youth and a postmodern sensibility rather than class, race, etc.—and to their music—which must somehow "express" and transcend the experience.[19]

Authentic rock is an expression of alienated youth. Once appropriated and commodified, it is reduced to mere entertainment and cannot be taken seriously. Taco Bell ads recently featured Little Richard and Willie Nelson singing lyrics that proclaim the pleasures of Taco Bell. Do these performers lose authenticity by participating in those ads or are they already seen as commodified entities? Performers have a history of signification and the media differentiates them on a hierarchy of authenticity. While pop entertainers (e.g., Michael Jackson, MC Hammer, Whitney Houston, New Kids on the Block) cannot lose authenticity, rock performers (e.g., Bruce Springsteen, John Cougar Mellancamp, and Bob Dylan) maintain their "integrity" by refusing to do commercials.

In contrast to the "codes" of authenticity used to represent Clapton in "his milieu," Little Richard is presented against a "fabricated" landscape of inauthenticity.

What happens when the auteur is concocted? A recent Gap commercial illustrates the pseudoauteur. In a smoky nightclub a man steps up to a microphone. A moment of screeching reverb from the mike, and across the screen appear the words: "What Fits by Max Blagg."[20] He reads aloud his poem.

> *"Sky fit heaven so ride it*
> *child fits mother so hold your baby tight*
> *lips fit mouth so kiss them*
> *And the face they adorn reminds you of someone you once knew some hot night*
>   *long ago*
> *familiar as these blue jeans that fit like a glove*
> *like an old lover coming back for more*
> *curved into the shape of your thigh like they were custom made to do just that."*

The reading is self-consciously stylized as a signifier of hip coolness. Blagg's reading underlines a cultural cliché about poetry as a vehicle for articulating depth and vision. Intercut with his reading are images of a chic audience, a female model in tight jeans, a motorcycle, and expressive female eyes. Framed by the male gaze, the female model and her jeans are eroticized and turned into an aesthetic object by aestheticizing the frame and making the jeans an object of poetry. Shot in fine-grain black and white, the formal elements of each frame (composition, lighting, angle, smooth cuts) predominate. Like the pictures in The Gap's campaign, the photographic style in this ad borrows from the "bohemian tradition of Richard Avedon."[21]

The aestheticization of authenticity is vulnerable to intertextual parody. The top pair of images appear in a Gap ad presentation of Max Blagg. The bottom pair of images, which match up shot for shot with the Gap ad, are from a Snapple ad that presents Jessica Mueller reading her poem to a not-quite-so-chic audience.

The aestheticized picture of the artist expressing his art does not fit with the obvious production of a commodity sign. Public criticism leveled at Max Blagg for performing in this ad amplified this contradiction. Because producing artistic discourse is valued as an authentic discourse, to commodify this discourse—even when maintaining a highly aestheticized form—violates the presupposition that authentic artistic production derives from a deep self, rather than one motivated by market forces. It calls into question the sincerity of the performance. The Gap appropriates poetry, closes off the space of the imagination by inserting preconstituted images and signifiers, and collapses these into a signified of cool sensuality. Poetry is reduced to the cultural role of selling commodities.[22]

Ironically, while authenticity has historically been associated with nonalienated relations, it has more recently also been linked to the aesthetics of alienation. While The Gap sought to embrace the auteur's vision as sign value, Pepe's competes in the same product category with moody expressions of self-imposed alienation. The badge of alienation can be presented as a sign of authenticity.

Auteurs in the Age of Flexible Accumulation

We have suggested that authentic styles emerge out of grounded spaces and relationships in social life. However, as Bourdieu argues, the bourgeoisie attempts to separate self-construction from historically grounded relations by privileging the auteur as someone who wills things to happen.[23] The auteur's creation (the original) is thus constituted as a sign of intense self-consciousness. Creativity is represented as a reflection of the inner life of the self, and not as a social act.

This 1993 Pepe Jeans commercial includes a nostalgic reference to the Beat generation's expression of alienation. Sandwiched between artsy, heavily grained, black and white photography of youthful interracial lovers are images referring to William Burroughs and his legendary expression of an alienated life in the novel *Naked Lunch*. We interpret the inclusion of these image-referents as a way of connoting the authenticity of alienation. More precisely, authenticity is defined by an aesthetic of alienation. Does the ad introduce Burroughs and *Naked Lunch* as signified or signifier? The commercial does turn them into second-order signifiers of "bohemian alienation," the romantic refusal to participate in the restrictive conventions of bourgeois civility or a lifestyle of commodity consumption.

In a world of mechanically reproduced commodity consumption, the capacity for distinguishing authenticity has signified an authentic self. The closer one is to the original, the greater the halo of authenticity. For the bourgeoisie, fashion shows and art shows provide opportunities to be in the presence of the original before anyone else. Benjamin saw mechanical reproduction of images as antithetical to authenticity because it negates uniqueness: "The presence of the original is the prerequisite to the concept of authenticity."[24] In a world of market relations, the original has meaning as a distant vessel of value. Copies have value in relation to it; the closer to the original, the more value the copy holds.

The original stands against mass consumption. But in the age of simulation and simulacra, the original becomes increasingly unrecognizable. In the system of corporate marketing, signs and simulations replace the original. Labels and designer names as sources of authenticity and cultural capital integrate the signature of the auteur with mass production and consumption. While production sites become dispersed across the planet, the designer logo claims to ensure quality and aesthetic consistency over the labeled image. How does authorship become located in the name brand? In the world of sign values, Benetton can stand for a sociopolitical awareness, Esprit for the environment, Patagonia for outdoor adventure. Or is the consumer the real auteur at this stage—responsible for picking and choosing the most authentic ensemble of signs—able to distinguish the quality of authorship and significance of this or that logo? The distinction at this stage is not the single sign but how one combines signs. The auteur and the bricoleur become one and the same, the individual who refuses to conform to convention in assembling and displaying their signs.

Nature as Authenticity

Extending commodity relations and instrumental rationality into all spheres of society has diminished the social spaces where authenticity can be experienced. This has happened because commodity practices reorganize nature itself. The historical result of organizing nature to support the commodity system has degraded nature as a space in which signs of the authentic can be accumulated. As noncommodified, natural spaces become scarcer, the sign of nature has been made a fundamental sign of the authentic. Advertising routinely attaches signifiers of nature to commodities as signs of authenticity or respect for authenticity.[25]

Capitalism treats nature as an alien force to be colonized and conquered, civilized and tamed; as a source of raw resources to be extracted. As capitalist development separated nature from everyday life, authenticity became expressed as a nostalgic desire to return to an unrepressed past (see Marcuse). Works such as Carolyn Merchant's *The Death of Nature* and William McKibben's *The End of Nature* decry the loss of pristine self-functioning natural environments.[26] Accordingly, nature has been socially reconstructed as a landscape uncorrupted by civilization, as a space where experiences of intensity, authenticity, and spontaneity can be located. When nature as an experiential realm disappears and society is experienced as overrationalized, nature is transformed into a representation that signifies a realm of freedom unencumbered by the constraints of civilization. Pristine nature has been mythologized as a replacement for God, as a space where individuals can have awe-inspiring experiences. While Western technology and economics continue to dominate the natural world, representations of nature construct a world of excitement, intensity, and risk. "The society of the spectacle" substitutes images of those experiences for the experiences themselves.[27]

Advertising presents spectacularized images of nature as it constructs a space in which authenticity can be pursued. A press release for the 1993 "Jeep Covers the Rest" television spot claims the ad strengthens the "legendary Jeep® brand image by extending the boundaries of nature to convey the 'go anywhere, do anything' attitude of Jeep vehicles." The Jeep-Eagle Division general-manager added that "more strongly than its competitors, the Jeep brand enjoys a strong identification with the cultural principles of authenticity, mastery, reach, and nature."[28] The commercial opens with a shot of a mountain range; as the camera pans across it, a male voiceover says, "Some mountains are over 500 million years old." But when two stingrays swim past the camera, the viewer realizes the scene is underwater. Swiftly, the camera rises out of the ocean and climbs a cliff where it discovers a line of Jeep vehicles as the voiceover finishes, "and while water covers two-thirds of them, Jeep covers the rest." Another ad shows a woman driving a

The sign of authentic experience equals distance from civilization.

Jeep up to a waterfall. The ad's soundtrack is conspicuously silent. The woman opens the door and the sounds of nature flow in. Jeep has positioned itself as the vehicle that can transport us back into immaculate nature for adventure or contemplation. Jeep advertising conceptualizes nature as a space to be experienced by privileged Jeep owners who now can travel deeper into nature than owners of other vehicles, but who are always in control of that nature because their Jeep controls nature. Jeep claims to effectively insulate and protect you from nature. The authentic experience (standing before the waterfall) is an experience superior to that of the crowd of tourists doomed to watching geysers at national parks. Though Jeep is a mass-produced and mass-marketed commodity, its advertising hails its audience as unique individuals who can appreciate the awe-inspiring majesty of nature and the satisfaction of conquering it.

Nature as a Sign of Distinction

Nature, pure and primitive, provides a source of signifiers for appellating the bourgeoisie. The Michelob Dry ad campaign with spots entitled "Whale watch," "Baja: Sea of Cortez," and "Serengeti" illustrates the celebration of authenticity as unmediated experience. These ads picture beautiful people who "thirst for adventure" while they encounter nature's wildness. They master nature's elements (wind, ocean, surf, desert) and then lean back to take satisfaction from the off-the-beaten-track beauty they have conquered. These texts address the young and wannabe bourgeoisie: the gods and goddesses who find themselves by exploring a pure and untrampled world.[29] Here is another version of the long-standing cultural contradiction between the bourgeois worldview and the forces of commodification. Though historically bourgeois class interests have been served by commodification,

Michelob people pursue genuine experiences, vivid and potent, outside of civilization.

they have sneered at its degrading impact on culture (witness the distinction in these ads between adventurers and mere tourists). Advertisers use nature to signify desires for intensity that the rationalization of the natural world has depleted.

Nature also offers a space for self-reflective meditations. Authenticity may be achieved through contemplating and appreciating nature's aesthetic. The 1989 introductory campaign for Nissan's Infiniti conspicuously omitted the car from the visual frame to construct nature as space for quiet contemplation. Each commercial dwelt on a single nature scene: a flock of geese, rain falling quietly on a pond, water rushing over rocks. A Zen-intoned voice spoke of the harmonious experience that driving an Infiniti offers. Nature's balance served as a metaphor for the automobile's functioning and its relationship with the driver. Leaving the automobile out of the frame further reinforced this aesthetic and cemented the name "Infiniti" to the signified of "tranquility" that comes from being in harmony with nature. The absent product coupled with the minimalist aesthetic differentiated the Nissan campaign from other ads that clutter television with images of frantic consumption that throw our lives out of balance.

The Infiniti campaign constructed a commodity sign by applying the codes of bourgeois nature photography to blend the rhetoric of aesthetics to the language of self. Like the photography of Ansel Adams or Eliot Porter, these nature scenes invoke the pure gaze that treats nature as a visual aesthetic object. In his analysis of bourgeois aesthetics, Bourdieu presents the detached gaze associated with the bourgeoisie as a product of a "life of ease—that tends to induce an active distance from necessity." For Bourdieu, "the pure gaze implies a break with the ordinary attitude towards the world which, as such, is a social break."[30] The Zen-ness of the narrator's voice connotes a consciousness unconcerned with economic necessity or conspicuous consumption. But such imagery signifies a self—supposedly unconcerned with status symbols—and certainly not the car (the Nissan Infiniti is a low-mileage power car). This construction of nature harkens back to the transcendental philosophies of Emerson and Thoreau that revered the self-reliant individual, so central to bourgeois

Bourdieu (1983:41) observes that "a certain 'aesthetic,' which maintains that a photograph is justified by the object photographed or by the possible use of the photographic image, is being brought into play when manual workers almost invariably reject photography for photography's sake (e.g., the photo of pebbles) as useless, perverse or bourgeois: 'A waste of film,' 'They must have film to throw away,' 'I tell you, there are some people who don't know what to do with their time,' 'Haven't they got anything better to do with their time than photograph things like that?' 'That's bourgeois photography.'"

economics. However, they sought an alternative outside the urban industrial world the bourgeoisie built. They looked to nature's quietude as an alternative to the noisy distraction of the city and society. Contemplating the purity of nature could enable the self to reach higher levels of fulfillment and self-awareness. This notion of transcendence privileges the bourgeois self by denying the social as a category of determination.

How nature is constructed as a sign of distinction depends on the class background of those being addressed. Now let's look at an Old Milwaukee Beer ad campaign in which nature appears as a landscape for vacations—or rather, as a prop for narrated musical travelogues. This ad celebrates friendship, not the discovery of self. A *Raising Arizona* visual style modeled after cartoon structures (wide angles, speeded-up motion, unnatural colors) turns the imagery of the natural landscape into a vehicle for a narrative that does not take itself seriously. Old Milwaukee Beer constructs a series of tongue-in-cheek ads in which two friends head off on the road to discover America, where they find quirky characters and hyperstylized nature. Set to the "Bonanza" theme song, a one-minute ad introduces Jack and Andy as they head to a national park in their 1970s-era Winnebago:

"Six wheels, a dish on top, two weeks in a Winnebago we go. Friends since the second grade, products of Altoona, PA. That's me, Jack, the Butch Cassidy of the Poconos. Big boots, big dog, big ideas. That's Andy, Mr. L.A. now, Mr. Poolside with Rayban shades. 'You can't see America by plane,' I say. You gotta go out and feel the dirt. So like Lewis and Clark, Stanley and Livingston, and Thelma and Louise, we took off for the great outdoors. 'It doesn't get any better than this' was Andy's refrain. Wide-open spaces, new friends and faces, a sunset you wouldn't find in L.A., and my thanks to a ranger named Beverly who assured us that bears don't like beer. But to Andy survival here is the same as

in L.A. You keep a cold supply of Old Mill on hand and you never travel out of range of a pizzeria that delivers anywhere. As Andy says, 'it doesn't get any better than this.' "

Jack's narrative pokes fun at middle-class consumer signs and their own status climbing—"Mr. Poolside with Rayban shades"—and takes an ironic stance toward commodification. These characters are at home in a commodified world and joke about being uncomfortable anywhere they cannot bring their conveniences. Jack's narrative, in conjunction with the video style, debunks the myth that one can have an authentic tourist experience of pristine nature in a national park. Andy further skewers this sensibility by watching TV at the campsite, sitting in a lounge chair on a mountain top, and ordering pizza. The ad's satirical tone does not deny authenticity, but instead relocates it in the durability of friendship rooted in the shared experience of a working-class community (Altoona, PA). That one can still construct a world *in spite of* the commodity form is a reoccurring theme in advertising.

Comfort and convenience take precedence over the authenticity of nature in Old Milwaukee's world.

Otherness

Revolt is the only mode of authenticity a repressive society allows; and when nature is repressed, revolt is inevitable.[31]

Historically, advertising has constructed messages that support the hierarchy of bourgeois values. Advertising defines desirability by attaching it to status—for example, fashion ads attempt to collapse sexuality and distinction. Advertising fuels consumption by attaching social signifiers of self-worth to commodities, constructing a model of self based on self-scrutiny in relation to a system of commodity signs. Reisman's category of "other-directedness" captured this style of conformity based on the discourses of mass consumption. Advertising contributed to a "national unified culture" organized around commodity consumption in which the bourgeois system of civility and its hierarchy of signs was extended to everyone.[32] Unlike traditional signs rooted in the social histories of class, modern advertising reworks signifiers of distinction to fit commodities. Distinction replaced class-consciousness.

As a hegemonic discourse, advertising redefines the parameters of bourgeois acceptability, while incorporating otherness into those parameters. Advertising discourse supports bourgeois perceptual, aesthetic, and moral codes while addressing the desires born of the repressive character of those codes. Bourgeois culture expresses an *ambivalence* toward those who live on the margins of bourgeois culture. Otherness is both romanticized and feared. This contradiction is rooted in the bourgeois codes of civility that repress the individual, for example, by defining sexuality as a matter of impulse control. The flip side of the lack of spontaneity is a demand for perfectibility, for control over the self: your every performance may be used to judge you. Codes of surveillance are both revered and cursed by this kind of socialization. Many have remarked at the self-policing panopticon imposed by consumerism applied to personal life. Middle-class youth feel judged and limited by a system that catalogues and orders their behavior. Their accumulation of cultural capital—which will eventually pay off for them in labor markets—feels dull and bland compared to the vibrancy and passion expressed by the alienated other. In America that other is defined by blackness. Blackness has become symbolically defined as wild, untamed, aggressively self-confident, dangerous, and rough. It is a culture full of braggadocio, or "trash talking." In the discourse of TV, otherness signifies an expressivity of the soul that is not locked up in accumulating signs of status and place. It also symbolizes the difference between inhibition and pleasure in one's relationship to the body.

Otherness is a social construction associated with definitions of desire: What is desired and what is undesirable? Initially, the other is defined as vulgar and obscene, the great cultural negations the bourgeoisie have repressed from their discourse. The mere physical presence of the other violates the system of civility that defines the bourgeoisie. Unlike the aristocracy that resorted to appeals to naturalism to explain their upper rank, members of the bourgeoisie must constantly prove their membership in the middle class by acts of self-control. Failure to control one's physical desires means loss of distinction or membership in bourgeois society. Fat, disfigurement, odor, and public sexual display are violations of bourgeois civility. Intentionality is inscribed on one's physicality and celebrated in the categories of grace, etiquette, and sophistication.[33] Self-scrutiny and self-consciousness makes impulsive spontaneous action difficult. The achiever in contemporary life leads a double life: a public life where a moral self is presented and a private life of desire. A sense of inauthenticity arises when the difference between public presentation and private desire becomes too great.

In bourgeois thought otherness signifies the unrepressed: the precivilized (Rousseau), the instinctual (Freud). While bourgeois morality devalues the other, bourgeois alienation celebrates it. Otherness is constructed as a romantic sign that speaks to the alienated psychological needs that result from obeying the regulative structure of civility, organization, and self-control. Middle-class society highly values individual achievement, self-awareness, and a sturdy, resolute inner self. Otherness emerges as a desirable sign born of the tensions generated by privileging the individual over the social and holding the individual responsible for regulating the body, its sensation, appearance, and expression. We read advertisements as expressing these tensions in bourgeois culture and commodity ideology. It is critical that we distinguish the bourgeois desire for otherness from the narrative structure of advertising that translates otherness into signs of authenticity.

As advertising advances into new territory to differentiate commodities, this hierarchy of signification fragments. Style that borrows heavily from otherness does not overthrow and replace the concept of social hierarchy but tries instead to revitalize the pursuit and consumption of commodity signs. The unpermissible (otherness) provides fresh signifying material for differentiating commodities. Style emerges out of marginalized subcultures. Subcultural movements such as the beats, the hippies, the punks, and more recently rap and grunge define themselves outside bourgeois codes. Within these movements small entrepreneurs and fringe artists turn out new signs that express disenchantment and alienated opposition to the hegemony of bourgeois cultural codes. These subcultural signs circulate on the periphery, but then a few are appropriated by mainstream cultural production and transformed into mass-produced icons of authenticity. The other is a necessary source of sign value for a commodity culture addicted to new styles and appearances. Advertising gives new, but certainly limited, voice to otherness. Ads celebrate, romanticize, and incorporate otherness, turning it into a nonthreatening, but well-paying, commodity sign.

The Spectacle of Ghetto Authenticity

In recent decades, subcultures have challenged bourgeois cultural codes by contesting the commercial semiotic process, while advertisers counter by trying to appropriate the signifying power of subcultures based on the extraction of semiotic otherness.[34] "Semiotic otherness" identifies a way of talking about who and what we are not. Identity is constituted by what it excludes. Fitting into the prevailing definitions of middle-class success means foregoing other possibilities. Otherness traditionally emanates from those who occupy the margins of society where they are subordinated and dominated. Out of these semiotic "struggles for possession of the sign" emerge commodity images "open to a double inflection."[35] When passed back and forth through the world of commodity images, desires for otherness tend to be translated into styles and surfaces.

During the 1992 Summer Olympics, Reebok hired Sinbad, a black comedian, to promote their new Blacktop basketball shoe. The campaign began with Sinbad explaining "the outdoor game . . . where legends are made," as the camera cut between Sinbad and inner-city youths showing off their best court moves. Sinbad's voicover exclaims:

> *"Let me tell you about the outdoor game . . . You shoot from anywhere . . . There ain't no rules . . . How do you know when you're out of bounds? . . . When you hit a trash can you've gone too far . . . ."*[36]

Structurally, the ad is simple. It correlates basketball shoes (commodities) aimed at youth with romantic signifiers of otherness: the athletic prowess of black ghetto ballplayers and the "no rules" setting of outdoor basketball. In another ad Sinbad tries to convince representatives from the International Olympic Committee to consider offering playground basketball as a sport in Barcelona. He addresses the viewer in street talk: "Yo! Sinbad here with the Blacktop shoe. I got my boys here from the International Committee. Schwinn and Schwinn." In contrast to Sinbad's looseness, the bureaucratic sports officials stand stiff and immobile. Sinbad's *talk*—his jawing and trash talking—contrasts sharply with the lack of expressivity in middle-class speech. Sinbad mocks the officials' inability to call for the next game, while behind him the game consists mainly of dunking displays. Real basketball is found in the *roughness* of "the outdoor game." Schwinn and Schwinn possess no glimmer of hipness. They lack the knowledge and appreciation of basketball aesthetics needed to judge the acrobatic, yet forceful dunks. They are out of their league in this nonwhite and noninstitutionalized territory

For marketing purposes, Reebok renames the city game "the outdoor game." This still frame represents the flavor of Reebok's visual mythology of a game they frame as black, wild, and unbounded but within the dense confines of an old inner city. The same signifiers recur: the chain-link fence, the side of a worn brick building, the laundry on the line, the realist codes. This is a moment in the black imaginary of television.

of "the Blacktop." The ad poses a binary semiotic opposition between the spontaneous (the nonwhite playground) and the official (the Olympics). Significantly, making Europeans the target of Sinbad's ridicule softens the assault on bourgeois categories, and allows American whites to identify with otherness without feeling put down.

In 1993 Reebok's Blacktop commercial revisited the outdoor court, this time depicted as a blacktop jungle. The setting is dark and threatening, illuminated by glaring lights against a background filled with swirling smoke. Visual signifiers consisting of graffiti, a chain-link fence, tattered paper, and billowing smokestacks suggest a decaying urban playground on the edge of an industrial wasteland. We enter with the crowd past an event title scrawled on a broken backboard, and we are suddenly brought face to face with the MC, who wears dark sunglasses and a black-hooded sweatshirt, trimmed in gold. He screams out, "Welcome to the 1993 Reebok Blacktop Slam-Dunk Fest." He might as well announce "Welcome to the spectacle of the ghetto." The first dunker is a white male wearing a blue headband (he is included, no doubt, to defuse criticism that this is a racist commercial). A rapid succession of black dunkers follows, the last one floating down to reveal an elongated product shot

of Reebok soles. But these are just the prelims. The MC thunders, "Clear the house! Look out y'all, Little Shorty rocks! Yo, check it out!" A shot of an opinion leader shows him gesturing "No way." Then, from behind two "fat boys," Shorty abruptly appears, and launches into somersaults as he flies toward the basket for slamdunks, with each dunk punctuated by a thunderous percussion. The dunks are a prelude to his real expression of mastery: hoisting

himself up to stand on the hoop, arms outstretched as victorious conqueror, while the two fat boys gesture their approval. The MC makes a ritualized hand gesture over his heart as he declares: "Thas wha I'm talkin about! This is Blacktop! You come on strong or you don't come at all!" The ad closes with a fade to black and the Reebok logo on the screen, as the MC's voiceover departs, "I'm gone. See!"

Combining harder edged rap language and gestures with signifiers of playground basketball marks off an authoritative and genuine space of otherness. Where Levi's had previously discovered the authenticity of alienation in the black blues guitarist, Reebok now seeks it in signifiers of ghetto hoops and rap. The language of this ad mimics the discourse of black male youth stylized in a rap video format. Like a rap song, the ad boasts of imaginary accomplishments. This ad revels in the stylized combativeness and braggadocio of rap, while basketball is reduced to an aggressive pregame bluff display, a dunk contest. Forget playing the game. As images, Shorty's slamdunks point to empowerment and social transcendence—flying, soaring, defying the laws of acceleration and gravity. Blacktop tries to signify blackness, virility, confidence, and potency. It also comes to signify membership in the hood (totem group) of wearers.

If this ad seems to address issues of authenticity, it is also undeniably about posturing and hype. But, rap too is about posturing and hype. Rap has developed out of a black cultural "street tradition called 'signifying' or 'playing the dozens' . . . where the best signifier or 'rapper' is the one who invents the most extravagant images, the biggest 'lies.'"[37] Blacks have historically played with the signifying power of language as a method of coping with material oppression. Rap has subsequently emerged as a contestation of public cultural forms and space by groups who have been marginalized in labor markets, political parties, housing, and elsewhere. Their bricolage, like that of the punks before them, constitute profound political statements in the only arena available to them, while the other arenas associated with political power have been closed off to them.[38]

Advertising is continually ripping off subcultures in the effort to turn a quick buck (a sign dollar) by appropriating new images that impart value. After Sinbad parted ways with Reebok, he commented on this kind of robbery and its reductionism. Sinbad objected to the "Yo, man" script genre:

> White marketing people think black is from the hood. We're all just gangsters. Advertising will grab that, and they don't care what it all does to the black community. . . . They don't know what the hood really is because it's not beneficial for them to go into our hoods. . . . The real hood brothers aren't doing commercials. They're in jail. They're selling drugs.[39]

Reebok found success in appropriating the language of the hood, and turning it into yet another reified signifier: "Yo, man!" Reebok sought sign value by licensing opposition and otherness to create a differentiated image for itself. Reebok appropriates only the surface markers of this otherness, while on the other side of the signifying coin rap artists must reproduce their authenticity by offending and outraging the norms and values of the middle class. Today's most aggressive style of rap, gangsta rap, rages against white institutions of domination—most notably, the police. In the TV videos, having a rap means having an attitude, as rappers vie with one another for status by "harshing" (put-downs) on one another and inflating themselves as "harder." The stakes rise steadily on both sides of the coin, for this is the currency of authenticity. Hardness is currency because the meaning of hardness functions as an index for authenticity.

Who buys rap records? "More than anyone else, white suburban males, the same 16- to 24-year-old audience that made MTV's program 'Yo! MTV Raps' an instant hit. Henry Louis Gates Jr. has suggested that these suburban listeners access black culture 'like buying Navajo blankets at a reservation road-stop'. . . . [They] buy nasty sex lyrics under the cover of getting at some kind of authentic black experience."[40] Several years ago amid the controversy about exploitation of ghetto youth by sneaker advertisers, John Morgan, basketball marketing director of Reebok International, justified putting blacks in basketball ads because "basketball is dominated by blacks and authenticity is really important. To have a basketball ad with all whites and Chinese doesn't make sense. Kids get turned off because it's not authentic."[41]

Reebok's Blacktop ad draws on more than the fact that black playground players are virtuosos of the game. It hails youth who romanticize the danger associated with being an outlaw and belonging to an exclusive, secret gang. This draws on a tradition in American culture associating the authenticity of otherness with black culture. Recall Jack Kerouac's ride along the edges of the underclass and Norman Mailer's glorified white hipster who "absorbed the existential synapses of the Negro." Later, Lou Reed's lyrics captured the desire and the frustration: "I wanna be black; I don't wanna be a fucked-up middle-class college student anymore." More recently, in the film *White Men Can't Jump*, William Horton (renamed Billy Ho) plays ball like the black athlete. He hustles. Racism protects the signifier of the other. It ensures the symbolic existence of the other, a fantasy necessary to support the repressive banality of middle-class life. To accomplish this, the other must be consistently degraded and romanticized, and then reduced to a signifier by the practices of those who have the power to define the other for both their economic and their psychological benefit.

Aestheticizing the Authenticity of Otherness

Ads represent otherness in the formal codes of the spectacle. Like any sign today, the sign of authenticity is driven by the logic of the spectacle. Debord comments that "in societies where the modern conditions of production prevail, all of life presents itself as an immense accumulation of spectacles. Everything that was directly lived has moved away into a representation."[42] First, signs supersede their referents. Once this process gains historical motion, the signifying representations used to shape the signifiers become subject to a creeping incrementalism: signs become more exaggerated, driven toward the representational superlative. Positioned against the spectacle everyday life seems boring and mundane. The spectacle robs everyday life of its richness by opposing it with the full development of every moment. Lefebvre's argument about "the annihilation of everyday life" addressed the way in which systems and signs organized outside of everyday life invade the discourses of everyday life until we only recognize daily life as it is refracted back to us through the codes of the spectacle.[43]

The spectacle violates the laws of space and time in images. In Reebok's version, gang members borrow from the spectacle to showcase themselves. Thirty-one shots are edited together to form Reebok's hyperstylized narrative, and each scene "authentically" steals a hyperstylized signifier from rap culture. The Reebok ad exaggerates traits and characteristics associated with black ghetto rap and turns actors into caricatures. Every signifier that appears in the frame has been placed there by design. The Reebok Slam Dunk Fest appropriates signifiers of the ghetto—lingo, gestures, basketball, chain-link fence, fat boys, and graffiti—in a calculated and cynical effort to oversignify the power of black alienation. The ad reifies signifiers of rap culture and fuses them into pure spectacle. Far from offering authenticity, the Reebok ad presents a burlesque of overencoded rap gestures and signifiers.

Reebok's ad, with its closed forms, its framing, and its overexposed backgrounds that obscure our sense of place, resembles a neoexpressionist video text. The neoexpressionist camera work relies on acute low angles with high-contrast lighting to produce distorted images. The ad offers an authoritarian celebration of the power of the leader, the cohesiveness of the gang, and the physical challenge as a form of initiation into the gang.[44] Yearnings for empowerment turn toward a neofascist sensibility.

Advertisers compete to capture the signifying power of otherness at the level of aesthetic codes. Within a sign war, the logic of differentiation tends to be determined by the spectacle. Advertising works by articulating—joining—disparate elements in the frame. It can take signifiers from anywhere and bleed out their meaning through aestheticization. The logic of the spectacle applied to authenticity finally mutates into highly aestheticized style. In contrast to Reebok's overtly spectacularized account of ghetto culture, Nike presents a vision that on first glance seems to stand outside the spectacle because it embraces a video style that connotes antiglamour and does not seem to deny the context of poverty.

A 1993 Nike ad correlates a soulful rendition of a traditional miners' lament, "Hardrock Miner," to scenes from a ghetto basketball court. This ad offers a textbook exercise in sign articulation: the joining together of discourses that have no necessary relation to one another in practice. The ad's narrative is ambiguous, in part because the ad draws more on codes than content. Although interpretation of this ad depends heavily on the meanings supplied by the viewer, we see this ad speaking to issues of authenticity at the level of Nike's thematic sign. The songs lyrics provide a metaphoric framework for interpreting the video:

> *"We are miners,*
> *Hard rock miners*
> *To the shafthouse we must go.*
> *With our bottles*
> *On our shoulders*
> *We are marching to the slope.*
> *O'er the land boys, o'er the land boys*
> *Catch the cage and drill your holes,*
> *Till the shift boss comes to tell you*
> *Put it all on the line for this mining for gold.*
> *Put it all on the line for this mining for gold."*

Nike's "Hardrock Miner": Do the codes of an unglamorous existence glamorize the ghetto?

"Hardrock Miner" speaks from the position of the oppressed about the drudgery of wage work that never ends. Slow motion and the fading in and out of black gives the video the texture of a journalistic photo essay, consisting of moments in time: portraits in a day-in-the-life series. These photographic moments seem nonconsecutive, but their meaning can be interpreted as sequenced by the song's metaphoric frames. The camera pulls against the flow of bodily movements on screen, impeding or restricting the flow of figures who seem to trudge past. Scenes in TV ads rarely linger on the screen; here lingering scenes record little action or movement—instead they offer poetics. Mixing the emotional color of the singer's voice with the flat, affectless black and white of the video creates a feeling of painfully slow and futile movement toward a goal.

The scenes convey a sense of exhaustion and fatigue, yet the music also suggests a sense of persistence. Born of working-class pain and despair, this song conveys sadness and hope, simple eloquence and sincerity. As hopeless and barren as each moment seems, the music conjures up a sense of resilience and hope. Though melancholy, the ad conveys a solemn and unbending quality: every day may be like the day before, but these guys never give up.

The hardrock miner's lot grew desperate as the gold industry expanded and became more corporate in the latter 19th century: hardrock miners were wage slaves, selling their labor for the dream of gold. The miner's dream was to get rich for himself. That kept him going. But are these basketball players workers? Theirs is not wage work, though we might easily infer this to be the daily labor of black male youth: working to develop their skills to play professional ball, while knowing full well the odds against their success. But still they persist. The ghetto kid's dream of mining for gold is making it big as a basketball player. How long will that dream keep them going?

Whether intentional or not, one subtext here is that their images have been mined for Nike's benefit, Nike's gain. What is the relationship between the mine and the ghetto? These lyrics speak of entrapment. Mine and ghetto are both prisons, the one a work prison, the latter a labor-market prison. But why would Nike risk using the rhetoric of the working class to position black youth in terms of class relations? Though Nike and every other shoe advertiser has presented basketball as a form of transcendence, perhaps Nike is attempting to differentiate themselves by politicizing the clichéd construction of the relationship between the black ghetto and basketball? Does this elevate Nike's authenticity quotient?

Perhaps the authenticity of this ad has nothing to do with any relationship between the ghetto blacktop and the ordeal of exploitation, but instead with the style of signification Nike uses. Correspondence between the music and the frame takes place at the level of aestheticization. While the sound track predominates, it is just one element in a highly aestheticized frame. Using slow motion, low-angle photography, black and white film stock, and a wide range of gray tones, Nike has created a miniartwork. The signifieds of alienation and authenticity are constructed out of aestheticized signifiers. Alienation is commodified (and contained) through this aesthetic reductionism.

In the context of the bleak and desolate ghetto wasteland, the music also strikes a transcendent chord. The miners' song has been modified by a gospel style; coupled with the visual setting it is easy to conjure up an image of the slave spiritual. Absent from the soundtrack is any trace of the playground. Because the only sound is the soulful lament framing the slow motion video, the piece takes on an ethereal—not an earthly—quality. The text connotes a legacy of spiritual resistance, an unwillingness to allow the yoke of oppression to completely dehumanize them. Yet the alienation represented here is strangely dematerialized—almost Hegelian.

Typically, shoe ads address the subject about moments of personal transcendence, while glossing over the social conditions of alienation. However, these lyrics do not hail us as individual consumers, but as members of a class relationship. Indeed, at ad's end the familiar black logo appears, but without the "Just Do It" slogan. Why is there no "Just Do It" injunction here? Why is there no injunction here about acting and making change, no imperative about making yourself anew (the core of the modernist self)? Or does this middle-class ideology look too out of place when applied to the conditions of being black, male, poorly educated, and living in the ghetto?

If this ad is read as a statement about Nike's commitment to authenticity, then various interpretations can work for Nike. For example, we might interpret the Nike ad as speaking to a more realistic form of transcendence in accepting one's fate. In this sense, it's a bit like religion: accept your alienation, and perhaps there'll be a better place by and by. Or perhaps the highest expression of authenticity comes when the ad mimics life and provides no magic moment of transcendence? At the same time, using this song to narrate images of a basketball court in a black ghetto, Nike romanticizes and mythifies that spiritual resistance. In semiotic terms, "spiritual resistance" gets turned into the theme of Nike's second-order commodity sign.

Antispectacular Awareness

Spectacularization jacks up the ante to maintain the same level of excitement. Why else would we see tire ads that feature airborne mechanics changing tires on a car carried along by a helicopter? As companies engage in sign wars, they enter the dialectic of the spectacle and must constantly create new images to differentiate themselves from competing brands. This presents a double bind. On the one hand, constructing authenticity as a commodity sign positions itself as antispectacle, or as the sign of everydayness. Within advertising, slices of life, references to the real, and realist production codes position the authentic against the spectacle. Nevertheless, the aesthetic codes of authenticity have shifted from realism to hyperrealism. Even within realist styles the logic of the spectacle moves the representation to the claim of being realer than real, that is, the hyperreal. At some point the codes replace the signified of the frame as the dominant source of significance. Despite operating according to the logic of the spectacle, the sign of authenticity is falsely positioned as existing outside the commodified spectacle. On the other hand, in an advertising world of clutter, the forces of differentiation align the exaggerated with the authentic in attempts to hold the viewer's gaze. The spectacular moment of real experience is edited out of its sociohistorical context to become a signifier of an experience of heightened intensity. As a second-order signifier of the experience named authenticity, questions of authenticity have become relocated within the spectacle as questions of aesthetic codes. The real becomes located within the spectacle.

In their sign wars, Nike and Reebok have each positioned themselves by appealing to antispectacle sentiment. Each has drawn heavily on the aesthetic codes of slow motion, black and white, and hypergrain to emphasize the semiotic opposite of spectacle. Nike presents a series of personal narratives spoken in first person, always with a wry sense of humor. Ads with Jim Courier deglamourize the tennis star's life by assembling clips of a day in the life minus music. Moral of the story: excellence is a product of grinding routine and sutained effort. A sepia-toned Nike com-

Backstage, in the empty gym, Nike presents Carlton Fiske doing the hard work of staying in shape.

mercial features a voiceover of Carlton Fiske as he does situps in an empty gym: "At my age I do everything I can to stay competitive. I run. I lift. I bike. I lace and unlace my cross-training shoes. There was a time when I didn't have to work this hard to stay in shape, but I'm not 40 any more." *Just Do It*. Advertising separates the self into two components, the authentic and the socially constructed. Through the first-person narrative, Nike constructs its spokesperson as an "I,"—a reflective, self-aware person. Nike supports a deeply American notion of individualism, the belief that one can *will* one's life to be different. In Fiske's case, resoluteness, the strength of personal character, transcends aging.

Nike's women's fitness ads celebrate the internal self of everyday consumers more than superstars. A series of ads construct the appearance of soothing, therapeutic spaces within a world that otherwise seems to be rushing past. In Nike's first ma-

Nike adopted the photographic style of André Kertész in "Don't Rush."

jor women's TV campaign, one ad shot in black and white in the photographic style of André Kertész follows a woman on a fitness walk through an urban setting. A woman's voice addresses the viewing subject in the second person: "Go slow," she cautions. "Don't rush. The world will wait for you. The world wouldn't spin nearly as well if you weren't in it." In the second person, the voice doubles as the walker speaking to herself and Nike speaking to us. Nike urges its target audience to construct similar narratives about "seizing the initiative to create oneself anew." This ad invites women to activate a true inner self and overcome the internalized social forces that now block that deep self from realizing itself. To the extent that Nike commercial messages sink down into our personal philosophies, they become another layer of socially constructed experienced and personal psychology. Nike's women's ads present the authentic as antispectacle by locating the Nike representations as the discourses of everyday life.

Nike presents its celebrity athletes as bearers of authenticity motivated neither by the desire for fame nor financial success, but by their love for the game. Michael Jordan shoots free throws in an empty gym. His voiceover frames the scene: "What if my name wasn't in lights? What if my face wasn't on the TV every other second? What if there wasn't a crowd around every corner? What if I was just a basketball player? Can you imagine it? I can." Shot in black and white, this commercial is saturated with the codes of authenticity. The first-person narrative form is a confessional form in which Jordan (the speaker) can relate personal intimacies to an audience. As one observer notes, "What the 'I' says is assumed to be 'true' because it suggests a candid revelation of the self's deepest concerns in front of an audience to whom the character has no reason to lie."[46] Authenticity is constructed as a deeper level of self from which motivation is drawn.[47]

Ads such as this also offer ruminations on the relationship between commodification, spectacle, and authenticity. In the same series, Andre Agassi drives through his hometown, Las Vegas, sharing with us his feelings about the neon glitter of Las Vegas and wondering aloud how he has been shaped by it. The ad invites the conclusion that even the spectacle itself—in this case, Vegas—can be a source of the organic and authentic. One can be a part of the spectacle without affecting the deeper self; alternatively, the deeper self may be the authentic product of the spectacle. Despite the overwhelming impact of commodification and spectacularization on sports, television and advertising construct sports as a space in which the authentic reigns as a motivating force.

Reebok used a similar technique in a black and white ad that presented NBA players in a pickup game. Instead of employing superstars, Reebok turned to veteran players such as Doc Rivers, Danny Manning, and Danny Ainge. Within the ad all the players are equals. The narrator calmly asserts: "A contract can make you rich, the fans can make you famous, the press can make you a superstar, and a championship ring can make you immortal. But only the love can make you a player. You got the love?" The final shot is of Doc Rivers, head tilted up, staring out of the upper corner of the frame with a concentrated transcendent gaze similar to the aesthetic gaze of the bourgeoisie who survey nature. This gaze refers back to the self. It expresses dis-

Reebok: "Only the love can make you a player."

tance from necessity. One does not play for money (survival) but for "the love"—the games defines your soul. As the screen fades to the Reebok logo, we hear a player saying, "Run it back." The narration venerates the purity of the players' motivation by denying external motivators. It devalues commodification (contracts), narcissism (fans), spectacle (press), and celebrity culture (the championship ring). Authenticity emerges as an internal quality, a quality that transcends the determinism of the commodity form: "only the love can make you a player."

Authenticity can also be signified by the relationship between a sponsor and its spokespersons. Dan Wieden of Wieden & Kennedy states:

> Back in 1980, when David and I first started working on the account, Nike made it very clear that they hated advertising. They had developed close relationships with athletes, and they didn't want to talk to them in any phony or manipulative way. They were obsessed with authenticity, in terms of both product and the communication.[48]

Nike ads mix humor, inside jokes, and personal narratives to authenticate Nike, its celebrity athletes, and its consumer. The "Bo Knows" spectacle discussed in Chapter 3 exemplifies Nike's approach to the subject of authenticity. Similarly, the 1993 Charles Barkley "I'm Not a Role Model" commercial positions Nike as a company that enjoys its relationship with its professional athletes, while allowing them space to speak as human beings and not just as brand representatives. Treating athletes as subjects shields Nike from the criticism of overcommodification, and Nike gains authenticity points for acknowledging controversial topics. Beneath this and their self-effacing tone in the Bo series, Nike's ads almost always hail viewers with the "Just Do It" philosophy—their call to action by invoking the powers of individual resolve. The ideology that willpower, determination, and hard work will prevail are deeply embedded in the fabric of American culture. Such idealist discourses ignore the social and material relations that structure and delimit life chances and create real boundaries to the personal transcendence Nike sells. In a series of critical articles, journalist Nena Baker shows how Nike's production process in South Asia contradicts Nike philosophy.[49] Assembly-line production at poverty wages in environmentally unregulated situations does not give rise to circumstances that many will likely transcend. Through their spokespersons, Nike responded that these are the requirements of staying competitive and that their contractors treat employees as well as anyone in the industry. This only makes the general point even more compelling. Capitalist production practices limit the chances of the many in the interests of the few, and the ideology of "Just Do It" is just that: an appropriate ethic for those who are already privileged in their life chances.

Authenticity as Representation

Launched in 1984, Levi's "501 Blues" campaign established the standard for simulating the look of authenticity in ads. Its use of nonmodels, street locations, and hyperreal camera and editing techniques created an advertising style still mimicked by advertisers who seek to correlate the sign of authenticity with their brand. The original campaign drifted from its urban blues image to three subsequent campaigns, all dedicated to the theme of authenticity. First came a series of ads that presented small groups of friends as extensions of place: Boston, Houston, Hollywood, Lake Charles, Chicago. Youths comment on their lives in reference to the specific social landscapes they inhabit. For example, an ad opens with "Lake Charles, Louisiana" written across the screen and we hear a youth state: "I

The Levi's "501 Blues" campaigns from 1984 to 1987 set the standard for representations of urban authenticity by drawing on the imagery of black bluesmen.

don't believe there's another place in the country that's like this. Free. It's got everything I want." Video shots of friends sitting on a porch, jeans hanging on a clothesline, and people riding an air boat on the lake, set against a Ry Cooder guitar in the

By rooting the identities of youth geographically, Levi's makes a claim for authenticity. This Levi's campaign symbolically located differences of identity and personality in the cultural and geographic specifics of place.

background, are transformed into signifiers of rural Louisiana. Levi's softens its usually jerky, uncertain camera movements to situate a grounded self within a small community setting. By contrast, their Hollywood commercial features heavily fragmented and disjointed dialogue and video as it focuses on a youthful wannabe director and a group of friends shooting video. In Hollywood, authenticity is situated in a cosmopolitan context as creativity, achievement, and success. When the youthful videomaker presents a fractured video stream of consciousness as insight into his soul, Levi's also calls attention to its own exaggerated reliance on fracturing the video into a stream of hypersignification. This is a document about self-aware youth seeking to express their creativity in bad video-poetry: "When I look at the sign / I think of / I need my motivation / five four three two / you say what / fine / it's over / fine / it's over / I am full of rage to have fun / you're not yourself / to have a good feeling about yourself / you can have good feelings about other people / one." Authenticity is associated with the budding artist who reaches deep into his being for inspiration. Unlike the Lake Charles commercial, the formal structure of this ad—stylized fragmentation—signifies authenticity as creativity.

After this campaign, Levi's 1990 "Is Your Fly Buttoned?" campaign turned to Spike Lee, who traveled America searching for the authenticity of real people. Each commercial in this series was formally equivalent, differing only by the character plugged into the interview formula: a fish thrower, a cartoonist, a grave digger, a lighting technician, a spelunker. All appear in their Levi's, all give themselves up to their activity. Immanence rather than transcendence signifies authenticity in these ads—take the world as it is and place oneself in the flow of being. In the best known commercial of the series, Lee interviews fish throwers at the Seattle Fish Market from off camera:

"Say who called the 800 number?"
"Bob did."
"I called the 800 number
and I told them I had a job throwing fish."
"What does it take to be a big-league fish thrower?"
"Gotta be a natural."
"What kind of fish do we have here?"
"This is a red snapper, king salmon, paper fish."
"Better throw it."
"Catch it."
"Better throw it."
"Use a fork."
"Do you like fish?"
"I hate fish, man."
"Three, four, five, six, seven."
"People eat that?"
"Sure."
Levi's 501 [written]
"Fly buttoned?"
"My fly's buttoned."

On the road with Spike Lee looking for the unique and different.

Though the campaign formula focused on offbeat vocations, the material conditions of work dissolve in the ads. The camera focuses on the performer, not the work, because panache and verve are determinant. Ironically, the ad celebrates authenticity, but was shot at the Seattle Fish Market, where fish throwing is stylized and staged for tourists. The work itself is theater staged to enhance the sign value of the tourist site, a practice called staged authenticity.[50]

When we celebrate the auteur, we define authenticity as an internal quality. Levi's hired Spike Lee, the celebrity auteur, to recognize and record authentic, but noncelebrity, personalities of America. Spike Lee and Levi's bestow the badge of recognition on individuals who demonstrate the personality to do the offbeat. Levi's associates themselves with real characters, whose appearance in turn valorizes Levi's as a sign of authentic individuality.

While this campaign siphoned sign value from Spike Lee's presence, it failed to establish the aura of authenticity that the original campaign had. Neither Spike's questions nor the glib replies seemed to plumb the depth of authenticity materialized by Nike's gritty exposition of personal narrative soundbites. Instead of biographical depth, Lee's interviews unintentionally located authenticity in the surface of personality. Except for Spike Lee's aesthetic sensibility itself, the campaign never valorized a coherent set of signifiers to correlate with its image.

Levi's recognized that their look and message had drifted, and rehired Leslie Dektor who had directed the 1984 campaign. Their 1993 campaign revived his aesthetic formula for encoding real selves being themselves. His aesthetic style effects a feeling of texture by combining hyperreal editing techniques with soundbites to create a collage of characters and spaces that connote authenticity. Making sense of these jagged montages of fragmented, disconnected images and soundbites depends on how we read the codes of authenticity. The aesthetic style of hypersignification binds the stream of images together with a metanarrative about finding personal identity qua authenticity. Levi's all-encompassing presence is reinforced by repetitive lyrics that celebrate the expression of true self-identity:

> *Nothin feels as good as laughter from the soul*
> *Got to feel*
> *Way it's gotta be*
> *Way it's gotta be*
> *I know who I am*
> *Got to be real*

Levi's 1993 campaign constructed authenticity through the middle-class gaze that recognizes the signs of authenticity.

Levi's constructs authenticity as something grounded in relationships. In an off-center frame, a middle-class youth philosophizes: "Hey / There's always two people / It starts out always two people and how they communicate." The ad then cuts to a shot of a Native American son and father who share the same frame. The boy addresses the camera: "Don't know of any friends that have fathers like mine. He's just one of the greatest guys you know, that you can know." Authenticity is expressed as shared intimacy based upon the hypersignified intensity of genuine moments. Despite the restless camera, authenticity is situated in relational terms as the empathetic moment when persons recognize and accept the other's unique subjectivity. These ads even drift toward the romantic, including hyperreal shots signifying an unstaged billboard marriage proposal: "Sabrina, will you marry me?"

But how has Levi's been able to turn a rapidly paced recitation of clichés into the fabric of authenticity? Because, in the blink of an eye, social relations are converted into coding practices.[51] Nowhere is this more evident than when dialogue (a fundamental element in social relations) is replaced by a formula of truncated soundbites and fragmented homilies. Constructing authenticity is *always* a matter of codes. Today this has become a matter of conveying an impression of context. Decontextualization is the enemy of bourgeois definitions of authenticity.

Consider, then, the irony that Levi's signifies authenticity by presenting exaggerated photographic decontextualization. Similarly, character structure emerges from the editing of soundbites and fragmented shots. Yet this surface one-dimensionality is able to stand for authenticity because it is presented through the codes of the authentic. Photographically, Levi's builds a polysemic structure based on hyperreal encoding techniques that include jump cuts, jerky peripatetic camera movements, off-center shots, grainy black and white film stock, and an elliptical structure that extends over the whole campaign.[52]

The critical element in this mix is Levi's use of hypersignifiers of subjectivity. These usually take the form of off-centered close-ups—hand gestures, partial glances, nervous rubbing, or an awkward pose—that serve as metonyms for the whole person. These hypersignifiers suggest a gestural honesty that replaces all but the fragments of language. Objects (e.g., a paper sculpture, goldfish in a bowl, bricks tied together to make a shotput) also become hypersignifiers of individual subjectivity. The objects apparently have meaning for the individual who holds them. But for the viewer, these have already become second-order signifiers of the deeper self. The deeper self is the sign Levi's wishes to join to their brand name.

Characters speak directly to the camera, acknowledging its presence along with the director's intent. Attention is drawn to the constructed nature of the advertisement, even as it provides the vehicle for allowing youth to exhibit deep selves. The Levi's ads locate subjectivity in the first-person speaker, permitting the self-reflective voiceover to vocalize a deep relationship between the audience and the inner self of the character. Unlike Nike's use of first-person narratives, Levi's fractures the discourse into soundbites about self-awareness and the importance of significant others: "Know who you are." "I let them see me how I am." "That's the way I am. That's the way I will be." "You have to have something to love, just got to." "If I can make people laugh that makes me feel good." But without narrative or character development to support them, these decontextualized aphorisms become shallow and tedious after multiple viewings. There is an oddly static quality to this pop psychology: though the lyrics speak of present and future, the future is nothing but more of the present.

Levi's 1984 campaign constructed otherness out of signifiers of the urban ghetto. Disconnected signifiers of less-urban poverty settings continue to function as organic landscapes minus the experience of poverty. Deteriorating brick walls and weathered wood invite a feeling of realist texture. They invoke the organic because they feel lived in. For Levi's, the stylized imagery of poverty settings represents an uncorrupted space for youth where the authentic still exists, where the dreamer can still dream.

Urban decay as a hypersignifier.

Levi's constructs an international, interracial, and multicultural set of tableaux, but unlike their 1990 campaign that located persons in specifically named places (Lake Charles, Chicago), this campaign embraces a postmodern sense of geography.

Multiculturalism as a signifier.

The landscape has no particular geographical markers. It is everywhere and nowhere. Its inhabitants are culturally diverse. In one ad three males playing hackey-sack introduce themselves and speak about their diverse heritages: "Polish-American / Born in Chicago / the Soviet Union." Levi's positions itself as ethnographer of this world. A recurring character in these commercials is the ethnographic photographer. In one commercial, a young photographer mentions his responsibility in photographing a disappearing American landscape: "I ride around and take pictures of all the people and places which are changing." This photographic ethnography also mythologizes multiculturalism, by selecting only images signifying tolerance of others and recognizing individuals' gestural uniqueness.

Unlike Levi's earlier campaign linking authenticity with alienation, this campaign situates authenticity in a humanistic recognition of species-being. We are all different and yet all the same. We might even recall the famous Coke commercial that gathered peoples of the world on a mountain top to sing of Coke as a totem of togetherness. Philosophically, Levi's presents a similar message but coded into a structure that denies commodification and spectacularization. Levi's links authenticity to the reenchantment of the world. But can there be authenticity without alienation?

In search of the authentic subject.

Sign Wars and Competing Constructions of Authenticity

Whereas Levi's positions us to identify with a speaker who appears confident, secure, and yet humble ("I know who I am"), Lee's jeans positions viewers to disidentify with an arrogant and conceited egotist who describes himself as "a complete package." Lee's draws attention to the inauthentic as a method of aligning their brand with the signifying theme of authenticity. Their "model" addresses the camera:

"What do I need an education for? you know I'm a model
Hey, can't we get any cold water over here
Of course I'm a perfectionist, look at me
Twice I've asked for cold water
What's my most attractive part?
I think you get a complete package, you know
I look good in jeans
How's my hair doin'?
Anyone looks good in jeans but I look tough in jeans
Some women are intimidated by my looks
I find that exciting, you know
I think when I'm done with modeling I'm going to be an astronaut."

The self-absorbed narcissist as Lee's anti-hero.

At ad's end, the screen reads, "**Look** like a model. Don't **think** like one. Lee's basic jeans."

Jolting video combined with screeching street sounds turns the ad into a collage of discordant images and sounds. The images portray an arrogant, self-centered, preening narcissist who displays his designer body as a weapon aimed at others: "Women are intimidated by my looks." The I isn't spoken with the humility of the Levi's characters. Instead, he represents self as pure ego and pure surface. Lee's constructs the model as someone so full of himself that he does not register as a model for the viewer: he is positioned as the anti-model. Lee's stereotypes the model as an object who lacks identity, subjectivity, and empathy. He is the logical conclusion of consumerism based on the currency of appearances.[53] He finds "exciting" the sense of sexual power his appearance gives him over others. He is truly a Hobbesian ego in a world where the conventions of consumer capitalism predominate. To ensure that we read him as a caricature of narcissistic excess, his discourse comically concludes by drawing attention to the absurdly grandiose side of his narcissism.

This Lee's ad attempts to provide a solution to a culture that celebrates appearance but which desires depth. The solution is to be both. Look like a model, but be a person with depth. Lee's ad holds up an appearance of the bad narcissism so that we can experience the joys of narcissism without being a narcissist. It attempts to solve the basic contradiction of youth: to be authentic in a culture that packages and privileges a commodified identity. One can work on oneself but it ought not to be obvious, or to be obsessive, or to restrict your humanity toward others. Here the Lee's ad pokes fun at Guess jeans and their slick images of glamour. Lee's positions themselves *with* the viewer and *against* the model.

The Authenticity of Death

In 1988 "reality" ads were the rage, usually shot in documentary style with a shaky hand-held camera to enhance the feeling that viewers were peeking into an unedited slice of someone's life. The best known of these were ads for AT&T business systems that earned the sobriquet "slice-of-death" ads, because of their grim and foreboding sense of finality (e.g., an ad that concluded with the ominous sound of a heavy metal door slamming shut). These ads spoke volumes about the stress and tension that middle-level managers experienced in the 1980s. The AT&T ads also spoke to a new turn in the way authenticity was signified. Ads became grittier. They began to acknowledge a phenomenological reality outside the commodity, but relieved by the commodity in question.

Five years later, the place has shifted from work to leisure, and the 1993 "Planet Reebok" series no longer uses shaky camera codes, but locates authenticity in a pure spectacular form, a montage of sports highlights constructed out of high-risk, intense athletic moments: a skier dropping out of a plane or a mountain bicyclist painfully crashing and careening down a rocky race course. Titles are intercut with shots proclaiming the not-values of Reebok's new global order:

> *No limits, no pain, no fear, no cupcakes, no wimps, no mercy, no fat, no subs, no beauty pageants, no gravity, no dirt, no excuses, no lawyers, no winners, no losers, no slogans.*

Each slogan hails a different market segment by gender, psychology, lifestyle, cynicism, and so on. Intense movement in each image substitutes for the missing predicate. Every scene is a decontextualized moment sewn together to represent the whole: Planet Reebok.

The ad's first image is a rocket leaving the Earth's atmosphere. Reebok hails itself as a global presence, the producer of a new universal world order built upon intense physical experience. Life on Planet Reebok is a visual smorgasbord of high-risk, emotionally intense experiences without the limitations of physical (no fat, no gravity), social (no beauty pageants, no lawyers), or psychological (no pain, no fear) boundaries. After this blizzard of title cards, the ad ends with the title "no slogans"—a sign wars reference to a world without Nike's "Just Do It" slogan. This is perhaps Reebok's fantasy.

Hailing diverse target audiences, the soundtrack draws together a montage

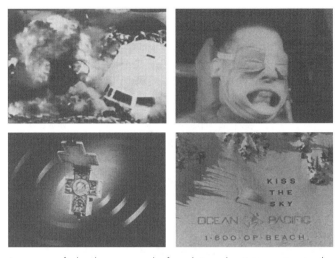

Imagery of death was rarely found in advertising prior to the 1980s. During the late 1980s that we have identified as the initial stage of hyperadvertising, images of death and destruction began appearing in ads. The images here, taken from an Ocean Pacific ad, look like scenes one might see in the *Faces of Death* films. In this particular ad, titled "Kiss the Sky," these scenes taken from archival footage are included to signify the intensity of experience of skiing on the extreme edge. Yet, following the scenes of being torn apart, an image of an ornate crucifix appears at the center of a serene ripple of water. The risk of annihilation seems to precede a moment of utter peace and tranquility—dare we say it, a moment of inner peace? Is this an appeal to faith?

of musical styles (punk, disco, pep band, heavy metal). Although the ad is constructed out of difference (titles, shots, and music genre), it collapses difference under the sign of Reebok. The sign itself has a coherency built around the theme of no limits. It locates authenticity outside internalized social boundaries and rules.

A Diet Mountain Dew ad features four Generation Xers who claim to have seen it all and done it all. Pepsi and other marketers are jumping on the bandwagon to hail this newly identified demographic lifestyle grouping. A Pepsi vice-president identifies this as a "vibrant, adventure-seeking group that is 40 million strong and spends $125 billion each year. To appeal to this group, the Dew ads feature four thrill-seeking young men who routinely perform death-defying "don't-do-this-at-home" stunts like base jumping from a cliff and boogie-board waterfall diving at locales representing Mount Everest and the Amazon. The free-falling feats, filmed in

Diet Mountain Dew's wannabe daredevil totem group and the consumption of staged danger.

Hawaii, California and Arizona, were actually performed by stunt professionals."[54] "People in their twenties are restless," the Pepsi vice-president added. "Dew's image—its bravado and connection to exotic adventure—plays to their quest for newness and adventure." After pounding fast cuts of action scenes from "Mt. Everest," spectacularized by thrash music and funky camera angles, the ad skips to close-ups of four guys who each stride forward to get in the face of the camera and then declare one after another: "Scaled it." "Jumped it." "Skied it." "Surfed it." This repeats with footage from the "Amazon" after which they lean forward to boast into the camera: "Rode it." "Dove it." "Flew it." "Crashed it." But when they encounter Diet Mountain Dew and experience its thrilling taste, they declare, "You've never done nothing till you do Mountain Dew."

Thrills are achieved by living on the edge. Nature provides the landscape where one's resolve to live at the edge can be tested, while commodities open up a world of intensity. These ads construct nature in the Hemingway tradition as the space in which humans can test their will and celebrate the qualities of physical strength and endurance. Hardship and suffering bring the greatest reward. There is no pleasure without pain. This is a masculine aesthetic, the tradition of the warrior, the hunter, the adventurer. The authentic self is one of pure will. Others aren't needed, only a wilderness. Advertising, however, modifies this tradition. The surface of the experience is lifted or abstracted. One sees an outstretched arm, the conquered mountain top, the exhilaration of flight, and even experiential intensity of a painful crash. Abstracted experience, however, is falsified. It denies the power of nature as an ever-present force that grinds its intended conqueror into submission. Nevertheless, these ads speak to the desire to construct an identity validated by the level of risk one takes.

Ironically, these images devalue the everyday experience that cannot compete with these spectacles. Indeed, these ads hail their audience by addressing a self so jaded that it doubts the possibility of new thrills to satisfy the desire for the new, the never-before-experienced. Finally, we encounter the two-century-long contradiction of the never-content bourgeois self. Obsessed with the new and different sensation, desire is now located in the vanishing moment of the novel experience. The moment gets shorter and shorter, until it is abbreviated in the nanosecond of the hypersignified adrenaline rush. Unintentionally, the Diet Mountain Dew ad registers the intertwined crisis of the bourgeois self and the reproduction of the commodity form. The authenticity of death foretells the death of authenticity. Here indeed is a self that does not look inside itself for depth: this is a self wholly dependent on the power and novelty of experience as a source of validation. Is the death-defying feat the only true test of authentic selfhood that is left?

The Death of Authenticity?

Postmodern critics view authorship and authenticity as myths that support class distinction. As cultural production accelerates and postmodern styles (pastiche, parody, plagiarism) proliferate, recognition of the original becomes more difficult. For example, the music group Milli Vanilli was awarded a Grammy Award before it was revealed that they lip-synched the words. After being stripped of their award, Milli Vanilli appeared in a Care*Free Sugarless Gum commercial where the two performers appear to sing a piece of operatic music. "How long will the flavor of Care*Free Sugarless Bubble Gum last?" asks the narrator. The record skips. The narrator responds to his own rhetorical question: "Until these guys learn to sing." Caught faking it again. Milli Vanilli grin at us. The joke is on those who believe in authenticity.[55]

Considering cover albums, ghost writers, speech writers, lookalikes, and so

This Care*Free ad was a clever maneuver within the field of sign value. Milli Vanilli had been in the news for cheating their fans by lip-synching—their celebrity tarnished, their sign value crashed in the advertising marketplace. Ahhh, but a negative could be turned into a positive by putting the right spin on it. How about a joke about Milli Vanilli as spokespersons for a pop culture saturated in artificial sweetness when we all know, and are reminded by the ad, that they are chronic fakers? Wink wink. Nudge nudge. As Lippert (1991, p. 37) points out, this gives the advertiser an opportunity to show off a "sense of humor and sophistication about irony, morality, and the nature of advertising artifice in general. It sure gets dubious and perverse."

on, authenticity appears to be a necessary myth. Despite cultural critics' declarations of the death of authenticity and authorship, in a capitalist culture the cult of the celebrity seems a necessary component to reproducing a climate of narcissistic desires. To many cultural analysts, Madonna represents a celebrity who has stretched the cult of celebrity with her carefully fabricated postmodern aura that seems to challenge the hegemony of authenticity as a category. She seems to epitomize the emergence of a decentered self that locates questions of identity and desire on the surface, in continually fluctating appearances. If there is any deep self, it is apparently constituted out of the chain of shifting signifiers she indulges in. The heart of authenticity shifts from the coherence of ego identity to the indulgence of desire itself.

The tensions between commodified identity, authenticity, and Madonna's decentered narcissism became manifest in a short-lived Pepsi commercial. Pepsi quickly yanked the ad because its linkage to her video version of "Like a Prayer" provoked outrage about its sacreligious sensibilities. This controversy concealed what was of greater interest to us about the ad: the uneasy mix between Pepsi's agenda of presenting images of identity and desire available via the consumption of Pepsi as a commodity sign (crudely paraphrased, "I wanna be like Madonna") and Madonna's ready willingness to join imagery of sensual liberation with visual signs of religiousity. The Madonna Pepsi ad lapsed back into the commercial theme of pseudoindividuality. Ideologically, it continued the well-established advertising tradition of appealing to our culturally constructed desire to articulate a distinctive and outstanding self. "Make a wish," Madonna counsels her younger self (who occupies the space in the ad for the youthful viewer to insert herself) as the ad concludes with an upbeat motivational message about achieving what we want.

Style has been described as the triumph of superficiality in which "surfaces themselves are lifted from an infinite number of sources."[56] The dominion of style dislodges signs from their referents and accelerates the circulation of signs. As signs are increasingly decontextualized and accelerated, the authenticity of all signs become suspect. Commodity signs used to construct a sense of authenticity no longer have the weight to sustain a coherent sense of self. While accelerated image production allows for the possibility of transcendence through the recognition of possibility, it also results in the replacement of meaning by fascination, disorientation, the waning of affect, and the inability to recognize substance. The pursuit of authenticity in this postmodern world may have become increasingly problematic, but the search for the substance of an authentic self lives on. The rise of cynicism, ironic detachment, nihilism, and even styles such as punk or grunge suggests the desire to construct an authentic sense of self outside of commodified social reality. Whether one takes a modernist position that authenticity was born and lost simultaneously in the swirl of modernity, or a postmodernist position that authenticity was always a myth, the use of signifiers of authenticity has proliferated. And while defining the authentic may be an impossible task in the postmodern swirl of simulations and signs and styles, as a culture we seem to still agree that it is better to be authentic than inauthentic.

6 *Green Marketing and the Commodity Self*

WE HAVE argued that to secure the necessary markets for capital to expand, 20th-century advertising has assisted in constructing a social world in which identity is expressed through consuming commodity signs. As the scale of corporate competition has increased and the circulation of signs has speeded up, the pressure on environmental resources has also gone up. Today, signs seem to zoom past our eyes, so fast at times that we have talked more about signifiers and hypersignifiers than completed signs.

Whenever actual consumption follows the circulation of commodity signs, there are real material consequences for the environment. We have argued that when previous distinctions between products are leveled by technology and technique, then commodity signs become a crucial ingredient in giving products value in the marketplace. Until now we have focused on the cultural resource demands of constructing commodity signs, but their institutionalization also has an impact on environmental resources. As long as commodity signs are the raw material for identity construction (i.e., authenticity), excessive production and consumption practices are probable. By stimulating the high levels of consumption necessary to support the logic of capital in the endless pursuit of increased profits, advertising aggravates tendencies toward environmental crises.

Prompted by the growth of the environmental movement and an awareness that overconsumption contributes to environmental destruction, mounting criticism has been directed at advertising. Advertising has responded by developing what has come to be known as "green" or environmental advertising. By appropriating signifiers from nature and transforming them into commodity signs, advertising repositions "thoughtful" consumption as a solution to encroaching environmental disasters. We argue that environmental marketing relegitimates consumption by buffering corporate practices from criticism and by alleviating the guilt associated with overconsumption by creating a distinction between good consumption and bad consumption. Ironically, advertising raids nature for the very signifiers it uses to justify continued incursions into nature.

The Commodity Self and the Death of Nature

This story has been a long time unfolding. The relationship between the commodity self and the capitalist political economy is now 8 decades in the making. During the 1920s, the technologies of mechanical reproduction, print, and photography reached a level of technical sophistication that permitted mass-produced advertising images to be nationally circulated.[1] This new institution emerged on the heels of a sea change in how work life was organized. Capital-intensive and mechanized economies of scale based on bureaucratically organized labor processes and the degradation of laboring activities aggravated class hostilities, but these economies of scale also multiplied industrial productivity until they outstripped the middle-class capacity to consume.[2]

In the early years of the 20th century, insufficient consumer demand threatened to throttle the circulation process of capital. Advertising and marketing took shape, in part, to resolve gaps between productivity and consumption by convincing people that homemade products were inferior to manufactured commodities. Thus ensued the social process of *branding* goods, that is, endowing goods with value and the capacity to fulfill a variety of desires.[3] Establishing brand names frequently involved associating signs of social status with products to simulate a fantasy world, which was nonetheless represented as being realistic and possible, where progress was defined as "convenience" and popularity was defined by "clear skin."[4] To establish brand identities, advertisers clothed their products in a "commodity aesthetic" so that styles expressed beauty, individuality, status, pleasure, and the fulfillment of desire.[5] Advertising sold the idea that identity is a product of how we consume, a product of the commodity badges we choose to wear.

This kind of advertising spoke to, and represented, an ideal middle-class life held in place by commodity relations. Working-class readers could look into advertisements and see all that was *absent* in their lives—alienated labor could be transcended and seemingly healed by purchasing commodities that other people would respect and envy. On the other hand, middle-class readers, anxious that they might be found inadequate when measured against their class ideal, could find in the same advertisements themselves made better by commodity acquisition. Advertising became culturally entangled in conceptions of self-identity. Recall that during the initial stages of industrialization the bourgeoisie as a social class based their self-identity on the accumulation of capital and achievements, while Protestant asceticism restrained consumption. But as industrialization became more capital-intensive, more centralized, and more concentrated, managers replaced entrepreneurs. By 1905, the Protestant emphasis on attaining salvation through denial and economic success was giving way to an emergent "therapeutic ethos" that ministered a "healthy" self achieved through consumption of commodity goods.[6] The shift to a fully capitalist urban society brought with it anxiety about self-actualization through one's producer status; it also cast into doubt what constituted the "real." Advertising of the period associated themes of self-actualization and self-realization with commodity brands by attaching them to frozen pictorial images concerning the satisfaction of psychological needs. In this way, advertising began to contribute to the manufacture of signs for constructing self-identity.[7]

Commodity-sign consumption thus developed as an institutional response to intertwined economic and cultural crises—on the one side overproduction, and on the other side the crises of self associated with mechanized and bureaucratized workplaces.[8] Advertising gave voice to frustrated social needs and desires that could ostensibly be remedied by going through the commodity form. Advertising articulated not just signs of success, but accelerated a general historical process in which signs replace what they stand for in all parts of our lives.

As industry banked more heavily on the arbitrary association of commodities with the social imagery of needs, one consequence was increased pressure to consume in general rather than to consume to meet specific needs.[9] The dialectic of market competition and the centralization of capital channeled the search for profits into the continued expansion of productivity on the one side, and the construction of untapped fields of value—namely, social sign values—on the other side. As mass production turned craftsmanship into a memory for many people, the sign values one consumed could be substituted for absent skills in the articulation of personal identity. Meshing the drive to augment surplus value on the production side of the equation with the need to extract an identity on the consumption side set in motion a self-reinforcing growth dynamic. This "dependence effect" was conditioned by the intervention of modern advertising into the relationship between products and the needs they satisfy. One consequence has been the construction of a perpetual artificial scarcity based on sign value.[10] And, since signs could be arbitrarily connected, disconnected, and reconnected to commodities, needs could become insatiable.[11]

Socially, the world of sign value took root in the context of the modern city's impersonal environment. The closeness and dependency characteristic of traditional communities was absent in urban life, so the cultural choices structured by mass markets began to turn privatized loneliness into a way of life. The Great Depression and World War II slowed the development of a consumer society, but its development accelerated after World War II, reinforced by the rise of the new middle class, suburbanization, the diffusion of television, the growth of state and corporate bureaucracies, the enlargement of the university, and expansion of U.S. capitalism onto a global plane. By the 1970s, consumer products were proliferating and the consumer marketplace began fragmenting into niche markets. Corporate competition for consumers' dollars saturated the marketplace with commodities and commodity signs. The increasing volume and turnover of commodity signs made the construction of self-identity based on the accumulation of packaged experiences and signifiers of experience more complex.

Marcuse argued that advertising fostered a second nature that tied the individual need structure "libidinally and aggressively to the commodity form."[12] The commodity form opened a Pandora's box of individuated pleasure and desire. Marcuse viewed the transformation of human needs into the commodity form as repressive insofar as it channeled the human impulse for freedom to fit the interests of capital—and those interests were always conditioned around the reproduction of unfreedom in the form of alienated labor. Popular resistance and contestation of the premises of pseudoindividualism had already become a part of the culture by the 1950s. The Beat movement protested the insipid conformism of mass culture. Rock 'n' roll went further: it threatened to cut the libidinal and aggressive cords to the commodity form and to undo restraint; it signified rebellion. Later, hippies would refuse to be style-conscious, refuse artifice, indeed, refuse sign values. But commodity culture has been able to domesticate and coopt these contestations by turning them back into commodity signs.

The more serious and enduring threat to the commodity self lay in its own internal logic: fragmented selves began to parallel fragmented marketplaces. By 1970, the phrase "future shock" described a self bewildered by the sheer quantity of decisions that everyday life demanded—a self dictated by the pace of change in markets, rather than by its own autonomous criteria.[13] As self-identity came to depend on how individuals presented themselves as an ensemble of aestheticized commodities, there ensued a generalized cultural slide toward narcissism.[14] Narcissism became normalized in a consumer society that defined well-being in terms of youth, style, and physical appearance. Privatized and serialized reception of the electronic media further collapsed formerly distinct social roles grounded in history (time), geography (space), and sociation (community).[15] Each additional decade of promoting the commodity self has brought forward the emergence of a postmodern self constructed out of constantly shifting signifiers that are arbitrarily and tangentially connected to signifieds. The relentless circulation of meaning undermines (collapses) the signifier–signified relationship, while the codes and referent systems that feed the meaning process are drawn less from daily life than from other media representations.[16] As shared, experiential referent points and traditional grounding recede, self-construction depends upon acquiring mass-mediated images that lose their value as quickly as they are accumulated.[17] Like a "Pacman" racing helter-skelter to chew up as many dots as possible before it is destroyed itself, the postmodern self is in a feeding frenzy, gobbling up commodities and the signifiers associated with them.

Capital kept itself growing by more efficiently dominating nature and reorganizing the sphere of culture around its own commodity logic. The long-term results were predictable. Linking individuated happiness and desire to limitless consumption has resulted in the expansion of a high-intensity market economy characterized by the association of personal and societal well-being with the economics of growth.[18] Linking individual identity to consumption may have helped counter the earlier crisis tendencies toward overproduction, but when both the logic of capital and the logic of self-construction are based on unlimited consumption, environmental degradation is inevitable.

From Nature Signifiers to Green Marketing

From its inception, modern advertising used nature as a referent system from which to derive signifiers for constructing signs.[19] Nature's landscapes were used to signify experiences or qualities that urban–industrial everyday life failed to provide. A familiar theme in 1920s advertising was "The Parable of Civilization Redeemed."[20] This scenario identified civilization with "images of sloth or decadence," work with drudgery, and modern existence with "nerves" and anxiety. Advertising located the solutions to these ills in commodities aligned with meanings associated with nature: essence and purity. Advertising suggested that civilization's deficiencies could be ameliorated by consuming commodities that contained the essence of nature.

The nostalgia for nature evident in the advertising of the 1920s and 1930s gave way to the fetish of gadgetry. Progress meant conquering climate and taming the out-of-doors—witness the recreational vehicle industry and even the shopping mall industry. Leisure well-being was linked to owning state-of-the art technologies (e.g., the goal promoted by *Playboy* was to own a sleek technologized playroom with remote controlled television, stereo, bar, etc.). In this world, there was no apparent trade-off between consumption and nature—every new act of private consumption appeared *de novo* and *in abstracto*. As the years went by and capitalist domination of the infrastructure intensified, modernist architecture and urban design annulled nature, boxing it out until the 1970s, when nature became an object of veneration incorporated inside cathedrals of consumption. Prefacing a critique of the Hyatt Regency, Gitlin observed:

Everywhere nature is consumed by capital, and everywhere the middle class reaches for its private share of the vulnerable and disappearing wildness. The spirit of the Seventies whispers: If the wilderness is going to be stripped away, plowed under and paved, let's grow our own. So do markets develop to make private appropriations of that which is growing scarce.[21]

Contemporary advertising is still littered with representations of nature that signify antimodern desires. Generally, these nostalgic narratives set up a semiotic opposition between nature (the countryside) and the city. Commodities like cars and cigarettes are placed in landscape settings, labeled "natural" and juxtaposed with natural objects. Using these associations, advertising disguises both the artificial and the negative characteristics of commodities by presenting idealized images of consumption and by refusing to acknowledge the relations of production that produce the commodity.[22]

Evian's ad theme, "Our Factory," situates commodity production in images of pure (unsullied by human activity) nature. As Williamson shows, ads cook nature in order to make it appear raw. The second image here comes from Instapure's effort to tap into the value of Evian's imagery—that is, their gadget on your faucet approximates the imagery of purity of Evian's nature factory.

While sponsors' use of environmental messages can be found in magazines such as the *National Geographic* since the 1960s, the television genre known as "green" or environmental advertising did not appear until the 1980s. Unlike traditional nature advertising, which used signifiers of nature to create signifieds of desirable human traits (e.g., a "peaches-and-cream" complexion), green marketing appears to position nature itself as the subject of the ad, while the signification of nature is actually positioned to hail the viewing subject. Both the commodity and the

This Hi-Tec shoe commercial frames images from national parks to position the viewing subject as well as the company and the product as sharing in a conservationist conviction and practice. Hi-Tec constructs its sign value as ecological consciousness.

FEMALE VOICE: I could not believe the size of these trees, they were incre . . . they were huge.

MALE VOICE: That park was so peaceful.

FEMALE VOICE: I know.

MALE NARRATOR: At Hi-Tec we cannot imagine life without our national parks.

MALE VOICE: Yeah, you protect the land and you know it takes care of you.

SECOND MALE VOICE: You gotta save it all.

FEMALE VOICE: I guess if this tree fell in the forest you would hear it.

MALE NARRATOR: We're working to protect the parks. Join us! Take the step!

corporation are spoken about in terms of their impact on the environment or their affection for nature, almost distracting attention from the subtle way in which nature signifiers are mythified, that is, turned into markers of commodity sensibility. Commodities are positioned as "environmentally friendly" and corporations as caring, concerned citizens actively involved in a leadership role to save the environment.

Like the nature advertising that first responded to the economic and the social-psychological crisis of the 1920s, green marketing also responds to an economic, and a corresponding social psychological, crisis. In a cultural climate characterized by a growing awareness of environmental hazards, the problem of corporate public relations is to reposition commodities whose production and consumption may be damaging to the physical environment as "earth-friendly." By placing the green consumer and the environmentally concerned corporation together on the same high moral ground, green marketing seeks to relegitimate commodity consumption. Green marketing serves the needs of capital by legitimating both bourgeois consumption practices and corporate power. We will explore this thesis by reading, first, commodity ads that link consumption to self-construction, and second, corporate legitimation advertising that proclaims the positive impacts of corporate practices on the environment.

Consuming to Protect the Environment: Commodity Advertising

Advertisers want to signify environmental concern because they see dollar signs in environmentalism. Think of fashion and the environment, and L. L. Bean's "durable, practical products for men and women who love the outdoors" spring to mind. The functionality of L. L. Bean's product coupled with a minimalist aesthetic speaks to values inherited from the Protestant ethic and New England pragmatism which rejected the fanciful fashions of consumerism. But even though L. L. Bean associates itself with function over style, in our semiotic culture this becomes a style in itself. The "prestige of the natural" has "nothing natural about it."[23] L. L. Bean–labeled clothes not only signify durability and an outdoor lifestyle, but also bourgeois authenticity.

All consumer goods have sign values characterized by difference and hierarchy.[24] Advertisers aim at differentiating their commodity sign from other commodity signs, thereby enhancing the value of their sign. Once signs are purchased and used, their sign value is passed on to the consumer, allowing one to construct an identity differentiated from others. For example, in Ellen Tracy ads natural settings are used to stage sign value. But, unlike the clothes in an L. L. Bean catalog, the clothing in an Ellen Tracy ad does not take on the signifieds of ruggedness and durability. A rocky seacoast serves as an ideologically necessary backdrop for Ellen Tracy fashions that are not meant to be worn in this setting. Ellen Tracy, however, *greens* this conventional approach by placing this copy under each image: "The clothing . . . perfect for Spring. The background . . . perfect forever." At the bottom of the page in small print, Ellen Tracy adds another layer of legitimacy to their nature aesthetic:

Ellen Tracy is vitally concerned about the destruction of the environment. We invite you to share and join with the Nature Conservancy, an international membership organization committed to the global preservation of the natural environment.

In the 1970s, the introspective, often melancholy, look replaced the smile in upscale advertising. The commodity sign associated with upscale

Body language expresses middle-class introspection and environment concern.

fashion was *depth*—of thought and feelings.[25] Ellen Tracy now offers a fresh object (sign) of concern: nature. Incorporating depth of concern about nature into the semiotics of fashion signifies sophistication, even as it devolves into conformism.

Esprit also associated environmental concern with its name. Its spring 1990 catalog consisted of full-page photographs of young models in Esprit fashions. Adjoining pages presented close-ups of a clothing ensemble framed by a grainy earth-tone border. Framing each photograph was a politicized question:

> *Ecology or Deep Ecology? Wildlife Habitats or an Astroturf World? The End of Nature or a Techno-fix? Star Wars or Eco-raiders? Conservation or Consumption? Personal Commitments or Group Apathy? Birth Control or Population Drawdown? Green or Greed? Eco-lmmunology or Techno-Medicine? Paper or Plastic? Recycle or Resource Waste? Human Solidarity or Personal Gain? Rainforests or Acid Rain? Earth First or Man First?*

The catalog's introduction contained a lengthy monologue proclaiming Esprit's environmental concern. Esprit addressed consumer alienation from the changing seasons caused by our out-of-control economic system, "where individuals, businesses, and governments have become slaves to the gods of expansion, 'progress,' profit and excess consumption." Esprit's environmental philosophy argued for "the need to return Nature to the center of the universe."

While Esprit regards itself as an environmentally conscious company, it is also a semiotically conscious company. Esprit's previous campaign, "Inform, Don't Conform," spoke to its audience as sophisticated sign users who, like Esprit, understood how sign ensembles are social statements of individuality. Knowing the code may be everything, but Esprit gave this a twist by congratulating its consumers for not giving into pseudoindividuality, and instead using their knowledge of fashion code to articulate and communicate their own unique differences. Now, Esprit appellates its audience as environmentally conscious by speaking in the discourse of the environmental movement. We might criticize Esprit for appropriating these politically loaded categories, but Esprit has anticipated this criticism, noting "that by 'piggy-backing' our message on to the same vehicle [this catalog] can save money and time and make us feel we give our fullest attention to all concerned." Esprit even raises the question of overconsumption and calls for consumers to "evaluate carefully what they need, and buy accordingly, whether it is clothing, cars, televisions, or whatever." Esprit is concerned because "world economics based on exponential growth and expanding consumptive appetites cannot be sustained forever." Esprit itself claims to be changing its business practices to better protect the environment. The copy notes that the catalog itself is produced out of recycled paper. By talking about the environment, Esprit cloaks a central contradiction: fashion and the status accrued by wearing it are based on the principle of waste, or continuous conspicuous consumption.

Advertising promotes semiotic obsolescence, geared to nullifying current sign values in the interest of establishing new sign values.[26] In spite of its politically correct rhetoric, the Esprit catalog participates in this process of "creative destruction" necessary for sign-capital to reproduce itself. Esprit seeks to transfer the images of socially desirable persons who are also environmentally conscious to the Esprit name. Could wearing Esprit commodities signify a wearer who is environmentally commited? What is the relationship of environmental activism to the environmentally concerned look? Do Esprit's upscale earth children signify political consciousness or narcissism?

Taken from a 1993 Pepsi "Clear" campaign, scenes like this hail the alreadyness of a politically correct consumer consciousness, or how is a picture of a rhinocerous a statement about your individual identity?

According to Ewen, "Style makes statements, yet has no convictions."[27] It takes surfaces (signs) and joins them to commodities that can be purchased and worn. But what is the relationship of the sign to the person who consumes it? Are L. L. Bean clothing wearers more authentic, Ellen Tracy wearers more sophisticated, and Esprit wearers more committed than anyone else? The ability to recognize each commodity sign speaks to middle-class membership, though each sign valorizes its correlated commodity by differentiation. Environmental signifiers do not challenge the code of fashion, but instead take a position along the chain of signifiers that already make up the code.

As environmentalists have drawn attention to the depletion of the earth's resources and to the reckless practices of a throwaway society, *recycling* has become a primary signifier of environmentalism and hence a catchword attached willy-nilly to products. In part because of long-standing public service ad campaigns, there is widespread popular acceptance of recycling consumer-goods packaging: glass, paper, aluminum cans, and plastic. The recycling of product containers affords many firms a glib opportunity to position themselves as both pro-environment and consumer-friendly. Products such as Tide and Downy hail women with images of container recycling done for their children's future well-being. An ad for Downy Refill presents a dramatization of the personal testimony of "Natalie Reid of Minneapolis" who begins by rededucating us: "Remember when we just threw it all away and figured there was just some big hole where trash would disappear. Well it hasn't."

Constructing the green consumer: The magic of Downy Refill can keep the environment's future clean and green, and your children healthy.

But of course the Downy Refill container can be crushed, compressed in front of our eyes and like a magic trick made to resolve that trash problem. Save money, cut down on waste, and "the best part is, I'm helping to make the future a little better for my kids." The salience of children as a signifier of environmental wellness cannot be overstated.

As an instance of how environmental rhetoric has been appropriated, "recycling" has increasingly become reduced to a signifier that can be attached to virtually any object. A Toro lawnmower ad appeared in *USA Today* on Earth Day 1990. Next to an image of piled grass clippings was this elaborate argument:

> ### *Introducing a lawnmower that can solve America's fastest growing recycling problem.*
>
> *Lawn debris. A healthy 1000 square foot lawn can generate up to 500 pounds of grass clippings a year. The solution isn't more landfills. It's a more effective lawnmower. The new Toro Recycler lawnmower. With the Toro Recycler, you get a lawn that's as beautiful and well-manicured as a lawn cut with a bagging lawnmower. But the real beauty of it is you don't have to bag. Since you don't generate lawn clippings, you won't be contributing to overcrowded landfills. You'll have no problem complying with lawn debris disposal laws. And you'll save time—mowing with the Toro Recycler is up to 38% faster than with a bagging lawnmower. The recycled clippings even help your lawn grow better by releasing beneficial nutrients and water to the soil as they decompose . . . unlike mulching lawnmowers, which can leave unsightly clippings on top of your lawn, the Toro Recycler injects clippings deep below the surface. . . . For more information, visit your Toro dealer. Ask him about environmental issues and the status of lawn debris legislation in your area. You'll be doing something good for the environment. And good for your lawn.*

Must we forego a beautiful lawn in the name of environmentalism? The dilemma between middle-class aesthetics and the greening of middle-class morality has, according to Toro, a technological resolution. The Toro Recycler conveniently reintegrates morality and aesthetics by providing a technologically superior device with "a unique airflow pattern that re-directs grass clippings downward." Unlike recycling that demands labor, the Toro does it for you. And as a bonus, "you'll have no problem complying with lawn debris disposal laws." Suburban environmentalism can be reconciled with one's life-style without changing that life-style. Bourgeois aesthetics (a beautiful lawn) and civic morality (complying with lawn debris laws) can be reconciled because "you'll be doing something good for the environment. And good for your lawn." This advertising pitch depoliticizes the recycling issue, turning it into a question of selecting the technically correct commodity. And yet the ad ends by encouraging the reader to politicize these issues, teaming with "your Toro dealer to do something good for the environment." There is absolutely no hint of conflict—no conflict of views, no conflict of interests. Recommending your Toro dealer as a source of objective, reliable information about recycling legislation suggests that the appropriate unit of political action is the act of consumption, and the appropriate opinion leader is your commodity dealer.

The Toro ad exemplifies how technological solutions take on meaning at the intersection of competing discourses. Middle-class consumption practices intersect with the social discourse of environmentalists—but this is all framed by the interests of a corporate capitalist firm.[28] Green advertising, like any advertising appeal, aims at stimulating demand for a product. Here, in the lawnmower industry, devising the new need still promotes obsolescence. While your new Toro Recycler "injects clippings deep below the surface," your old lawnmower is headed for the dump. Toro has taken a real problem, the overcrowded landfill, and invented a solution that co-opts the politics of recycling.

Greening product lines serve two agendas: to expand market share by using green respect as a sign that appeals to consumers who have environmental concerns, and to position companies as socially and environmentally responsible. Linking these agendas is another approach that promises to give a portion of every purchase to an organization that works to preserve the environment. The logic of this appeal is to increase the volume of consumption in order to do the most good for environmental protection.

Now The Card
That's Accepted In More Places
Also Protects More Places

This headline frames a collage of scenes: a whale skimming along the surface of still water, a single blue egg in a nest, a raccoon clutching the bark of a tree, a herd of grazing bighorn sheep, silhouetted wildebeests at sunset, and a family of four. The text goes on to explain:

> *Every time you use the Sierra Club Visa Card, you'll be helping the Sierra Club—the group that's charged with preserving the environment. And since our card is accepted in more places around the world, it's easier than ever for you to help save the most beautiful places on Earth.*

Mortised in the copy is the Visa Card with an image of a mountain lake on it. Operating in a marketplace that runs on the notion that everything should not only be available to anyone who has the credit to afford it, but also be available instantaneously, a never-quite-quenched *sign appetite* results in consumption levels that go beyond what a functioning social and physical environment can tolerate. The time and space between the desire for a commodity and access to that commodity has shrunk to the vanishing point when all one needs is a credit card, a cellular phone, and Federal Express. The world economy now works on the related principles of immediate gratification and convenience. Where the global economy can join electronic and phone transactions with just-in-time production systems (a.k.a. flexible accumulation), it completes the circulation cycle the most quickly. Ironically, capitalism thwarts itself in achieving this "perfect" circulation process, precisely because it is exhausting its ability to environmentally reproduce itself—it is running out of unspoiled nature to convert into exchange values. The acquisitive culture of the bourgeoisie has turned into a global commodity culture with global environmental impacts.[29]

A primary goal of green marketing is the legitimation of production and consumption practices. Marketing strategies not only weave their way through the contradictions inherent in an economic system driven by profit and expansion, but also through a cultural system driven by bourgeois no-

As the technology of the cellular phone shrinks the world to the vanishing point, rustic and rural landscapes appear as prominent signifiers of space for MobiLink and Cellular One. Is this because "the peak of speed is the extermination of space"? (Virilio and Lotringer, 1983, p. 74).

tions of individuality in which self-construction is understood as an outcome of consumption.[30] The Sierra Club Visa Card offered by Chase Bank legitimates consumption as an Earth-protecting strategy since using one's Sierra Club Visa Card means monies will be donated to that environmental organization every time one makes a purchase. Plastic credit cards simultaneously make accessible formerly remote spaces, while also claiming to protect them. Like ecotourism, this permits further gratification of individual desires while allowing consumers to see themselves as ecologically aware. It also defines activism as the giving of contributions to *the* official national organization "charged with preserving the environment." Purchases are transformed into political tokens and chits. Ads like this reposition the expression of individuality through the accumulation of commodity signs as a positive ethic, so that consuming *for a purpose* differentiates oneself in relation to other sign wearers.

Deflecting Green Criticism: Legitimation Advertising

Since Earth Day in 1989, legitimation ads with environmental messages have become part of the television wallpaper of daily life. Corporations concerned about governmental regulations and restrictions on resource extraction and commodity production have adopted television ads as a method of contesting state-enforced restrictions.[31] Usually, environmentally motivated legitimation advertising is joined to a multipronged strategy: First, establish a powerful lobbyist presence at the political center. Second, support front groups that take on names that appear to signify environmental concern for the purpose of subverting legislation that might prove adverse to corporate profit rates. Advertising is the third tool and the locus of public relations campaigns aimed at neutralizing public support for environmentalist legislation—in a sense, the advertising provides covering fire so the lobbyists can quietly do their work. The battles are often won in the lobbying trenches, but they cannot be won if public opinion, or more importantly, public opinion amplified by the television media, keeps attention focused on images of environmental degradation.

Corporations have put considerable energy into trying to harness the political momentum of the environmentalist movement by coopting its institutions and appropriating its symbols. Environmental organizations currently possess high sign value because of their concerns about preserving the natural environment, other species, and human health. The value of an organizational sign draws on the organization's history, its philosophy, its level and form of activism, its size, its cultural productions (magazines, films, photographs), its political practices, and its own sign associations.[32] The environmental organization market is a competitive market in which image construction is essential to organizational vitality. To accumulate capital through memberships, donations, and marketing commodities, environmental organizations must position themselves as legitimate, potent, and effective.[33] One source of capital is the corporation. When an organization accepts corporate funding it risks devaluing its own political credibility due to its association with the corporate donor, and worse, it also risks coopting its political practices.[34] Simply to allow the name of an environmental organization to appear in a corporation's ad allows for the association and transfer of value to be made. Association, sharing the same advertising frame, is the process by which currency is transferred and sign value is accumulated. The environmental organization gets a little capital and publicity, a free mention, while the corporate firm draws on the moral currency of supporting just and popular environmentalist causes. For example, Beatrice/Hunt-Wesson distribute World Wildlife Fund Greeting Cards as a promotional strategy. Other strategies hail consumers by allying them to the corporation as partners devoted to nature: "You can help preserve the beauty of America's parks. James River Corporation and your local retailer will jointly make a donation to your state parks when you buy Brawny Towels, Northern Napkins, or Bathroom Tissue for a limited time." Still another strategy involves corporations creating their own front organizations and their own logos of environmental presence.

The sign of Coors's in-house environmental organization, "Pure Water 2000."

Preserving the Image of Nature

With the proliferation of cable channels, the market for nature specials has greatly expanded. The Discovery Channel, the Learning Channel, Turner Broadcasting Services, as well as the Public Broadcasting System, sustain a continuous flow of nature programs. The specials with the most prestige tend to be produced by the National Geographic, the National Audubon Society, and the Cousteau Society. Nature programming is framed as educational rather than entertaining, and its upscale audiences are targeted by advertisers because they are opinion leaders.

Chevron's ads sponsoring a National Geographic Special on PBS position Chevron as a responsible corporate citizen. One ad pictured the fiery blush of a sunset sky and a peaceful swampscape reflecting the red hues. In the distance, a silhouetted row of trees separate swamp from sky. Identified as a delta in the Kalahari Desert in Botswana, this scene is boldly framed: "WE THINK TELEVISION SHOULD CELEBRATE THE ENVIRONMENT NOT POLLUTE IT." The ad goes on:

> *"Many would argue the airways are contaminated. Clogged with the irrelevant belching the irresponsible. Still there is an alternative. One that lets you escape your own world to exciting new ones. It's public television. And the National Geographic Special with their celebration of the planet and all who share it. The people of Chevron are proud to bring you every joyous dramatic enlightening minute of them."*

GIVING THOUGHT TO TELEVISION

The Chevron logo punctuates and completes the text. While the photograph of the Kalahari appears realistic, it has been selected and constructed to meet the needs of *National Geographic* and Chevron, and the logic of advertising. The image is driven by the logic of spectacle. Nature is located someplace else; it is foreign, exotic, and untouched by human activity. Real nature, defined in terms of less developed regions such as Africa, has the power to let "you escape your own world," a world of bad television "clogged with the irrelevant belching the irresponsible." Nature is defined as the space outside the spectacle.

The spectacular quality of the photograph is as much a function of filter, f-stop, film stock, and printing as it is a quality of any actual relationship of light to landscape. The foreground is completely blackened to provide space for the bold white copy that frames the landscape without appearing to intrude into it. As much as this is a representation of an actual landscape, it is also an image of an image that stands for a National Geographic special.

Like PBS documentaries, this Epson computer ad uses cinema codes such as aspect ratio, exotic signifiers of nature and culture, and an "environmental consultant" who functions as an anthropologist tour guide.

There is a second reading of the Chevron ad. The ad does not just promote a National Geographic special, but an energy corporation. The "We" in the ad may refer to National Geographic, PBS, or all of us who celebrate the planet, but it is spoken by Chevron. The ad offers the analogy that just as PBS stands in contrast to commercial television, so Chevron stands in contrast to irresponsible industrial corporations. Just as PBS provides an alternative to contaminated airways, "clogged with the irrelevant belching the irresponsible," Chevron positions itself as an alternative to environmentally irresponsible businesses.[35] This is the same Chevron that was a principal backer of the campaign against California Proposition 128, known as "Big Green." In this ad, Chevron has appropriated National Geographic's vision of nature which they then celebrate as a visual experience. The audience can partake in this celebration by watching the special and experiencing pleasure and enlightenment. Indeed, Chevron's observance of nature's visual beauty is dedicated less to its preservation than to buffering their business practices that run counter to the integrity of nature's delicate balance. The spectacle of nature has replaced lived nature as an object of concern.

The Restorative Power of Science

The oil, chemical, and plastics industries confront perennial public relations problems over their pollution-producing practices. Accidents such as that at the Union Carbide plant in Bhopal or with the *Exxon Valdez* have spurred efforts to push for increased government regulation of these industries, so firms in this industry consider it imperative to appear responsible and public-spirited. A pervasive theme in their advertising campaigns is the narrative of how their corporate direction of science has already created enlightened solutions to aid in the restoration of the planet. One ad for Du Pont purported to show an "overwhelmingly positive" response from seals, otters, ducks, geese, penguins, and dolphins as they "applaud" (clap, bark, honk) the environmental safety and cleanliness made possible by "Du Pont's pioneer[ing] use of new double-hulled oil tankers in order to safeguard the environment." The ad registers a joyful, sunny sequence of sea species choreographed and framed by the stirring music of Beethoven's "Ode to Joy."

Du Pont resorts to spectacular nature photography to create amnesia about their interventions into nature.

The ad concludes with the screen overlay of Du Pont's familiar tag line, "Better things for better living" which has, for years, been Du Pont's way of assuring us that their technology will make the other discomforts of capitalist relations palatable. Unfortunately, as Doyle has detailed, this Du Pont ad is an egregious distortion of the Du Pont record of environmental stewardship. Du Pont's Conoco division did not actually have either of its double hulled ships in operation until 1992, and since double-hull ships have been in use for more than 20 years, the claim to be "pioneers" was an exaggeration.[36] More importantly, this ad misrepresents the general environmental record of Du Pont. Du Pont remains the leading corporate polluter in the United States, with its many subsidiaries producing pollution discharges four and one half times greater than the combined total of other significant polluters including Dow, Union Carbide, W.R. Grace, and PPG in 1989. According to Doyle, "Among the Fortune top ten in 1989, Du Pont had the highest ratio of pollution to profit and the lowest value of sales generated per pound of pollution."[37] And Du Pont continues to engage in ocean dumping of toxic chemicals and in the production of chemicals that deplete the ozone layer.[38] There is considerable irony in the fact that Du Pont's ads chronicle their lifesaving technological contributions in the field of early cancer detection (improved mammography devices), while they remain silent about the ways in which their science may have unleashed toxicological and carcinogenic risks.

A Phillips Petroleum ad featuring a sketch of an empty eggshell and a bird's footprint likewise endorses managed science:

The eagle has landed.

. . . where few bald eagle nests have produced young in the last 50 years. Using precious eggs and dedicated effort, the Sutton Avian Research Center is successfully raising eaglets from fuzzy to fierce. And releasing them into the habitats bald eagles used to call home. Phillips Petroleum supports this unique program to re-establish our endangered national symbol. After all, if Man can land an Eagle on the moon, he can surely keep them landing on earth.

Saluting the space program's technological achievement is meant to reassure us that we can control and manage earth's environment. The lunar landing provides a symbolic achievement to signify generic Man's scientific omnipotence. By using the correlative "eagle," the space program and the avian program are placed in nominal equivalence. If science can put a spacecraft named *Eagle* on the moon, it surely can return eagles to their habitats. Equivalence is established by association, not by logic.

Since the bald eagle is a national symbol, it provides an ideal indicator species for any corporation that professes concern for the environment. But, the Phillips ad campaign conveniently glosses over why bald eagles had such trouble producing young in the last 50 years. What has been the impact of the energy industry on the bald eagle's habitat and the habitat of other species? Have fertilizers and pesticides produced by chemical companies weakened eggshells so that eagles now have to be hatched in captivity?

A comparable TV ad by Weyerhaeuser pictures the bald eagle as "the overseer of the land below" while Weyerhaeuser presents themselves as the "overseer" of the Eagle, and by symbolic extension, of nature:

> *"The bald eagle. Symbol of freedom. Ruler of the sky and keen overseer of the land below. A stately reminder that we must manage our commercial forests so that they are compatible with the basic needs of wildlife. It's the job of Bob Anderson, Weyerhaeuser wildlife biologist to develop procedures to protect the eagles residing on Weyerhaeuser lands . . . ."*

Using science and technology as tools for more efficiently extracting raw resources has had side effects on species, like eliminating their habitats, but this vanishes in corporate narratives of restoration and preservation.

In contemporary Western society, Marcuse perceived that "in the realm of culture, the new totalitarian manifests itself precisely in a harmonizing pluralism, where the most contradictory works and truths peacefully coexist in indifference."[39] Corporate legitimation advertising with environmental themes often juxtaposes opposites in an effort to rehabilitate the environmental impacts of corporate practices. The mechanized clearcutting of forests can be renamed "managed harvesting," for practices destructive to natural areas can be framed to appear beneficial, and actions mandated by law can be made to appear voluntary. Observe how another oil company, Chevron, claims to go beyond restoration

The bald eagle is a frequently abstracted signifier in TV ads. Match these eagle images to their corporate sponsors: Anheuser Busch; Hi-Tec; Weyerhaeuser.

Answers:
1): Hi-Tec
2): Anheuser Busch
3): Weyerhaeuser

to create a superior habitat. A Chevron ad in *Audubon* magazine frames a sketch of birds, and reframes the magnitude of their pollution impacts:

The shorebirds who found a new wetland.

There's a saltwater wetland in Mississippi at the edge of a pine forest. It's a place nature might have made. But it actually was created a few years ago by people who work in the nearby refinery. They not only agreed to replace an existing wetland but made it even more valuable as a wildlife habitat. Now herons and whimbirds, egrets and plovers are among more than a dozen kinds of birds that congregate there to rest and feed. Do people need to create new places so that nature can spread its wings?

People Do

Though the *Chevron* plant in Pascagoula, Mississippi, is ranked at number 290 for toxic releases on the National Wildlife Federation's Toxic 500 list, Chevron presents itself as a corporation that serves wildlife interests.[40] The ad's "People Do" tag line pushes a voluntaristic environmental agenda. Yet when asked for information about its restoration project, Chevron responded with a one-page sheet noting that Chevron needed to expand its facility and so filled in wetlands areas "in accord with state and federal permit conditions," took "measures to mitigate adverse effects" on others, and "offset any unavoidable impacts" by "construction of a replacement habitat" that is a mere 25 acres in size.

A consistent theme in these advertising narratives is that progress and nature coexist because the corporation cannot only replace the habitat, but improve on nature. Weyerhaeuser counters concerns about clear-cutting of old-growth timber and the destruction of forest habitats by claiming that "we can grow better forests than nature" on planned tree farms. Chevron has "excavated a new marsh from a planted pine forest to a range of depths and grades comparable to those found on the natural marsh," transplanted grasses "fertilized to accelerate colonization," built an "artificial dune" and "stabilized (it) against erosion."

Science and technology are represented in corporate ads as the mechanism of progress, the power behind humanitarian advances. What's more, they are always called on to clean up the messes that "people" have made for themselves. Pollution and environmental degradation are normally presented as things that "just happened." Sometimes an ad will attribute human agency to the generic human condition. More often, the forces that created ecological pollution are unspecified. Few—very few—corporate ads actually include any photographic images of environmental pollution. Crucial to understanding these ads is what is visually absent. The Du Pont ad is a perfect example: the part of the world that Du Pont claims responsibility for is nothing but clean seas, sunny skies, and happy wildlife species. An exception to the rule is an Archer Daniels Midland ad that openly confronts the imagery of air pollution with a story about carbon monoxide.

Archer Daniels Midland (ADM) surprised viewers with an ad campaign that squarely addresses the crisis of air pollution and landfills in our country. These ads typically appear on Sunday morning interview shows, and begin as if they are public service advertisements that critically address a public problem. One such ad begins by violating a key rule of corporate ads: it directly acknowledges air quality problems and attributes them to our history of burning hydrocarbons in our automobiles. A trustworthy male voiceover narrates:

> *"For as long as we've been pumping gasoline, we've been pumping poisonous carbon monoxide into the air. It wasn't a major problem at first, there were simply fewer cars on the road. But over the years as we pumped more gasoline, our carbon monoxide emissions have grown too. And even though today's cleaner burning cars have helped reduce carbon monoxide levels, the problem persists [pause] for everyone."*

History does have another side! The car as a means of dominating nature imperils future generations of children. Our cars—those gleaming totems that have been made to signify our identities and anchor the commodity self—have environmentally destructive side effects. Damage to our atmosphere is signified by combining tense, foreboding music with black and white film footage. Still, the ad recovers this ground by proclaiming a clever, scientific, practical solution that will allow us to hold on to our cars as a basic engine of our capitalist political economy. The voiceover continues:

> *"But part of a solution is already here. Ethanol blended fuels. Ethanol blends reduce deadly carbon monoxide emissions significantly and help hold down ozone pollution in our cities. And a detergent in ethanol helps keep engines burning cleanly. That makes one thing perfectly clear: the more ethanol blends we pump into our cars, the less carbon monoxide we pump into our lungs."*

When ADM's ethanol product enters the scene to resolve the problem of air pollution, the music shifts to an airy, melodic piano counterpart to a naturally colored world. The decisive moment of transition comes when a young boy's face is replaced by a dissolve overlay of the imagery of "Superunleaded." The structure of signification is worth dwelling on here. The narrative of the ad has been made to pivot symbolically on the boy's face: he represents that which is endangered by our past pollution sins. His value is the measure of what ethanol is worth to us. The pictorial superimposition of the boy's face and the ethanol gas pump produce this ad's commodity sign. This blond child's face connotes "the heartland," "the future," and "American" (he becomes a signifier of all that is golden and full of possibility in America)—the signifiers joined together compose a signified on the paradigmatic axis. The boy's face signifies the product, and the product signifies his cherubic face.[41] This obvious narrative turning point of the ad is reinforced by the next scene which literally centers the meaning of Superunleaded/everyman's child in the blended fluid that comes from the gas nozzle. During the first part of the ad devoted to defining the problem of air pollution, ominous music built while traffic mounted in volume and density; this pictorial narrative was

Superunleaded Boy. This blended overlay of the dissovled signifiers of Superunleaded gasoline and childhood marks the dramatic turning point in the ADM ad away from the dangers of pollution to a healthy environmental future because of the new ethanol blend. Combined with the blond cherubic face, the baseball cap provides a powerful signifier of Americanicity. In color, green tones replaced ominous gray shadings. The overlay allows the Superunleaded to be both part of the foreground and the background. Its presence as a heading clearly frames our negotiation of this picture, if only because Superunleaded is now the emblem on his cap and the stamp across his head.

assembled to point to a historical pattern from the 1920s to the 1980s. Whereas the first half of the ad carefully matched visual signifier and verbal signifier in every scene, after the watershed scene of the boy/overlay with "Super-Unleaded," the spoken signifiers of emissions and gasoline are framed by nonthreatening visual signifiers of greenery and safety—in other words, they are made to signify their opposite.

Implicitly, ads like this fall back on an ideology of nature that goes back to the Enlightenment: nature is a mechanism that can be studied, mastered, and then adjusted to make it run better. We are left to marvel at the ingenuity of the ADM solution: scientifically unwrapping the secret of turning corn—a renewable resource—into a fuel that burns with less carbon monoxide by-product relieves us of those messy and irrational political solutions, and reminds us that our problems can best be handled by the marriage of the two most rational forces known to Western *man*: markets and science.[42]

The everyday operation and reproduction of capital entails costs that are manifest as social and governmental costs. As long as it was not defined as a problem and could be ignored, air pollution was a hidden cost. But eventually it became perceived as reducing the quality of life and became a matter of concern for the urban middle classes. As they politically registered their concerns on the state, there ensued increased regulation, which meant increased economic costs.[43] By the latter decades of the 20th century, capitalist rationalization of production has become so well developed in its ability to effectively dominate nature that it has impaired its own ability to sufficiently reproduce nature (air, water, soil, trees, etc). The constant drive to expand productivity ultimately negates itself, until the costs of protecting and remedying prior decades of environmental damage constitute unproductive expenditures from a capitalist perspective—that is, they are both a drain on new capital investment and a barrier to increased productivity or profitability.[44]

Over time, the continuous cycle of capitalist production has depleted the environmental conditions of production to the point that it imperils productivity. In the past relationship between capitalist civil society and the state, some costs of reproducing the labor force and the natural resources that premise continuous production were passed along to the state. Though capitalists have extracted raw resources as if they were commodities, they have not historically had to bear the costs of replenishing the stock of nature. All that has changed in recent decades as new scarcities have been generated. Increasing state regulation of public resources such as forest timberlands, the oceans, water, and air has placed limits on profit growth. Because the politically charged process of state regulation has introduced exogenous factors into their market calculus, capital has battled politically against environmentalist forces seeking to restrict intrusions into nature. These industrial forces have been seeking the leeway to turn the process of replenishing resource supply (e.g., tree farms, ethanol) into new avenues of capital investment, while minimizing or eliminating existing regulatory restrictions. Corporate giants like Weyerhaeuser, whose primary commodity is a raw resource, trees, use television ads to promote themselves as far-seeing managers of the environment, and thereby attempt to ideologically neutralize social movements which seek to politicize the environmental conditions of production.

The Spectacle of the Environment

An eruption of consumer ads celebrated the 20th anniversary of Earth Day by attaching themselves to issues of environment concern. Advertising banners in *USA Today* trumpeted, "this year McDonald's wants to buy $100,000,000 worth of recycled materials," and "Everyday is Earth Day for American Cattleman." Filtered through the mass media, Earth Day spectacularized our relationship with the environment, just as the Super Bowl spectacularizes our relationship with sport, and Mother's Day spectacularizes our familial relationships. The National Cattlemen's Association, McDonald's and the many other Earth Day advertisers signified their concern by buying ad space to position themselves as benevolent, caring entities who believe in the well-being of the social whole, if not now, at least in the future (or was it the past?).

The relationship of the spectacle to actual practice is always suspect. Cattle production, for example, although an inefficient way to produce protein, is framed as an environmentally sound practice because cattle consume grass and water. Putting aside the health costs set in motion by serving saturated fat to 30 to 40 million people a day, the volume of ground beef necessary to keep the hamburger industry growing has taken an enormous toll on the environment and on impoverished populations in Central and South America.[45] Industrialized beef entails clearing forested areas, which has forced peasants to migrate to areas unsuited to agricultural production, where soils are further ruined by their efforts to produce commodity values. This part of the story was conveniently left out by McDonald's and the Catttlemen's Association. Instead, McDonald's has used marketing and advertising techniques to associate itself with core American values: the family, the achieving athlete (the Olympics), seriously ill children (Ronald McDonald's House), and now the environment (McRecycle USA). While McDonald's publically declared the commitment to the environment by volunteering that they had spent $100,000,000 on buying recycling materials, in 1989 they spent $774,400,000 in U.S. advertising alone, and were ranked 7th in U.S. advertising expenditures. Their worldwide sales exceeded $6 billion, while systemwide sales were over $17 billion.

The spectacle presents the isolated appearance as having greater significance than the actual relationships engaged in getting their product to market.

Extravaganzas such as Earth Day can easily distract from the routine character of the spectacle in everyday media. Indeed, we see so many spectacularized images of nature that no single image any longer appears all that spectacular. Like the production of commodities, the production of representations is influenced by market logic and shaped via media codes. The spectacle is not simply an event but a relationship between representations and reality in which exaggerated or dramatized repre-

This Weyerhaeuser ad used opera music to frame tree replanting as a quasi-religious experience. The radiant beams of light streaming down onto the forest floor signify a romantic reverance for God's nature that Weyerhaeuser claims its stewardship preserves.

This image from a US Air ad not only exemplifies the spectacular representations that the tourist industry routinely commodifies, it also reminds us that the geography of the spectacle is placeless. It is, to paraphrase Roland Barthes, "everywhere and nowhere."

sentations frame commodity interests. In the society of the spectacle, nature is conceptually carved into discrete scenes. Just as easily as the familiar imagery of a nuclear mushroom cloud can be relocated within a sequence of images in a sneaker ad, so too the spectacle sets nature signifiers free to roam.

Decontextualized images take on such importance in the spectacle that they eclipse the places they refer to. This gives rise to generic images of nature: floating signifiers that can be bent to the political interests of those who sponsor and narrate these spectacular moments. Spectacularized images of nature become dislocated and place-

less. The beautiful picture of a mountain range becomes just that, a beautiful picture of a mountain range in search of a meaningful association. Disjointed from geographical space, spectacular nature is nature distilled, available to signify the semiotic opposite of civilization. Supported by inspirational music drawn from opera and classical music, firms such as Weyerhaeuser and Du Pont frame the majestic beauty of nature as standing for the ways in which these corporations behave with regard to the environment. In the spectacle of nature assembled by Anheuser-

Anheuser-Busch positions themselves as a contemporary Noah: "The future belongs to the young, but its promise rests in all our hands today. At Seaworld and Busch Gardens we're working for a brighter tomorrow. By establishing the Busch wildlife preserve and the Seaworld Research Institute, we're moving to preserve that which has been given to us in trust. At Anheuser-Busch we realize that if we're to make way for the generations to come we must all work to preserve what we have today." These spectacular images omit all sense of context—namely, theme parks and caged habitats. In the spectacle every image becomes roughly equivalent—each is a thing of beauty or an object of cuteness; in this ad, each animal photograph is made to stand for the goodness of the Anheuser-Busch sign.

Busch, nature is presented as equivalent to the sum of the scenes rather than as relationships. Nature is never negated in the spectacular space of television commercials. Indeed, the power of frames creates critical absences: for example, the Anheuser-Busch ad pictured above has gone to great lengths to not show the caged conditions in which animals are kept. The emotional presentation of these species' images encourages viewers to forget that Sea World is a theme park where species are packaged and presented for tourist consumption as a simulated experience of nature. Sea World is a humanly constructed reenactment of nature designed to simulate the real thing in such a way that it can be rationally managed day after day. The Sea World ad presents a replica twice removed from its connoted referents.

Personal testaments or testimonial soundbites from corporate employees appear to ground the spectacle by reinstituting the codes of realism. These present themselves as not being part of the spectacle, but of course, insofar as they rest on coded framing practices, they are. The following 1992 GM commercial mixed/alternated hyperreal codes to indicate the scientific testing of the electronic engine controls, catalytic converters, and alternative fuels with heavily colorized and aestheticized scenes of nature enhanced in beauty—nature that has had a facelift—nature that is less real than real, but more beautiful than the places we inhabit. The hyperediting style takes us to Debbie Madigan, GM electrical engineer, who looks directly into the camera while riding a stationary bike and bluntly asserts: "Friends ask me if I believe this company is committed to the environment. I don't believe it, I know it because it's people like me who are General Motors." Similarly, the presumption in ads for Georgia Pacific and the Committee on Nuclear Awareness and Waste Management, Inc., is that employees identified by name testify to a higher level of authenticity of corporate concern for the environment.

From left to right: GM scientists presented in grainy hyperreal codes. Next is a shot of a computer-generated screen included as a signifier of advanced science. Third is employee Debbie Madigan, interviewed in the codes of straight realism. Fourth is the hyperstylized and hypercolorized image of nature—a pond in which the car is perfectly mirrored. The car is thus aestheticized by its place in nature, a presence not only mirrored in romanticized nature, but a presence that leaves nature pristinely undisturbed, as perfect as art.

The Greening of Commodity Signs

Although unable to gain control of state environmental policy, a diverse group of environmental organizations did gain a foothold in the news and entertainment media during the 1980s. Environmental politics has created a cultural climate in which the appearance of being environmentally *unfriendly* can be poison to corporate profits. Because of their vast power, corporations require either a shield of invisibility or of public legitimacy, and the environmentalist movement threatens to tarnish that legitimacy. Diminished legitimacy limits the ability of corporate lobbies to block expanding state regulation of industrial production practices as they impact the environment. So, too, the stigma of environmental indifference can also negatively impact sales. When it comes to the environment, image has become a precarious commodity in the world of political economy.

Green marketing has responded to the perceived moral authority of the environmental movement. Corporations and ad agencies now consult opinion polls and surveys to gauge the life-style importance of environmentalism: Are environmental issues likely to influence changes in purchasing practices? As a marketing approach, *green* aims to sweeten the corporate image along with the product.[46] But corporate environmental practices are bounded by the structure of global capitalist markets, the history of technology, consumer demands, and regulatory politics.[47] The desire to appear environmentally friendly and the ability to actually operate in an environmentally friendly manner and still maintain acceptable profit margins may result in significant distance between the commodity practice and the commodity sign.[48] In a media society the only thing worse than having no sign is having a besmirched sign. Remember when Mobil Chemical Co. was exposed for deceptive advertising and consumer fraud because they claimed their Hefty garbage bags were biodegradable and they weren't?

Green marketing sanctions consumption by separating the act of consumption in general from its impact on the environment. Suggesting that credit card purchases are benign when a donation is made to an environmental group, or positioning recycling as the panacea for environmental destruction are tactics that legitimate middle-class consumption practices and life-styles. By hailing and naming the consumer as environmentally aware, green marketing legitimates consumption as environmentally positive action: to consume *green commodity signs* is to consume with a sophisticated and "clean" political consciousness. While environmental advertising does not necessarily increase consumption, it legitimates life-styles based on overconsumption. People can eat at McDonald's, wear fashionable clothes, mow their lawns, use cosmetics, and go into debt all in the name of environmental concern.[49] Does it really make a difference whether we buy fast food at Burger King or Wendy's or McDonald's, or pump gas from Chevron or Phillip's or Exxon? Green marketing insists these are important choices because rational consumption stabilizes a balanced and healthy environment. More consequential, green marketing confuses and blurs the issues of what are environmentally destructive practices, thus making it difficult for most people to evaluate which corporations are environmentally friendly.

Do consumers have the power to transform economic–social–environmental relationships via their commodity choices? This position is being translated into popular literature (Shopping for a Better World), labeling (Green Seal vs. Green Cross), and legislation (*The Green Report: Findings and Preliminary Recommendations for Responsible Environmental Advertising*). The Earth Day media hype of television educating individuals to become "earth-friendly" consumers was readily redirected by corporate marketing into green labels and signs. We suspect the reliance on green labels has self-contradictory consequences: they may marginally increase environmental awareness as a general catchphrase; but they also cloud political discourse regarding the environment in a swirl of commodity signs that blocks out critical questions about control over the means of production! Barry Commoner argues that "what a green seal does is to obviate a need for understanding. It lets the public off the hook again, and puts the responsibility for determining what is environmentally correct back in the hands of others."[50] Corporate capital's disproportionate access to, and control over, the means of producing signs enables them to redirect these signs to depoliticize environmental issues—thereby permitting the most important issues to be negotiated by government technocrats and corporate technocrats. A related problem that emerges from the debate on green signs is the degree of abbreviation created by the process of substituting a sign for a body of knowledge. Setting aside for the moment the question of whose evaluation process is valid and superior, slapping a Green Seal or a Green Cross across a package has contradictory social implications. Initially, this may be a method of politicizing the act of consumption, but we have also observed its quick routinization—an act of faith that the self-proclaimed trustees of environmental conscientiousness know their business and will not compromise their standards for financial gain.

Relying on signs to fight for environmental change is a double-edged sword: they may provide a tool for fighting the ideological war of opinion polling and so on, but they continue to fight the battle on the terrain staked out by capital.[51] A more realistic strategy for countering the structural roots of environmental destruction begins with Leiss's (1976) call for the formation of a conserver society built on principles of decentralized production, reconstruction of the socialized self around nonconsumption strategies, demilitarization, and the reduction of multinational corporate power. The stimulation of desire by advertising will not likely blunt social and ecological catastrophe. As long as the construction of self-identity is based upon the accumulation and display of commodity signs, it is unlikely that the formation of a conserver, ecologically sound society will occur. By assuring us that if we consume properly, the Earth can sustain a global economic order based on high levels of consumption, green advertising glosses over these central contradictions.

7 *The Corporate Politics of Sign Values*

THE POWER of advertising lies in its ability to photographically frame and redefine our meanings and our experiences and then turn them into meanings that are consonant with corporate interests. This power to recontextualize and reframe photographic images has put advertising at the center of contemporary redefinitions of individuality, freedom, and democracy in relation to corporate symbols.

Television advertising campaigns have become a primary venue in which corporations stage public relations campaigns devoted to corporate image building. As Harvey states:

> Competition in the image-building trade becomes a vital aspect of inter-firm competition. Success is so plainly profitable that investment in image-building (sponsoring the arts, exhibitions, television productions, new buildings, as well as direct marketing) becomes as important as investment in new plant and machinery. The images serve to establish identity in the marketplace.[1]

This competition in the television image-building trade centers on the production of *sign values*. As we have already argued, ads arrange, organize, and steer the meanings of images into signs that can be inscribed on products; they are always geared to transferring the value of one meaning system to another. Corporations are no different than commodities in this regard. Just as consumer-goods ads are structured to engineer an exchange of meanings, corporate ads are structured by the same principal of exchange to generate *currency* for a corporate name. Whereas consumer-goods ads help arrange commodity sign production, corporate advertising engages in corporate-sign construction, especially the construction of *legitimation signs*.

Business publications use the term *corporate advertising* as a catchall category

A GE corporate sign value formed at the conclusion of GE ad celebrating the "light of freedom" in Hungary.

that includes *image advertising, identity advertising,* and *advocacy* or *issue advertising.*[2] Corporate ads tend to be non-product-oriented, geared not to producing immediate sales, but to positioning a company for better sales. The marketing of corporate image usually involves managing visual perceptions of corporate personalities. Among the subsets of corporate advertising, we propose the terminology of *legitimation ads* to designate those ads that address general themes about the relationship between corporate business morality and the public trust. The overarching agenda of these ads—whether they stress the social benefits of private profits, or promote the compatibility of industry with a healthy environment, or deny corporate political clout—is the legitimation of corporate economic and political power.[3] What we call legitimation ads combine two well-known practices of contemporary advertising and marketing: *packaging* and *spin control.* Each practice aims at controlling the way issues are framed and how they are perceived. As one expert on corporate image advertising counsels, "*Perception* is what counts; it's not necessarily the reality of a situation but what your target audience *believes to be reality* that creates corporate image."[4]

Advertising for the purposes of marshaling corporate legitimacy began when AT&T pioneered *institutional advertising* in 1908 in an effort to create the appearance of a beneficent national monopoly. A 1917 advertising textbook called this style of advertising "molding public opinion" copy. AT&T adopted a long-term institutional strategy in which corporate image was employed as a "protective shield." Directed by Theodore Vail, AT&T sought to counter the public impression of an impersonal and "soulless" bureaucratic corporation with an image campaign that stressed leadership of technological progress and commitment to a "close-knit personalized society." AT&T's campaign strategy deflected issues of monopoly power and ownership by trumpeting themselves as a corporate "democracy." In the following decades, the railroad, meat-packing, and steel industries used corporate ads as an aggressive weapon against government regulatory efforts.[5] Today, 85 years after AT&T began the practice, corporations continue to strategically employ advertising to block efforts at state regulation of industrial practices.

Since the 1920s, advertising has evolved as a crucial agent in defining our relationships to others, to nature, to our work lives, to our leisure, and indeed to our very bodies. Post–World War II television advertising became the preeminent encoder of a universal way of life and its cultural values. In a fundamental sense, consumer advertising since the 1920s has also tacitly been legitimation advertising. In addition to the obvious sales pitch, consumer ads usually carry taken-for-granted assumptions about the arrangement of our lives and about what we value. Advertisements of the 1920s and 1930s explicitly depicted commodities as providing the best way to solve personal needs.[6] Since then, this has become an unspoken, and nearly universal, presupposition in advertisements. Ads depict our commodity system not as a system of wage workers and private property ownership, nor as a source of conflict and inequality, but as a fountain of personal freedom and satisfaction. Whether intentionally or not, the formative decades of modern advertising during the 1920s and 1930s offered working people a perspective other than class consciousness by constructing a new political ideology of consumerism grounded in a notion of consumer democracy.

Advertising has so fully saturated us with this ideology that the words "citizen" and "consumer" have become roughly interchangeable in their usage.[7] This premise of consumption as the basis for democracy makes it easier to accept a corollary process in which political imagery is corporately privatized, their products legitimated by democratic leanings. A Goodyear ad refers to itself as "a symbol of security for millions of Americans"; Goodyear's "promise" to its customers draws on the language of democratic political rights to "guarantee your rights" in "every

Father and son stand in reverent appreciation of "The Goodyear Promise."

state of the nation." With the Goodyear "guarantee" of consumer rights visually encased in the kind of protective glass display usually reserved for great "historical" documents like the Declaration of Independence, this ad draws on the legitimacy of the nation to identify Goodyear as possessing the same virtues as the democratic state.

After nearly a quarter century of robust economic growth, U.S. GNP and corporate profit rates sagged in the early 1970s. Correspondingly, a 1972 Conference Board survey found remarkably little public confidence in business institutions.[8] This spurred leading U.S. corporations to organize the Business Roundtable as a corporate lobbying organization in 1972.[9] Negative attitudes toward business precipitated two broad corporate coalition ad campaigns during the mid-1970s. One was a collaboration between the Business Roundtable and *Reader's Digest*; the second was the "American Economic System" campaign produced by the Advertising Council and the Department of Commerce. Both campaigns drew on the premise that the public needed to be "educated" about the unappreciated virtues of a privately owned business system.[10]

The 1973 OPEC oil embargo turned into a media spectacle that provoked public concern about the practices of giant oil companies. The brief supply crisis and consequent surge in fuel prices prompted by the oil embargo fueled a new era of *legitimation advertising.* Dramatic surges in fuel prices shattered confidence in the social contract of familial–vocational privatism.[111] The promise of privatized consumer freedom enshrined in the automobile constituted an anchor of this familial–vocational privatism. When the cheap oil vanished and the oil corporations passed along the sharp price increases plus a little something for themselves, a deep public mistrust of the major oil companies ensued as issues of corporate greed and self-interest, quiescent for years, resurfaced.[12] The oil companies responded with a barrage of ads that sought to educate the public about all that they provided.

Stung by inflation, sinking consumer confidence in corporations, and widespread worker apathy, the leading sector of the corporate community launched a counteroffensive aimed at restoring popular confidence and legitimacy in multinational corporate capital: or, as Bob

Beginning in July 1973, Exxon ran a series of ads on network evening news broadcasts. These ads featured stories about how Exxon serves European communities; how Exxon works at "responsible technology" to prevent oil spills; how Exxon's labs turn petrochemicals into consumer conveniences; how Exxon's years of investment and work transport oil across the world to your doorstep; how fish prefer Exxon's undersea drilling platforms; how Exxon supports the arts; how Exxon develops new energy technologies. Each ad closed by shrinking the film frame and then dissolving it into the Exxon logo shown here. How simplistic this 1973 effort at constructing corporate sign value looks compared to today's norm.

Hope—himself an institution—repeatedly assured us in behalf of Texaco, "We're working to keep your trust." Since 1971, when annual recordkeeping began, corporate advertising expenditures have increased every year. Corporate advertising cost $157.6 million in 1971; by 1977 this had grown to $329.3 million. But the most significant growth was yet to come: by 1989, $1.4 billion was spent on company corporate advertisements, and by the mid-1980s television advertising comprised nearly half of all mass media expenditures for corporate advertising.[13] Corporate campaigns aimed at boosting favorable awareness of corporate identities became ever more reliant on TV in the 1980s. Cable TV's segmenting of audiences made corporate TV advertising a more affordable option. Interviewed in 1989, James Foster, president and CEO of Brouillard Communications, added that "TV is the quickest way to build awareness. Print can give you depth, and corporate ads will always need a print base to reach the targets TV misses, but TV can deliver more emotion and simplified messages through effective soundbites."[14] By the 1990s, the emotional and simplified spaces of network and cable television had become the predominant media in which corporations play out public relations and legitimation strategies.[15]

Because in a media society legitimation problems are presented through the screen, they become manifest as image problems. Hence, the goal of corporate image campaigns is usually to blunt and disperse oppositional discourse, rather than to convert the masses. Unlike the sometimes abrasive and proselytizing ideological tone of advocacy advertising in magazines and newspapers, television ads are not usually geared to promoting public debate. Image campaigns on television are more often *aesthetic* and *anesthetic* in an effort to keep issues depoliticized and in the private realm. Like the rest of television, corporate ads tend to turn issues into entertainment and spectacle. Further, TV advertising tilts the playing field to give corporate interests a political advantage, because access to television advertising today is restricted to those who possess substantial financial resources. Of course, the payoffs can be equally substantial: a well-placed advertising spot can reach millions of privatized and separated viewers in their homes. This gives corporate class interests a disproportionate opportunity to play on (not necessarily influence) the values and beliefs of the American populace. Effective free speech has become an expensive commodity. As commodity discourse, corporate image ads and advocacy ads have contributed to a significant reshaping of public discourse in terms of soundbites and visual "signbites."

Hybrid Ads

Neat and tidy boundaries of corporate advertising are elusive because ads can appear to be both product-and image-oriented. A McDonnell-Douglas advertising director offered this pragmatic distinction: corporate ads "are based on the premise that McDonnell-Douglas is eternal, product ads on the premise that tomorrow we must eat." Too often, however, media analysts behave as if only the former are ideological. True, corporate ads may trade more openly in ideological discourse, and there are obviously some ads dedicated to championing an idea and not a product (e.g., the W. R. Grace "Debt Trials" ad), but a primary lesson of social semiotics is that all images carry signifieds, and no ad can segregate purely denotative meanings from subjective connotations. Further, even when ads are constructed around multiple agendas such as building consumer and investor awareness, they are composed of ideological materials and carry ideological weight. Every ad is an exercise in the framing of meaning, and those who control the frames of meaning tend to exercise a disproportionate power on the conceptual frameworks used to publicly interpret and make sense of our world.

During the early 1980s, corporate image ads became increasingly difficult to differentiate from product ads. *Hybrid ads* were corporate ads with a product twist.[16] This critical shift did not diminish the salience of legitimation in ads, but it did cement the link between commodity hegemony and corporate hegemony. Ads do not have to be explicitly political, adversarial, or controversial in order to register as political ideology. A case in point was a 1984 Aetna Life and Casualty Company commercial that no network challenged on the grounds of fairness or having to provide time for opposing viewpoints. The ad promoted Aetna's industrial insurance services by registering a Reagan-like policy position on labor–management relations and a hands-off regulatory strategy concerning occupational health and safety in industrial manufacturing. Aetna's ad presented a narrative about an industrial plant where welders are suddenly stricken by illness while on the job. This rash of workplace illness is portrayed as a mystery and a cause for alarm. An "Aetna environmental expert" is summoned to the scene to "take charge" and investigate the source of this mysterious spate of disabling illnesses. Aetna's youthful professional expert wears glasses and carries a bag containing scientific instruments. At the industrial site he magically waves a measuring device through the air—his technocratic expertise is apparently derivative of his status as a corporate medicine man. The Aetna expert's scientific examination of the plant site cuts to "a series of laboratory tests [that] leads to a startling discovery." Aetna has solved the mystery: "vapors from the solvent heated by the welding produced a deadly gas." When informed by the Aetna expert of the problem's source, the plant manager's face expresses shocked dismay. But Aetna's command of scientific expertise easily saves the day: "Aetna solves the mystery. The workers return to work safely." Management is gratified because disruptions to the production process are minimized, and smiling workers are likewise happy because they can return to work without fear of injury to their health. Indeed, the ad concludes with a burly welder slapping his arm around the Aetna expert's shoulder and giving voice to what supposedly one third of America's largest corporations say: "Aetna, I'm glad I met ya." And then it's back to work as he snaps his work goggles down.

This ad pictures workers and managers working together in harmony and without antagonism when they have the appropriate corporate expertise and science behind them. It depicts workers and managers preferring the commodification of occupational health and safety issues because it is quick, efficient, and trustworthy. Joined to this pitch for market solutions to occupational health and safety issues is the conspicuous absence of either an adversarial labor union or bureaucratic, government regulatory agencies such as OSHA. Corporate advertisers discovered it was no longer necessary to write extensive copy or to take a belligerent stance when they could abbreviate their agenda into emotionally charged narratives. The shift to hybrid ads was in full swing by 1984 and coincided with a decisive upswing in corporate ads on network television because of the Olympics and the Reagan presidential campaign.[17]

During the 1970s, capitalist political organizations advertised to demonstrate their commitment to a classwide politics aimed at protecting corporate class interests.[18] Capitalist firms used advertising campaigns to defend "the private property system" in the 1930s, 1940s, and even the 1950s, and yet private property was scarcely mentioned in 1980s ads.[19] Was capitalist legitimacy so secure in the 1980s that corporate leaders no longer felt a need to justify the system? Given their bolstered material hegemony, the corporate business community was certainly more confident in 1984 than in 1976, and they took a page out of the Reagan media strategy and began to embed their ideological discourse in emotionally charged images. The Reagan advertising campaign in 1984 set the tone for corporate ads during the next few years. Based on image and emotion, the Reagan campaign ads were interchangeable with ads during the same period by GE, Budweiser, International Harvester, and many other corporations:

"It's the kind of advertising we've seen for products," said Alvin Hampel, chairman of D'Arcy MacManus Masius, New York. "Pure imagery by and large, it surrounds

What did a major parity product, a longtime corporate giant and producer of heavy industrial equipment, and the U.S. president have in common? These ads for Miller beer, International Harvester, and Ronald Reagan all shared a reliance on grandiose symbolic imagery—here, the mechanized golden harvest, a symbol of prosperity in the heartland. Pure imagery was the product of a reductive media semiotics looking to score impression victories—hey, "it's big, uplifting."

him [Reagan] with beautiful pictures, America. A lot of products tie into America. It's big, uplifting. It is the kind of advertising that is usually used for a parity product. . . . If you took some of the Reagan footage and put in some other voiceover and soundtracks, you could have the commercial for another product, and vice versa."[20]

Like all other advertising, corporate ads became more finely targeted during the 1980s, allowing advertisers to address the business community and opinion leaders through print media, while television provided the vehicle for addressing wider audiences of consumers, citizens, and employees. Did corporate advertising strategies become more image-based in the 1980s because corporate legitimation requirements shifted from the 1970s to the 1980s? Whereas corporate print ads of the latter 1970s harped on the moral and material superiority of the "free enterprise" system, the formal rhetoric of free enterprise became less immediate in television ads, replaced by glossy, stylized images that objectified freedom. But the glossy signs that dominated TV through the 1984 Summer Olympics and Reagan's reelection so cluttered the airways that there ensued a counterreaction against the encoding practices of "commodity perfection." By 1986, "realism" emerged as a more credible encoding practice, but cynicism continued to swell until only one basic legitimation claim could be consistently invoked in ads (con-

After the technicolor musicals that dominated corporate advertising in the mid-1980s, advertisers circa 1987 began to shift to the same realist codes that we have talked about in ads for jeans and shoes. The prototypical corporate ad of the 1980s, like the International Harvester and Miller ads referred to above, was set to a vibrant, inspiring musical soundtrack, its scenes filled with sweeping iconic monumentalism. The above scenes from a Drexel Burnham ad, circa 1988, built around realist codes and a down-to-earth tone. It follows a single working mother, Sally Brinkman, trying to get her three children ready for daycare and school, and testifies to the daily chore (reality) of having a family. Drexel traded in the flash for a cross between documentary and a home movie complete with the ambient sounds of toys, breakfast dishes, and sibling conflict. A problem is shown—affordable daycare that working parents can feel safe and secure with—and Drexel claims to have helped fashion an answer. When they invest capital, little people like Sally and her children benefit.

sumerism = the good life). All others were now hooted down—or zapped—by increasingly cynical viewers armed with remote control devices.

Building Corporate Sign Values

Advertising in the United States has historically been charged with multiple, and conflicting, agendas. It aims at stimulating desire, often by fostering personal anxieties and doubts, while also trying to promote an atmosphere of corporate trust. Advertising has played a primary role in establishing commodity hegemony, the worldview that presumes all needs and problems have a commodity solution, and turns a blind eye to the full social implications of commodity relations. And yet, in contributing to commodity hegemony, advertising leaves behind a trail of discarded ideological systems after they have been picked clean of signifiers and signifieds. The competition to establish the preeminent sign value of the moment (whether in commodity markets or political candidate markets) has a long-term side effect: it becomes another force cultivating generalized skepticism and cynicism, and thus indirectly, a weak and unstable democratic polity. There emerged a growing

> disjuncture between hegemony and legitimacy in the 1980s. Legitimation crises have become a near-permanent institutional feature of U.S. society, but these crises have not imperiled the rule of corporate capital. Today, legitimation claims have lost credibility, exhausted by overuse by the corporate mass media and the Presidency, so that . . . these claims merely excite cynical skepticism or boredom (a yawn). In the absence of credible legitimation claims, the hegemony of the *knowing wink* encourages us to be savvy but private interpreters of the world— this fractures discourse, blocking the capacity for public discursive exchanges. Interpretation is treated as a private act that may be converted into discrete units of sales or points in opinion polls.[21]

But if advertising yields a hegemony of fractured discourse, then why do we see so many corporate ads aimed at securing legitimation claims? The answer lies in the fact that corporate giants are caught in a bind. They compete at producing signifiers of value, and in the contemporary marketplace dominated by constant turnover these signifiers of value are, at best, fleeting. At the same time, corporate giants "value a stable (though dynamic) image as part of their aura of authority and power."[22] Legitimation ads are those that cultivate an aura of stable values in order to lay claim to the signifieds of enduring solidity and authority. In our terminology, *legitimation advertising aims to establish corporate sign values.* These corporate images or sign values constitute a currency of legitimation: these values are not a guarantee of public legitimacy but tokens played to buffer the corporate firm against the accumulation of legitimation claims. What has been observed of Dow Chemical TV ads can be generalized to many other campaigns: they sanitize the company's image and cultivate social and historical amnesia.[23] Ironically, Dow's cloying narrative presentations breed cynicism as well as amnesia. Though probably not intentional, the resulting consumer cynicism may prove to be the more effective legitimation strategy.

The syrupy Dow "Lets You Do Great Things" ad campaign illustrates an image campaign that lies at the cusp of multiple motives. Though public memory is normally fleeting at best, the legacy of Dow's involvement in producing napalm and Agent Orange during the Vietnam War had dimmed very little over time. This be-

Framed by a chorus singing, "Yes, you can make a difference in what tomorrow brings, cause Dow lets you do great things," a graduating scientist chooses a future of service to humankind. This ad hailed a skeptical public, future scientists, and Dow's own employees.

came more than an inconvenience to Dow after 1985 when a major restructuring and acquisition program put them squarely into consumer products and pharmaceuticals. Their goal of establishing a kinder, gentler public image was aimed at ensuring that largely female consumer audiences perceived them as humane, but they were also concerned to cheer employee morale and bolster Dow's future recruitment of engineers and scientists from the hostile college campus scene.[24]

Frequently, corporate ads in the 1980s targeted companies' own employees. This continues a tendency begun in the institutional advertising of GE and GM in the 1920s, aimed not simply at the general public, but also "directed inward to its own organization." In those early days of national advertising, GE pursued institutional advertising to "stamp the GE logo, the 'initials of a friend,' upon the entire organization and its affiliates and . . . unite them behind the vision of the company that it represented."[25] Today many institutional ads continue to address these twin motives: establish a trusted corporate emblem while motivating employees with flattering self-images.

Another prime agenda behind corporate television advertising has to do with positioning the firm for greater market share. Corporate name identity and awareness, reputation building, or shifting an identity (Rockwell, Unisys, Shearson Lehman Hutton, International Harvester/Navistar) can be critical elements in a comprehensive business strategy. During the economically volatile 1980s, the surge of corporate takeovers, mergers, and acquisitions created a continuously shifting corporate geography and iconography; in this economic world, it became imperative that corporations seek a stable image and a stable identity. TV ad campaigns for diversified conglomerates often look and sound like the 1984 Tenneco campaign:

> *"Tenneco is a leading oil and gas producer. Tenneco is America's successful shipyard. Tenneco is the world's leading exhaust system manufacturer. Tenneco is premium fruit, nuts and vegetables. Tenneco is one of America's largest natural gas pipelines. The Tenneco family. Building on quality."*

Corporate identity and name recognition can have a substantial bearing on future earnings, and since the 1980s campaigns geared to adding awareness have concentrated more heavily on television.[26]

Of course, not all firms are equal in their reliance on corporate ads. The larger the firm, the more likely it is to spend on corporate advertising. In 1984, 51% of the Fortune 500 companies used corporate ads. When the statistics are broken down more closely, 98% of the top 50 firms used corporate ads, 96% of the top 100, and 78% of the firms ranked 100 to 200.[27] Corporate image ad campaigns have been the product of multiple motivations and agendas, including public relations damage control; enhancing company reputation and name awareness; boosting employee morale and employee recruitment; nourishing a climate of growth; addressing local, state, and national government officials; and even advancing stock values.

Though there is disagreement as to their effectiveness in boosting stock prices, there can be no doubt that corporate ads (especially in business publications) target investors. Can corporate ads add an increment of value to stock prices? One 1980 study claimed 4% of the variability of stock prices could be traced to a rationalized program of corporate advertising.[28] Garbett claims that "an improved reputation may make securing capital easier . . . or the right campaign may improve the price–earnings ratio."[29] Market analysts recognize that investor perception is critical in making judgments about the market value of commodities and securities. And usually the better a firm's reputation, the lower its cost of raising capital.[30] While claims about the influence of corporate advertising on stock prices should be viewed with healthy skepticism, there's little doubt that some CEOs target campaigns at institutional investors and lenders with the objective of building confidence. Further, there is anecdotal evidence that CEOs of takeover targets in the 1980s often resorted to corporate ads to keep stock prices up, a practice known as "shark repellent."[31]

We must not lose sight of the theoretical implications of this. Here, the historical relationship between signs and capital comes full circle. Signs and images now influence the capital formation process. Signs are no longer simply commodified in service to the interests of capital: they are now a commodity deployed to stimulate capital formation. In our studies on consumer ads we have observed that commodity signs are the historical product of capital, and a currency through which capital reproduces itself. In the world of corporate advertising, the sign is not merely the product of capital: capital is now also the product of signs.[32]

Turning legitimation claims into corporate sign values locates questions of legitimation in the spectacle rather than in society itself. For example, a 1991 campaign for TCI cable television touted cable television as replacing our intellectuals, our philosophers, and our historians. At a time when American educational achievement had been steadily eroding—some would argue because television turns all public discourse into entertainment—the cable industry ads proclaimed cable TV as our educators and mentors, the backbone of a democratically pluralist society! These ads present images of a peaceful, tolerant, small-town Jeffersonian democracy whose lifeblood is its cable television. Questions of corporate hegemony over society and culture

TCI's vision of mind-broadening education, with the tag line "We're taking television into tomorrow," neatly turns citizenship into consumption. "And it's interesting, isn't it, how today our eyes get opened, and our minds get broadened, where our heroes come from, and our dreams begin. As television grows up with us, some feel better knowing there's one television company with the knowhow to have already brought nearly 200,000 miles of cable to more than 8 million homes, servicing it with over 10,000 people. Because as we head into the future, maybe the secret lies not so much in trying to know what tomorrow will bring, but just in making sure we know someone who does." This sounds a lot like what Habermas called the model of civil-privatism based on the legitimacy of technocratic rule.

evaporate in these ads, to be replaced by images of benevolent corporate entities whose primary mission is to serve community needs and human potentialities. Legitimation ads draw on our love of family, community, sports, environment, and patriotism to legitimate corporate activities in the workplace, the marketplace, and the polity. These ads hail us as citizens, but citizens redefined as consumers. Paradoxically, this advertising offers us consumption as a way out of alienation and as a way of reestablishing public spheres of discourse. But this is a public sphere defined by commodity discourses.

Selling Capitalism

Legitimation ads make claims about corporations as institutions, and not just as institutions that serve the individual consumer's needs, but as institutions that promote public well-being, the greater good. Over the past decade a broad spectrum of advertising fits into our rubric of legitimation ads. Advertising as a medium of legitimation stresses grand, but amorphous, ideological themes of "free enterprise" or the "American economic system" as euphemisms for capitalist economic relations. Most ad campaigns that promote ideas are print-based, like the Advertising Council's "American Economic System" campaign of the 1970s and the advocacy advertising of Mobil, Smith Kline, and United Technologies. Such ad campaigns attempted to limit public agendas by framing issues around abstract ideological slogans of the free market and free competition, and thereby minimize public debate about questions such as the importance of corporate profits, the distribution of corporate stock ownership and the relationship between American industry and the public trust.[33] However, the "American Economic System" business advocacy campaign of the 1970s taught media practitioners that an "education model" was *not* effective in changing attitudes, and that "advocacy efforts should become highly personal in tone."[34] On television, W. R.

Robert E. Brennan, President
First Jersey Securities

Robert Brennen performed as a cheerleader for capitalist growth without once mentioning capitalism. Here the vulture, or rather, venture, capitalist poses in front of his helicopter (the perfect metaphor) after surveying from the air the strong value of America's railroads.

Grace addressed the fiscal crisis of the state with a series of ads that attributed government debt to tampering with the laws of free markets, while Shearson Lehman Hutton ads philosophized about the optimistic spirit and vision of capitalism and First Jersey Securities positioned itself as a cheerleader for free enterprise and the American growth machine: "Come Grow with Us." Roughly comparable ad campaigns justify entire capitalist industries: for example, a campaign in behalf of America's insurance companies attributes the triumphant historical expansion of the United States to the steady, guiding hands of America's insurers, "always there and working" to keep us rooted, safe, and secure while we took the risks necessary for growth.

Because corporate leaders felt the private enterprise system was neither sufficiently understood nor appreciated, corporate advertising in the late 1970s and early 1980s more aggressively sold capitalism as a value-laden system. A 1978 Textron television campaign proposed a historical narrative of hard work, innovation, ingenuity, and progressive technology aimed at showing how the "American system of industry is designed to reward those who find better ways to meet people's needs." The male voiceover recounts a trajectory of progress:

"Back when America was picking up speed, most of the bearings it rolled on had to come from Europe. A group of Connecticut Yankees decided to change all that and started the Fafnir Bearing Company. Their first target: 150 ball bearings a day. But American industry was just starting to take off. Soon an amazing parade came along because the American system is designed to reward those who find better ways to meet people's needs. And all these new machines need bearings that will keep out dirt or turn at one half million rpm or operate at extreme heat and cold. So today Textron's Fafnir Bearing division makes 19,000 varieties of bearings a day and Fafnir has grown from 7 people to 7,000, and expects to keep on growing as it continues to find new ways for what people want done. That's what private enterprise is all about. And that's what we do in every division of Textron."

Textron retold the history of private enterprise and technology to create a place for themselves as a signifier of successful private enterprise (a corporate actor that respects the laws of free markets and human needs). Here is civil privatism at its clearest. The scenes composing this narrative are connected by dissolve edits to convey *the history* of American industry and Textron, as one of smooth transitions driven by the continuous advancement of mechanized technology to achieve "better ways to meet people's needs." Textron arrives on the scene so unobtrusively that we might suppose Textron embodies the spirit of those old "Connecticut Yankees" who started Fafnir Bearing but have long since been replaced by corporate bureaucracies.[35]

Warm, Fuzzy, and Inspirational

Relatively few TV corporate ad campaigns actually mention the word "capitalism." More often, the relations of capitalism are represented as sentiments or feelings. Take the example of International Harvester in 1984. Deep in crisis, this grandfather of corporate capitalist firms was going down for the last time, but not before one last spirited collage of images set to vibrant music proclaimed the eternal presence of capital and its dedication to its employees. Meant to reassure its own corporate labor force that their jobs were secure, the ad hails the International Harvester family of employees:

SINGER: *Your pride is strong. You won't just make it do. With every job you leave a little bit of you.*
VOICEOVER: *We started with an idea, a promise, a commitment to American farming and trucking. We've been building for over a 150 years. And now we're honoring it in more ways than ever before. International Harvester. The commitment is forever!*

Though absent in name, capital is visually represented as a luminous and glossy presence rather than as impersonal market relations. Its claim to legitimacy draws on *your* willingness to embrace the ideological referent system of pride in work well done. For nearly a century, this mythic imagery of small-town and rural America as the heartland has constituted the locus of American moral virtue in advertising, and is often utilized to signify American pride. In turning to the flash of spectacle, International Harvester cannot say the word "capitalism" because to do so would betray the promise of eternal commitment. Instead, capital masquerades here behind glib populism, going so far as to picture an International

The International Harvester ad's crowning symbolic moment was also its terminal symbolic moment. The luminous red-orange glow of a rising sun represented eternal commitment. The greater truth of symbolized corporate politics lies however in the fact that the decontextualized image of the sun's red-orange glow can just as easily be a sunset as a sunrise.

Harvester flag waving proudly, standing over and behind the heartland of America.

Throughout the 1980s a steady stream of musical spectaculars featured the warm, fuzzy, feel-good imagery of pluralism, harmony, community, and tradition. In the early 1980s, ads for consumer corporations like McDonald's, Coca-Cola, GE, and Bell Telephone employed sophisticated photographic techniques and formulaic lyrics to link highly charged emotional valences to the consumption of mass products and services.[36] For example, McDonald's campaigns in the early 1980s tied their sign to sanitized images of traditional American institutions such as the family and private property in the interest of restoring a sense of continuity and stability—a sense of shared identity. This advertising style typically features flashy upbeat video editing in conjunction with feel-good lyrical tag lines. This scene from a Coke ad celebrating "Operation Desert Storm" illustrates the prototypical warm and fuzzy moment, joining claims about the legitimacy of the nation-state with the charged emotional valence of a serviceman returning to his child.

Crucial to these ads is the continuous pronoun slippage between the individual and the corporation—from the personal "you" to the inclusive, homogenizing "we," "us," and "our."[37] The indeterminate "we" invites viewers to share in the interests of the corporation and vice versa. "Our" abundance, peace, and safety thus appear to be realized in their growth and profit. Whereas crisis management ads combine ambiguous pronoun references with a passive linguistic construction so that questions of agency and responsibility appear indistinct, these consensus-oriented ads use the active voice to take credit. Like the conventional methods of addressing viewers of consumer-goods ads, these corporate ads hail the individual (or household) as "hey you" with imagery of social alreadyness, before shifting to an inclusive "we" that beckons the consumer to join the corporate totem group of sign wearers. Memorable ad campaigns in this genre include GE's "We Bring Good Things to Life," Prudential's "You Work Hard, So Do We," Chevrolet's "The Heartbeat of America" and The Equitable's "We Are The Equitable, We Can Help You Live the Good Life. We Can Help Your Dreams Come True." Corporate capital represents itself as "nowhere and everywhere, like the sky,

Reductive tag lines like "Can't Beat the Real Thing" organize an equivalence exchange between multiple signifying elements—here, the sacred feeling of family life, love of the nation-state, and Coca-Cola—by forcing them all through a common denominator.

the horizon, an authority which at once determines and limits a condition."[38] Here is a social world in which *difference* has been abolished, but diversity honored. Here is a social world where omnipresent, yet unintrusive, corporate entities appear in the form of signs to protect and serve, providing the necessary superstructure for personal and familial gratification.

Sometimes the arrested development of American ideological themes obscures

The *Wall Street Journal* turns to song while drawing on historical footage of immigrants to romanticize "the American dream."

MALE SINGING VOICE: You are a dreamer until your dreams come true . . .
VOICEOVER: And while most haven't brought riches, they have brought dreams.
MALE SINGING VOICE: . . . then you're a leader and they're all looking up to you. You have the courage to see your dreams through. The dreamer, the leader. They're one and the same in you.
VOICEOVER: At the *Wall Street Journal* we believe that the most precious resources a country can have are the hopes of its people, because tomorrow's achievements grow out of today's dreams.
MALE SINGING VOICE: You have the courage to see your dreams through. The dreamer, the leader. They're one and the same in you.
VOICEOVER: The *Wall Street Journal*, the daily diary of the American dream.

fundamental changes in the organization of social, political, and economic life. According to Reid, "[The] remnants of an old individualistic liberal tradition persist to inhibit collective economic and political awareness and action among a variety of socioeconomic groups."[39] Corporate ads throughout the 1980s persistently invoked ideologies (abbreviated into slogans) of individualism, equality, and success braided into the "American dream." Events like the Reagan reelection, the 1984 Olympics, and the restoration of the Statue of Liberty offered corporate sponsors ideal opportunities to tap into the ideological resonance of this American dream. Paying homage to the social mobility imagery of immigrants realizing the American dream has continued to be one recurrent way of glossing over the inequities of venture capitalism (First Jersey Securities), blocking out critique of public policies that reconcentrate wealth (Reagan Reelection Committee), or glorifying the spirit of entrepreneurship and opportunity in a world now dominated by concentrated corporate bureaucratic power and finance capital (*Wall Street Journal* commercials).

Rhetoric of ardent sincerity and moralism is also prominent in politically motivated public service campaigns such as the recent collection of clichés used to promote George Bush's "Points of Light" campaign for volunteer community service. It is imperative that we take note of what is consistently absent in this advertising style: these ads make no mention of strict market calculations or the never-ending search for higher rates of profits, nor the ways in which market forces push us into a Hobbesian "war of all against all." Absent are the social problems of poverty, homelessness, drug abuse, rape, child abuse, or a healthcare system that cannot take care of those in need. This advertising genre permits capital to employ pseudonyms ("The Equitable") to musically decontextualize its social contributions in spectacle form.

It must be stressed that ads do not fulfill a legitimation function in a single showing. However, when this formula is shown repeatedly, day after day, the cumulative sense of these spectacular displays overshadows—nay, eclipses—the social irrationality of "free markets." In particular, the heavily rationalized corporate system of

Male-oriented legitimation advertising uses handshakes to signify a community of friendship and a code of noncontractual integrity and honesty. The handshake shown here punctuated a spirited anthem by Miller beer with these lyrics: "Where I come from folks stand proud and tall. You know they're always sincere. It's where your word is your word, a friend's a friend, and Miller's the beer. Miller's made the American way. Born and brewed in the U.S.A."

free markets that characterizes the emerging system of flexible accumulation is anathema to the social relations of family, neighborhood, and community idealized in these ads.[40]

Ironically, the purest form of commodity discourse (advertising) is the discursive form used by corporate powers to publicly address questions of social responsibility. Yet corporate ads as commodity discourse usually prefer not to acknowledge that the continuous institutional expansion of markets to all spheres of social life has proven socially irrational in reshaping daily life. Whereas consumer-goods ads usually celebrate the extension of the commodity form into social life, corporate image ads pretend that commodification does not exist, preferring instead to picture the bonds of community and friendship.

Combating Crises: Image as Spin Control or Prophylactic

Legitimation ad campaigns are most clearcut when they respond to crises that imperil public confidence. Recent crises include the savings and loan ripoffs costing taxpayers billions of dollars; the *Exxon Valdez* oil spill and ecological crisis; International Harvester and its crisis of corporate bankruptcy and reorganization; Johns Manville and the health crisis of asbestos and cancer; and Weyerhaeuser and environmental crisis, endangered species, regulation, and the loss of jobs. A further reason for a general decline in corporate confidence has been the steady news of corporate violations of law in recent years. In the post-Watergate era there has been greater vigilance in exposing illicit activities. Few industries have been untouched by accident or scandal. The Three Mile Island accident turned public opinion against the nuclear power industry. Check-kiting schemes by E. F. Hutton, stock manipulation and insider trading by Drexel Burnham, and so on, have tarnished the reputations of major corporate brokerage firms. Reports of price-fixing and bid-rigging in the bond markets and in the defense industry have become so commonplace that it defines public perceptions of how the "big boys play." In the chemical industry Du Pont has been charged with toxic dumping, Dow is forever tainted by Agent Orange, and Union Carbide plants are infamous for deadly gas leaks. Between 1975 and 1984, 62% of the Fortune 500 corporations were involved in one or more illegal incidents.[41] In this light, one critical agenda in corporate advertising is *spin control* over bad news. Ad campaigns that respond to crises are usually motivated by concerns that diminished public consumer confidence can put a damper on future earnings.

Drexel Burnham Lambert's 1988 advertising campaign ran on the same TV news shows that carried negative news stories about Drexel's legal troubles (charges of insider trading, stock manipulation, defrauding customers, and violations of securities laws). The ads were part of a broad public relations effort aimed at countering public perceptions of Drexel Burnham as greedy wheeler-dealers in junk bonds. As exercises in spin control, the Drexel Burnham ads stress how their expertise in junk bonds has raised funds so that a small company can make daycare centers for working women a possibility, or help bring jobs to local communities, or provide middle-income housing. One ad quietly narrates the story of Vidalia, Louisiana, where high unemployment led Drexel Burnham to help finance a hydroelectric plant with high yield bonds, thus reducing unemployment by 20%. The narrator sets up Vidalia's hard times by accenting the word "unemployment" keyed to a photo of a poor white woman's face (reminiscent of Depression-era photos by Dorothea Lange). Then a soft transition occurs, keyed to a light guitar background and a peaceful scene of a man, a boy and their dog casually walking down a dirt road in a warm green countryside. Scrolling text on the screen narrates the rest of the story:

> In December 1986, the Catalyst Energy Corporation began construction on the Vidalia hydroelectric plant, financed with the help of high yield bonds provided by Drexel Burnham. Today this project has helped reduce unemployment by over 20%. Proof that high yield bonds are not just good for business. But for everyone.

The ad ends with the tag line: "Drexel Burnham—Helping people manage change." Targeted at regulators, Congress, clients, employees, the press, and the pub-

The illegitimate legitimation ad. "Before" and "after" signifiers summarize Drexel Burnham's narrative of their corporate "virtue and Public spirit" (Lippert, 1988, p. 28). Well, not so quick. The Vidalia image ad backfired because it turned out to be doubly fraudulent. Drexel Burnham not only tried to distract the public from illegal insider-trading practices, they also faked the ad. It turns out that the ad wasn't even shot in Vadalia, but 300 miles away in Fort Smith, Arkansas, perhaps on the premise that Southern poverty is Southern poverty. Once this was revealed, not even the documentary realism style could prevent the transparent insincerity of Drexel Burnham from shining through.

lic, this image-building ad presents spin control at its most recognizable, substituting a positive connotation of "high yield" for negative connotations associated with "junk" bonds.

Following the acute scare about the dangers of nuclear power at Three Mile Island, and later at Chernobyl, the nuclear power industry was faced with pacifying public fears and buffering the political community of government regulators and decision makers from negative public opinion. Here is an industry wholly vulnerable to public policy decisions. Hence, the U.S.

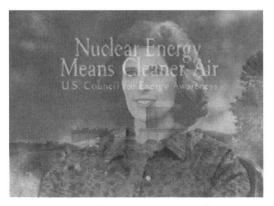

NUCLEAR MOM: "When I was in college I was against nuclear energy, but I've reached a different conclusion. It means cleaner air for this planet."

Committee for Energy Awareness, a confederation of firms with capital investments in the nuclear power industry, ran television ad campaigns to lobby for energy policy favorable to the nuclear and coal industries.[42] Their campaigns concentrated photographically on scenes of nuclear- and coal-based energy production that appear completely unobtrusive on nature: the golden warm glows of sunset skies or the clear, clean peaceful lake set against a nuclear plant in the background. After explaining that their science "is still many tomorrows away" from efficiently harnessing the sun's energy, the ad concludes: "That's why we need other ways. Like conservation. Coal. Nuclear energy. Energy Americans can count on today." Against the panorama of three birds soaring across the beautiful reds and oranges of a sunset sky, soprano voices sing "I Love You . . . Tomorrow." The proof is in the pictures: energy from coal and nuclear sources *appears* clean, non-polluting, healthy, and loving.

The largest corporations in extractive resource industries consistently confront criticisms about damage to the environment and a lack of commitment to community life. Sun Company responded to these exploitation criticisms by producing a campaign that joined themes of corporate stewardship and corporate good neighbor. Sensitive to criticism that outside ownership is insensitive to local needs, their ads told the corporate story in the voices of local employees. For example, the story of Ft. McMurray, Canada, is told by Ken Flaherty, Sun employee and little league hockey coach:

"Under the snow there's more oil than in Saudi Arabia. Twenty years ago Sun Company developed a process to get oil from tar sand. Since then a lot's devel-

oped around here—jobs, a community, hockey teams. The energy's not just under the snow, its everywhere, even on the ice. [Pause] At Sun we think that putting our energy back into a community is just as important as getting it out."

MALE SINGER: *"Where there's Sun, there's energy."*

Sun's extractive industry thus appears to promote affluence, a stable community, and strong family values without violating the environment.[43]

Another style of legitimation advertising is to flatter and salute working people. Safeway inaugurated its "You Work an Honest Day" campaign while Safeway management pursued union-busting activities with its own grocery workers. Here, legitimation is not an abstract principle but an essential part of making profits. On the other hand, Budweiser's salutes "to all the men and women who keep . . . (fill in the industrial sector) . . . going" have little to do with existing crises. They are rather a hedge against future problems, a calculated effort at redirecting the real and valid sentiments of adult worker solidarity to mesh with the consumption interests of Bud. Take, for example, a Bud ad that paid tribute to the men who mine coal. The ad's workplace scenes are narrated by miner Dan Jigelski who speaks of the mining tradition passed along from one generation to the next, and of the occupational pride and solidarity he shares with his buddies. The Budweiser voiceover then constructs a correspondence between the miner's pride and Budweiser's pride: "It's for guys like Dan Jigelski that we make sure that every Budweiser is the best it can be . . . brewed with the kind of pride that Dan puts into his work. So for Dan and all you guys out there like him," [singer] "For all you do, this Bud's for you." Almost every major player in the beer industry produced ads that saluted America's industrial workers in the 1980s: You've got pride, we've got pride, hey we were made for each other. Like Budweiser's campaign, the "Miller Time" campaign offered the imagery of occupational community in a bottle, with their beer as the reward for a job well done. These ads redirect the sentiments of worker solidarity toward nation-state icons, which are, in turn, placed in relations of equivalence with corporate icons and logos.

Safeway: "You work an honest day, you want an honest deal."

Such ads address the relationship between reward structure and motivation in our society, though they refuse to acknowledge the existence of alienated labor. The salute-to-workers style of advertising relies solely on images of unalienated labor. These ads fetishize and objectify images of excellence minus the process it takes to achieve excellence, glossing over the material relations of production. Why would people be motivated to produce excellence when their real income has been dropping for over a decade, when they fear being laid off from jobs, when they are denied health and pension benefits? What motivates workers when they are treated as objectified factors of production?

Motivation Ads: Championing the Work Ethic

A related genre of legitimation advertising combines homilies about the virtues of the nation-state and the bourgeois character structure with the stirring imagery of individual transcendence. Frequently, this type of advertising spotlights sporting heroes because sports are used to represent achievement and motivation and to bolster perennial bourgeois norms that have fallen on hard times. The presence of motivational themes in corporate ads echoes the homilies sung about in product ads: for example, "It takes a little more, to never say never. It takes a little more of what is deep inside. . . . It takes a little more to make a Champion." Before he appeared in spots for Starter sporting apparel explaining what it takes to become the best, Larry Bird appeared in Raytheon's "Mastering the Fundamentals" campaign that used Bird to link itself to the virtues of practice, hard work, and a desire to be the best. By endorsing individual character, firms like Raytheon try to create the impression that their corporate organizations are not only suffused by these character traits, but that their corporate goal is the cultivation of such character and values. Budweiser, Miller, and Coors all wrap themselves in the banner of support for *our* Olympic athletes, while identifying themselves with the spirit of excellence that supposedly marks the character structure of Olympians. Sport, spectacle, and legitimacy all converge with the Olympics, where firms treat athletic success like bankable currency that can be drawn upon to maximize corporate sign values.

But corporate ads that engage in moralizing are hardly confined to the subject of sports. The gospel of motivation regularly surfaces in ads that depict a corporate "We" that supports a public and private morality rooted in flag, family, and an eternal small-town atmosphere. They typically define the corporate presence as the penultimate good citizen, usually as a kindly overarching, patriarchal, and patriotic presence. In the late 1980s, Burger King and McDonald's began to shift the locale of such image campaigns, more and more often situating their motivational sagas in urban black communities. In 1990, McDonald's ran an ad entitled "Second Chance" about a black teenager saved from gang life by working at McDonald's, where he discovers the sturdy old-fashioned virtues of hard work, responsibility, belongingness, community, and a smile for others.[44]

The steady decline into deindustrialization has required corporations to address questions of motivation—our will to perform—alongside the issues of institutional legitimacy. This advertising style is hackneyed by now—early versions appeared from Whirlpool ("Is this country in the autumn of its time? They say that we have lost our pride, and quality no longer is a way of life . . . ") and Budweiser ("They say nobody cares about quality anymore, but 'made in America,' that means a lot to me. So here's to you America. I pledge my best to you. Cause I still care about quality"). These ads substituted, as the semiotic opposite of mediocrity, the signifier of the soaring eagle as a marker of corporate pride and achievement. More recently, General Motors' slide from its pedestal to an also-ran company elicited new inspirational halftime speeches. During Super Bowl XXVI, GM ran an ad set in an American classroom that heralds a return of confidence in American industry, of which General Motors is cited as the key example. The ad inadvertently reveals the poverty of corporate public leadership as it confuses education with the threadbare platitudes of a pep talk equating individual character traits such as courage and willpower with the well-being of our people and our nation. Unlike the previous round of corporate ads aimed at restoring pride in the products of our labor, this ad is shot using the codes of hyperrealism (swish pans, blurring, overexposed film, etc.). This ad aims at distancing itself from the earlier "unreal" exhortations of 1980s corporate ads that substituted overblown symbols for the temporal space of the everyday. A teacher addresses her class:

> "OK guys, so we've read all the articles about how American industry has lost its edge, about how our workers don't care anymore. Well listen to this [starts to read from a newspaper]: 'There's a profound change taking place. American workers are proving they can deliver quality products; for example, at General Motors new products are so improved it gives real hope for the future.' [Pause, as she finishes reading and turns to address the class] Now, there's a lesson here, and not just for industry. If anybody ever tells you that you can't be the best at something, if you believe that person you will fail. But if you have courage and willpower, there is nothing any one of us can't achieve."

Why does GM feel compelled to sell the work ethic? Why yet another lesson in an achievement ideology composed of personal willpower and the motivation to prove yourself to others? We call this stirring moral lesson sponsored by GM a *motivation ad* that invites us to join in the spirit of commitment with the GM team. Motivation ads like this frequently have their origins in the goal of bolstering employee

This is a story about Calvin and salvation. No, it isn't about religion; its about a black inner-city youth and the power of McDonald's to change his life for the better. The ad opens with Calvin striding down the street, hat on backward, as we overhear two black women, presumably from the neighborhood, in conversation about Calvin. There is a slouching saunter to his gait and we are unsure whether he might be a young tough or not.

> WOMAN 1: Isn't that Calvin?
> WOMAN 2: I haven't seen him for a while. I wonder where he's headin?
> WOMAN 1: I heard he got a job.
> WOMAN 2: Is that right? Well it's about time he got himself a job.

He is approaching a group of older and larger black males occupying the area near a playground gate. This is a dramatic visual turning point in the narrative, as we see the menacing look of a gang member, followed in the next edit by his grasping hand reaching out after Calvin to grab the boy back, but the boy is resistant to the lure of the gang and its criminal morality, for he now has himself a job. He turns to wave them off, and is shown in profile in a self-virtuous smile. We next see him approaching an older woman struggling with her loaded grocery cart. She is initially threatened by his appearance, but when he assists her she beams in gratitude.

> WOMAN 1: Now that you mention it, there is something different about him.
> WOMAN 2: Just goes to show you can't judge a book by its cover.
> WOMAN 1: Looks like responsibility's been good for him.
> WOMAN 2: Well I'm just glad somebody believed in him enough to give him a chance.
> WOMAN 1: Wonder where he's workin?
> CALVIN: Welcome to McDonald's. May I help you.

Until this final scene there is no mention of McDonald's, either as a corporation or as a fun eating place. Only when Calvin sets foot through the door and those familiar colors materialize does he turn his cap around; then we realize that McDonald's has given Calvin a second chance, and it is being a member of the McDonald's family that gives him the moral integrity to withstand the evils of street life.

morale by publicly acknowledging them as the "salt of the earth." But others, like the 1992 Bank of America campaign, aim their inspirational moments at consumers. Even without the stirring musical accompaniment to the Bank of America ad, note the difference in narrative tone as the "Banking *on* America" ad hails potential consumers with a flattering image of a self determined to succeed in spite of disadvantages of either social station or body.

"Banking on America" voiceover: "The father of the sculptor was a steelworker, the mother of the writer can't read English. The man who owns the restaurant used to wash the dishes there, and the son of the farmer now turns corn into fuel. As long as Americans believe there's nothing they can't do, we'll keep helping them do it." These lines are delivered alongside images of women, ethnics, farmers, and working-class people, and we mustn't forget that penultimate TV ad signifier of individual transcendence: a wheelchair-bound person.

In the early history of capitalism, the appeal to fairness made by capitalism's defenders focused on the personal freedom to choose, especially in the performance of labor. Capitalist legitimacy drew on claims of uncoerced labor and personal freedom insofar as the individual could choose where and to whom he sold his labor. As the class relations of capitalist societies developed over the first 100 years, open class conflict made it difficult to sustain the credibility of this claim. The experience of many laborers was that their perpetual dependence on wage labor for survival made them wage slaves. Gradually, capitalist legitimacy reconfigured itself, as the motivation to perform became the carrot of consumption and the promise of better carrots down the road. Alienated labor could be justified as the price of future freedom.

In the latter 20th century, the conduct of daily life in our society has not usually involved open consideration of questions of motivation and legitimation. Such questions remain in the background until they become problematic. A highly individuated market society depends on individuals being motivated to perform their roles: as breadwinner and worker, as consumer, as parent, as athlete, as sign-wearer, and so on. How do ads address us about our motivation to work and about our motivation to produce excellence? Corporate TV ads construct idealized visions of these social and economic roles as well as idealized scenarios of our motivation to perform. All structural limits and constraints neatly disappear in these narratives.

Corporate ads differ from product ads in the way they address us about our "alreadyness," and about our motivations to work and consume. Consumer-goods ads hail us with a sense of how we could be socially if we ate *their* bread, wore *their* shoes, drank *their* beer, and the like. They offer us a self we want to be. Consumer ads try to persuade viewers to try on—or identify with—the image presented. These ads frequently position viewers to be motivated by fear: fear of being socially undesirable, fear of being alone, fear of rejection. We recognize that consumer ads speak to our motivations by holding out the carrot of desires fulfilled and the promise of pleasure.

Corporate legitimation ads also offer us images of ourselves and our families and our communities that we dream of being—but there is an ever-so-slight twist that we all pick up on when we view these ads. The people presented to us in corporate ads look like *who we are already.* Of course, like the selves offered to us by commodity signs, the communities and families that corporate ads hold out to us are not who we are, but instead stylized representations of who we *wish* we were—they are no more or less socially real than what is shown in any other ad. But the corporate ads hold up a mirror that is much less likely to dwell on our envy of others, or on our dissatisfaction with selves and family relations that are flawed or abusive. This is not a self, family, or community made better by commodities, this is *your* self, family, or community as it already is. Corporate legitimation ads rarely try to motivate us by individuated fears, but by encouraging us to share in a set of overarching moral convictions. Legitimation ads tap into an "alreadyness" of popular sentiments and values, and then proclaim themselves as patrons of those sentiments, defenders of our values.

Corporate legitimation ads frequently reverse the direction of sign value construction: a company tries to draw the value of its name from its association with our images, and from the virtues that our images appear to signify. *Our* images give *their* corporate aura respectability; corporations seek to enhance their legitimacy by embracing our own best characteristics.[45] To be sure, the sense of social well-being these ads depict is presided over by the overarching presence of corporate capital; not simply by the sum total of its products/commodities, but by a sense of capital as sui generis. In these ads, Capital = Society!

Still, beneath the GM ad runs a current of fear. The peace treaties signed between labor and capital in the early 1950s cemented the expectation of a trade-off of privatized consumerism for alienated labor. Thus were sown the seeds for our current crisis of motivation. Now, despite our constant repetition of the mantra of "America the Great," we continue to flounder economically. Does declining productivity mean we are becoming second best or third-rate? When the Japanese indicted American workers as lazy, this characterization threatened some cherished images of ourselves as a people who take pride in their work, who are devoted to producing the best? What made America great, so the myth goes, is courage, willpower, and our work ethic. The work ethic, however eroded by the spirit of consumer capitalism, remains a basic part of our conviction about ourselves.[46] Corporate ads champion the work ethic, while consumer-goods ads sell us appearance and sign values.

In the wake of the Japanese devaluation of the American work ethic, Budweiser ran two ads during the 1992 Winter Olympics defending the American worker and the American work ethic. One ad began with a closeup of a golf ball in what looks like a sand trap. There is no music, only a male voiceover:

> *"It has been said that American workers are lazy. We want high pay without working. And give too little attention to quality. The fact is that U.S. workers are the most productive in the world. And then some. For all the hard work and achievements of the American worker, thanks from Budweiser."*

As the camera pulls back, we recognize the famous scene of astronaut Neil Armstrong hitting a golf ball during the American moon landing. This imagery reminds us that what might superficially look like a fixation on leisure is, in fact, evidence of our superior achievements. The second Budweiser ad reprised a commercial that appeared regularly for 5 years during the mid 1980s. Hence, it opened with a preface on the screen: "Because we believe some messages are timeless. . . . ":

> MALE SINGER: *If I thought that no one cared about the things I do in life, well I'd still care about working hard and making it turn out right. Made in America, that means a lot to me. Well I believe in America and American quality.*
>
> CHORUS: *Here's to you America.*
>
> MALE SINGER: *My best I give to you.*
>
> VOICEOVER: *At Budweiser we salute with pride what all Americans know in their hearts, the American worker's commitment to quality is stronger today than ever.*
>
> CHORUS: *Here's to you America*
>
> MALE SINGER: *My best, I give, to you.*
>
> VOICEOVER: *Nothing beats the quality of the American spirit.*

The dominant tone of the ad is sincerity. In the singer's voice, "I" is the American worker, while the chorus hails "you" as America the collectivity. There is no nihilism here, as the singer, in our behalf, dedicates "my best" to society. When the official Budweiser voiceover speaks, the distinction between the individual and the collective consciousness is dissolved and unified from the third-person perspective of Budweiser. The new tag line refers back to Budweiser's long-standing tag line, "Nothing beats a Bud." The new tag line substitutes "the quality of the American spirit" as the functional equivalent of "Bud." Through this ad Budweiser both champions the work ethic and invests our collective spirit in their sign value at the same time.

Patriotic Homilies

It is common for legitimation ads to contain a dose of nationalist pride and sentiment. In their struggles to fend off the takeover of U.S. markets by Japanese cars, American automakers gravitated toward characteristic themes of family, community, and country choreographed to stirring music and lyrics (e.g., Chevrolet, "There Are Some Things in This Life We Can Count On"; Plymouth, "The Pride Is Back, Born in America"). The 1980s witnessed several surges of patriotic fervor in ads. Reagan's incessant use of the patriotism button prompted ad campaign after ad campaign to wrap itself in the emotion of flag and fatherland: for example, Miller's "Made the American Way" campaign. Patriotism is rarely out of favor as a legitimation strategy, but it can be overdone: witness the hyperpatriotic General Dynamics Memorial Day ad in 1990, so heavy in sentimental syrup that it provoked derisive laughter. Patriotic ads invariably rely on the same stock signifiers and stock methodology of signification, so that ads for Coors, Maxwell House, the U.S. Army, and Shearson Lehman blur together in both form and substance. "Memorial Day," a 1986 Shearson Lehman Brothers ad, presented an emotional story of tradition and remembrance and its transmission from generation to generation. Such narratives are dominated by imagery of an America unconflicted, united by a mutually shared cultural bond. The ad opens with scenes of a parade with elderly veterans waving from an open convertible. Behind them are Marines marching in military regalia and, of course, the red and

Shearson Lehman intertwined the generational gestures of family and patriotism to create a unity they called a "family named Americans."

white stripes of an American flag. A solemn corporate voiceover frames the sequence of scenes:

> *"There are some who see Memorial Day as just a welcome excuse for a barbe-*
> *cue. At Shearson Lehman Brothers, however, we see it as the day to remember*
> *those who are part of the family named* Americans, *and who in defense of the*
> *family gave of themselves on battlefields and beaches, in the skies and on the*
> *seas. Let them hear the bells, let freedom ring."*

The voiceover begins by lamenting the trivialization of Memorial Day and its transformation into leisure privatism. But rather than counterpose allegiance to the nation-state against familial privatism, Shearson Lehman relocates the love of family to the public sphere where memory and freedom live on in this reenactment of the ritual tradition of the military parade. This text is tinged with nostalgia for that which is absent in a society structured around commodified privatism. It speaks to matters of duty and honor. In narrative counterpoint, the aging World War II veteran is pictured proudly marching and exchanging heartfelt glances with the father and son watching the parade. The linchpin of this ad is the heartwarming interaction be-tween father, son, and the elderly veteran (grandpa?). When grandpa proudly salutes and smiles, the following scene shows the young boy returning his own little salute. Three generations are united by national devotion; the family unites us, because it is what we defend the nation-state for, just as dedication to the nation-state is a family affair. The nation gives meaning to our familial relations, while the family represents the meaning of freedom.

The patriotic endorsement has been a stock response from firms and business associations facing credibility problems. As an icon, the U.S. flag comes equipped with a powerful valence: the stars and stripes signify national pride and an associa-tion with a mythic historical past dominated by signifiers of Main Street U.S.A. and parades. Its mere presence in an ad permits a syllogistic association between corpora-tion and country. Of course, corporate ads dissociate patriotism from imagery of the federal government, even when these ads draw heavily on signifiers of the American military tradition. Soldiers, and especially veterans, connote the greater glory of "Fa-therland" and not "the State" in these ads. A late 1980s Merrill Lynch campaign in-vented historical vignettes situated circa World War I to intertwine the history of Merrill Lynch with that of our nation-state in war and peace. Presented as a minidocudrama in the film style of Frank Capra, Charlie Merrill is shown leading the campaign to "buy Liberty bonds" to support the United States in World War I. Like its founding father, Charlie Merrill, cast as an ardent patriot and soldier, Merrill

Lynch is represented as trustworthy because it is an authentic American institution that has withstood the test of history.

Science and Technology

Another recurring type of legitimation ad dwells on how the corporate direction of science and technology ensures progress, solves problems, and guarantees a brighter, more humanitarian future. Du Pont has long covered its diverse activities with the tag lines "Progress is our most important product" and "Better things for better living." Corporate advertising equates "progress" with scientific advancements; firms identify themselves not as capitalist political–economic entities, but as the historical summation of scientific contributions to humanity. Siemans presents itself as this historical steward of science from 1908 through the present: "Creating technologies to keep America and the world moving in the right direction. Siemans: Precision thinking." ITT ads do not focus on problems at all, but on the stark white imagery of advanced scientific labs. In their ad, "The Hyperclean Room," ITT presents science in its purest and most hyper significations: "ITT engineers are hard at work at advanced technology centers. . . . They are making things that are already changing the ways people live here on earth. And someday, who knows where else?"

Corporate ads for firms such as Burroughs, ITT, Bell, TRW, United Technologies, Allied Corporation, GE, Du Pont, Siemans, and GTE, regularly recount how their science and technology will heal you, make better medicines, keep you from danger, feed you, permit you to realize personal goals while making your children's future brighter, and so on. Corporate science is routinely associated with consumer freedom. The imagery of science provides a shield for corporate bureaucracy by substituting the imagery of people-oriented corporate technogods for that of bureaucrats. Over the years, corporate ads have shifted from the authority of the father to the corporate bureaucratic father to the corporate technician. The corporate technician appears in ads as a signifier of well-organized competence and honesty. "Mr. Goodwrench," for example, presents a corporate sign for a place where high-tech manager/mechanics perform the role of superdad by making certain we are looked after. Or, in AT&T's version of "Somewhere Over the Rainbow," neutered, well-dressed, female and male technocrats supervise the operation of a pristine, secure high-tech world.

Ironically, corporate ads address the moral and practical problems of legitimacy and the solidarity of social relations by making claims about the ability of corporations to practice technical–instrumental control of nature. Yet it is precisely the consequences of such technical–instrumental control that create a demand for constant relegitimation.[47] For example, Du Pont's ads chronicle their lifesaving technological contributions in the field of early cancer detection (improved mammography devices), while they must remain silent about the ways in which productivity through science has unleashed toxicological and carcinogenic risks into everyday life.

Where does this perpetual tail-chasing take us? Does it engender public gratitude or public disaffection? What is the relationship between corporate ads and opinion poll results? Do ads touting scientific advances play well to audiences because technological change has been a tangible experience? Lipset and Schneider note:

> One of the strongest themes running through the polls is an appreciation of the technical and economic accomplishments of business, including "big business." [Four times] "between 1966 and 1978, the Harris Poll asked Americans to give their "impression of the job business is doing" in a long list of areas. The strongest positive evaluations were for its technological and economic performance: developing new products and services through research, improving the production process, developing new markets, and expanding growth opportunities.[48]

In contrast, ads that represent the corporation as socially responsible do not significantly enhance corporate credibility, as measured by the polls, probably because they do not correspond to material performance. Indeed, the same opinion surveys reveal that "business did not score well on conservation of natural resources, honesty in advertising, dealing with shortages, controlling pollution, or helping solve social problems."[49]

Going Global

Corporate ads, as we have seen, show "capitalism at its best." This phrase from a 1986 Shearson Lehman Brothers campaign explicitly verbalized the subtext of most corporate television ads. Of course, there is also the matter of "capitalism at its worst"—for example, the persistent abuse of social and environmental relations. But capital investment is not aided by focusing on negatives, so corporate ads try to purge negation from their narratives. Some firms now position themselves as global: Yeah, we are big, but that's good for you the consumer or you the investor. Ads stressing the diversified presence of multinational firms became more common during the mid-1980s. Throughout the evening of Reagan's landslide reelection in 1984, the Reagan victory was repeatedly punctuated by a Manufacturer's Hanover Trust ad that featured global imagery of an integrated worldwide network supremely capable of consumer financing and efficiently overseeing businesses. Spanning the imagery of a global topography, still focused in the United States, nothing too big or small escapes their integrated expertise. Economic bigness is thus translated from a problem to a benefit: for example, "a tool and die firm selects our treasury management system in St Louis. Our bank's financial management system subsidiary developed it!"

The totalizing, but personalized approach to depicting global multinational capital is exemplified in a 1991 GE ad about the omnipresent network of benevolent technology and social relations made possible by GE's corporate empire. A gentle male voiceover narrates this web of connections:

> *"[He] works at the power plant which produces its energy far more efficiently as it lights up the city and powers the hospital with its lifesaving images where Sam [a cute black boy] was found healthy in time for the game [pro football] held under the lights and broadcast to millions by a satellite system designed with precision and shipped by powerful locomotives that passed by a factory that helped build a car with advanced thermoplastics that sits in the drive at the home of Patricia [a cute little white girl] who went to the fridge and got a drink for her dad who works in the room where he turns out the light as he puts his young daughter to bed."*

A more authoritative voiceover sums things up: "Everyday, GE technology touches the lives of just about everybody." Those familiar with the concentration of corporate resources in the world today know that GE *does* indeed touch many lives everyday. Simple ideology critique suggests, however, that not every point of contact is as uniformly positive as this sequence of relations would suggest. Omitted from this portrait of contemporary life is the contested history of GE's nuclear weapons production or their involvement in nuclear waste disposal at the infamous Hanford site; nor is there reference to worker layoffs that are the flip side of GE's technologies and acquisitions. What about the prodigious market might and political power necessary to permit the network of relations described above?

Missionaries of Capitalism

Another variant of the "We are global, but that's good" approach emerged after the fall of East Germany and the Soviet Union. One such ad by Shearson Lehman Brothers featured a symbolic representation of consumer freedom (a brightly clothed skateboarder) doing wheelies around a gray stone monument to the defunct and discredited legacy of communism. The voiceover then equates the joys of consumerism with democracy and freedom and notes that Shearson will provide the capital necessary to extend free markets to everyone in the world. This is *in-your-face legitimation advertising*: Shearson turns the tables on Khrushchev's boast of decades past that "we will dance on the grave of capitalism," so that now the symbol of consumer freedom dances around the grave of communism.

Another GE ad titled "Bringing the Light of Freedom to Hungary" stresses GE's corporate role in extending the promise of democracy and freedom where previously there was only cold, gray authoritarianism. Set to Franz Lizst's "Hungarian Rhapsody," the ad narrates the story of the Hungarian people stirring from the symbolized dark night of communism to celebrate the light of liberation. GE represents itself as a partner with the Hungarian people in bringing the light of freedom to Hungary. Though unnamed as such, capitalism is unmistakably present in this ad in the symbolic form of GE that suffuses the intensity of feeling named "freedom." GE *means* freedom and democracy. This GE ad sells a corporate sign-value instead of an immediate product. In fact, to paraphrase an old GE slogan, at GE *corporate sign value is their most important product.*

The text intertwines testimonial soundbites of Hungarian speakers: "Freedom is all that matters . . . freedom is everything" and "freedom is something we [Hungarians] have to work very hard for" with GE's corporate voiceover: "There's a new light shining over Eastern Europe. A light of hope, joy, and most of all, of freedom." GE's corporate voice then announces that "in this spirit, GE has entered into an historic partnership with a company called Tungsram, Hungary's leading lighting company." As the pace and crescendo of the music builds, images of native-costumed Hungarians dance, smile, cheer, and otherwise exult, as the GE voiceover states, "At GE, we're proud to play even a small part in helping the Hungarian people to build what promises to be a brilliant future." This advertisement implies that GE's $150 million purchase of a 50% share in Tungsram was a philanthropic investment in the future of freedom in Eastern Europe. But the real reasons for GE's investment are avoided: to stop Tungsram from undercutting GE in the American market and to give GE a low-cost competitor in Europe with which to challenge Phillips (Holland) and Osram (owned by GEC, Siemans, and Thorn EMI). "To go after Western Europe—that's why we're here," stated a GE senior vice-president. Indeed, GE's acquisition of Tungsram amounted to a hostile takeover, resulting in 2,700 unemployed workers, while the remaining labor pool remains a relatively cheap one for GE.[50]

The GE ad raises the category of history, but their narrative of history is composed by hollowing out actual existing production and class relations.[51] The ad constructs a binary symbolic visualization of the historical transition sweeping Eastern Europe. Symbolic metaphors of daybreak, candles, bridges, folk dancing, and ballet are placed in semiotic opposition to darkness as a way of signifying a movement from socialism to freedom. The ad invites viewers to focus not on the referent system of Hungarian history but on our own ideological assumptions. After turning the meaning of history and freedom into a thoroughly symbolic construction, the ad then substitutes (replaces) this meaning with that of GE's presence. This is precisely what Barthes identified in his theory of myth: here, Hungarian freedom is turned into a second-order signifier of GE. "Myth deprives the object of which it speaks of all history. In it, history evaporates."[52]

Abbreviating Public Discourse

In the 1930s Bertolt Brecht theorized that didactic theater could help to politically educate the working class. Brecht felt drama could effectively raise class consciousness if it was "quotable"—if it contained easily remembered and reproduced phrases, gestures, and images. Brecht called this quotable moment the Grundgestus, meaning a unified compound of sound, vision, and gesture.[53] In an era of mechanically reproducible images, enormous cultural value can be packed into such concentrated units of meaning. Ironically, this approach to cultural praxis has received its greatest expression in the corporate TV commercials that try to distill all that is culturally dear to us into musically framed and emotionally loaded scenic moments. Brecht's theory of applying the principles of abbreviation and condensation to the production of politically salient signs has proven more effective in the hands of the capitalist culture industry than in the plays of socialist revolutionaries. After years of this a generic set of ideological frames and panoramic signifiers, both musical and visual, reign across corporate TV ads, mixing motivational themes with a landscape that is free and open—from Chevrolet's "Like a Rock" series with its "land of rugged individualists," to Bank of America's portraits of self-directed upwardly mobile Americans for whom the word "can't" is absent from their vocabularies, to Bud's snapshots of "Dedication and a Real Sense of Pride."

Corporate television ads often draw on subjectively significant "paleosymbolic" scenes to produce these quotable moments. As Gouldner explains, "On the sociological level, the paleosymbolic . . . implicates central persons, nuclear social relations, and the affectively laden gratifications and securities associated with them."[54] Paleosymbolic scenes are often presented as if they simulate comparable moments from viewers' own lives. This advertising practice steers the private, subjective meanings encapsulated in paleosymbolic scenes toward the service of corporate ideological interests, thus collapsing the formerly private language of paleosymbolism and the public language of ideology into a neither–nor discourse. Though they easily fit the category of "publicity," corporate image ads construct a public language that is composed of discontinuous and decontextualized paleosymbolic scenes. GE television ads excel in capsulizing such scenes. In the final scenes of GE's ad about how their global network of technology practices positively touch "your" life everyday, a father puts his little girl to bed while the camera slowly scans across her little ballet slippers which carry a deeply subjective significance because we've just watched her stretch on her little tippy-toes to reach a drink from the refrigerator for her daddy. The camera scans up to her cherubic face peacefully asleep on the pillow and GE's frame encloses her image to bring that total paleosymbolic moment within its domain.

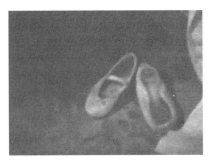

Corporate advertisers redirect the discontinuity of personal photographs to construct paleosymbolic moments that might lend value to their company identity. By reworking the meaning of photographic moments so that they can be made meaningfully equivalent to the corporation in question, this kind of advertising blurs the boundary relations between private and public life, making them appear indistinguishable. Such ads siphon off political meanings, yet by isolating intensely personal and subjective moments, they *appear* to have no ideological dimension whatsoever. These ads confuse the meaning of "public," in part, by confusing the matter of what is "private." Two kinds of private spheres are at work in these ads: one explicit and manifest—the domestic sphere, the sphere of personal and familial relations, and one tacit, the sphere of private capital—the sponsor themselves. Sponsors of TV legitimation ads rarely identify themselves as private self-interested capital, but as a quasi-public guardian of the personal private sphere. This is important and bears repeating: corporate television commercials gloss over the corporate organization of private property operating in a market economy. Instead, a majority of corporate ads adopt a tone of civic republicanism, the goal of which is ostensibly to promote the

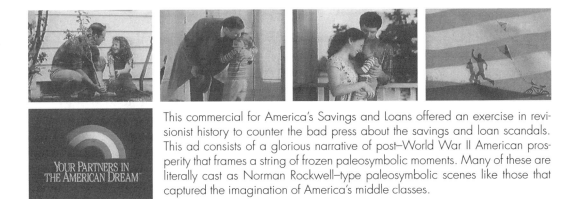

This commercial for America's Savings and Loans offered an exercise in revisionist history to counter the bad press about the savings and loan scandals. This ad consists of a glorious narrative of post–World War II American prosperity that frames a string of frozen paleosymbolic moments. Many of these are literally cast as Norman Rockwell–type paleosymbolic scenes like those that captured the imagination of America's middle classes.

"common good" framed from the unifying vantage point of an all-embracing corporate "We." By adopting the voice of civic republicanism, corporate ads tend to transform corporate interests from those of self-seeking, profit-maximizing private property owners and managers into participants of a public-spirited collectivity, where self-interest is submerged to the benefit of the symbolic common good and paleo-symbolic personal happiness.

We have returned a number of times to what happens when advertisers intentionally encode the metacommunicative level to steer viewer questions about the agenda of the message away from questions of power, control, and inequality. Turning the personal photograph into a corporate paleosymbol frequently involves just such a process of falsified metacommunication. A subtext of many corporate ads is the power relationship between the consumer and the corporation. Many ads reframe corporate power as simply the capacity to do good deeds, while other ads plead innocent to any monopoly of power by assuring us that real power lies with "you," the individual consumer. Of greater ideological significance, however, is that ads like those about corporate science invoke the rationality of scientific technique both as a justification for trust and as the common ground on which to base consensus formation. Instead of acknowledging that the corporate management of science is geared to generating profits, firms such as Bell Atlantic frame it as "managing complex technologies to meet your needs. We make technology work for you." The premise of consensus formation is a veneer covering the goal of control: in these ads, the invocation of scientific rationality is a means of reproducing distorted communication, and hence domination.[55]

Corporate advertising based on building sign values out of emotionally charged paleosymbolic scenes have significantly altered the character of public debate and dialogue. No less than Herbert Schmertz of Mobil Oil, a leading corporate ideologue and producer of corporate advertising, describes these ads as "conclusatory emotional appeals" that close off rational public debate. Paleosymbolic scenes such as the one encoded by GE's advertiser as signifying the "light of freedom" further debilitate public discourse by atrophying the capacities for argumentation necessary for rational public debate. In his study of radio music, Theodor Adorno identified a "regression of hearing" as a "growing inability to concentrate on anything but the most banal and truncated aspects of a composition."[56] The fetishism of vision practiced by advertising has brought forth a corresponding *regression of seeing* whereby concepts such as freedom and democracy become semiotically truncated and abbreviated. This visual abbreviation is the result of historical processes of viewing television ads. Once we accept the associations offered by these ads, we can make sense of the ads without referring back to the combination of material and moral premises that initially justified making and accepting the connection. The GE strategy of defining freedom in terms of framed paleosymbolic scenes testifies to the withering impact of commodified semiotics on public discourse.

° Corporate Ads and Public Debate

What kind of public sphere of debate does such corporate television advertising promote? And how *free* is a "free market of ideas" when the field of discourse is governed by the rules and practices of commodification, where corporate interests have disproportionate access to the field of discourse? In our estimation, corporate television ads promote what Nancy Fraser calls "weak publics, publics whose deliberative practice consists exclusively in opinion-formation and does not also encompass decision-making."[57] These ads may address opinion leaders and opinion followers, but the publics they address are barely publics at all: instead, they are pseudopublics composed of privately situated spectators related to one another through the mass media they view and the public opinion polls that "construct" them. Though corporate advertisers wrap themselves in the cloak of civic republicanism as their model of a public sphere of discourse, their ads continue to tightly compress public discourse into corporate signs of reassurance and legitimacy. Quite apart from whether or not any viewer is persuaded by any of the legitimation claims embedded in these signs, corporate advertisements comprise a space in which only signs of corporate legitimacy circulate.

In contrast to print advocacy ads that express a "company's own point of view on controversial public policy issues that affect their business,"[58] television image ads are soft and mushy, conveying emotional feelings and the relationships between corporations and consumer lifestyles through images. Image ads seem designed to put a democratic sphere of public debate to sleep. The same cannot be said of prickly print advocacy ads that have sometimes opened up subjects for public debate. Yet this is rarely, if ever, a sphere of *democratic* debate since the resources are so skewed that it creates an unbalanced playing field. Consider Mobil Oil's use of "advertising as a weapon" from the late 1970s through the early 1980s. Mobil ran op-ed pieces in nine leading U.S. newspapers each week; columns in 400 Sunday supplements; two–three minute commercials on an ad hoc network of TV stations not affiliated with the networks; and (beginning in August 1980) minute-long advertisements that simulated a news format during network evening news shows. No activist political group, no environmental group, no opposing interest to Mobil Oil could muster the funds to match even one plank of the Mobil campaign. Nonetheless, to compete at all in this new public sphere of discourse, noncorporate interests such as the AFL-CIO and

NOW were forced in the 1980s to make use of limited ad campaigns to fight for legislation they considered important to their interests.

But when David actually challenged Goliath on the field of television ads, Goliath cried "foul." In 1990 a small political advocacy group called Neighbor to Neighbor challenged the Bush–Reagan policy of support for the El Salvador regime by organizing a consumer boycott of corporate-brand coffees distributed in the United States. Neighbor to Neighbor's consumer boycott strategy was organized around buying advertising time on local TV stations to present ads that narratively symbolized how an American consumer product, coffee, was connected to the deadly civil strife in El Salvador. The ad argued that Folgers (a Proctor & Gamble brand name) "brews misery, destruction and death" when it purchases Salvadoran coffee beans because wealthy coffee growers in El Salvador subsidize the right-wing death squads. The concluding image showed dripping blood from a coffee cup turned upside-down. The side of the cup read "Sale of Salvadoran Coffee." When the ad ran on a Boston station, Proctor & Gamble (P&G) became incensed and threatened to withdraw all product advertising from offending stations. At the time, P&G spent in excess of $600 million annually on television ads, so their threats carried weight. Only 3 stations accepted the Neighbor to Neighbor ad, while 25 stations capitulated to P&G's threats and rejected the Neighbor to Neighbor spot.[59] This led to Proctor & Gamble "being portrayed as a corporate bully that denies its critics the right of free speech—even when they are willing to pay for it."[60]

In the last quarter century the only possible place for democratic public debate has been in the sphere of paid-for speech. As an abstract principle, this rule of law is laudable—the sphere of public debate is open to any party or interest that can afford to join in—but as an actual political practice it favors the dominant class in structuring the terms and agenda of any public debate. To paraphrase Anatole France: *The law in all its majesty allows the poor as well as the rich to run television ad campaigns.* Unfortunately, treating ideas as commodities precludes the necessary conditions for enacting an unconstrained, free, and open marketplace of ideas. This does not mean the sphere of public debate goes wholly uncontested, but it does mean that if popular opinion is the basis of legitimacy, and the basis of that opinion is structured by the rule of commodities, then we should probably rethink what it means to talk about a public sphere of democratic discussion.

When corporate elites pursue legitimation strategies rooted in the management of corporate sign values, they may put to sleep a public sphere of debate where opposition interests can challenge corporate policies by making rationally discursive arguments. However, these same signifying strategies may also open the door to unanticipated forms of political opposition that are anything but rational. As we have observed, corporations have collapsed both their commodity interests and their legitimation interests into the decontextualized imagery of their signs. Ironically, because the corporate trademark has emerged as the pivotal signifier in "postmodern signifying culture," such floating imagery can become the focal point of nonrational opposition on the part of dispossessed and marginalized populations. Coombe addresses one version of this postmodern politics—the rumor—as she retells the story of how Proctor & Gamble eventually surrendered its symbolic logo because of rumors linking it to Satanism: "Rumor is elusive and transitive, anonymous, and without origin. It belongs to no one and is possessed by everyone. Endlessly in circulation, it has no identifiable source. This illegitimacy makes it accessible to insurgency."[61]

The Era of Chronic Legitimation Crisis?

The mere fact of corporate advertising can in no way be taken as a guarantee of renewed legitimacy. Even the grandiose campaign undertaken by the Ad Council in behalf of the "American economic system" failed to achieve its "educational goals."[62] But the impact of corporate ads cannot be calculated solely on whether or not they are successful, because spanning the bandwidth of competing products, corporate television advertising promotes the imagery of capitalist institutions. In corporate ads from the late 1970s through the 1980s, recurring iconic images such as the soaring eagle or the warm, enveloping orange glow of sunrise and sunset symbolized an overarching and omnipresent sense of well-being made possible by interchangeable corporate entities. The aesthetics of symbolically sculpted signifiers has deflected debate away from actual issues. This style of advertising contributes to a thin, but generalized, halo of corporate stewardship and a sense of corporate interchangeability. In this sense, corporate advertising plays out a classwide corporate political legitimation agenda.[63]

By relying on orchestrated collages of images, corporate ads muddy questions about how huge corporations exercise their power or whether they do so in accord with generally accepted notions of the public interest.[64] We have argued that corporate advertising has contributed to a public sphere of discourse characterized by ideological and conceptual confusion. Compounding this ideological disarray, corporate advertising is guided by opportunistic invocations of almost any hot ideological sign that has value at any given moment. The result is a public ideological swamp that effectively clogs the articulation of coherent alternative views, and hence stymies rational public debate. Reinforcing this point, our research shows that television image campaigns in the 1980s and 1990s have turned to heavily aestheticized representations as a strategy for keeping issues depoliticized and in the private realm.

What happens when legitimation crises become chronic, indeed, continuous? In the society of the spectacle, crisis has become a necessary ingredient for high ratings. The media's commodity interests automatically elevate controversy into crisis. As one revelation displaces the last in a long string of revelations, public memory becomes attenuated and the citizenry grows more disillusioned, cynical, and apparently disinterested. Crises in the basic institutions of daily life reinforce the sense of something gone awry. Yet, the notion of legitimation crisis—based on the Weberian theory that some societally shared consensus must exist in order for a political regime to govern in the modern nation-state—now almost seems to carry the ring of nostalgia. We have begun to wonder along with Kellner (1990) whether the capitalist state any longer requires a widely shared consensus in order to govern, so long as commodity culture and privatized consumerism replace it as the social cement.[65]

Some 20 years ago, in *Legitimation Crisis,* Jurgen Habermas argued that efforts at managing legitimation crises tend to be self-defeating when there is a deliberate manufacture of normative commitments. He noted: "There is no administrative production of meaning. Commercial production and administrative planning of symbols exhausts the normative force of counterfactual validity claims. The procurement of legitimation is self-defeating as soon as the mode of procurement is seen through."[66] However, the historical record of corporate intervention into the public realm to shore up legitimation deficits suggests that while commodification of cultural traditions may "exhaust" the normative force of validity claims, Habermas underestimated the ability of corporate interests to discursively appropriate the meanings of cultural traditions to "procure" legitimation. We are distinguishing between the corporate appropriation of normative commitments and attempts to manufacture such commitments. Effective sign values cannot be constructed *de novo*: they depend on the appropriation of existing cultural values as raw materials. However, this appropriation carries a cost of cultural and political desensitization: "A crisis of meaning is generated by the fact that symbols are not as effective as they once were in compelling loyalty to the society."[67] Habermas presumed this normative exhaustion would exacerbate legitimation crisis; instead, it has fueled a rising tide of cynicism that surrenders to a perception of institutionalized anomie as the inevitable condition of contemporary society. Relying on television advertising to counter legitimation problems has contributed to a far more pervasive crisis: a crisis of meaning, as signs circulate without much respect for communities of meaning.

Conclusion: Sneakerization and Hyperculture

THE ADVERTISING landscape of the 1990s is thematically fractured compared with that of 30 years ago. Although there are far fewer appeals to God and country, themes of character, hard work, and integrity still abound in TV commercials. Alongside such appeals, obviously, are the barely differentiated, soulless, commodity personalities abuzz on toothpaste or perfume or cereals. Television is still dominated by this latter kind of advertising that sells a commodity self. The pervasiveness of this advertising formula has, in turn, precipitated two major responses: one fixed around themes of authenticity, another embracing an ironic and jaded attitude toward advertising and commodity consumption.

On the surface at least, television advertising seems to be a much more contested ideological space than it was even 15 years ago. The ideological fractures and divisions in television advertising correspond to the modes of address that arise when marketers divide consumers into target audiences based on lifestyles or any other psychocultural category that might garner an additional increment of market share. Advertisers today practice the art of appropriation in an ecumenical way: any manner of cultural expression is permissible when it can be turned into an effective method of hailing an audience.

Today's advertising is also marked by the extraordinary turnover rate of positioning categories associated with brand names. Paralleling this acceleration on the product side is the proliferation of niche markets, what some have called "sneakerization," or niches within niches. According to Goldman, Nagel, and Preiss, "Sneakerization is shrinking product lifetimes, as competitors quickly seek to imitate successful, high-margin goods. At Panasonic, consumer electronic products are now replaced with new models on a 90-day cycle."[1] The accelerating circulation of sign values and their vehicles—the ads themselves—has emerged as a defining feature of the land-scape of commodity culture.

In the high-velocity advertising wars we have discussed, ideologies become reduced to the role of adjectives used to boost the flavor of this or that commodity. If the mechanical reproduction of images gave rise to mass culture, then the analog and digital reproduction of images—in conjunction with the relentless organizing principle of commodity logic—has helped spawn *hyperculture.* Within the regime of hyperculture, raiding ideological referent systems for eye-catching signifiers has relatively little to do with ideological commitment to a cause or a perspective. Where once commodity culture consistently affirmed a watered-down version of bourgeois ideology, it has now become a space in which ideological constancy can, as often as not, be a liability.

In brief historical perspective, since the 1950s, opposition or resistance to capitalist institutions has shifted from the sphere of production to the cultural sphere—and particularly into the realm of styles and commercial symbols. Style emerged as the space within which working-class youth could express their dissatisfactions. Without real opportunities to challenge the arrangement of production relations, youth redirected their energies into modifying and recoding the signs inscribed on consumer goods. The practice of bricolage permitted at least a symbolic expression of those relations that capitalist society blocked. Youth would rearrange signifiers and signifieds to subvert the commodity imprinting we have been talking about. Advertisers and marketers eventually responded to youth's bricolage by trying to reincorporate into commodity form the modified stylistic expressions founded by subcultures.[2] Thus began a two-step dance of bricolage and commercialized counterbricolage.

Cultural appropriation is an essential component in producing successful sign values. Advertisers can never rest in their search for culturally resonant meanings that can be used as resources for constructing new sign values. Commodity sign culture provides a site where youth often contest and reinterpret the meanings of commodity signs, until the culture industry reaches back to reappropriate the bricolaged sign. In this sense, advertising feeds off of opposition to the machinery of style. At the same time it has grown culturally cannibalistic as it chews up and recycles earlier images and styles. After repeated rounds of this process over the years, it was predictable that the next stage of signs and styles would be concocted by recycling and splicing together signifiers of previous media images and styles. Moreover, the next generation of ads have also had to address viewer resentment.

The logic of sign wars drives the process of cannibalizing signs and images. As the referential domain of everyday life became more and more picked over, sign competition shifted to a stage of hypersignification based on an obsession with encoding practices. This has been accompanied by an increasingly pervasive practice of rummaging through the old bins of television images in search of image fragments that can be recycled and reframed. This practice is akin to what Olalquiaga calls the construction of "second-degree kitsch" in the memorabilia shops. Just as the retrieval of decades-old home movie footage spoke to a higher level of authenticity, second-degree kitsch ironically turns both the plastic religious icon and the plastic stiffness of a 1950s deodorant commercial into signs of a refined sensibility. In Olalquiaga's view,

> This kitsch is self-referential—a sort of kitsch-kitsch. . . . It capitalizes on an acquired taste for tackiness. It is a popularization of camp sensibility, a perspective wherein appreciation of the "ugly" conveys to the spectator an aura of refined decadence, an ironic enjoyment from a position of enlightened superiority.[3]

The ability to appreciate old kitsch represents a higher order of consumer authenticity. But once again we must stress the ransacking quality of this process. Even in this media-referential recycling, images are plucked from their media contexts for the purpose of highlighting their referential status and drawing attention to a sponsor capable of recognizing the value of empty images that have long since been discarded. When semiotics enters the equation, meaning can be disassembled into signifiers and signifieds—not just in theory, but in advertising practice. This practice has cultural consequences insofar as it contributes to a linguistic universe characterized by a wide pool of radically decontextualized signifiers and signifieds. What's more, as sign war competitions have escalated over the years, the circuit of decontextualization has sped up. Indeed, it has been reported that the style arbiters at MTV already are abandoning grunge in favor of a retro 1950s look defined by the swank design of "swizzle-stick aesthetics."[4]

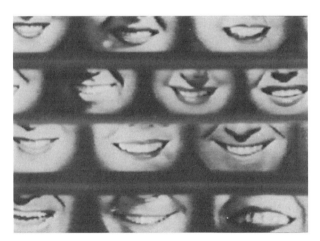

What is the referent here? The worst excesses of image cannibalism can be found in a 1992 LA Gear "Pressure/Release" TV campaign constructed around rapid-fire editing of a hodgepodge of images plucked from 1950s mass culture. The sole logic guiding the arrangement of these images is the repetitive semiotic opposition of "pressure" versus "release." The ad centers on the pleasure of kitsch.

Thus, as we have stressed, the appetite of the commodity sign industry—advertising—is voracious. Producing and reproducing sign values necessitates a continuous quest for cultural matter that can supplement simple commodity value. Today advertising depends on cultural opposition in order to keep the malls open. Subcultural opposition to middle-class values, whether it be punk or rap or grunge, provides the basis for new styles and looks. For decades, advertising drew on predominantly middle-class values and cultural preferences, but commodity culture can no longer replenish itself without drawing on oppositional cultural expressions. To put it bluntly, the retail sector of capital has grown reliant on the circulation of expressions of cultural alienation.

In fact, the circuit between commodity images and the appropriation of rebellious subcultural expressions of style has become nearly seamless. As sign contests came to revolve more tightly around a culture of appearances, corporations have institutionalized the process of identifying and appropriating the hippest looks and styles that circulate on the underside of the commodity system. Within the system of sign value, the images that have the highest exchange value are those that come from marginalized populations: queer culture, renegade subcultures, and poor black youth. One young fashion observer hired to ferret out the not-yet-commodified youth styles states the obvious: "Big companies are realizing that if they are going to make money, they have to be on top of what is going on."[5] Thus firms like Converse hire people to scout cool kids and design sneakers inspired by their various forms of bricolage: "They are sourcing drag queens and club kids." At Converse, Baysie Wightman is a style hunter, staking out clubs on the edge: "Of particular interest to Wightman are styles of skateboarders and transvestites, often the most innovative and experimental of dressers. . . . She then runs back to the Converse Inc. headquarters in North Reading, Mass., far from the smoke-filled rooms, pulsating acid jazz music, and 20-year-olds of the clubs, and tries to translate urban counterculture into marketable sneaker ideas."[6]

The colonization of graffiti.

The effort to build advertising value out of signs of cultural resistance is cast in sharp relief by a 1994 billboard campaign for Neon, a new subcompact car from Chrysler. The billboard campaign drew attention, because "in a guerrilla warfare tactic, the company has 'tagged'—added graffiti—to its own displays."[7] This simulated tagging is not even done with a spraycan, but with boom trucks that permit paper hangers to overlay the billboard with the preconstituted panels that include the "graffiti."[8] This illustrates several points we've been talking about. First, it reminds us of the considerable effort devoted to contesting the sign landscape and—wink, wink—joking about it with the spectator. Second, notice how the advertiser thus layers and appears to recode the meanings of the ad. In their television and billboard blitz campaign, Neon had punctuated every ad with the word "Hi" beside the car. By drawing a red mohawk hair icon across the car's roof and adding a "p" to turn "Hi" into "Hi*p*" the advertisement now speaks to viewers about how even the denizens of subcultural hipness recognize Neon's hip aura. For a brief moment during the summer of 1994 the Neon billboards stood out as a site of differentiation—a novel signifying gambit. This campaign extends the war of bricolage and counterbricolage into preemptory tagging, a form of manufactured bricolage based on coopting mythified signifiers of subcultural vitality and resistance.

The pace and aggression of sign war competitions has continued to increase in intensity, force, and speed, while a growing proportion of advertisers attack advertising in general in order to differentiate themselves from their brethren and acknowledge their sympathy with viewers. RC Cola's current campaign illustrates this kind of sign wars agenda. RC Cola held only a 2% market share of the U.S. cola market, and was dwarfed by Coke and Pepsi sales. But under new leadership, RC Cola boosted its 1994 advertising budget by 64% to mount an aggressive symbolic attack on the signs of Coke

RC Cola's "Fish-o-Rama" symbolized Pepsi and Coke as fishermen displaying hooked, landed, and hung consumers as the trophies of their sign war.

and Pepsi. RC Cola executives literally speak of their new campaign as a "guerrilla war" campaign.[9] The RC Cola campaign's most attention-getting TV ad, titled "Fish O'Rama," attacks the cola industry behemoths: Coke and Pepsi. The ad pictures competing fishing boats representing smug Coke and Pepsi executives reeling in "hooked" Coke and Pepsi drinkers. Competing fishing crews dressed in Pepsi and Coke colors bait their hooks with Coke and Pepsi cans and cast their lines. Then with yells of "Fish on," the crews are shown reeling in not fish, but humans flying through the air as if they were marlins. Once hauled in and netted, these consumers are displayed as game fish hanging upside down on the dock, the trophies of Coke and Pepsi advertising. "Hey," the voiceover exclaims, "you don't have to swallow that." The ad hails Generation X consumers as potential nonconformists weary of being "fed the same old line for years." In dark comic style, "Fish O'Rama" addresses consumer misgivings about how advertisers bait and hook them. And yet no sooner does RC hail this cynical sensibility and attack the advertising methodologies of Coke and Pepsi as treating consumers like fish to be caught, than RC's last image in the ad confirms they are after their own fish.

Competing to Hail the Channel Surfer

A survey conducted for *TV Guide* found that 88% of poll respondents own remote controls, which makes for "a lot of channel surfing," which spells trouble for any programmer trying to deliver "half an hour of an audience."[10] Moreover, advertisers have come to believe that younger viewers are fed up with ads. "I don't think you can grow up in America today without being cynical about advertisers' messages, which means we have to be cagier about how we present the message to the younger generation," said Bill Stenton, creative director at Ketchum Advertising in Los Angeles.[11] Similarly, the director of global media for Coca-Cola views the Generation Xers as "professional channel surfers:" "You have to entertain or inform or amuse them. You can't just sell."[12]

Corporate marketers quickly strangled the life out of what Douglas Coupland named Generation X. It promptly devolved into "Generation Y," a set of demographic categories focused on consumers who are 17 to 49 and predominantly urban. When put through the prism of marketing studies, Generation X shifted from a cultural constellation to a more inclusive constellation of youth who are urban, black, Hispanic, and white members of the working class. This has resulted in campaigns that have indulged heavily in media-referential constructions, such as Taco Bell's revival of the Rocky and Bullwinkle cartoon characters. Similarly, Budweiser has hailed the babybusters with cheerfully nostalgic recollections of media memories from the TV sitcoms of the mid-1970s. Other campaigns combine media-referentiality with a heavily ironic tone of voice. At the extreme end, Coors Light has adopted a winking approach that

Joe the Slacker refers to an imaginary TV show on an imaginary TV network: the Coors Light Channel.

makes the whole of television culture its playground. The "Coors Light Channel" campaign pushes media referentiality to the limit by compressing the entirety of television into their Coors Light Channel icon. It's like a Saturday Night Live parody of television. After a female telephone voice advises that "You're watching the Coors Light Channel," a voice similar to that of network promos informs us that "Up next, its Coors Light Sports. Then Joe buys a flannel on a very special Joe the Slacker. But first these messages." Ah, finally we reach the heart of the matter, the advert within the advert. "What do you think of Coors Light?" An elderly silver-haired woman interviewed on the street blurts out, "Never drank a glass of beer in my life." Without skipping a beat the commercial male voiceover—the familiar hard-sell voice of TV ads—declares, "Coors Light: The most popular beer in the world!" Juxtaposing hard-sell hyperbole over a testimonial from someone who has never sampled the product and doesn't care about it is intended to be funny. This is like the Toyota Paseo ads, discussed earlier, that seek to deny their agenda by mocking it. To remind the viewer that this is a parody of the television experience, the scene quickly shifts to an obvious mock-up of television hucksterism: "Introducing Coors Light trading cards featuring the Coors employees you know and love. Not available in stores." Coors Light's joke about TV kitsch confirms what we have already seen; the entire ad is fashioned as a knowing wink that acknowledges the absurdity and inauthenticity of television culture, a culture we are now urged to consume in a different way—with a postmodern sensibility that can appreciate it as kitsch. The "Coors Light Channel" commercial ends with the tag line "Always On" (which is an abbreviation of "There's always something going on.") Here, then, is another campaign designed for youthful audiences who have seen it all on television, but who continue to watch. This ad speaks to the contradictory nature of television watching in contemporary culture; there is "an incredible reliance on television as a presence in people's lives. But the engagement of the viewer is declining."[13]

Coors Light Kitsch

Throughout these essays, we have tried to show what sign wars look like in the context of specific niche competitions. Obviously, the corporate players in both the beer and soft drink industries are competing to hail Generation X/Generation Y. In the soft drink industry, it has become commonplace for campaigns to push the envelope when it comes to constructing ads aimed at taking the side of jaded young spectators who will no longer abide fantasies of commodity euphoria. Leading the assault on conventional advertising ideologies of commodity fetishism is a Sprite campaign that hails the cynical view-er by declaring that "a soft drink is not a magic potion, a status symbol or a badge that says who I am," while the screen flashes across a collage of packaged brand names like Talent, Bravery, Magnetism, and Forever Young. "It won't make me run faster or jump higher, and it won't make me more attractive to the opposite sex, though I wish it would. . . . " In summation, the young black narrator declares, "Thirst is everything," before he commands, "Obey your thirst."[14] Sprite presents the young black narrator in a way that bridges the cultural constellation labeled as Generation X with the demographic clustering of Generation Y. The emergence of the nonwhite and noncelebrity narrator is a significant advertising shift prompted by this new marketing category. Choosing a black, noncelebrity narrator was far from haphazard for Sprite. Though he doesn't rap, he has the aura of the authentic rapper: one of the lone images of the organic intellectual available on commercial television. He is a generic urban black who can talk with the authority of experience and cannot be construed as talking down to the audience. On the television news, rap is demonized and linked in the public consciousness with drugs and gang vio-lence; but on MTV and in the world of TV ads, rap has emerged as the number-one vehicle for expressing authenticity. Rap offers a signifier of unpackaged and un-tamed authenticity. Though he's not rapping, Sprite's "Brother" speaks to his audi-ence with the clipped no-bullshit tones of a Brother who is "gonna lay out 'the truth' for us." This is why Sprite chooses to represent the narrator by his black lips—because he "shoots from the hip."

Sprite's "Image Is Nothing—Thirst Is Everything—Obey Your Thirst" cam-paign is only one of many to imitate the Nike antihype ads we have already dis-cussed, including ads in which Spike Lee and Charles Barkley directly address what the Nike product can and cannot do. Most re-cently, Barkley refuses to repeat the commodity fantasy talk of advertising ("Dreams come true with my new shoe"). Instead, Barkley—who has cultivated a public persona as a no-nonsense kind of guy—tells kids that his Nike shoes "won't make you dunk like me, won't make you rich like me, they'll just give you shoes like me."[15] In the athletic shoeindustry, recall how Reebok tried to counter Nike's sign strategy of labeling them-selves as the only shoe signature (the swoosh) with the courage to challenge the fetishism of sign purchases. Reebok's "No Slogans" campaign

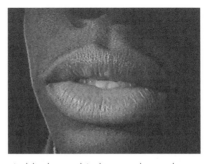

A black youth's lips and mouth are made to stand for Sprite's image and voice: "Image Is Nothing!"

was a grandiose sign war effort aimed at calling attention to Nike's "Just Do It" signature tag line. But young viewers were quick to suspect that this was yet another ad scam because they had learned their semiotic lessons well: they understood that "No Slogans" was in fact Reebok's newest slogan. In sign wars, there seems to be no Archimedean point where one can stand outside the world. By posturing as if they were eschewing any sign position, the Reebok campaign actually upped the distrust level of youthful viewers and further upped the ante in these advertising wars.

The tone of voice in Sprite's ads is savvy, calculated to appease the anger of potential consumers who have been hailed way too often. A Sprite print ad aimed at women begins by conventionally hailing the viewer before shifting to a wry and knowing tone so that the ad's metacommunication is (in sympathy with the viewer) "give the rhetoric a rest!" Like so many of the ads we have looked at, this one is deliberately self-reflexive about the relationship between the ad and the viewer.

> You're *a woman*
> *of the* **90's.**
> **Bold**, *self-assured and empowered.*
> *Climbing the ladder of success at work*
> *and the Stairmaster at the gym.*
> *You're socially aware and politically correct.*
> *But you probably know all this already*
> *because every ad and* **magazine**
> **NO** *has told you a* zillion *times.*
> **wonder**
> **you're**
> **thirsty.**

In advertising, themes of pseudoindividuality appear to annul authenticity. The Sprite campaign has positioned itself precisely as the critique of fictive advertising claims for preconstituted individuality. One ad, for example, narrates the struggle of a middle-class youth seeking to find his identity through the appropriation of subcultural signifiers. The ad parodies the impulse among the mass of advertisers to invite the viewer to try on the totem identities of this or that subculture. The youth stands at a busy urban traffic intersection as he narrates his search for a "cool" identity, trying on, in turn, the identities of a homeboy, a skateboarder, a preppie, and a boombox-carrying fatboy. With the assistance of innovative photographic techniques, he visually transmutates into and out of these identities, rejecting each in turn, until he is left alone with himself and thirsty:

Sprite tells the story of a youth who is in quest of a more interesting identity. He tries on the stereotyped looks of various youth subcultures. In these scenes, he becomes a stoner skateboarder and a boombox-toting fatboy before returning to his own puzzled self.

A YOUTH'S INNER VOICE: *What is cool? Does who ya hang with make you cool?* (He tries on the guise of a wannabe black dude in black homeboy voice.) *Yo, B. Check me out! I'm funky.*

INNER VOICE: *Maybe not. Hey wait, these dudes are cool* (referring to long-haired, stoned skateboarders)

SKATEBOARD VOICE: *Yo, brruuuhhd. Totally cooool.*

INNER VOICE: *Nah! Maybe going prep is cool?*

PREP VOICE IN BLOND TENNIS ATTIRE: *Hey Buffy! Ha. Ha. Ha. Ha.*

INNER VOICE: *Now, that is not cool.*

INNER VOICE: *If I was like this guy [fat boy with boombox], then I'd be cool.* (now weary from his search, he sighs.) *I need a cold drink. What should I drink?*

BLACK NARRATIVE VOICEOVER RESPONDS: *Give your brain a rest. Obey your thirst.*

The Brother's voice is that of authenticity, and he's telling us that this is a bogus search. One cannot satisfactorily locate self-identity in signs of authenticity that have been abstracted from other people's lives and turned into magic icons by ad wizards. To those familiar with contemporary TV advertising, there is more than a touch of irony to this Sprite campaign. After all, Sprite's sappy "I Love the Sprite in You" campaign has long defined the parameters of signifying teenage pseudoindividuality: Drink Sprite and have a special personality. In spite of all its irreverence, Sprite chooses not to acknowledge the specter of its own inauthentic advertising past.

Coke is test-marketing a product named "OK" soda, a carbonated, fruity drink for teenagers and young adults. With a new product launch, the task of differentiating the product image and sidestepping the intense skepticism of youth becomes even more manifest. According to Greenwald, Calabresi, and Van Tassel, "With OK's deliberately drab cans and pseudo-Zen profundities ('What's the point of OK soda? Well, what's the point of anything?'), Coke hopes to capture a generation . . . inoculated against pitches from having grown up with television jingles at breakfast." Coke's marketing managers perceive their audience as "very versed in participating in the commercial world. . . . Probably their main area of power is as a consumer."[16] Coke has devised an elaborate set of strategies to deny its own advertising and marketing agendas. To wit, Coke's advertising agency, Wieden & Kennedy, created a hotline and planted messages such as the following "trashing its own claims" for OK:

> *"Ah, this is Pam H. from Newton, Massachusetts, and I resent you saying that everything is going to be O.K. You don't know anything about my life. You don't know what I've been through in the last month. I really resent it. I'm tired of you people trying to tell me things that you don't have any idea about. I resent it. [Click!]"—Message left on the 1-800 line set up to promote OK soda.*[17]

The 1-800 number was motivated by Coke's perception of teenagers sharing an "inveterate cynicism about corporate messages." The hotline permits the teens themselves to more actively define the product and their relationship to it. This is a campaign designed to lure back skeptical viewers by inviting them to participate, and thus invest socially (via hotlines and chain letters) in the meaning of the product:

> Armed with its findings, Coke set out to address the very real problems that teens face without seeming, on the surface at least, to exploit them. The OK trademark struck company marketers as the ideal solution. "It underpromises," says Brian Lanahan. "It doesn't say, 'This is the next great thing.' It's the flip side of overclaiming, which is what teens perceive a lot of brands do." At the same time, the OK theme attempts to play into the sense of optimism that this generation retains. ("OK-ness," says a campaign slogan, "is the belief that, no matter what, things are going to be OK.")[18]

Campaigns such as this revisit arguments Marcuse made about one-dimensionality, where oppositional arguments are prepared in a preconstituted format. Coke's hotline of recorded messages is really quite remarkable in the way it visits and corrals each reason for opposing this new drink. These recorded messages even include a well-stated critique of Coke's commodification of the language of daily life. Dennis J. of Aurora, Colorado, states:

"Listen, I got something to say to you people. I think it's stupid that I can't say the word OK now. What, you own the words OK now? Yeah, I own the words 'Have a nice day.' All right? [Click!]"

So real, you don't even know if its Memorex. This is the alienated spectator with a vengeance. Ads like these offer the viewer a posture of knowingness with which to present themselves in a world beyond their daily control. Sure, you're still getting screwed, but now you can count yourself one of the select few who are hip to how it happens. The knowing wink that began with Levi's in the 1980s has widened into a knowing shrug.

A Commodity Community?

Saturn's current "Homecoming" ad seems to move in precisely the opposite direction of the wave of cynicism discussed above. This is what we previously referred to as the flip side of jadedness.

"This summer we invited everyone who owns a Saturn to visit Spring Hill, a Saturn Homecoming. They could see where their cars were built and meet the people who built them. We could thank them for believing in us. 44,000 people spent their vacations with us, at a car plant. . . . "

The aura of community and a desire to belong are in the air. A softly melodic country twang to the music (reminiscent of Crosby, Stills, and Nash) frames the imagery of cars caravaning along two-lane country highways toward the new "Mecca," with the lettering on their rear windows telling the story: "Spring Hill or Bust." This ad smacks of the memory and nostalgia themes we have discussed, but like so many other recent ads, this one situates that nostalgic moment in the present and not the past. Saturn presents itself as a company that reintegrates the relationship between producers and consumers; they are not, in other words, another global firm that remains impersonally distant through the vast market nexus. This ad epitomizes what it means to talk about belonging to a commodity totem group as it depicts 44,000 people spending their vacations to form a community based not on geographical locale nor occupational similarity nor religious convictions, but on their common status as consumers of the totem sign/car named Saturn.

Has Saturn pioneered a new kind of commodity community? Sure, capitalist society has long since seen company towns organized around the production practices of the early capitalist steel and railroad barons. Half a century later, corporately de-

The Saturn "Homecoming" ad is full of images of Saturn consumers meeting and greeting Saturn workers, of tents and food lines à la a country fair or a church picnic, of people mingling together in their search for community and their search for meaning.

signed and organized suburbs laid the foundations for commodifying the whole of social life. Today, nearly a century after Pullman's coercive efforts to materially integrate his workers into the commodity form, we see a higher, more spiritual, sense of community as consumers voluntarily commit themselves to the spirit of the totem group. Could this be the postmodern community that emerges from the "logic of late capitalist society?"

Saturn's imaginary new social order is structured around a political economy of signs grounded in "models, codes and signs."[19] There can be no doubt about this. However, images of Saturn's totem-car community are not simply a figment of their simulacrum: they also represent a GM strategy for climbing out of its deindustrialization doldrums with a reindustrialization plan located in the previously nonindustrial South. Saturn started with a special agreement between the UAW and GM's spinoff organization and a non-GM system of management.[20] Another Saturn ad narrated by a Saturn worker explains how workers at the Saturn plant are given the responsibility to "pull the rope" and "stop the line" when they spot any problem. The Saturn campaign strategy has focused on a symbiotic spirit of goodwill between Saturn workers and Saturn consumers.

The Saturn "Homecoming" ad seems to contradict much of what we have argued about the collapse of history, geography, sociability, and narrative in ads. Though time and space are the very real and material coordinates of social life, in the advertising spectacle the primary kind of time is simultaneity, and space most often appears to be disconnected from material forces. Hence, a wide range of ads depict a world in which individual consumers move without constraint and without encountering any interventions from others. Even other campaigns aimed at reconstructing a sense of community—such as MCI's "Family and Friends" campaign that claims to help sustain important personal bonds and relationships—construct sociality through video codes. Put another way, it is difficult to know any longer which direction the causal arrow is pointing: do real social relations translate into sign values or do the efforts by Saturn and MCI turn their sign values into real spatial and social relations?

A wide range of 1990s campaigns visualize culture as if it is autonomous and unlinked to material production. As opposed to the Saturn style, these ads represent postmodern culture as simultaneously global and individuated, as a culture that pivots on the actions of the consumer and not the producer. Far more frequent than the Saturn approach is an advertising representation of a postmodern social and cultural world that pictures our most important relationships as free-floating. In the worlds constructed by 1993 campaigns for Diet Coke ("Taste It All"), AT&T ("The I Plan"), Reebok ("No Slogans") and Levi's free-floating series, the only social relations worth noting were monads and dyads. Individuals float through homogenous spaces that have been completely abstracted from place. In these spaces un-

Total individual freedom? The Levi's ads imagine individuals as free-floating through a space marked only by the presence of their sign. Total individual freedom is also the subject and the sign of Diet Coke's imagery.

governed by the laws of gravity, souls blessed by commodities transcend the conventions and constraints of daily life by way of visual clichés. Such scenes are hardly new. Over the years, these decontextualized representations have grown so commonplace that we scarcely take notice anymore. These ads emphasize totalizing individual freedom in a world where the only bond people share is their pursuit of self-satisfaction under the banner of an aestheticized corporate presence, ultimately represented by a brand sign or the corporate sign: GE, Coke, AT&T, and the like.

These advertising representations depict a new global order sensitive to combining multiculturalism with the primacy of the individual. The geographical space represented in these ads is a space that instantly encompasses everywhere, yet has no spatial coordinates in the social, political, or economic world. Production has been quietly, but firmly, banished from these representations. Instead, montages of isolated individuals provide the legitimation corollary to flexible accumulation—flexible distribution and consumption is individually tailored to your needs by the technocratic rationality of firms like AT&T: "What is this? It's your life made easier." AT&T's "I" campaign isolates the always moving individual as the focal point in today's world. Colorfully portraying a new age of global multiculturalism by placing society and community in absentia, in AT&T's world the individual shifts continuously from Asian to European to female to male. The rhetoric of individualism is visually represented in an ethnically heterogenous world unified by the presence of AT&T. AT&T's voice is reassuring: "What makes us all the same is that we're all different." Consumers need no longer fear the forces of massification nor need they fear the dominance of one culture over another, since corporate capital is now equipped to unify our diversity. AT&T will tailor a package of phone service to your needs "because it's based on your life."

The 1993 "Taste It All" Diet Coke ad campaign built on many of the same conventions that have marked advertising culture for the last 30 years, but it also registered a significant completion of an ideological transition that had been taking place for some time. Like AT&T, Diet Coke offered an idealized representation of a postmodern social landscape—a landscape dedicated to the privatized consumption ethic sponsored by corporate capital, a landscape where community obligations have withered away to afford maximum freedom for individuals to construct their own identities. Diet Coke endorsed the freedom to go beyond conventional ideological boundaries about how individuals construct themselves. One ad opened with references to "a minister who surfs," followed by "a surgeon who sculpts" and an "insurance agent who speeds." True freedom is thus located in the figure of what Benetton's magazine, *Colours,* calls the "cultural transvestite": members of a new global generation who make consumption choices that stand at odds with their ascribed identities (e.g., Polish cowboys, Japanese rappers, and white Rastafarians).[21] To be sure, Diet Coke offers timid versions of this "cultural transvestism" to indicate that we live in a time when anything goes. Diet Coke offers a world in which there is no hint of domination, a place where the absence of work activities crucially defines the flavor of freedom. The regulated character of work no longer blocks individuals from being what they want to be. Occupational identity is not completely irrelevant, but neither is it any longer the dominant source of identity in a leisure society. Occupation is something we can transcend in our leisure lives where our personal choices replace occupation as source of identity. This comes at the same time that Americans are actually working more hours and not fewer.[22]

Production vanishes and leisure becomes omnipresent against a backdrop of nature that is perfectly rationalized and tamed. With nature settings as the stage, speed and risk signify freedom. Here individuals can experience transcendent moments with arms outstretched or uplifted. They dive, leap, and soar, their heads tilted back to suggest the orgiastic ecstasy that their life-style affords. Arms extended upward suggest a similar transcendent sense of satisfaction. The pleasure of transcendence replaces the desire for sexuality. It is not surprising that this ad ends on a mountain top, site of magically transcendent moments. In the middle of the Diet

Coke ad, text on the screen reads: "Some people live their life as an exclamation not an explanation." This exemplifies the way in which advertising has usurped the traditional role of philosophy, albeit here the philosophy is Don't Think. With "You got to taste it all," Coke mimics Pepsi's philosophical imperative, "You gotta have it." Coke's imperative to live your life for the moment preaches self-actualization minus self-knowledge. You don't have to know anything, because all you need to know has been entered in preconstituted form into Diet Coke.

The Spectacle in the Fractured Marketplace

We are frequently asked: "Well, who's winning the sign wars these days?" It's always difficult to point to a single winner since sign wars are fought out in market niches. Nevertheless, over the past few years Nike and its advertising agency, Wieden & Kennedy, have defined the cutting edge of the field more than anyone else. Before them, Levi's dominated their sign niche with a comparable authority. In the early 1980s, Pepsi seized the rudder in the so-called cola wars. Of course, before them one of the early giants in the field of sign values was Coca-Cola. Coca-Cola was the first company to develop a global advertising image. Few of us are unfamiliar with "I'd Like to Teach the World to Sing in Perfect Harmony" ad, made in 1971 and reshot in 1989. The ad featured a chorale of young people gathered on a mountain top, costumed as if they came from all corners of the Earth, learning to sing the words "Coca-Cola" in perfect harmony while happily beaming. According to Glancey, "The idea behind the advertising is that we really are part of some global village: we all want the same things, we all have access to them and we all respond to the same imagery. Coca-Cola sells itself as democratic, international and liberating; no wonder it's good for you."[23]

In the 1970s, Pepsi copied the same advertising approach used by Coke to present soft commodity fetishes—for example, adorable scenes of little boys being licked by puppy dogs, their soft focus cuteness overlaid with the Pepsi logo. But in the 1980s, Pepsi scored heavily in their advertising vis-à-vis Coke by creating a campaign involving more visually memorable sexual fetishism, with images such as the infamous abstracted red lips around a straw in the Pepsi can. Second, Pepsi began to tell different kinds of commodity narratives, and told them in different ways. Frequently, the stories turned out to be jokes. The butt of the jokes was the Coke emblem. Third, they jacked up the celebrity fetishism level. The tables had turned: Pepsi no longer mimicked Coke, now Coke copied Pepsi, trying to match celebrity power with celebrity power (Pepsi had Michael Jackson while Coke weakly countered with New Kids on the Block). Still possessor of the best known brand sign in the world, Coke's once hegemonic advertising approach was now sapping their strength. In an effort to sustain and spread their unitary global sign, they had become inflexible. The sameness of their imagery, previously their strength, was now a factor of a slow erosion of strength in newly expanding global markets. The nadir of Coke's advertising came with a mechanical global campaign during the 1992 Olympics that featured pop culture celebrities such as Randy Travis guiding viewers on quick tours through nationalist cultures around the world, always focused on how Coke plugs into these cultures without disrupting them. Still trying for perfect harmony, Coke's stress on a monolithic image was now way out of whack with their audiences.

Finally, in 1993, rampant channel surfing convinced Coke to abandon its reliance on traditional ad agencies in favor of Creative Artists Agency, a Hollywood talent agency, to generate dozens of TV ads with the focus on entertainment. This moved Coke from their long-time strategy of promoting one great global aesthetic, to a new, wildly polyaesthetic campaign based on the principle of entertainment. Coke moved from building ads around semiotic formulas to constructing ads based on the pleasure of the text. Their semiotic formulas had always aimed at steering viewers toward a single set of meanings, but their recent campaigns emphasize varied aesthetic styles and narrative conventions. These ads no longer steer viewers toward a single interpretation, but open the door to polysemic (many meanings) interpretations. Every ad in the campaign differed in look, feel, and tone. Usually, viewers learn to recognize the aesthetic of a campaign so that after they have seen one or two ads in a series they can spot any other ads in the series at a glance. The 1993 Coke campaign defied this with ads that ranged from an icehouse percussion dance to the whimsy of animated polar bears watching the aurora borealis to avant-garde photographic games accompanying pieces of music that seemed rather indifferent to the agenda of the advertising.

Perhaps this Coke strategy defines one wave of the future in sign wars. It provides a new mode of differentiation, while avoiding the deep cynicism that is emerging as a central voice of advertising. Of course, as we have shown, Coke has also put some of their eggs in the cynicism basket with new brand lines such as OK cola, which brings us back to Wieden & Kennedy. While Wieden & Kennedy may specialize in authenticity, their work also epitomizes the new cynicism. In fact, their versions of authenticity and media-referential irreverence seem to be joined at the hip. On the one hand, Nike's astonishing success with their sign, the swoosh, has been rooted in their ability to stake themselves better than any other advertiser to themes of authenticity. And yet they are even willing to desecrate their own logo. This has given their voice credibility, and makes them likeable because nothing seems sacred to them, not even their most precious commodity: their swoosh sign. Is this why Wieden & Kennedy features William Burroughs in a Nike campaign? Why would Nike (athletic shoes) feature the same William Burroughs whose past includes antibourgeois writings such as *Naked Lunch*, homosexuality, heroin use, mental illness, and manslaughter? Is it because as we've already noted with respect to a Gap ad (in chapter 5) that Burroughs has become reduced to a signifier that evokes the authenticity of alienation? If you can no longer express your alienation, at least you can embrace a signifier of it.

A decade ago, Fredric Jameson observed that "aesthetic production today has become integrated into commodity production generally: the frantic economic urgency of producing fresh waves of ever more novel-seeming goods . . . at ever greater rates of turnover, now assigns an increasingly essential structural function and position to aesthetic innovation."[24] We expect the feverish intensity of sign wars to continue for some time yet. There will continue to be innovators such as Coke and Nike, and there will also be legions of imitators. As long as this dialectic of differentiation and imitation continues, so too will the problems of clutter and acceleration continue to haunt the sign war industry. Our concerns, as the reader has surmised by now, lie less with the continuing profitability of the sign war industry than with the toll it takes on what is conventionally known as public culture. This volume has pursued the thesis that when capital annexes culture as a semiotic universe and directs the meanings of images to obey the logic of commodity relations, it also introduces into culture the contradictions of the commodity form. By turning to culture to expand the range of exchange values, capital has exported its crisis tendencies into the cultural sphere.[25] The capitalist ideal of overcoming barriers to capital circulation has bred a commodity culture driven by an amazingly rapid turnover of signifiers and signifieds. Free-flying signifiers and signifieds are continuously recirculated into a still newer pastiche combo of the day. The combinations inflate, the combinations deflate, and the process starts again, hinging and unhinging signifiers and signifieds to define new signs.

As more competitors squeeze in, the velocity of this process accelerates because it becomes very difficult to hold on to a differentiated sign position for very long. Advertising's own unremitting efforts to reproduce and sustain a system of sign values contributes to breakdowns in the signifier–signified circuit. Signifiers trade places so readily

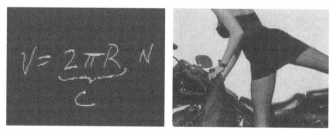

This reference to velocity comes from a short-lived Reebok compaign called "The Physics of Physique." The formula for velocity illustrates much of what we have been talking about.. It is difficult to imagine a much more free-floating signifier. In the ad, the formula is turned into a second-order signifier of the sculpted designer body (achieved through the application of Reebok physics). But now we have chosen to rip this image even from that context, so that we can make it testify against the culture industry and its velocity of sign turnover.

with signifieds that it grows impossible to tell which end is which. But with the relationship between signifier and signified reduced to a state of equivalent indifference, differential meaning drifts. In the "simulacrum" of television advertising, the sign of difference replaces difference. In the whirl of sign wars, advertising generates a glut of signs that makes it difficult to differentiate those signs. Fueling this motor of cultural appropriation requires the constant sacrifice of "unpolluted meaning systems." This pollution process and the constant rerouting of meanings of authenticity, identity, and resistance has taken a deep toll on our culture: it has cost us our faith. Leslie Savan quotes "a fellow media malcontent":

> "Veal, that's what we've become, especially the young 'uns." That's what anyone raised by the corporations, fed their version of "fun," "excitement," and above all, "hip," becomes—pale, docile, and unmuscled, a creature finely attuned to the aesthetics of its own flesh but incapable of standing on its own legs. Your movement beyond the TV box may be restricted, your opportunity to frolic in uncommercialized fields may be nil, but it's OK, being veal: All your life, the corporate stock feeders bring you sugar food and hormone entertainment. Raised to consume, kept soft in head and belly—the modern spirit is slaughtered early.[26]

Sign wars represent a maturing stage of the political economy of sign value. Driven by processes of accelerated decontextualization of meanings, are sign wars contributing to a generalized crisis of meaning in our culture? Today's evolving economic formations, usually described as flexible accumulation, seem to place an even greater premium on turning culture into sign value. If the chronic tendency of advertising to cannibalize culture has already driven us to new heights of cultural cynicism, where will this next stage of mobile (placeless) capital push commodity culture, and what new cultural contradictions will arise? We end in what seems a conundrum: On the one hand, we see advertising as continuing to provide ideological frames that support the hegemony of capital, and most importantly, the commodity form. On the other hand, as the logic of capital penetrates the sign, it introduces the conditions for crises of meaning amid alienated audiences. It remains to be seen what kind of cultural politics and practices will emerge out of the cultural contradictions and semiotic hemorrhaging that accompany sign wars.

Notes

Introduction

1. John Berger, 1972, p. 134.
2. Judith Williamson, 1978; see also Stuart Hall, 1980.
3. Judith Williamson, 1978, p. 43.
4. P. M. Fischer et al., 1991, pp. 3145–3148.
5. Semiotics is well suited to the tasks of both constructing and deconstructing sign values because it mimics the structural mechanics of both the commodity form and the advertising form. The "preferred" interpretive conventions of the advertising form reproduce the logic of the commodity form. The latter consists of three intertwined moments: (1) abstraction, the removal of a meaningful action or relationship from its context; (2) equivalence exchange, the formal relation of universal exchangeability between items that are otherwise not comparable; and (3) reification, the conversion of human attributes and relations into the characteristics of objects or things. Advertisements routinely abstract meaning systems from their contexts, place them into relations of formal exchange, engineer a transfer of meanings to construct an equivalency, and propose a reified commodity sign. In this sense, we see the advertising framework replicating the logic of the commodity form.
6. Martha T. Moore, June 15, 1993b, p. B1.
7. Nena Baker, April 28, 1991, pp. K1, K5.
8. Roland Barthes, 1972.
9. Nena Baker, March 14, 1992, p. B1.
10. Stuart Elliott, May 10, 1991, p. D1.
11. "'93 Camaro Advertising Arrives with Rock 'n' Roll Beat," March 29, 1993.
12. See Theodor Adorno, 1941; Bernard Gendron, 1986.
13. Richard Sennett and Jonathan Cobb, 1972.
14. Dick Hebidge, 1979.
15. See Robert Goldman and Stephen Papson, 1991.
16. Bruce Horovitz, July 16, 1991, p. D6.
17. Dick Hebidge, 1988, p. 237.

18. Judith Williamson, 1978, p. 13.
19. See Terry Eagleton, 1991, p. 1.
20. Herbert Marcuse, 1964.

Chapter 1

1. "Director of the Year: Bay," May 1993, p. 9.
2. We suspect this is changing. Over decades, Coke has established itself as the paradigm of the unified sign and unified advertising themes and executions. But the 1993 Coke campaign departs from this tradition with a campaign based on multiplicity. Every ad is aesthetically different. Rather than producing globally encompassing, but reductionistic, campaigns such as their 1980s blockbuster approach "Coke Is It!," Coke now hails each market segment in a different voice. Thematic unification is still supplied, of course, by the tag line "Always Coca-Cola." Recognizing that ads must now entertain trigger-happy remote-control users, Coke turned to Hollywood to make these ads. Until recently, the leading firms tended to pursue strategies based on maintaining market share via brand awareness, but Coke's experiment may encourage other leaders to be less conservative. In a different fashion, industry leader Nike under the direction of Wieden & Kennedy has been able to establish themselves as a metasign. Though Nike ads range widely in substance and message, all their ads speak with a common subtext—an overarching sensibility—summarized in the Nike swoosh symbol.
3. After MCI snuggled up to viewers with home movie encodings of our personal lives, AT&T responded by producing ads that appeared relatively undifferentiated from the MCI ads. We might read this as an example of research-driven advertising, since marketing focus groups expressed a preference for greater realism in the ads. Or we might view it as a self-conscious strategy to confuse consumers, a view shared by some marketing experts. After all, confused consumers who could not tell whose ad was which would be unlikely to make changes in their long-distance carrier.
4. AT&T's hostility level peaked in the Fiji wrong number ad when a snide operator from another company says "You're not dealing with AT&T," to which the angry consumer responds, "Well, I am now!" and slams down the phone. See also AT&T's "The Siren Song Is Just a Myth" ad.
5. Bruce Horovitz, January 19, 1992, D1.
6. See Alex Castellanos, April 20, 1992, p. 24.
7. Bruce Horovitz, January 19, 1992.
8. "Back in 1980, it took AT&T nearly a year to get a commercial from concept to completion. By 1984, that time period had been compressed to seven months. And by 1989, it had shrunk to two months. Most recently, AT&T has shown the ability to respond within a few weeks to the competition. But the competition continues to be quicker. In January, 1990, after an AT&T snafu with its switching network caused its long-distance network to fail in some areas, Sprint reacted within two days with an AT&T–bashing print ad that

said 'other options exist' besides AT&T" (Horovitz, 1992). The impact of computers on producing advertising cannot be underestimated here.

9. George Zinkhan and Rudy Hirshleim, 1992, pp. 80–88.
10. Reebok CEO Paul Fireman, quoted in Gary Strauss and Martha T. Moore, June 24, 1993, B2.
11. Allan J. Magrath, 1992, p. 26.
12. Martha T. Moore, August 12, 1992, pp. B1, B7; Richard F. Chay, 1991, pp. 30–37; Diane Crispell and Kathleen Brandenburg, 1993, p. 26. Brand value can influence crucial variables such as shelf placement in the supermarket.
13. Peter H. Farquhar, Julia Y. Han, and Yuji Ijiri, 1992, p. 16.
14. Bill Saporito, March 23, 1992, p. 68.
15. We wish to thank Julia Reid for bringing this example to our attention.
16. Bob Garfield, March 1, 1993, p. 48.
17. Randall Rothenberg, October 20, 1991, section 6, p. 30.
18. Peter Carlson, November 3, 1991, p. W15.
19. Peter Carlson, November 3, 1991, p. W15.
20. Nancy Millman, August 16, 1992, p. 1C.
21. "'More Is Less' Approach Cuts into Ad Clutter at Magazines," May 29, 1989, p. 27. "'It's easy to get lost in ad banks and it's easy to become invisible,' says Lori Osiek, advertising manager for Esprit, which ran a 10-page ad portfolio last spring. 'Our strategy of late has been multiple pages coming out with a bang.'"
22. Robert Hughes, 1980.
23. Dennis Rodkin, June 5, 1989, p. 38. See also Randall Rothenberg, December 10, 1989, p. L11.
24. "Advertising Everywhere!," 1992, p. 752.
25. See Robert Goldman, 1992, ch. 7, "This Is Not an Ad."
26. Randall Rothenberg, January 21, 1991, p. 6D.
27. There has even been an attempt to revive the much despised "unique selling proposition" as a response to the crisis of differentiation in parity markets. See Joanne Lipman, September 11, 1992, p. B20.
28. Stuart Elliott, February 19, 1993, p. D18.
29. Harry Berkowitz, January 25, 1993, p. 27.
30. Cited in Harry Berkowitz, January 25, 1993, p. 27.
31. Victoria Bushnell, June 15, 1990, p. 8B.
32. Ira Teinowitz, April 29, 1991, p. 50
33. Bob Garfield, quoted in Dennis Chase, September 21, 1992, p. 58.
34. Bob Garfield, quoted in Dennis Chase, September 21, 1992, p. 58.
35. According to figures provided by Goldberg Moser O'Neill, the San Francisco agency that created the ad (see Jamie Beckett, 1991).
36. Bob Garfield, March 18, 1991, p. S8.
37. See Bob Garfield, May 31, 1993, p. 46, and December 7, 1992, p. 53.
38. Martha T. Moore, March 18, 1993, p. B10.

39. Tony Wright, president of McElligott, Wright, Morrison, White, quoted in Dan Wascoe, July 28, 1991, p. B9.

40. "Sometimes You Win, Sometimes You Lose. . . . Anheuser-Busch Loses Suit over Parody Ad," April 5, 1993, p. 3.

41. Kim Foltz, February, 20, 1991, p. 17D. See also Cindy L. Yorks, June 13, 1990, p. E1; Edward Kiersh, March 22, 1992, p. 28; Pamela Swanigan, May 2, 1993, p. H1.

42. Marcy Magiera, January 29, 1990, p. 16.

43. See Robert Goldman and Steve Papson, 1994.

44. Brian Bagot, 1990, pp. 61–66.

45. David J. Jefferson, 1991, p. 114; Rich Wilner, February 1, 1992, p. S12; Marcy Magiera, June 8, 1992, p. 8.

46. Glenn Rifkin, February 10, 1993, p. D7.

47. H. Peter Goehrig, an Asics vice-president, cited in Chris Woodyard, September 4, 1991, p. D3.

48. Kim Foltz, February 20, 1991, p. D17.

49. Leslie Savan, April 2, 1991, p. 43.

50. See Marcy Magiera and Pat Sloan, February 25, 1991, pp. 3, 54.

51. Leslie Savan, April 2, 1991, p. 43.

52. More than a half-billion pairs of Converse All-Stars have been sold since 1917. "All-Stars came to be called 'Chucks' because they were endorsed by Chuck Taylor, a semi-pro basketball player and Converse salesman. Chucks became the overwhelming preference in the National Basketball Association. George Mikan, Wilt Chamberlain, Oscar Robertson and Bob Cousy never wore anything but All-Stars. When the Boston Celtics won eight consecutive NBA titles between 1959 and 1966, they all wore black Chucks. . . . Today Chucks, like Keds, are alive and kicking as fashion items. They have become big with certain rock stars, such as Duran Duran and Bruce Springsteen. The Rolling Stones chose All-Stars as their official 'Steel Wheels' tour shoe, and there is even a rock group that calls itself "Men Who Wear Chucks" (William Ecenbarger, April 18, 1993, p. 27C.).

53. Bob Garfield, April 19, 1993, p. 44.

54. The conjuncture between difference and individual freedom of choice is located in the positioning concept of "style." Style works to contain the antagonism between class and culture by turning the latter into a series of commodity signs that we may select to try on, wear, display, and even own.

55. "Rat on Dinosaur Rip-Offs; Help Universal Get Richer," July 12, 1993, p. A2.

56. Nick Fielding and Larry Black, July 19, 1992, p. 6.

57. Steve Woodward, July 7, 1992, p. 12C; see also Jamie Beckett, July 15, 1992, p. B1.

58. "The conflict leaves the IOC and national Olympic teams in a quandary, even if they could legally enforce their ambushing claims. Many of those acused of 'piggybacking' on the Olympic sponsorship of their rivals are valuable backers of individual teams. An IOC crackdown would therefore amount to cannibalism, according to marketing analysts" (Nick Fielding and Larry Black, July 19, 1992, p. 6).

59. See Bernard Edelman, 1979; James Gaines, 1991.

60. Jeff Jensen, January 17, 1994, p. 43. Terry Lefton, January 31, 1994, p. 1.
61. "Judge Denies Everready's Request to Ban Coors Commercial," May 15, 1991.
62. Cited in Stuart Elliott, April 29, 1991.
63. How can there be a false association in the world of commodity signs where nearly every association is arbitrary? The implication here is that truth begins and ends with the condition of commodity (image) ownership.
64. "Judge Denies Everready's Request to Ban Coors Commercial," May 15, 1991; George Lazarus, May 16, 1991, p. 4.
65. Cited in Dennis Rodkin, June 5, 1989, p. 38.
66. Judith Graham, September 11, 1989, p. 3.
67. Leslie Savan, January 9, 1990, p. 56.
68. Bruce Horovitz, June 2, 1992, p. D1.
69. Alison Simko, January 13, 1992, p. S22.
70. John Berger and Jean Mohr, 1982, p. 100.
71. Leslie Savan, November 24, 1992, p. 47
72. Gary Levin, February 17, 1992, p. 62.
73. Guy Debord, 1977, p. 9.
74. Leslie Savan, November 24, 1992, p. 47.
75. Leslie Savan, November 24, 1992, p. 47.
76. Leslie Savan, November 24, 1992, p. 47.
77. See Dean Baker, November 6, 1991, p. E1; Alix M. Freedman, May 31, 1989, p. B12.

Chapter 2

1. Robert Goldman and John Wilson, 1983.
2. Theodor Adorno, 1941; Max Horkheimer and Theodor Adorno, 1972; Marcuse, 1964.
3. John Wilson, 1988.
4. Jean Baudrillard, 1983a.
5. Dick Hebidge, 1988, p. 211.
6. Still, the cultural contradictions continue to proliferate. Advertising efforts to deny media hegemony draw on new media technologies such as video synthesizers, computer–video linkages, and digitized images that permit still greater manipulation of frames. Television has become increasingly dominated by the fetishism of technique. The prototype of fetishized TV is MTV which cultivates media reflexivity and jadedness by relying upon familiarity with television codes to subvert and one-up those codes. MTV cuts up the codes and edits (pastes) them into an ironic pastiche of the code.
7. John Fiske, 1987, p. 24.
8. See Kevin Goldman, June 9, 1993, p. B6; Alan Liddle, January 29, 1991, p. 12.
9. Erving Goffman, 1959, p. 112.
10. "Come backstage with me darling, and I'll show you the wires and gizmos. You'll like that! You'll be in on the secret. And that's part of the secret, see—American audiences love to be in the know. They love to go backstage. They want to see the machinery that

fools them, the back projections, the special effects. Right? Right! They don't realize that showing them the machinery is the show, and while they're hypnotized by the gears going round, the micro-chips blinking on/off, while you let them see the marketing surveys that reveal their kinky emotional ratchets and levers, you can really get your hands deep down into their pockets. They get hypnotized thinking they are learning how the rubes get hypnotized" (Jay Cantor, 1987).

11. Erving Goffman, 1959, p. 128.
12. Judging by the reaction, many rock 'n' roll fans felt betrayed that Clapton had sold out. He later apologized to his fans, explaining that he was abusing alcohol at the time.
13. See John Caughie, 1981.
14. Karl Heider, 1976.
15. The jerky and searching camera can signify different moods. With rapid-fire editing techniques, it can convey a sense of energy, but without editing it can connote the strained tedium of daily life. Witness the difference between AT&T ads that dwelt on a single scene to draw out the anxiety and tension of work in a vicious corporate world, whereas Michelob combined the restless camera with flashy editing practices to furnish a feeling of gritty glamour in leisure life.

   Advertising for airlines and rental cars aimed at business people communicates a hyperreal style by creating a sense of blurred, rapid horizontal camera movement through a negative space—*space-in-between*—flash-panning past hypersignifiers, such as fragmented glimpses of flight schedule monitors, baggage, and mechanics' limbs in motion. Space-in-between is designed to pass through as rapidly as possible. It is space governed by norms of efficiency, and emptied of warmth, personality, or desire. These scenes have their semiotic flip side in personal-touch scenes that punctuate these rapidly paced vignettes aimed at the postmodern nomad: for example, a flight attendant takes a traveler's drink, careful not to wake him.
16. Karel Reisz and Gavin Millar, 1968.
17. See Alfred Schutz, 1967.
18. This produces opposing interpretive tendencies. Hypermagnified objects and gestures are presented to viewers loaded with significance. After being freighted with layers of meaningful association from years of viewing ads, well-versed viewers who skim across the surface of magnified signifiers can bring forth meaningful associations. On the other hand, hypersignifiers are by nature spectacularly decontextualized and hence confusing.
19. Debbie Seeman, June 13, 1988, p. 28.
20. When pop and rock 'n' roll music saturated ads in the late 1980s, advertisers turned to opera to find differentiated musical soundbites.
21. Henri Lefebvre, 1971.
22. Guy Debord, 1977.
23. See Marshall Berman, 1982.
24. See Wolfgang Fritz Haug, 1986.
25. The Energizer campaign is thus both critical and parasitic: it has lampooned ads for soaps, deodorants, network trailers, and Slim Whitman–style record offers.

26. The Sprite ads were actually shot by the high school students who appear in them. They used a video camera given them by the Burrell agency of Chicago. On the other hand, the Surf ads by Ogilvy and Mather were mock-up home movies that featured real people.

27. Advertisers no longer presume a consensus about social definitions of need. Trendy magazines catering to the avant-garde, such as *LA Style* and *Details,* now openly mock the meaning of consumption. Meanwhile, advertisers (e.g., K-Mart) aiming at working-class audiences seek to reassure viewers that the needs they service are not manufactured, but correspond to those of actual people like yourself.

28. Richard Parker and Lindsey Churchill, 1986.

29. Gregory Bateson, 1972.

30. Jean Baudrillard, 1983a.

Chapter 3

1. Another force influencing the semiotics of alienation may have to do with the advertising people themselves and not their audiences. DDB Needham Worldwide's consumer behavior lifestyle study uncovered an interesting finding when they ran an abridged version of their questionnaire with an in-house publication staff. The agency people differed significantly from the general population surveyed. The title of the report, "I Have Met the Customer and He Ain't Me," summarizes nicely. In particular, only 28% of agency people acknowledged that "TV is my primary form of entertainment," while 53% of the general survey population said it was. And yet 82% of the agency people agreed that "I want to look different from others," far more than the 62% recorded in the rest of the survey (reported in Joseph Winski, "Study: The Customer Ain't Me," Advertising Age, January 20, 1992, p. 18.).

2. Rickie Windle, March 2, 1992, p. 1.

3. Joe Mandese, May 4, 1992, p. 18.

4. Gary Strauss, June 7, 1993, p. B1.

5. Bob Garfield, June 6, 1993, pp. C1, C4.

6. Herbert Marcuse, 1964.

7. Stuart Ewen, 1976.

8. See Robert Goldman, 1992; Judith Williamson, 1978.

9. Kim Foltz, July 26, 1990, p. C15.

10. Patricia Greenwald, cited in Jeffrey Tractenberg, December 26, 1988, p. 120.

11. Kim Foltz, September 28, 1990, p. C1. Not coincidentally, each of these ads came from Chiat/Day. "The Energizer Bunny commercials work because Chiat/Day is thumbing its nose at advertising. It does what many television viewers would like to do—literally jump in and stop a stupid commercial dead in its tracks."

12. See, for example, A&W Root Beer's recent campaign featuring TV ad characters from yesteryear such as Madge (Palmolive) and Mr. ("Please don't squeeze the Charmin") Whipple. Each endorser is seen lapsing into the obsessive behaviors learned from their previous campaigns: Madge lets her hands soak in the root beer while Mr. Whipple ha-

bitually squeezes the root beer cans while the director's voice from offscreen implores them to just pour the drink. This combination of references to the history of silly TV ad campaigns (nostalgia) coupled with exposing the process of producing ads produced an off-beat positioning strategy. See Barbara Lippert, January 7, 1991, p. 45.

13. As Barkley says this, the screen cuts to a kid who says, "Good." This provides another moment of self-deprecating humor—in this case, directed against the celebrity athlete.

14. Judith Williamson, 1978.

15. An Avia campaign in 1991 made news when it declared that smokers need not apply for their totem group. What appeared for a moment as negative appellation was actually a means of shoring up identification with Avia's totem group—that is, I belong to a totem group that *excludes* smokers.

16. See Julie Tripp, February 12, 1992, p. D1.

17. "U.S. Bancorp Brad and Tina Ads Praised," December 11, 1992, p. E13.

18. Michael O'Rourke of Borders Perrin and Norrander, quoted in Bill MacKenzie, April 14, 1991, p. R1.

19. Peter Howell, March 4, 1993, p. G3.

20. The toothpick is a substitute for Leary's trademark cigarette which is obviously still too inappropriate for a Nike ad. The chain-link fence has developed into a recurring signifier of urban alienation in TV commercials.

21. T. J. Jackson Lears, 1983.

22. Cyndee Miller, August 17, 1992, p. 1.

23. Edward Walsh, November 30, 1991, p. A3.

24. Cyndee Miller, August 17, 1992, p. 2.

25. It helps, however, to have a cultural historian unpack the dialectic of tight lacing and moral respectability. The corset as an instrument of torture and the many pounds of petticoats, hoop skirts, and crinoline were more than merely ways of displaying women as objects, they were also part of a morality of domination. Perversely, Victorian woman "needed to be at once supported and confined, in a many-layered, heavily reinforced costume that would make undressing a difficult and lengthy process" (Allison Lurie, 1981, pp. 219–220).

26. Richard Herskovitz, 1979, p. 182.

27. Robert Goldman and Steve Papson, 1991.

28. Whereas Joe Isuzu was an oily huckster, Toyota has made it entirely technique.

29. These are the dynamic, shape-changing fonts that we discussed in chapter 2.

30. Gregory Bateson, 1972, p. 178.

31. Kathleen Deveny, March 8, 1990, p. B1. See also Don Oldenburg, August 15, 1993, p. L12.

32. Mary Gottschalk, September 9, 1992, p. D1.

33. Hugh Hart, September 9, 1992, p. 5C.

34. Bruce Horovitz, May 11, 1993, p. D1.

35. Cited in Bruce Horovitz, May 11, 1993, p. D1.

36. Dick Hebdige, 1979, p. 114.

37. Dick Hebdige, 1979, p. 115.

38. Greil Marcus, 1989, p. 213.
39. We wish to thank Edward Ames for making this argument.
40. Adrienne Ward, February 24, 1992, p.4.
41. See Penelope Spheeris's movie, *The End of Western Civilization.*
42. Frank Browning, quoted in Elizabeth Kastor, April 25, 1993, p. F1.
43. See Susan Willis, 1991, on the representation of the commodity fix in mass culture.
44. "Pepsi's New Ads Reflect Old Theme," January 26, 1993, p. D2.
45. We wish to thank Doug Kellner for pointing this out to us.
46. Dick Hebdige, 1988, p. 150.
47. Barbara Lippert, July 15, 1991, p. 29.
48. Dick Hebdige, 1988, p. 148.

Chapter 4

1. Roland Marchand, 1985, pp. 335–341.
2. Randall Rothenberg, November 29, 1989, p. C1.
3. When the signified is nostalgia, advertisers tend to reach into the bin marked "popular culture"; when the signified is history, the primary referent is the quality and texture of the image. Whatever the signified is, the signifier is plucked from historical context to serve commodity maximizing interests.
4. See Benedict Anderson, 1991.
5. Roland Barthes, 1972, p. 143.
6. Robert Goldman and David Dickens, 1983, p. 585.
7. See Ann Game, 1991. Turning memory into visual signifiers invariably elevates the spatial over the temporal. "The memory of duration is not the memory of images: any representation consists in a spatialization, a cutting out, an immobilisation. Representation of past, present or future is a denial of time" (pp. 97–98).
8. Judith Williamson, 1978, p. 158.
9. John Berger and Jean Mohr, 1982, p. 119.
10. Susan Sontag, 1977, p. 9.
11. Neville Wakefield, 1990, p. 125.
12. George Lipsitz, 1990, pp. 80, 79.
13. Robert Bellah et al., 1985. p. 153.
14. Roland Barthes, 1972, p. 143.
15. Bob Garfield, June 17, 1991, p. 50.
16. Nikki Tait, January 14, 1993, p. 15.
17. Stuart Ewen, 1988, p. 255.
18. Guy Debord, 1977, p. 157.
19. The term "swish pan" is the film version of a "saccadic" eye movement. This refers to the imperceptible blurring that occurs when the eye shifts from one object to another.
20. Judith Williamson, 1978, p. 158.
21. As Barbara Lippert notes about Coke's newest campaign: "Gone is the Wally Cleaver

earnestness of previous Coke spots set on Little League fields and in Connecticut kitchens. The new spots successfully draw on some of that 1950s nostalgia. (The original Coke logo, which appears in many of the spots, is as powerful as Elvis.)" (March 1, 1993, p. 61).

22. Professor Fred Davis, quoted in Randall Rothenberg, November 29, 1989, p. C17.
23. Walter Benjamin, 1969, pp. 158–161.
24. "Hoover's Largest Advertising Investment Ever Will Continue Building Brand Recognition," April 5, 1993.
25. Nike's use of the Beatles's song "Revolution" accomplished both outcomes simultaneously.
26. Herbert Marcuse, 1964, p. 61.
27. See Walter Benjamin, 1969; Henri Lefebvre, 1971.
28. Donald Lazere, 1987, p. 98.
29. Roland Barthes, 1977, pp. 17, 44.
30. John Berger and Jean Mohr, 1982, pp. 97, 87, 91.
31. Guy Debord, 1977, p. 24.
32. Elaine Underwood, April 1, 1991, p. 24.
33. Walter Benjamin, 1969, p. 261.
34. Fredric Jameson, 1991, p. 20.
35. Jean Baudrillard, 1987.
36. "In a consumer capitalist economy, where unmet needs and individual isolation provide the impetus for commodity desires, legitimation is always incomplete. Even while establishing dominance, those in power must borrow from the ideas, actions, and experience of the past, all of which contain potential for informing a radical critique of the present" (George Lipsitz, 1990, pp. 67–68).
37. Stuart Ewen, 1988, p. 258.
38. Christopher Lasch, 1975, p. viii.

Chapter 5

1. T. J. Jackson Lears, 1983, p. 8.
2. How will this change with interactive TV? Is interactive TV the path advertisers will take in trying to bypass the current contradictions of clutter and nondifferentiation?
3. Roland Barthes, 1972, p. 129ff.
4. Indeed, just as we were finishing this manuscript in August 1994, *Newsweek*'s cover story was "Everyone Is Hip!" The story's hook was that if everybody is hip, how hip can it be to be hip? How can there be a hip if there is no mainstream to judge it against anymore? Oh my god, to be hip is to be mainstream!
5. The authentic is defined here in terms of contextualized experiences and meanings. Commodity signs are based on decontextualization and decontextualization is the absolute enemy of authenticity. Commodity signs also undermine the status of being an outsider who possesses an elect (secret) knowledge.
6. "Until this Mastercard campaign, credit cards were sold as passports to glamour, luxury

and prestige. American Express, through most of the 1980's, sniffed that 'Membership Has Its Privileges.' Visa combed the world for intriguing locales that didn't accept the Amex card, claiming 'Visa. It's Everywhere You Want to Be.' Even Mastercard centered its previous campaign on people who 'Master the Moment' through not-quite-so-conspicuous consumption" (Saul Hansell, March 7, 1993, p. 1).

7. See C. Wright Mills, 1951, pp. 257–258.
8. Marshall Berman, 1970, p. 21.
9. Marshall Berman, 1970, p. 16. Ironically, with the emergence of the designer body, the correctness of nakedness is replaced by an abstracted form.
10. See Marshall Berman, 1982.
11. Marshall Berman, 1982, p. 94.
12. T. J. Jackson Lears, 1983, pp. 9–17.
13. Ferdinand Tonnies, 1963, p. 35.
14. Pierre Bourdieu, 1984, p. 6.
15. See C. Wright Mills, 1951, pp. 220–224.
16. Lindsay Chappell, October 8, 1990.
17. Another Saturn ad follows a Saturn employee who travels to remote Alaska with a replacement seat for a defective one in a woman's new Saturn. Advertisers for products as varied as Honda, M&M, MCI, Midas, and UPS feature comments by workers or customers concerning the company's dedication to delivering a quality product or service. Workers work weekends, inspect with care, deliver on time, and are concerned with quality—not because they get paid, but because they care about "you" personally.
18. Jean Baudrillard, 1981, p. 103.
19. Lawrence Grossberg, 1992, pp. 206–207.
20. Max Blagg was a little-known and, judging by his Gap performance, probably a second-rate Chicago-area poet who was criticized roundly by other poets for caving in so shamefully to the crass commercial lures of easy money and 30 seconds in the spectacle spotlight.
21. Henry Allen, May 23, 1993, p. G1.
22. See David Dishneau, September 26, 1992, p. L8.
23. Pierre Bourdieu, 1984, p. 5.
24. Walter Benjamin, 1969, p. 220.
25. Opportunities for unmediated experiences of nature have diminished. Nature now appears mostly in "cooked" form. Administered simulated environments in theme parks crop up to satisfy the need to detox from the frustrations, anxieties, and tensions of the social world.
26. Carolyn Merchant, 1983; William McKibben, 1989.
27. Guy Debord, 1977.
28. "Jeep Brand Extends Boundaries of Nature in New Advertising Campaign," April 5, 1993.
29. Levi's Dockers similarly bestows its product with bourgeois subjectivity, authenticated by the abstracted style of movement through natural settings with exotic background sounds. Nature does not function well as a bourgeois sign until it has been aestheticized.
30. Pierre Bourdieu, 1984, pp. 5, 31.

31. Marshall Berman, 1970, p. 32.
32. See Roland Marchand, 1985; Stuart Ewen, 1976.
33. Stuart Z. Charme, 1991, pp. 17–41; John Fiske, 1989, pp. 69–102.
34. Fashion semiotics, as noted earlier, always look for signs of resistance to tame. Naming a brand to reflect resistance is a common practice. For instance, Protest Clothing drew on the imagery of nose piercing, and a legion of examples can be found in *Details* magazine of advertisers' appropriation of Grunge and its logic of disorder to rename pseudo-individualist fashion choices. See V. N. Volosinov, 1986 (p. 23) on the relationship between the sign and class struggle.
35. Dick Hebdige, 1979, p. 17.
36. "Sinbad to Star in Reebok's New Advertising Campaign to Promote the Blacktop Series," May 2, 1991.
37. Henry Louis Gates Jr., June 19, 1990, p. A23.
38. See Brian Cross, 1993.
39. Quoted in Cyndee Miller, November 23, 1992, p. 2.
40. Howard Reich, July 26, 1992, p. 4.
41. Bill Brubaker, March 10, 1991, p. A1.
42. Guy Debord, 1977, p. 1.
43. Henri Lefebvre, 1971.
44. See Leo Braudy, 1977. See also Siegfried Kracauer, 1947.
45. Kertesz captured the beauty of the mundane in everyday life, for example, the light glancing off a puddle of water in the street, the cracks in the sidewalk.
46. Barbara Stern, 1991, p. 9.
47. Perhaps this commercial also functions to combat the apparent overuse of Jordan in other commercials (Hanes, Gatorade, McDonald's) by reminding consumers that Jordan is successful because of his dedication to a game he loves.
48. Dan Wieden, 1992, p. 97.
49. Nena Baker, August 9, 1992, pp. A1, A10–11.
50. Dean MacCannell, 1976, pp. 91–108.
51. These are social relations built on idealism and voluntarism. Though the encoding style draws attention to material artifacts, this is not a materialist world but a surprisingly ungrounded sensibility.
52. Levi's and Dektor failed to duplicate one element of their earlier coding success. The Levi's code requires noncommodified music, music that does not serve the master of commerce. Levi's earlier success in signifying authenticity drew on the blues for its evocation of alienation and otherness. Here, both music and lyrics sound concocted and thus fail to articulate a credible emotion of authenticity.
53. Frederick Wiseman's film *Model* depicts how models are reduced to objects by the work structures they inhabit. Narcissistic discourse surrounds the model's life. Often it is used by directors and photographers to direct the model into a specific pose. Wiseman presents modeling as unexciting work, as a highly routinized form of labor that is controlled by the agency. Nevertheless, modeling is about surface and appearance, and as the word

suggests, the model is an object, even though he/she is a highly aestheticized one. Authenticity, on the other hand, is synonymous with depth of being.

54. "Mountain Dew's 1993 Ad Campaign Debuts with 14-Minute Single-Night Advertising Schedules," March 17, 1993.
55. See Barbara Lippert, July 1, 1991, p. 37.
56. Stuart Ewen, 1988, p. 16.

Chapter 6

1. Walter Benjamin, 1969; Stuart Ewen and Elizabeth Ewen, 1982.
2. Harry Braverman, 1974. Industrial capitalists faced both political crises of legitimacy and class rule, as well as a looming economic crisis.
3. Alfred D. Chandler Jr., 1977; Stuart Ewen, 1976.
4. Susan Strasser, 1989; Erich Fromm, 1955.
5. Wolfgang Fritz Haug, 1986; Stuart Ewen, 1976, pp. 177–184.
6. The bourgeoisie was caught between a definition of individuality that extolled autonomy, and a market environment where bureaucracy was necessary to integrate production, distribution, and consumption (see T. J. Jackson Lears, 1981, pp. 55–58; Daniel Bell, 1976).
7. T. J. Jackson Lears, 1983, pp. 7, 17–19.
8. Stuart Ewen, 1976; T. J. Jackson Lears, 1981; James O'Connor, 1987.
9. James O'Connor, 1984, pp. 164–165.
10. Jean Baudrillard, 1981, pp. 82–87.
11. William Leiss, 1976, pp. 24–28.
12. Herbert Marcuse, 1969, p. 11.
13. See Alvin Toffler, 1970.
14. Christopher Lasch, 1979.
15. Joshua Meyrowitz, 1985.
16. See Jean Baudrillard, 1983a and 1983b.
17. See Mike Featherstone, 1991.
18. William Leiss, 1976, p. 13.
19. Roland Marchand, 1985; Stuart Ewen, 1976; Stuart Ewen and Elizabeth Ewen, 1982; T. J. Jackson Lears, 1983.
20. Roland Marchand, 1985, pp. 223–226.
21. Todd Gitlin, 1979, p. 291.
22. Judith Williamson, 1978, pp. 134–137.
23. Jean Baudrillard, 1981, p. 46.
24. Jean Baudrillard, 1981, pp. 37–39; Douglas Kellner, 1989a, pp. 19–25.
25. Stephen Papson, 1986.
26. William Leiss, Stephen Kline, and Sut Jhally, 1986.
27. Stuart Ewen, 1988, p. 16.
28. Andrew Feenberg, 1990.

29. Arjun Appadurai, 1990; Mike Featherstone, 1990.
30. Pierre Bourdieu, 1984.
31. This list of corporations includes: Du Pont, Arco, American Cyanimid, Dow, GM, AT&T, IBM, WR Grace and Co., Exxon, Shell, Mobil, Chevron, Phillips Petroleum, Monsanto, Union Carbide, Kerr-McGee Corp., Texaco, Sun, Amoco, BP America, Ciba-Geigy, Proctor and Gamble, and Adolph Coors.
32. Roderick Nash, 1989.
33. Brian Tokar, 1991.
34. Environmental organizations have good reason to be cautious. Greenpeace accepts no corporate funding. The Sierra Club and later the National Audobon Society turned down $700,000 from McDonald's to sponsor an environmental education project (Eve Pell, 1990). With corporate donations to environmental organizations have come corporate executives who sit on the environmental organizations' boards of directors. Note the example of the relationship between Waste Management, Inc., and the National Wildlife Federation. WMI used NWF to help influence waste disposal policy decisions by EPA administrator William Reilly (see Eve Pell, 1991).
35. The relationship between educational programming, the corporation, and the Public Broadcasting Service is an extension of the formation of the commercial network system (Erik Barnouw, 1978). The Reagan administration expanded the domain of corporate influence when it reduced federal funding for the Corporation of Public Broadcasting (Herbert Schiller, 1986, pp. 38–41).
36. Jack Doyle (1991, p. 6) also notes that the remaining four ships in Conoco's fleet will not be double-hulled until the year 2000. Further, when the relatively small size of Conoco's fleet is considered in relation to the number of oil and chemical tankers sailing the oceans, it is unlikely to "influence the environmental safety of oil transportation overall."
37. Jack Doyle, 1991, pp. 13–15.
38. Du Pont, of course, pioneered the use of Freon aerosols; these chlorofluorocarbons used as propellants have been a prime cause of ozone layer depletion. Based on the EPA's Toxic Release Inventory data, Du Pont's water release pollution for 1989 was 1,966,863 pounds and its air release pollution for the same year was 52,460,458 pounds! (see Jack Doyle, 1991, p. 16).
39. Herbert Marcuse, 1964, p. 61.
40. Norman Dean, Jerry Poje, and Randall Burke, 1987.
41. The photographic overlay represents the narrative interface between two signifying systems—that is, this face functions as a metasign linking the well-being of your children to "Super-Unleaded" ethanol.
42. It must be emphasized that ads like this are not meant simply to legitimate ADM. Such ads clearly address at least two general target audiences. They are intended to attract the attention of investors watching the news show: the pitch here is we are a huge operation with fresh new ideas that address today's challenges, so why not put your capital behind us? A second audience is the general citizenry: the pitch here is we are a large company that is quietly doing our part to produce a better world for our/your children.

43. For example, in the late 1970s 30% of Du Pont's annual new investment went into pollution control equipment to comply with federal regulations (see David Hounshell and John Smith, 1988, p. 585).
44. James O'Connor, 1988, p. 26.
45. Daniel Faber, 1993.
46. See "The Green Marketing Revolution," June 19, 1991.
47. See Stefan Bechtel, 1990.
48. Debra Lynn Dadd and Andre Carothers, 1991.
49. Indeed, the first electric cars will be marketed to upscale target audiences as the ultimate sign of environmental concern and commitment since their price tag will be nearly double that of comparable autos with standard combustion systems.
50. Cited in Dick Russell and Owen DeLong, 1991, p. 33.
51. In the late 1980s, a coalition of environmentally aware companies emerged called "Act Now: Business for a Change." Their stated goals include redirecting the "peace dividend" to environmental and social programs. These companies have a vision of environmental education that might lead to political activism and increased governmental investment in the environment. The companies involved are exclusively focused on consumer goods (Ben and Jerry's, The Body Shop, Patagonia, Tom's of Maine, Seventh Generation, Esprit) and all emerged out of entrepreneurial efforts by individuals who were part of the 1960s counterculture. Is it possible that this represents a coalition of "left"-oriented capital?

Chapter 7

1. David Harvey, 1989, p. 288.
2. S. Prakash Sethi, 1977; Thomas F. Garbett, 1981; James R. Gregory, 1991.
3. A leading practitioner of corporate ads bluntly says that all corporate campaigns "seek social support and understanding" (Thomas F. Garbett, 1982, p. 104).
4. James R. Gregory, 1991, p. 22.
5. Thomas F. Garbett, 1981, p. 9, Roland Marchand, 1987.
6. Stuart Ewen, 1976; Roland Marchand, 1985.
7. See Stuart Ewen, 1988.
8. See Walter A. Hamilton, 1973. The 1972 survey recorded high approval from only 18% of respondents, a figure that dipped even lower by September 1974. Opinion polling throughout the 1970s confirmed a general loss of confidence in business (see also Thomas F. Garbett, 1981; Seymour M. Lipset and William Schneider, 1983; Leonard Silk and David Vogel, 1976).
9. Circa 1980, the 196 Roundtable CEOs represented firms whose collective annual revenues equaled half of the U.S. GNP (Michael Useem, 19984, p. 35; G. William Domhoff, 1990, p. 267).
10. Mark Green and Andrew Buchsbaum (1980, pp. 97–98) found "the dominant *leit-motif* of Roundtable lobbying is behind-the-scenes advocacy—the private meeting rather than the public argument." Ironically, advertising afforded another avenue whereby these cor-

porate leaders could turn matters of public debate into private musings. "Supported by the Business Roundtable, the editors of *Reader's Digest* prepared a series of advertisements for publication in the *Digest* and reprinted in pamphlet form for further circulation. They address issues on which public acceptance is most needed but least firm: how multinational corporations are helping 'to create a peaceful and prosperous world,' why government spending spurs inflation, what large companies offer that small ones cannot, and, the oldest adage of all, that corporate profits are the lifeblood of American capitalism" (Michael Useem, 1984, p. 107).

11. Jurgen Habermas (1970) argues that this social contract, rooted in the dual ideologies of privatized commodity consumption and technocratic expertise, has anchored the legitimacy of corporate capitalism since the 1920s.

12. A year later, revelations about ITT's involvement in the military overthrow of Chile's democratically elected government cast a pall of further mistrust over the corporate community. See Erik Barnouw, 1978, pp. 84–86, on how ITT countered its crisis of legitimacy with the "Big Blue Marble" ad campaign.

13. See Thomas F. Garbett, 1981, pp. 68–69; "Corporate Advertising Costs," 1984; Josephine Curran, 1985; Meryl Davids, 1987; Joan Reisman, 1989; "Corporate Advertising Expenditures," 1990; Paul H. Alvarez, 1993.

14. Joan Reisman, 1989, p. 28.

15. Network television's centrality peaked in the mid-1980s before part of its share shifted to cable, spot, and syndicated television (corporate ad spending on cable television increased 91% in 1989). The percentage of expenditures for corporate television advertising on network TV fluctuated between 58% in 1984 and 46% in 1989 (see "Corporate Advertising Expenditures," 1990).

16. See Michael Winkleman, 1985, p. 22; Meryl Davids and Michael Winkleman, 1987, p. 34; Joan Reisman, 1989, p. 27.

17. In 1984–1985 the increase in image ads was particularly noticeable among banks and major consumer-goods corporations. In 1984, the fourth leading corporate advertiser on network television was the Reagan Election Committee. Well behind AT&T, the Reagan Committee barely trailed GM and Ford in corporate television ad spending at $21.9 million (see Curran, 1985, p. 30).

18. Michael Useem, 1984.

19. Roland Marchand, 1987, pp. 148–152.

20. Quoted in Philip Dougherty, 1984, p. D29.

21. Robert Goldman and Steve Papson, 1991, p. 91.

22. David Harvey, 1989, p. 288.

23. Mark Crispin Miller, 1990.

24. Sal Vittolino, 1988.

25. Roland Marchand, 1989, pp. 188, 192.

26. Pat Botwinick, 1984. Corporate advertising articulates corporate identity both to external target audiences and to internal constituencies of stockholders and employees. Building better awareness of the corporation is the most cited objective of corporate ad cam-

paigns (Joan Reisman, 1989; "ANA Tracks Growth of Corporate Ads," October 12, 1981; Celia K. Lehrman, 1987, p. 33). Beatrice exemplified an umbrella firm that took over known firms but was itself unknown. Beatrice spent $23.28 million on their 1984 "We Are Beatrice" campaign, of which $18.98 million went toward network television ads (Josephine Curran, 1985, p. 30). An example of a corporate TV campaign targeting investors was Internorth's "Annual Report" (1984–1985).

27. "Corporate Advertising Costs," 1984, p. 22.
28. About whether corporate advertising, and especially corporate image ads, can positively influence a company's stock prices, see B. G. Yovovich, 1981; George Guimaraes, 1985; James K. Gregory, 1991.
29. Thomas F. Garbett, 1981, p. 90.
30. George Guimaraes, 1985.
31. James K. Gregory (1991, p. 60) quotes a senior vice-president at J. Walter Thompson's corporate communications division, and Joan Reisman (1989) uses the term "shark repellent" to describe the use of advertising for this purpose.
32. Winthrop Neilson, 1981, pp. S10–S11 presents a strategy called "Investorism" based on "capital formation communications." The strategy consists of three tenets:
    1. "A favorable capital market environment with government understanding and support must exist in order to encourage investment incentives. These would provide monies for productive facilities to meet society's needs and to offer meaningful rewards to those who make the commitment."
    2. "The average person must willingly commit himself to ownership by placing his money in capital formation. In doing so, he expresses support of the corporation for responding to economic challenges facing society."
    3. "Businesses must make decisions and then communicate them in ways that will rekindle trust in business."
33. No less critical in channeling the flow of public debate are those frames that are *absent* or *excluded*; see Robert Goldman and Arvind Rajagopal, 1991.
34. Karen Fox and Bobby Calder, 1985, p. 11.
35. See Madison Social Text Group, 1979, pp. 178–179.
36. See Michael Arlen, 1980.
37. See William Lutz, 1977, pp. 864–865.
38. Roland Barthes, 1972, p. 51.
39. Herbert G. Reid, 1974, p. 154.
40. See Barry Bluestone and Bennett Harrison, 1982, on the social costs of deindustrialization.
41. Amitai Etzioni, 1985.
42. Knight-Ridder News Service, 1983.
43. Another ad in this series cools out concerns about "the future of the land" around a strip-mining facility at Powder River Basin, Wyoming. Sun anticipated such problems and "developed this land reclamation center to make sure the land is properly restored. At Sun we think that putting our energy back into the land is just as important as getting it out."

44. See Stuart Elliott, April 16, 1990, p. B4.
45. Similar to Feuerbach's (1957) view of how humans projected (and hence alienated) their own best qualities on to gods.
46. Ads about pride in one's work are aimed at men about their work role and their ability to support their families. How many women are nostalgic about the "good old days" of work when few women had decent jobs? Are men more anxious about their loss of status, their loss of authority in the workplace?
47. See William Leiss, 1974.
48. Seymour M. Lipset and William Schneider, 1983, p. 164.
49. Quoted in Seymour M. Lipset and William Schneider, 1983, p. 168.
50. See "Rednecks Redux," July 21, 1990, p. 316; Jonathan Levine, 1990. GE sought Tungsram because it provided "a low-cost backdoor" to gaining a foothold in Western Europe. Tungsram had been producing a standard incandescent bulb 30% cheaper than that made by any Western competitor.
51. Along with the absence of production relations, the GE ad presents a gentrified middle class gleefully celebrating the demise of Hungarian socialism.
52. Roland Barthes, 1972.
53. Martin Esslin, 1982, pp. 236–237.
54. Alvin Gouldner, 1982, p. 225.
55. See Ben Agger, 1985.
56. See Martin Jay, 1984, p. 123; Theodor Adorno, 1978.
57. Nancy Fraser, 1990, p. 75.
58. In Walter P. Margulies, 1981, p. S-12.
59. See "Brewing Trouble," May 26, 1990, p. 70; Judann Dognoll and Laurie Freeman, 1990; Anthony Ramirez, 1990.
60. "Brewing Trouble," May 26, 1990.
61. Rosemary J. Coombe, 1992, p. 101.
62. Karen Fox and Bobby Calder, 1985.
63. See Michael Useem, 1984.
64. Leonard Silk and David Vogel, 1976, p. 128.
65. Douglas Kellner, 1990.
66. Jurgen Habermas, 1975, pp. 70–71.
67. Alan Wolfe, 1977, p. 252; see also Daniel Hallin, 1985, pp. 136–139.

Conclusion

1. Steven Goldman, Roger Nagel, and Kenneth Preiss, October 9, 1994, p. F9.
2. Dick Hebdige, 1979.
3. Celeste Olalquiaga, 1992, p. 51.
4. Kristi Turnquist, October 27, 1994, p. E1.
5. Jennifer Steinhauer, May 22, 1994, p. 1.
6. Jennifer Steinhauer, May 22, 1994, p. 1.

7. Paul Duchene, June 30, 1994, p. B1.
8. Paul Duchene, June 30, 1994, p. B1.
9. Larry Jabbonsky and Tim Davis, 1994, p. 22.
10. Jack Curry of *TV Guide,* quoted in Claudia Montague, 1993, p. 18. As Dallas Smythe argued, the audience is the essential commodity being packaged and sold on television.
11. Harry Berkowitz, July 25, 1993, p. 72.
12. Harry Berkowitz, July 25, 1993, p. 72.
13. Jack Curry of *TV Guide,* quoted in Claudia Montague, 1993, p. 18.
14. "I Hate the Sprite in You, Fool," 1994, p. 6.
15. Harry Berkowitz, May 9, 1994, p. C02.
16. John Greenwald, Massimo Calabresi, and Jane Van Tassel, May 30, 1994, p. 50.
17. Greenwald, Calabresi, and Van Tassel, p. 50.
18. Greenwald, Calabresi, and Van Tassel, p. 50.
19. See Steven Best and Douglas Kellner, 1991.
20. The separate arrangement even carried over into the advertising; see Raymond Serafin, March 7, 1988, pp. 1, 78.
21. Alison Simko, January 13, 1992, p. S22.
22. See Juliet Schor, 1991.
23. Jonathan Glancey, January 23, 1993, p. 37.
24. Fredric Jameson, 1984, p. 56.
25. Turning cultural meanings into exchange values has generated contradictory side effects that create real barriers to the reproduction of commodity signs. We have identified broad sets of such contradictory tendencies. First, the intensely competitive minting of sign values may hike the value of specific commodity signs, but at the cost of depreciating the currency of signs. The first rule of sign wars for advertisers is to undermine the sign exchange value of their competitor while boosting (via differentiation) the value of their own commodities. Routinized glamour also reinforces this tendency for the rate of sign value to decline: saturate a currency and you devalue it. Second, in a mature political economy of sign value, the mechanics of sign construction and reconstruction draw attention to the very category of value: value becomes relativized and the authority of the value production process becomes transparent. Under these circumstances, the category of value has exhausted its truth claims. Thus it is not accidental that in recent years an increasing number of ads address viewers by openly acknowledging that sign value is plastic and transitory, based on artifice and superficiality. Third, the same competitive situation encourages a circuit of sign differentiation followed by sign imitation: a differentiated sign translates into a marketplace advantage, while imitations reduce the sign's value. Round after round of competition generated distinctive images that stand out. It also produced a diminishing half-life of sign values, ad campaigns, and viewer attention spans. Fourth, from the 1950s on, advertisers rationalized and overstructured advertisements in order to secure competitive sign values. This approach to advertising involved positioning the viewer to participate in the meaning of the ad, by encouraging the viewer to identify with the subject of the ad. But the repeated positioning of viewers has bred a

sense of alienation and resentment. Since the mid-1980s, advertisers have incorporated criticism of advertising and commodity-sign fetishism into their ads by adopting postures of reflexive self-awareness about the project of advertising itself. (See Goldman, 1994).

26. Quoted in Leslie Savan, September 6, 1994, p. 50.

Bibliography

Adorno, Theodor. (1941). "On Popular Music." *Studies in Philosophy and Social Science,* 9, 117–148.

Adorno, Theodor. (1978). "On the Fetish Character of Music and the Regression of Listening." In A. Arato and E. Gebhardt (eds.), *The Essential Frankfurt School Reader* (pp. 270–299). New York: Urizen Books.

"Advertising Everywhere!" (1992, December). *Consumer Reports,* p. 752.

Agger, Ben. (1985). "The Dialectic of Deindustrialization." In J. Forester (ed.), *Critical Theory and Public Life* (pp. 3–21). Cambridge, MA: MIT Press.

Allen, Henry. (1993, May 23). "Are You Cool Enough for the Gap?" *Washington Post,* p. G1.

Alvarez, Paul H. (1993, August). "Corporate Advertising Review: Overall Media Buying Stagnates but Targeted TV Booms," *Public Relations Journal,* pp. 14–15.

"ANA Tracks Growth of Corporate Ads." (1981, October 12). *Broadcasting,* p. 82.

Anderson, Benedict. (1991). *Imagined Communities.* Rev. ed. London: Verso.

Appadurai, Arjun. (1990). "Disjuncture and Difference in the Global Cultural Economy." *Theory, Culture, and Society,* 7(2–3), 297–310.

Arlen, Michael. (1980). *Thirty Seconds.* New York: Penguin.

Associated Press. (1984, February 17). "Health Groups Call Reynolds Ad Campaign a Smoke Screen." *Lexington Herald-Leader,* p. A6.

Avenoso, Karen. (1992, November 23). "Trapped by Self-Actualizing Ads: Young Women Shape Up at the Expense of Greater Goals." *Advertising Age,* p. 18.

Bagot, Brian. (1990, June). "Shoeboom!" *Marketing and Media Decisions,* pp. 61–66.

Baker, Dean. (1991, November 6). "OLCC Bans Poster for Malt Liquor." *Oregonian,* p. E1.

Baker, Nena. (1991, April 28). "If Nike Lost a Shoe, It'd Still Have T-Shirt for Its Back." *Oregonian,* pp. K1, K5.

Baker, Nena. (1992, March 14). "Nike's Ready to Go All Out to Promote Latest Sneaker." *Oregonian,* p. B1.

Baker, Nena. (1992, August 9). "The Hidden Hands of Nike." *Oregonian,* pp. A1, A10–11.

Barnouw, Erik. (1978). *The Sponsor.* New York: Oxford University Press.

Barthes, Roland. (1972). *Mythologies.* New York: Hill and Wang.

Barthes, Roland. (1977). *Image—Music—Text.* New York: Hill and Wang.

Bateson, Gregory. (1972). *Steps to an Ecology of the Mind.* New York: Ballantine.

Baudrillard, Jean. (1981). *For a Critique of the Political Economy of the Sign.* St. Louis: Telos Press.

Baudrillard, Jean. (1983a). *Simulations.* New York: Semiotext(e).

Baudrillard, Jean. (1983b). *In the Shadow of the Silent Majorities . . . Or the End of the Social.* New York: Semiotext(e).

Baudrillard, Jean. (1987). "The Year 2000 Has Already Happened." In A. Kroker and M. Kroker (eds.), *Body Invaders* (pp. 35–44). London: Macmillan.

Bechtel, Stefan. (1990). *Keeping Your Company Green.* Emmaus, PA: Rodale Press.

Beckett, Jamie. (1991, September 12). "Ad Shops Seek More Cachet." *San Francisco Chronicle,* pp. C1, C2.

Beckett, Jamie. (1991, October 14). "Controversial Ads Are Sometimes the Most Effective." *San Francisco Chronicle,* p. B3.

Beckett, Jamie. (1992, July 15). "Struggle Over Olympic Ads Heats Up: Advertisers Who Avoid Paying Fees Infuriate Organizers." *San Francisco Chronicle,* p. B1.

Bell, Daniel. (1976). *The Cultural Contradictions of Capitalism.* New York: Basic Books.

Bellah, Robert, et al. (1985). *Habits of the Heart: Individualism and Commitment in American Life.* Berkeley and Los Angeles: University of California Press.

Benjamin, Walter. (1969). "Art in the Age of Mechanical Reproduction." In Hannah Arendt (ed.), *Illuminations* (pp. 217–252). New York: Schocken.

Berger, John. (1972). *Ways of Seeing.* New York: Penguin.

Berger, John, and Jean Mohr. (1982). *Another Way of Looking.* New York: Pantheon.

Berkowitz, Harry. (1993, January 25). "Listen Up and Follow the Floating Type." *Newsday,* p. 27.

Berkowitz, Harry. (1993, July 25). "'Twentysomething' Consumers Are New Focus of Advertising Agencies." *Newsday,* p. 72.

Berkowitz, Harry. (1994, May 9). "Advertisers Turn to Antihype Hype." *Newsday,* p. C02.

Berman, Marshall. (1970). *The Politics of Authenticity: Radical Individualism and the Emergence of Modern Society.* New York: Atheneum.

Berman, Marshall. (1982). *All That Is Solid Melts into Air.* New York: Simon & Schuster.

Best, Steve. (1989). "The Commodifications of Reality and the Reality of Commodification." *Current Perspectives in Social Theory,* 9, 23–51.

Best, Steven, and Douglas Kellner. (1991). *Postmodern Theory: Critical Interrogations.* New York: Guilford Press.

Bluestone, Barry, and Bennett Harrison. (1982). *The Deindustrialization of America.* New York: Basic Books.

Blumenfeld, Laura. (1992, July 20). "Black Like Who? Why White Teens Find Hip-Hop Cool." *Washington Post,* p. C5.

Bonney, Bill, and Helen Wilson. (1990). "Advertising and the Manufacture of Difference." In M. Alvarado and J. O. Thompson (eds.), *The Media Reader* (pp. 181–198). London: BFI.

Botwinick, Pat. (1984, November). "The Image of Corporate Image." *Public Relations Journal,* pp. 12–14.

Bourdieu, Pierre. (1984). *Distinction: A Social Critique of the Judgment of Taste.* Cambridge, MA: Harvard University Press.

Braudy, Leo. (1977). *The World in a Frame: What We See in Films.* Garden City, NY: Anchor.

Braverman, Harry. (1974). *Labor and Monopoly Capital.* New York: Monthly Review Press.

"Brewing Trouble." (1990, May 26). *Economist,* p. 70.

Brubaker, Bill. (1991, March 10). "The Sneaker Phenomenon, Part 1 of 2. Athletic Shoes: Beyond Big Business; Industry Has a Foothold on Defining Societal Values." *Washington Post,* p. A1.

Buck-Morss, Susan. (1977). *The Origins of Negative Dialectics.* New York: Free Press.

Bushnell, Victoria. (1990, June 15). "Doing the Bunny Hop: Chiat/Day/Mojo Advertising Campaign for Everready Battery Co." *Back Stage,* p. B8.

Cantor, Jay. (1987). *Krazy Kat.* New York: Macmillan.

Carlson, Peter. (1991, November 3). "It's an Ad Ad Ad Ad World." *Washington Post Magazine,* p. W15.

Castellanos, Alex. (1992, April 20). "Subaru for President: Look Who's Running Negative Advertising!" *Advertising Age,* p. 24.

Caughie, John. (1981). "Progressive Television and Documentary Drama." In T. Bennett, S. Boyd-Bowman, C. Mercer, and J. Woollacott (eds.), *Popular Television and Film* (pp. 327–352). London: British Film Institute.

Chandler, Albert D., Jr. (1977). *The Visible Hand: The Managerial Revolution in American Business.* Cambridge, MA: Harvard University Press.

Chappell, Lindsay. (1990, October 8). "Dealers Cheer about Saturn Pricing." *Advertising Age,* p. 85.

Charme, Stuart Z. (1991). *Vulgarity and Authenticity: Dimensions of Otherness in the World of Jean-Paul Sartre.* Amherst: University of Massachusetts Press.

Chase, Dennis. (1992, September 21). "Can Unique Selling Proposition Find Happiness in a Parity World?" *Advertising Age,* p. 58.

Chase, Dennis. (1991, January 29). "Ad Age: Gallop Surveys." *Advertising Age,* pp. 8–10.

Chay, Richard F. (1991, June). "How Marketing Researchers Can Harness the Power of Brand Equity." *Marketing Research,* pp. 30–37.

Coombe, Rosemary J. (1992). "Postmodernity and the Rumor: Late Capitalism and the Fetish of the Commodity/sign." In William Stearns and William Chaloupka (eds.), *Jean Baudrillard: The Disappearance of Art and Politics* (pp. 98–108). New York: St. Martin's Press.

"Corporate Advertising Costs." (1984, November). *Public Relations Journal,* pp. 20–21, 24–25.

"Corporate Advertising Expenditures: Steady Growth Continued in 1989." (1990, September). *Public Relations Journal,* pp. 26–30.

Crispell, Diane, and Kathleen Brandenburg. (1993, May). "What's in a Brand?" *American Demographics,* p. 26.

Cross, Brian. (1993). *It's Not about a Salary: Rap, Race, and Resistance in Los Angeles.* New York: Verso.

Curran, Josephine. (1985, December). "The 14th Annual Review of Corporate Advertising Expenditures." *Public Relations Journal,* pp. 28–30, 40.

Dadd, Debra Lynn, and Andre Carothers. (1991). "A Bill of Goods? Green Consuming in Perspective." In C. Plant and J. Plant (eds.), *Green Business: Hope or Hoax?* (pp. 11–20). Santa Cruz, CA: New Society Publishers.

Dagnoll, Judann, and Laurie Freeman. (1990, May 21). "Coffee Boycott Boils." *Advertising Age,* p. 6.

Davids, Meryl. (1987, September). "Tough Stuff: 16th Annual Review of Corporate Advertising Expenditures." *Public Relations Journal,* pp. 28–31.

Dean, Norman, Jerry Poje, and Randall Burke. (1987). *The Toxic 500.* Washington, DC: National Wildlife Federation.

Debord, Guy. (1977). *Society of the Spectacle.* Detroit: Red & Black.

Deveny, Kathleen. (1990, March 8). "An Esprit Ad Crosses into Gray Racial Area." *Wall Street Journal,* p. B1.

"Director of the Year: Bay." (1993, May). *Advertising Age,* p. 9.

Dishneau, David. (1992, September 26). "Critics Question Poet's Integrity Because of TV Ad Selling Jeans." *Oregonian,* p. L8.

Doane, Mary Ann. (1989). "The Economy of Desire: The Commodity Form in/of the Cinema." *Quarterly Review of Film and Video,* 11(1), 23–33.

Domhoff, G. William. (1990). *The Power Elite and the State: How Policy Is Made in America.* New York: Aldine de Gruyter.

Dougherty, Philip. (1984, November 8). "Reagan's Emotional Campaign." *New York Times,* p. D29.

Doyle, Jack. (1991). *Hold the Applause!* Washington, DC: Friends of the Earth.

Duchene, Paul. (1994, June 30). "Chrysler 'Vandalizes' Own Neon Ads." *Oregonian,* p. B1.

Eagleton, Terry. (1991). *Ideology: An Introduction.* New York: Verso.

Ecenbarger, William. (1993, April 18). "A Trend Afoot: America's Love Affair with Athletic Shoes Is Growing by Leaps and Bounds." *Chicago Tribune,* p. C27.

Edelman, Bernard. (1979). "Ownership of the Image: Elements for a Marxist Theory of Law. London: Routledge & Kegan Paul.

Elliott, Stuart. (1990, April 16). "It's Back to the Attack as Ads Get Tough Again." *USA Today,* p. B4.

Elliott, Stuart. (1991, May 10). "Hey, Dude, That's One Serious Pitch." *New York Times,* p. D1.

Elliott, Stuart. (1991, November 25). "Coke Escalates Cola Wars in International Campaign." *New York Times,* p. D7.

Elliott, Stuart. (1992, June 12). "Tough Old-Style Campaign for Pepsi's 'New Age' Drink." *New York Times,* p. D9.

Elliott, Stuart. (1993, February 19). "TV Spots You Read Have Become a Popular Production Technique." *New York Times,* p. D18.

Esslin, Martin. (1982). *Mediations.* New York: Grove Press.

Etzioni, Amitai. (1985, November 15). "Shady Corporate Practices." *New York Times,* p. A35.

Ewen, Stuart. (1976). *Captains of Consciousness.* New York: McGraw-Hill.

Ewen, Stuart. (1988). *All-Consuming Images.* New York: Basic Books.

Ewen, Stuart, and Elizabeth Ewen. (1982). *Channels of Desire: Mass Images and the Shaping of the American Consciousness.* New York: McGraw-Hill.

Faber, Daniel. (1993). *Environment under Fire: Imperialism and the Ecological Crisis in Central America.* New York: Monthly Review Press.

Farquhar, Peter H., Julia Y. Han, and Yuji Ijiri. (1992). "Brands on the Balance Sheet." *Marketing Management,* 1(1), 16.

Featherstone, Mike. (1990). "Global Culture: An Introduction." *Theory, Culture, and Society.* 2(3), 1–14.

Featherstone, Mike. (1991). *Consumer Culture and Postmodernism.* Newbury Park, CA: Sage.

Feenberg, Andrew. (1990). "The Critical Theory of Technology." *Capitalism, Nature, Socialism*, 5, 17–45.

Fielding, Nick, and Larry Black. (1992, July 19). "Ambush at Barcelona." *Independent,* p. 6.

Fischer, P. M., M. P. Schwartz, J. W. Richards Jr., A. O. Goldstein, and T. H. Rojas. (1991). "Brand Logo recognition by Children Aged 3 to 6 years: Micky Mouse and Old Joe the Camel." *Journal of the American Medical Association,* 266(22), 3145–3148.

Fisher, Christy. (1992, May 25). "Wrangler Makes Brand Imprint via Rodeo Scene." *Advertising Age,* p. 33.

Fiske, John. (1987). *Television Culture.* London: Methuen.

Fiske, John. (1989). *Understanding Popular Culture.* New York: Unwin Hyman.

Foltz, Kim. (1990, July 26). "As Baby-Boomers Turn 40, Ammirati and BMW Adjust." *New York Times,* pp. C1, C15.

Foltz, Kim. (1990, September 28). "The Unruly Ads that Made an Art of Smart Alecky." *New York Times,* p. C1.

Foltz, Kim. (1991, February 20). "Campaign for British Knights to Escalate Sneaker Wars." *New York Times,* p. D17.

Foltz, Kim. (1992, March 12). "Reebok Fights to Be No. 1 Again." *New York Times,* pp. C1, C3.

Foster, Hal. (1985). *Recodings: Art, Spectacle, Cultural Politics.* Seattle, Bay Press.

Fox, Karen, and Bobby Calder. (1985, January–February). "The Right Kind of Business Advocacy." *Business Horizons,* pp. 7–11.

Fraser, Nancy. (1990). "Rethinking the Public Sphere: A Contribution to the Critique of Actually Existing Democracy." *Social Text,* 25–26, 58–80.

Freedman, Alix M. (1989, May 31). "Sexy Ads for Malt Liquor Brew Criticism." *Wall Street Journal,* p. B12.

Fromm, Erich. (1955). *The Sane Society.* New York: Holt, Rinehart & Winston.

Feuerbach, Ludwig. (1957). *The Essence of Christianity.* New York: Harper.

Gaines, Jane M. (1991). *Contested Culture: The Image, the Voice, and the Law.* Chapel Hill: University of North Carolina Press.

Game, Ann. (1991). *Undoing the Social: Towards a Deconstructive Sociology.* Toronto: University of Toronto Press.

Garbett, Thomas F. (1981). *Corporate Advertising.* New York: McGraw-Hill.

Garbett, Thomas F. (1982, March–April). "When to Advertise Your Company." *Harvard Business Review,* pp. 100–106.

Garfield, Bob. (1988, June 13). "Kool-Aid's 'Group Talk' Height of Faddishness." *Advertising Age,* p. 72.

Garfield, Bob. (1988, June 20). "Joe Pytka's Scope as Master Director Dwarfs Gold Lions." *Advertising Age,* p. 104.

Garfield, Bob. (1991, March 18). "Most Directory Ads on the Wrong Page." *Advertising Age,* p. S8.

Garfield, Bob. (1991, June 17). "Maxwell House 1892 Ad Brews Up Bad Memories." *Advertising Age,* p. 50.

Garfield, Bob. (1992, December 7). "Chiat Clones Lexus Ad to Good Effect, But . . . " *Advertising Age,* p. 53.

Garfield, Bob. (1993, March 1). "MasterCard Ads Get Style but Substance Still MIA." *Advertising Age,* p. 48.

Garfield, Bob. (1993, April 17). "Converse Tells the Truth About Its Chuck Taylors." *Advertising Age,* p. 44.

Garfield, Bob. (1993, May 31). "BMW's Attack on Lexus Doesn't Quite Make Sense." *Advertising Age,* p. 46.

Garfield, Bob. (1993, June 6). "TV's Dark Ads." *Oregonian,* pp. C1, C4.

Gates, Henry Louis, Jr. (1990, June 19). "2 Live Crew, Decoded." *New York Times,* p. A23.

Gendron, Bernard. (1986). "Theodor Adorno Meets the Cadillacs." In Tania Modleski (ed.), *Studies in Entertainment* (pp. 18–36). Bloomington: Indiana University Press.

Gitlin, Todd. (1979). "Domesticating Nature." *Theory and Society,* 8, 291–298.

Glancey, Jonathan. (1993, January 23). "I'd Like to Teach the World to Sell." *Independent,* p. 37.

Goffman, Erving. (1959). *Presentation of Self in Everyday Life.* New York: Anchor.

Goldman, Kevin. (1993, June 9). "Nuveen Hopes to Win Your Heart with Gentle Ads from Real Folks." *Wall Street Journal,* p. B6.

Goldman, Robert. (1992). *Reading Ads Socially.* London: Routledge.

Goldman, Robert. (1994). "Contradictions of a Political Economy of Sign Value." *Current Perspectives in Social Theory,* pp. 183–211.

Goldman, Robert, and David Dickens. (1983). "The Selling of Rural America." *Rural Sociology,* 48(4), 585–606.

Goldman, Robert, and Steve Papson. (1991). "Levi's and the Knowing Wink." *Current Perspectives in Social Theory,* 11, 69–95.

Goldman, Robert, and Steve Papson. (1994). "The Postmodernism that Failed." In David Dickens and Andrea Fontana (eds.), *Postmodernism and Social Inquiry* (pp. 223–254). New York: Guilford Press.

Goldman, Robert, and Arvind Rajagopal. (1991). *Mapping Hegemony.* Norwood: Ablex.

Goldman, Robert, and John Wilson. (1983). "Appearance and Essence: The Commodity Form Revealed in Perfume Advertisements." *Current Perspectives in Social Theory,* 4, 119–142.

Goldman, Steven, Roger Nagel, and Kenneth Preiss. (1994, October 9). "Why Seiko Has 3,000 Watch Styles." *New York Times,* p. F9.

Gottdiener, Mark. (1986). "Recapturing the Center: A Semiotic Analysis of Shopping Malls." In M. Gottdiener and A. Lagopoulos (eds.), *The City and the Sign* (pp. 288–302). New York: Columbia University Press.

Gottschalk, Mary. (1992, September 9). "Liz Claiborne Wants to Stop the War at Home." *Oregonian,* p. D1.

Gouldner, Alvin. (1982). *The Dialectic of Ideology and Technology.* New York: Oxford University Press.

Graham, Judith. (1989, September 11). "Benetton 'Colors' the Race Issue." *Advertising Age,* p. 3.

Gramsci, Antonio. (1971). *Prison Notebooks.* New York: International Publishers.

"Green in Marketing." (1991, January 29). *Advertising Age,* Special issue.

Green, Mark, and Andrew Buchsbaum. (1980). *The Corporate Lobbies: Political Profiles of the Business Roundtable and the Chamber of Commerce.* Washington, DC: Public Citizen.

Greenwald, John, Massimo Calabresi, and Jane Van Tassel. (1994, May 30). "Will Teens Buy It?" *Time,* p. 50.

Gregory, James R. (1991). *Marketing Corporate Image: The Company as Your Number-One Product.* Lincolnwood, IL: NTC Business Books.

Grossberg, Lawrence. (1992). *We Gotta Get Out of This Place: Popular Conservatism and Postmodern Culture.* New York: Routledge.

Guimaraes, George. (1985, June 10). "The Corporate Ad: Wall Street's 'Supersalesman.' " *Industry Week,* pp. 38–39.

Habermas, Jurgen. (1970). *Toward a Rational Society.* Boston: Beacon Press.

Habermas, Jurgen. (1975). *Legitimation Crisis.* Boston: Beacon Press.

Hall, Stuart. (1980). "Encoding/Decoding." In Stuart Hall et al. (eds.), *Culture, Media, and Language* (pp. 128–138). London: Hutchinson & Co.

Hallin, Daniel. (1985). "The American News Media." In J. Forester (ed.), *Critical Theory and Public Life* (pp. 121–127). Cambridge, MA: MIT Press.

Hamilton, Walter A. (1973, March). "On the Credibility of Institutions." *Conference Board Record,* p. 31.

Hansell, Saul. (1993, March 7). "The Man Who Charged Up Mastercard." *New York Times,* Sunday Magazine, section 3, p. 1.

Hart, Hugh. (1992, September 9). "Profits or Prophets? A Growing Number of Capitalists Get into the Business of Championing Causes and Advocating Awareness." *Chicago Tribune,* p. 5C.

Harvey, David. (1989). *The Condition of Postmodernity.* Cambridge, MA: Basil Blackwell.

Haug, Wolfgang Fritz. (1986). *Critique of Commodity Aesthetics.* Minneapolis: University of Minnesota Press.

Haworth, Lauren. (1993, May 17). "What Makes Nike Shoes Fly? Scott Bedbury Explains It All." *Business Journal of Portland,* Section 1, p. 17.

Hebdige, Dick. (1979). *Subculture: The Meaning of Style.* London: Methuen.

Hebdige, Dick. (1988). *Hiding in the Light: On Images and Things.* London: Routledge.

Heider, Karl. (1976). *Ethnographic Film.* Austin: University of Texas Press.

Held, David. (1982). "Crisis Tendencies, Legitimation, and the State." In J. B. Thompson and D. Held (eds.), *Habermas: Critical Debates* (pp. 181–195). Cambridge, MA: MIT Press.

Herskovitz, Richard. (1979). "The Shell Answer Man and the Spectator." *Social Text,* 1, 182–185.

Hodge, Robert, and Gunther Kress. (1988). *Social Semiotics.* Ithaca, NY: Cornell University Press.

"Hoover's Largest Advertising Investment Ever Will Continue Building Brand Recognition." (1993, April 15). *PR Newswire.*

Horkheimer, Max, and Theodor Adorno. (1972). *Dialectic of Enlightenment.* New York: Seabury Press.

Horovitz, Bruce. (1991, July 16). "Cost-Conscious Agencies Turn to Rental Photos." *Los Angeles Times,* p. D6.

Horovitz, Bruce. (1992, January 19). "Long-Distance Overload: Marketing. The Big Three Carriers Put on a $1-Billion Advertising Blitz Last Year. They Are Blasting Consumers— and Each Other—to Win Market Share." *Los Angeles Times,* p. D1.

Horovitz, Bruce. (1992, June 2). "Can Ads Help Cure Social Ills?" *Los Angeles Times,* p. D1.

Horovitz, Bruce. (1993, May 11). "Shock Value Helps an Obscure Jeans Maker Be Not So Obscure." *Los Angeles Times,* p. D1.

Hounshell, David A., and John K. Smith. (1988). *Science and Corporate Strategy: Du Pont R&D, 1902–1980.* Cambridge: Cambridge University Press.

Howell, Peter. (1993, March 4). "We've Got Two Words for You: Denis Leary Blows Smoke Rings at Pop Culture." *Toronto Star,* p. G3.

Hughes, Robert. (1980). *The Shock of the New.* New York: Knopf.

"I Hate the Sprite in You, Fool." (1994, May 2). *Advertising Age,* p. 6.

Jabbonsky, Larry, and Tim Davis. (1994, March). "Born Again to Be Wild: Royal Crown Company Reorganizes under New Owners Triarc Companies Inc." *Beverage World,* p. 22.

Jameson, Fredric. (1984). "Postmodernism, or The Cultural Logic of Late Capitalism." *New Left Review,* 146, 53–92.

Jameson, Fredric. (1991). *Postmodernism, or The Cultural Logic of Late Capitalism.* Durham, NC: Duke University Press.

Jay, Martin. (1984). *Adorno.* Cambridge, MA: Harvard University Press.

"Jeep Brand Extends Boundaries of Nature in New Advertising Campaign." (1993, April 5). *PR Newswire.*

Jefferson, David J. (1991, December). "Don't Walk a Mile in His Shoes: Can Disney Magic— and Money—Put Former L.A. Gear Shoe King Robert Greenberg Back on Fast Track?" *Los Angeles Magazine,* p. 114.

Jensen, Jeff. (1994, January 17). "Nike Kicks Apex over NFL 'Spatting.' " *Advertising Age,* p. 43.

"Judge Denies Eveready's Request to Ban Coors Commercial." (1991, May 15). United Press International, news release.

Kastor, Elizabeth. (1993, April 25). "Holy Chic: A Crossover Culture." *Washington Post,* p. F1.

Kellner, Douglas. (1989a). *Jean Baudrillard: From Marxism to Postmodernism and Beyond.* Stanford, CA: Stanford University Press.

Kellner, Douglas. (1989b). *Critical Theory, Marxism and Modernity.* Baltimore: Johns Hopkins University Press.

Kellner, Douglas. (1990). *Television and the Crisis of Democracy.* Boulder, CO: Westview Press.

"Kevin Johnson Demands Grudge Match with Grandmama and Larry Johnson Puts 'the Rock in the Hole' in Converse TV Ads." (1993, March 8). *PR Newswire.*

Kiersh, Edward. (1992, March 22). "Mr. Robinson vs. Air Jordan: The Marketing Battle for Olympic Gold." *Los Angeles Times,* Sunday Magazine, p. 28.

Kleiner, Art. (1991, July–August). "The Three Faces of Dow." *Garbage,* pp. 52–58.

Knight-Ridder New Service. (1983, April 22). "Nuclear Power Proponents to Launch Advertising Blitz." *Lexington Herald-Leader,* p. A11.

Kracauer, Siegfried. (1947). *From Caligari to Hitler: A Psychological History of the German Film.* Princeton, NJ: Princeton University Press.

Lasch, Christopher. (1975). "Introduction." In Russell Jacoby, *Social Amnesia.* Boston: Beacon Press.

Lasch, Christopher. (1979). *The Culture of Narcissism.* New York: Warner Books.

Lash, Scott. (1988). "Discourse or Figure? Postmodernism as a Regime of Signification." *Theory, Culture, and Society,* 5, 331–336.

Lazarus, George. (1991, May 16). "Judge Rules Coors Can Beat Its Drum." *Chicago Tribune,* p. 4.

Lazere, Donald. (1987). "Capitalism and American Mythology." In D. Lazere (ed.), *American Media and Mass Culture* (pp. 97–105). Berkeley and Los Angeles: University of California Press.

Lears, T. J. Jackson. (1981). *No Place of Grace: Antimodernism and the Transformation of American Culture, 1880–1920.* New York: Pantheon.

Lears, T. J. Jackson. (1983). "From Salvation to Self-Realization." In Richard Fox, and Jackson Lears (eds.), *The Culture of Consumption: Critical Essays in American History, 1880–1980* (pp. 3–38). New York: Pantheon.

Lefebvre, Henri. (1971). *Everyday Life in the Modern World.* New York: Harper.

Lefton, Terry. (1994, January 1). "Can't Fake This?" *Brandweek,* p. 1.

Lehrman, Celia K. (1987, April). "Questionnaire Results: Corporate Advertising." *Public Relations Journal,* p. 33.

Leiss, William. (1974). *The Domination of Nature.* Boston: Beacon Press.

Leiss, William. (1976). *The Limits of Satisfaction.* Toronto: University of Toronto Press.

Leiss, William, Stephen Kline, and Sut Jhally. (1986). *Social Communication in Advertising.* New York: Methuen.

Levin, Gary. (1992, February 17). "Benetton Brouhaha; $60M Campaign Ignites More Controversy." *Advertising Age,* p. 62.

Levine, Jonathan. (1990, July 30). "GE Carves Out a Road East." *International Business Week.*

Liddle, Alan. (1991, January 28). "Real People' Ads Give Authenticity to Campaign." *Nation's Restaurant News Newspaper,* p. 12.

Lipman, Joanne. (1992, September 11). "Backer Spielvogel to Revive 'USP' idea." *Wall Street Journal,* p. B20.

Lippert, Barbara. (1988, February 28). "How the Grubby New Realism in Ad-Land Reflects Our Election-Year Doldrums." *The Washington Post,* p. C1.

Lippert, Barbara. (1991, January 7). "A&W's Golden Oldies." *AdWeek's Marketing Week,* p. 45.

Lippert, Barbara. (1991, July 1). "Milli Vanilli Fakes It for Care*Free Gum." *Adweek's Marketing Week,* p. 37.

Lippert, Barbara. (1991, July 15). "Nike Learns to Use Overexposed Celebs." *Adweek's Marketing Week,* p. 29.

Lippert, Barbara. (1993, March 1). "Coke, Hollywood Style." *Newsweek,* p. 61.

Lipset, Seymour M., and William Schneider. (1983). *The Confidence Gap: Business, Labor, and Government in the Public Mind.* New York: Free Press.

Lipsitz, George. (1990). *Times Passages: Collective Memory and American Popular Culture.* Minneapolis: University of Minnesota Press.

Lukács, Georg. (1971). *History and Class Consciousness.* Cambridge, MA: MIT Press.

Lurie, Allison. (1981). *The Language of Clothes.* New York: Random House.

Lutz, William. (1977). "'The American Economic System': The Gospel According to the Advertising Council." *College English,* 38(8), 860–865.

MacCannell, Dean. (1976). *The Tourist: A New Theory of the Leisure Class.* New York: Schocken.

MacKenzie, Bill. (1991, April 14). "U.S. Bank Ad Campaign Focuses on Financial Reality." *Oregonian,* pp. R1, R6.

Madison Social Text Group. (1979). "The Media and the New Right." *Social Text,* 1, 169–180.

Magiera, Marcy. (1990, January 29). "Nike Again Registers No. 1 Performance." *Advertising Age,* p. 16.

Magiera, Marcy. (1992, June 8). "Small Rivals Leap as L.A. Gear Stumbles." *Advertising Age,* p. 8.

Magiera, Marcy, and Pat Sloan. (1991, February 25). "Rivals' Ads Hammer Nike." *Advertising Age,* pp. 3, 54.

Magrath, Allan J. (1992, August). "Lessons from the Heavyweights: Marketing Management." *Sales and Marketing Management,* p. 26.

Mandese, Joe. (1992, May 4). "TV Clutter: Who Has the Most, Who's Hurt the Worst." *Advertising Age,* p. 18.

Marchand, Roland. (1985). *Advertising the American Dream.* Berkeley and Los Angeles: University of California Press.

Marchand, Roland. (1987). "The Fitful Career of Advocacy Advertising: Political Protection, Client Cultivation, and Corporate Morale." *California Management Review,* 29(2), 128–156.

Marchand, Roland. (1989). "The Inward Thrust of Institutional Advertising: General Electric and General Motors in the 1920s." *Business and Economic History,* 18, 188–196.

Marcus, Greil. (1989). *Lipstick Traces: A Secret History of the Twentieth Century.* Cambridge, MA: Harvard University Press.

Marcuse, Herbert. (1964). *One-Dimensional Man.* Boston: Beacon Press.

Marcuse, Herbert. (1969). *An Essay on Liberation.* Boston: Beacon Press.

Marcuse, Herbert. (1970). *Five Lectures.* Boston: Beacon Press.

Margulies, Walter P. (1981, July 6). "A Stepsister to Consumer." *Advertising Age,* pp. S12–S13.

Marx, Karl. (1967). *Capital.* New York: International Publishers.

Marx, Karl. (1973). *Grundrisse.* London: Penquin.

Mayer, Martin. (1958). *Madison Avenue, U.S.A.* New York: Harper.

McKibben, William. (1989). *The End of Nature.* New York: Random House.

Mellencamp, Patricia. (1990). "TV Time and Catastrophe; or, Beyond the Pleasure Principle of Television." In P. Mellencamp (ed.), *Logics of Television* (pp. 240–266). Bloomington: University of Indiana Press.

Merchant, Carolyn. (1983). *The Death of Nature: Ecology and the Scientific Revolution.* San Francisco: Harper & Row.

Meyrowitz, Joshua. (1985). *No Sense of Place.* New York: Oxford University Press.

Miller, Cyndee. (1992, November 23). "Comedian Sinbad Decries Lack of Opportunities for Blacks." *Marketing News,* p. 2.

Miller, Cyndee. (1992, August 17). "Liberation for Women in Ads: Nymphettes [sic] June Cleaver Are Out; Middle Ground Is In." *Marketing News,* p. 1.

Miller, Cyndee. (1993, February 1). "Trendy Marketers Want Consumers to See Right through Their Products." *Marketing News,* p. 1.

Miller, Mark Crispin. (1990, September). "How Dow Recycles Reality." *Esquire,* p. 110.

Millman, Nancy. (1984, March 12). "Four A's Tackles Ad Image with Ads." *Advertising Age,* pp. 1, 62.

Millman, Nancy. (1992, August 16). "Pop Dollar." *Chicago Tribune,* p. C1.

Mills, C. Wright. (1951). *White Collar.* New York: Oxford University Press.

Montague, Claudia. (1993, March). "How Viewers Feel about TV." *American Demographics,* p. 18.

Moore, Martha T. (1992, August 12). "What's in a Name? Billions." *USA Today,* pp. B1, B7.

Moore, Martha T. (1993, March 18). "Roy Rogers Has a Ball with Ad Spoof." *USA Today,* p. B10.

Moore, Martha T. (1993, June 15). "Visual Overload: Fleeting Ad Images Catch Viewers." *USA Today,* p. B1.

"'More Is Less' Approach Cuts into Ad Clutter at Magazines." (1989, May 29). *Advertising Age,* p. 27.

Morse, Margaret. (1990). "An Ontology of Everyday Distraction: The Freeway, the Mall, and Television." In P. Mellencamp (ed.), *Logics of Television* (pp. 191–221). Bloomington: University of Indiana Press.

"Mountain Dew's 1993 Ad Campaign Debuts with 14-Minute Single-Night Advertising Schedules." (1993, March 7). *PR Newswire.*

Mulvey, Laura. (1975). "Visual Pleasure and Narrative Cinema." *Screen,* 16, 6–18.

Nash, Roderick. (1989). *The Rights of Nature: A History of Environmental Ethics.* Madison: University of Wisconsin Press.

Nielson, Winthrop. (1981, July 6). "Keeping Good Relations." *Advertising Age,* pp. S10–S11.

"Nike's Olympian Trademark Fight." (1992, July 11). *New York Times,* p. 17.

"'93 Camaro Advertising Arrives with Rock 'n' Roll Beat." (1993, March 29). *PR Newswire.*

O'Barr, William. (1994). *Culture in the Ad: Exploring Otherness in the World of Advertising.* Boulder, CO: Westview.

O'Connor, James. (1984). *Accumulation Crisis.* New York: Basil Blackwell.

O'Connor, James. (1987). *The Meaning of Crisis.* New York: Basil Blackwell.

O'Connor, James. (1988). "Capitalism, Nature, Socialism: A Theoretical Introduction." *Capitalism, Nature, Socialism,* 1, 11–38.

Olalquiaga, Celeste. (1992). *Megalopolis: Contemporary Cultural Sensibilities.* Minneapolis: University of Minnesota Press.

Oldenburg, Don. (1993, August 15). "New Ads Deliver Shock to System." *Oregonian,* p. L12.

Papson, Stephen. (1986). "From Symbolic Exchange to Bureaucratic Discourse: The Hallmark Greeting Card." *Theory, Culture, and Society,* 3(2), 99–111.

Papson, Stephen. (1990). "The IBM Tramp." *Jump Cut,* 35, 66–72.

Parker, Richard, and Lindsey Churchill. (1986). "Positioning by Opening the Consumer's Mind." *International Journal of Advertising,* 5, 1–13.

Pell, Eve. (1990, April–May). "Buying In." *Mother Jones,* pp. 23–25.

Pell, Eve. (1991). "Stop the Greens: Business Fights Back by Hook or by Crook." *E: The Environmental Magazine,* 2(6), 33–36.

"Pepsi's New Ads Reflect Old Theme." (1993, January 26). *Atlanta Journal and Constitution,* p. D2.

Philips, Michael M. (1992, July 7). "Nike to Appeal Spanish Court's Ruling." *Oregonian,* p. D6.

Phizacklea, Anne. (1990). *Unpacking the Fashion Industry: Gender, Racism, and Class in Production.* London: Routledge.

Polan, Dana. (1985). "A Brechtian Cinema? Towards a Politics of Self-Reflexive Film." In Bill Nichols (ed.), *Movies and Methods* (Vol. 2, pp. 661–672). Berkeley and Los Angeles: University of California Press.

Ramirez, Anthony. (1990, May 12). "Proctor & Gamble Pulls Some TV Ads over Slur to Coffee." *New York Times,* pp. 1, 6.

"Rat on Dinosaur Rip-Offs: Help Universal Get Richer." (1993, July 12). *Orlando Sentinel,* p. A2.

"Rednecks Redux: America's Corporate Flag-waving." (1990, July 21). *Economist,* p. 68.

Reich, Howard. (1992, July 26). "No Rapprochement!" *Chicago Tribune,* p. 4.

Reid, Herbert G. (1974). *Up the Mainstream: A Critique of Ideology in American Politics and Everyday Life.* New York: McKay.

Reisman, Joan. (1989, September). "Corporate Advertising Expenditures: Steady Growth Continued in 1989." *Public Relations Journal,* pp. 28–31.

Reisz, Karel, and Gavin Millar. (1968). *The Technique of Film Editing.* New York: Focal Press.

Rifkin, Glenn. (1993, February 10). "The Machines of a New Sole." *New York Times,* p. D7.

Rodkin, Dennis. (1989, June 5). "Retro Active." *Advertising Age,* p. 38.

Rosenberg, J. M. (1991, December 15). "Consumers Turning from Malls to Small Centers, Discount Stores." *Oregonian,* p. K10.

Rothenberg, Randall. (1989, July 13). "With Media Losing Mass, What's Left?" *Oregonian,* p. G1.

Rothenberg, Randall. (1989, October 3). "The Turmoil on Madison Avenue; Shifts in Marketing Stretegy Jolting Advertising Industry." *New York Times,* pp. A1, D23.

Rothenberg, Randall. (1989, December 10). "Nostalgia Becomes a Craze of the Present." *Oregonian,* p. L11.

Rothenberg, Randall. (1991, January 21). "In Ads, Simple Is Replacing Slick." *New York Times,* p. D6.

Rothenberg, Randall. (1991, October 20). "Seducing These Men." *New York Times,* Section 6, p. 30.

Rubin, Maureen. (1990, September). "Threat to Corporate Image Advertising Left Unresolved." *Public Relations Journal,* pp. 37, 39.

Russell, Dick, and Owen deLong. (1991). "Can Business Save the Environment." *E: The Environmental Magazine,* pp. 28–37, 57.

Saporito, Bill. (1992, March 23). "Why the Price Wars Never End." *Fortune,* p. 68.

Savan, Leslie. (1990, January 9). "The Shock of the Hue." *Village Voice,* p. 56.

Savan, Leslie. (1991, April 2). "Sneakers and Nothingness." *Village Voice,* p. 43.

Savan, Leslie. (1992, November 24). "Logo-rrhea." *Village Voice,* p. 47.

Savan, Leslie. (1994, September 6). "Naked Lunch: Ads from the Underground." *Village Voice,* p. 50.

Schiller, Herbert. (1986). *Information and the Crisis Economy.* New York: Oxford University Press.

Schor, Juliet. (1991). *The Overworked American: The Unexpected Decline of Leisure.* New York: Basic Books.

Schutz, Alfred. (1967). *The Problem of Social Reality.* The Hague: Martinus Nijhoff.

Seeman, Debbie. (1988, June 13). "Johnson's New Big Baby Look." *Ad Week,* p. 28.

Sennett, Richard, and Jonathan Cobb. (1972). *The Hidden Injuries of Class.* New York: Vintage.

Serafin, Raymond. (1988, March 7). "GM's Saturn Breaks Mold: UAW Helps Select Ad Agency." *Advertising Age,* pp. 1, 78.

Sethi, S. Prakash. (1977). *Advocacy Advertising and Large Corporations.* Lexington, MA: Lexington Books.

Silk, Leonard, and David Vogel. (1976). *Ethics and Profits: The Crisis of Confidence in American Business.* New York: Simon & Schuster.

Simko, Alison. (1992, January 13). "Do the Left Thing: At Tibor Kalman's Design Firm, M & Co., Office Politics Has Definitely Transcended the Water Cooler." *Advertising Age,* p. S22.

"Sinbad to Star in Reebok's New Advertising Campaign to Promote the Blacktop Series." (1991, May 2). *PR Newswire.*

Smythe, Dallas. (1977). "Communications: Blindspot of Western Marxism." *Canadian Journal of Political and Social Theory,* 1(3), 1–27.

"Sometimes You Win, Sometimes You Lose . . . Anheuser-Busch Loses Suit over Parody Ad." (1993, April 5). *Modern Brewery Age,* p. 3.

Sontag, Susan. (1977). *On Photography.* New York: Dell.

Steinhauer, Jennifer. (1994, May 22). "Feet First into the Clubs." *New York Times,* section 9, p. 1.

Stern, Barbara. (1991, September). "Who Talks Advertising? Literary Theory and Narrative 'Point of View.' " *Journal of Advertising,* pp. 9–29.

Strasser, Susan. (1989). *Satisfaction Guaranteed: The Making of the American Mass Market.* New York: Pantheon.

Strauss, Gary. (1993, June 7). "X Marks Advertisers' Spots: Discerning Post-Boomers Elusive Target." *USA Today,* p. B1.

Strauss, Gary, and Martha T. Moore. (1993, June 24). "New Fashions Slam-Dunk Sneakers." *USA Today,* pp. 1–28.

Swanigan, Pamela. (1993, May 2). "The Selling of Basketball." *Toronto Star,* p. H1.

Swartz, Herbert. (1986, December). "Clout." *Public Relations Journal,* pp. 26–28.

Tagg, John. (1982). "The Currency of the Photograph." In V. Burgin (ed.), *Thinking Photography* (pp. 110–141). London: Macmillan.

Tait, Nikki. (1993, January 14). "Why the Friesian Lady is Feeling Full of Beans: How Standardized Packaging Has Helped Sara Lee to Sell Its Coffee." *Financial Times,* p. 15.

Teinowitz, Ira. (1991, April 29). "Coors in a (Rabbit) Stew over Parody." *Advertising Age,* pp. 1, 50.

Toffler, Alvin. (1970). *Future Shock.* New York: Random House.

Tokar, Brian. (1991). "Marketing the Environment." In C. Plant and J. Plant (eds.), *Green Business: Hope or Hoax?* (pp. 42–51). Philadelphia: New Society.

Tonnies, Ferdinand. (1963). *Community and Society.* New York: Harper & Row.

Tractenberg, Jeffrey. (1988, December 26). "Viewer Fatigue?" *Forbes,* p. 120.

Tredre, Roger. (1992, March 7). "Denim's Journey Back to the Badlands." *Independent,* p. 37.

Tripp, Julie. (1992, February 12). "U.S. Bank Ads Tackle Reality of Hard Times." *Oregonian,* p. D1.

Turnquist, Kristi. (1994, October 27). "Cocktail Culture." *Oregonian,* p. E1.

Underwood, Elaine. (1991, April 1). "Campaign Trends: Pitching a Rosy Past." *AdWeek's Marketing Week,* p. 24.

"U.S. Bancorp Brad and Tina Ads Praised." (1992, December 11). *Oregonian,* p. E13.

Useem, Michael. (1984). *The Inner Circle: Large Corporations and the Rise of Business Political Activity in the United States and the United Kingdom.* New York: Oxford University Press.

Virilio, Paul, and Sylvère Lotringer. (1983). *Pure War.* New York: Semiotext(e).

Vittolino, Sal. (1988, February). "Dow Chemical's Formula for Acquiring a New Image." *Human Resource Executive,* pp. 14–16.

Volosinov, V. N. (1986). *Marxism and the Philosophy of Language.* Cambridge, MA: Harvard University Press.

Wakefield, Neville. (1990). *Postmodernism: Twilight of the Real.* Winchester, MA: Pluto.

Walsh, Edward. (1991, November 30). "Stroh Workers Charge Ads Fuel Harassment; 'Bikini Team' TV Spots Prompt Lawsuits." *Washington Post,* p. A3.

Ward, Adrienne. (1992, February 24). "'Socially Aware' or 'Wasted Money': AA Readers Respond to Benetton Ads." *Advertising Age,* p. 4.

Wartzman, Rick, and Kathleen A. Hughes. (1990, February 2). "Northrup's Image Ads, Televised on Trial's Eve, Spark U.S. Objection, but Appeals Court Lifts Ban." *Wall Street Journal,* p. A22.

Wascoe, Dan. (1991, July 28). "Ads That Tweak Other Ads Now Part of the Game." *Chicago Tribune,* p. B9.

Wernick, Andrew. (1991). *Promotional Culture: Advertising, Ideology, and Symbolic Expression.* London: Sage.

Wieden, Dan. (1992, July–August). "A Sense of Cool: Nike's Theory of Advertising." *Harvard Business Review,* p. 97.

Williamson, Judith. (1978). *Decoding Advertisements.* London: Marion Boyars.

Williamson, Judith. (1986). *Consuming Passions.* London: Marion Boyars.

Willis, Susan. (1991). *A Primer for Daily Life.* London: Routledge.

Wilner, Rich. (1993, February 1). "The Battle for #3: Athletic Shoe Manufacturers." *Footwear News,* p. S12.

Wilson, John. (1988). "The Stages of Advertising." Unpublished Paper.

Windle, Rickie. (1992, March 2). "Ads that Target like Smart Bombs." *Austin Business Journal,* p. 1.

Winkleman, Michael. (1985, December). "Corporate Advertising." *Public Relations Journal,* v. 41, pp. 22–25.

Winski, Joseph. (1992, January 20). "Study: The Customer Ain't Me." *Advertising Age,* p. 18.

Wolfe, Alan. (1977). *The Limits of Legitimacy.* New York: Free Press.

Woodward, Steve. (1992, July 7). "USOC Targets Unofficial Advertisers." *USA Today,* p. C12.

Woodyard, Chris. (1991, September 4). "Sneaker Firm Gains U.S. Foothold." *Los Angeles Times,* p. D3.

Yorks, Cindy L. (1990, June 13). "Shoe Business's Star-Studded Sneaker Wars." *Los Angeles Times,* p. E1.

Yovovich, B. G. (1981, July 6). "How To Woo Wall Street." *Advertising Age,* pp. S4–S5.

Zinkhan, George, and Rudy Hirschheim. (1992). "Truth in Marketing Theory and Research: An Alternative Perspective." *Journal of Marketing,* 56(2), 80–88.

Index